Dostoevsky's Convictional Theology Expressed in His Life and Literature

Dumitru Sevastian

Langham
MONOGRAPHS

Published 2021 by Langham Monographs
An imprint of Langham Publishing
www.langhampublishing.org

Langham Publishing and its imprints are a ministry of Langham Partnership

Langham Partnership
PO Box 296, Carlisle, Cumbria, CA3 9WZ, UK
www.langham.org

ISBNs:
978-1-83973-202-7 Print
978-1-83973-460-1 ePub
978-1-83973-461-8 Mobi
978-1-83973-462-5 PDF

British Library Cataloguing-in-Publication Data
A catalogue record for this book is available from the British Library.

ISBN: 978-1-83973-202-7

Cover & Book Design: projectluz.com

Working on the life and writings of Fyodor Dostoevsky, Dumitru Sevastian has produced an instructive exercise in reconstruction of this influential Russian writer's theology. The book employs James Wm. McClendon's "biography as theology" approach which provides the necessary interpretive lenses through which Dr Sevastian discovers Dostoevsky's convictions and the communities which stood behind them and shaped them. This book demonstrates how life events and communities of influence leave their imprint on one's convictions and embedded theology. This is a good example of how to do theology biographically.

Oleksandr Geychenko, PhD
Rector,
Odesa Theological Seminary, Odesa, Ukraine

It was a pleasure to read this systematically worked through material by Dumitru Sevastian of Dostoevsky's novels. Often I have looked at the question of Dostoevsky and his faith struggles and convictions, reflecting more personally on the Eastern European context and Christianity. This research, that speaks so well to an Eastern Slavic soul, has helped me to see a clearer picture of Dostoevsky and his faith. I very much look forward to seeing this dissertation as a book to be read by many others.

Peter Penner, ThD, Dr Habil
Director of Advanced Studies,
Euro-Asian Accrediting Association

Dr. Dumitru Sevastian's book is excellent research, showing a new perspective on the theology of Dostoevsky through his life experiences and convictions. It is an investigation of character in community through Dostoevsky's main books (*The Poor Folk*, *The House of the Dead* and *The Brothers Karamazov*). Dr. Sevastian has demonstrated how the convictional theology of Dostoevsky can be an example for the life and mission of modern people living in different cultures.

Sergiy Sannikov, PhD
Emeritus President,
Euro-Asian Accrediting Association

Contents

Abstract ix

Acknowledgements xi

Abbreviations xiii

Chapter 1 1

Introduction

    1.1 Foreword 1

    1.2 Moldavian Contemporary Society 1

    1.3 Moldavian Church – Its Mission and Vision 8

    1.4 Survey of Criticisms of Dostoevsky's Religious Views 13

    1.5 Convictional Theology 18

    1.6 The Structure of the Study 21

    1.7 Conclusion 22

Chapter 2 23

Pre-Siberian Period: The Quest

    2.1 Introduction 23

    2.2 Dostoevsky's Convictions Shown in His Own Life During

        the Pre-Siberian Period 23

        2.2.1 Under Family Influence (1821–1834) 24

        2.2.2 The Academy of Engineers (1834–1843) 36

        2.2.3 Merging into Literary-Political Circles (1843–1849) 51

        2.2.4 Imprisonment (1849) 62

    2.3 Theological Motifs in *The Poor Folk* 66

        2.3.1 The Perfect World 67

        2.3.2 The Distorted World 70

        2.3.3 The Tragic End 89

    2.4 Conclusion 92

Chapter 3 97

The Siberian Period:

The Regeneration of Convictions

    3.1 Introduction 97

    3.2 Dostoevsky's Convictions Shown in His Own Life During

        the Siberian Period 97

        3.2.1 On the Way to Siberia (1850) 98

        3.2.2 Katorga (1850–1854) 99

3.2.3 Service in the Tsar's Army (1854–1859)....................104
3.3 Theological Motifs in *The House of the Dead*...................106
    3.3.1 The Sinfulness of Man.....................107
    3.3.2 Freedom.....................121
    3.3.3 The Image of God in Each Person.....................129
    3.3.4 Repentance – The Only Way to a Radical Life Change....135
3.4 Conclusion 142

Chapter 4 147
Post-Siberian Period: Self Sacrifice
4.1 Introduction.....................147
4.2 Dostoevsky's Convictions Shown in His Own Life During
    the Post-Siberian Period.....................147
    4.2.1 Arrival in Petersburg (1859–1863).....................148
    4.2.2 Significant Losses (1863–1866) 153
    4.2.3 Success and Acknowledgement (1867–1881).....................156
4.3 Theological Motifs in *The Brothers Karamazov*.....................168
    4.3.1 The Sinfulness of Man.....................169
    4.3.2 The Image of God in Every Person 182
    4.3.3 Faith in God 190
    4.3.4 Rebellion against God.....................199
    4.3.5 Christ-Like Living of Life.....................205
4.4 Conclusion 217

Chapter 5 221
Dostoevsky's Theology
5.1 Introduction.....................221
5.2 Synthesis of His Life and Writings 221
    5.2.1 Scripture 221
    5.2.2 Christ.....................223
    5.2.3 Man 226
    5.2.4 Redemption.....................230
    5.2.5 The Church.....................232
5.3 Conclusion 234

Chapter 6 235
Influence of Dostoevsky's Theology on Society
6.1 Introduction.....................235
6.2 Influence of Dostoevsky's Theology on the Society
    of His Time.....................236
    6.2.1 Influence on Slavophilism: K. Leontiev.....................236
    6.2.2 Influence on Westernism: M. Antonovich.....................244

6.2.3 Influence on the Narodnik Movement:
N. Mikhailovskiy 250

6.2.4 Influence on Radical Christian Thinkers: V. Soloviev 255

6.3 Influence of Dostoevsky's Theology on a
Baptistic Community..261

6.3.1 Faith in God 261

6.3.2 Rebellion against God..263

6.3.3 On the Way to God 264

6.3.4 Life in God..265

6.3.5 The Mission of the Christian 268

6.4 Conclusion 269

Chapter 7 271

*Conclusion: The Challenge of Dostoevsky's "Christ's Way" for
the MECBC*

7.1 Introduction 271

7.2. Challenge for the Life of the MECBC..............................272

7.3. Challenge for the Mission of the MECBC in Its
Orthodox Context 276

7.4 Conclusion 281

Bibliography..283

Abstract

The theology of F. M. Dostoevsky is the focus of this investigation. Quite often the theology of Dostoevsky has been viewed with a desire to define Dostoevsky as one of "them" or as "foreign" to Russia. In assessing his beliefs, researchers often came from their personal viewpoints of acceptance or rejection of those beliefs. The present research proposes a new perspective. It focuses on the expression of theology in the life experiences and convictions of Dostoevsky as revealed in his own personal context and in his writings. It is an investigation of character in community.

The book divides logically into seven chapters: following an introduction in chapter 1, the first part of chapters 2–4 investigates the life of Dostoevsky. For this task primary sources were used: F. M. Dostoevsky's memos and notebooks; "Diary of a Writer"; a collection of his letters; memoirs of his wife and daughters; and reminiscences of Dostoevsky's co-workers, acquaintances and friends. The conclusions arising from the first part show that Dostoevsky's convictions changed from faith in God to disbelief in the pre-Siberian period, and then in the Siberian period his convictions changed again with a return to faith in Christ. In the post-Siberian period Dostoevsky's life of faith can be seen when he conquered many of his former doubts. During this period "Christ's Way" was the dominant image in Dostoevsky's life.

The second part of chapters 2–4 investigates three of Dostoevsky's novels: *The Poor Folk, The House of the Dead* and *The Brothers Karamazov*. The motifs of these books are evidence of his theology. The primary sources which were used in this part are these three novels. In these novels Dostoevsky illustrated a deep and implicit theology in some detail by using the life stories of the characters in his novels.

The investigation in chapters 5–7 is intended to bring together the theology of Dostoevsky, the things observed in his life and those things he proclaimed through his writings. An investigation is also undertaken into his influence on his society and on a contemporary baptistic community. Finally, because this research has been done by a member of the Moldavian Evangelical Christian Baptist Church, the research looks at the ways the MECBC can learn from Dostoevsky's living theology.

This research shows that Dostoevsky's convictional theology is a Christ-centred theology. The image of Christ's suffering and resurrection is the centre of his vision and mission. I would argue that his convictional theology can be an example for the life and mission of MECBC.

Acknowledgements

I am very grateful to many people for their support over many years, which made possible the writing of this book. First, I express my gratitude to the International Baptist Theological Seminary (IBTS) academic community. Each meeting with the leadership of IBTS has been productive in the writing of the book. Here I need to point out two particular persons who invested much in my study. I give thanks to Dr Parush Parushev who supervised my work and offered me any support that I needed along the way. He not only explained to me the "secrets" of doing good research, but he also is very familiar with the life and works of Dostoevsky, who is the subject of my research. I found Dr Parushev to be the best supervisor I have ever met in my life. Second, I appreciate the great support of Dr Peter Penner, who was for me the best example of living Christianity when I was a student at Saint Petersburg Christian University and afterwards during my study at IBTS.

I want to mention the librarians at IBTS, who contributed to my writing in different ways. My research was done in Moldova. So I cannot omit mention of my colleagues and students at the College of Theology and Education in Chisinau, Moldova, who showed great patience listening to my "messages" about the research. I thank Vladimir Ubeivolc who is my colleague at CTE and also at IBTS. Our discussions were very helpful. Also I thank the members and leadership of Bethany Baptist Church in Chisinau where I am a pastor. They kindly understood my absences for the research colloquia and they always supported me in prayer. There are also particular persons who prepared me for writing this book long before I ever envisioned starting this research. One was Pastor Mikhail Botnari who invested his time and life to help me grow spiritually and encouraged me in the beginning of my ministry in the church. Also there were my teachers from the first Chisinau Bible School:

Donald Winch, Dr Haith and Feodor Mocan. While writing my dissertation I often thought of them and hoped they would be proud of me.

Also, I want to thank Nancy Lively, Alec Gilmore, Dr Ian Randall and Dr Tim Noble, who read my work attentively and made many critical and constructive comments, helping me to improve the language and clarity of the text.

Finally, I thank my wife Liubovi Sevastian and my three children: Elena, Marin, Olga for their daily support and patience.

Abbreviations

Bednye Lyudi	F. M. Dostoevsky's novel *The Poor Folk*
Brat'ya Karamazovy	F. M. Dostoevsky's novel *The Brothers Karamazov*
CTE	College of Theology and Education
Dnevnik Pisatelya	F. M. Dostoevsky's *Diary of a Writer*
IBTS	International Baptist Theological Seminary
MECBC	Moldavian Evangelical Christian Baptist Church
MECBU	Moldavia Evangelical Christian Baptist Union
PCRM	Communist Party of Republic of Moldova
PD	Democrat Party
PL	Liberal Party
PLDM	Liberal Democrat Party of Moldova
Pis'ma	F. M. Dostoevsky's *Letters*
USSR	The Union of Soviet Socialist Republics
Slovo Istiny	"Light of the Truth" – the periodical of the MECBU
Stat'i i Zametri	F. M. Dostoevsky's "Articles and Notes 1845–1861"
Svet Zhizni	"The Light of Life" – the periodical of the MECBU
Zapiski iz Mertvogo Doma	F. M. Dostoevsky's novel *The House of the Dead*

Introduction

1.1 Foreword

The goal of this book is to discover and analyze Dostoevsky's theology expressed in his life and literature and to indicate its possible relevance for the life and mission of the Moldavian Evangelical Christian Baptist Church (MECBC). This research was inspired by my personal interest in Dostoevsky's living theology. I do this research as a member of MECBC and that is why it is important to me to see what MECBC can learn from Dostoevsky's theology.

1.2 Moldavian Contemporary Society

To achieve the goal of the book, it is necessary to provide a picture of the most widespread challenges that Moldavian society faces. Moldova is a small Eastern European country, located between Romania and Ukraine. The country gained its independence from the Soviet Union in 1991. It is home to 3.5 million people. An additional half-million people live in the breakaway region of Transnistria.[1] Most of the Moldavian population is Orthodox Christian. About 93 percent of the population belongs to this faith.[2] Despite this, the Moldavian society faces the issues that are far from the Christian living society.

---

1. "Children of Moldova" (UNICEF, 1 January 2011), 11 February 2012, http://www.unicef.org/moldova/Children_of_MD_for_web.pdf.

2. "Moldova – Religion" (Mongabay.com, January 2010), 12 February 2012, http://www.mongabay.com/reference/country_studies/moldova/SOCIETY.html.

Poverty is one of the main issues of the Moldavian society and has been so during the last 20 years. In 2010, the minimum living wage on average per person was 1,373 MD lei. The monthly income per person was 1,273 MD lei, which represented 92.7 percent of the minimum living cost.[3] Old people are in deep poverty, especially in rural areas. A woman who worked in the fields for 45 years receives a pension equal to 380–400 MD lei.[4] Their monthly pension does not cover half of the living cost.[5]

Poverty has negative consequences for the population of Moldova. Because of poverty, parents have left their children and have looked for any kind of work in other countries, leaving children with family but often without the emotional support they need. Many of them have become slaves. For poor families without migrant parents, residential care is too commonly used. Twenty percent of Moldavian children grow up without the care of one or both parents due to migration or family breakdown. Ninety-seven percent of children in institutions are not parentless.[6]

Moldova is one of the main countries of origin for women and children trafficked for sexual exploitation to other parts of Europe, Russia, and the Middle East.[7] Tatiana Jardin, IOM[8] expert, confirmed that in her organization alone in 2010, advice was sought for over 20 women and adolescents who were victims of human trafficking.[9] Violence at home is widespread and fuels the trafficking trade. Eighty percent of trafficking victims from Moldova were

---

3. "Minimul de existenţă în Moldova a revenit la nivelul anului 2008" [Subsistence Minimum in Moldova Came Back to the Level of 2008] (INFOTAG, 7 April 2011), 22 May 2011, http://www.azi.md/ro/print-story/17619.

4. "Pensia medie lunară nu acoperă minimul de existenţă" [Average Monthly Pension Does Not Cover Living Subsistence] (Info-Prim Neo, 21 December 2009), 23 February 2011, http://www.azi.md/ro/print-story/7923.

5. "Studiu IDIS: 2008 a fost dominat de tensiuni politice, regrupari pre-electorale si saracie" [IDIS Research: 2008 was Dominated by Political Tensions, Pre-election Grouping and Poverty] (Info-Prim Neo, 29 January 2009), 2 May 2011, http://www.azi.md/ro/print-story/1121.

6. "Children of Moldova" (UNICEF, 1 January 2011), 11 February 2012, http://www.unicef.org/moldova/Children_of_MD_for_web.pdf.

7. Alexandru Eftode, "Freedom House: R. Moldova – libertatea şi drepturile politice în declin" [Freedom House: R. Moldova – Freedom and Political Rights in Decline] (Radio Europa Libera, 17 July2009), 14 April 2011, http://www.azi.md/ro/print-story/4516.

8. International Organisation for Migration.

9. "Creşte numărul de persoane traficate în Moldova" [The Number of Trafficked Persons in Moldova Is Increasing] (INFOTAG, 16 June 2011), 12 June 2011, http://www.azi.md/ro/print-story/19072.

exposed to family violence as children. Children who grow up in institutions are ten times more likely to be trafficked than other children.[10]

Excessive alcohol use is a serious problem in Moldavian society. Without work, many people become discouraged and resort to an excessive use of alcohol. According to a recent report, the Moldavian population in 2010 consumed the most alcohol per person in the world.[11] Alcohol use causes much damage to individuals and families.[12]

Another important issue of current Moldavian society is the increasing number of illnesses and sick people. In 2002 out of every one hundred thousand persons there were 167 cancer patients, but in 2004 this number had increased to 190 out of each one hundred thousand.[13] Moldova is in the top three countries with the highest infection rate of tuberculosis. Every day in Moldova two people die of tuberculosis. In the last two years, the situation remains unchanged.[14] In Moldova there are about 25,000 HIV-positive.[15] Also, the number of invalid children is increasing. In 1991 there were 9,673, and in 2004 there were 13,225 invalid children.[16] Services often fail to reach those most excluded from society. The poorest children, children with disabilities and Roma children are the worst off. More than four in ten Roma children do not attend school; more than sixty percent of children with disabilities do not attend school; children from poor families seek medical care half as often as children from non-poor families.[17]

---

10. "Children of Moldova" (UNICEF, 1 January 2011), 11 February 2012, http://www.unicef.org/moldova/Children_of_MD_for_web.pdf.

11. "Samaya p'ushchaya natsiya v mire: ne russkie" [The Nation That Drinks the Most in the World Is Not Russia], 25 February 2011, http://health.passion.ru/l.php/samaya-pustcaya-natsiya.htm.

12. S. K. Ivanets, *Alkogol'naya zavisimost'* [Alcohol Dependence], (Novosibirsk, 2006), 7.

13. "Indicii premilinari ai activitatii institutiilor medico-sanitare pe anii 2002–2004" [Preliminary Indications of Medical Institution Activities for the Years 2002–2004] (Chisinau, 2004).

14. "V Moldove ne hvataet vrachey fitiziatrov" [A Lack of Tuberculo-Therapists in Moldova], 13 December 2010, http://vesti.md/?mod=news&id=3012.

15. "Zlye dziny immonodifitsita" [The Evil Jinn of Immunodeficiency], 20 March, 2011, http://noutati.md.

16. A. Racu, *Interventia recuperative-terapeutica pentru copii cu dizabilitati multiple* [Recuperative-Therapeutic Intervention for Children with Multiple Disabilities] (Pontos, Chisinau, 2006), 18.

17. "Children of Moldova" (UNICEF, 1 January 2011), 11 February 2012, http://www.unicef.org/moldova/Children_of_MD_for_web.pdf.C

Corruption is also a big issue in Moldavian society. "Corruption in the Moldavian society has penetrated all spheres of the state," said Mihai Ghimpu, a member of the Moldavian Parliament.[18] Economics and business have been corrupted. Businessmen who are close to authorities are privileged. Those businessmen who do not support the authorities are pressured in order to capture their business. This was also a common practice during the rule of the PCRM .[19]

Justice is corrupt in Moldova. An indication of the corruption of injustice in Moldova is the number of cases won by citizens of Moldova against the government of Moldova in the European Court of Human Rights (ECHR). Since 1998, Moldova has lost 180 cases in the ECHR.[20] The ECHR ordered the Republic of Moldova to pay €9.7 million to citizens who have been harmed by the Moldavian courts.[21] According to an expert in European justice, Dovydas Vitkauskas, Moldova needs an urgent reform of justice, police, courts, prosecutors, and investigating committees because of their corruption.[22]

The above-mentioned issues and the widespread lying and selfishness indicate a lack of virtue in Moldavian society. Lying is another problem within Moldavian society. Unfortunately, it has become the principal means to which Moldavian citizens resort to justify their selfish and evil actions. Anastasia Naryshkina, in her article about the political situation in Moldova, stated that lying is a chronic disease of Moldavian society. She came to this conclusion by watching how political parties, guided by personal interests, interpret the history of Moldova. Thus, the pro-Russian Communist Party has denied the

---

18. "Instanțele judecătorești economice dispar, dar nu consolidează alianța de guvernământ" [Economic Courts Disappear, but Do Not Strengthen the Ruling Alliance] (Info-Prim Neo, 6 July 2011), 23 July 2011, http://www.azi.md/ro/print-story/19514.

19. "Guvernantii moldoveni intensifica presiunea asupra businessului, Financial Times" [Moldavian Authorities Step up Pressure on Business: Financial Times] (Info-Prim Neo, 29 May 2009), 14 March 2011, http://www.azi.md/ro/print-story/3350.

20. "Statul va plăti despăgubiri cazurilor în instanțe, pentru a reduce numărul dosarelor depuse la CEDO" [The State Will Pay Compensation to Court Cases, to Reduce the Number of Cases Submitted to the ECHR] (Info-Prim Neo, 13 April 2011), 2 February 2011, http://www.azi.md/ro/print-story/17740.

21. "Lista persoanelor vinovate de pedepsirea R. Moldova la CEDO" [The List of the People Who Are Guilty in Condemning of R. Moldova by the ECHR] (INFOTAG, 19 February 2009), 25 November 2010, http://www.azi.md/ro/print-story/1422.

22. "Experții europeni au prezentat strategia de reformare și coordonare a sectorului justiției" [European Experts Presented Their Strategy and Coordination of Justice Reform] (INFOTAG, 7 July 2011), 28 July 2011, http://www.azi.md/ro/print-story/19562.

negative consequences of the Moldavian deportation by Soviet authorities in 1940–1948.[23] They are lying to protect their image because they are followers of the Communist Party of Russia.[24]

Lies are often diluted with the truth. So are the media in Moldova. This was evident before the Parliamentary and local elections. Research showed that in the period before the local elections, which took place on 5 June 2011, each party's representatives in Parliament controlled one or more newspapers, TV, or radio stations. Their people appeared on the programs more than other candidates, and moderators were always talking positively about them.[25]

The Moldavian society is permeated with selfishness. This is especially noticeable in the desire of one man to be lifted up above the others. In this case, egotism and vanity are intertwined. Thus, while the majority of citizens are in deep poverty, the president of Moldova (from 2001 to 2009), Vladimir Voronin, has spent 33 million lei from the state budget to repair his residence in Condrita and has been allocated 507 acres of forest.[26]

Not only has the former president had a tendency to lift himself up to the rank of master, the leaders of AEI[27] are doing the same. Members of the first Parliament consider that one of the main problems of Moldova now is the lack of real leaders. In their view, the chairmen of the Moldavian political parties behave more like masters than leaders.[28]

Because of selfishness and poverty, annual more than 2,700 women's first pregnancies are terminated. As a result, 12–15 percent of young families

---

23. "Deportarea romanilor din Basarabia, Bucovina, Herta" [Deportation of Romanians in Bessarabia, Bukovina, Herta], 24 June 2011, http://civicnet.info/Procesulcomunismului.asp?ID=204.

24. "Comportamentul infantil al clasei politice din Republica Moldova" [Infantile Behaviour of Politicians in Moldova], 14 May 2011, http://www.azi.md/ro/print-story/12916.

25. "Spre sfârșitul campaniei electorale, presa devine tot mai partizană" [Towards the End of the Campaign, the Press Is Becoming More Partisan] (Centrul pentru Jurnalism Independent (CJI) (Moldova Azi, 2 June 2011), 4 June 2011, http://www.azi.md/ro/print-story/18743.

26. "33 milioane de lei pentru 'reamenajarea' complexului Condrița" [33 Million Lei for "Rearrangement" of Condrița Complex] (Timpul, 18 August 2009), 22 May 2011, http://www.azi.md/ro/print-story/5133.

27. The Alliance for Europe Integration.

28. "Deputatii primului Parlament sint ingrijorati de situatia social-economica si climatul politic din R. Moldova" [First Parliament Deputies are Concerned about the Socio-economic and Political Climate of R. Moldova], (INFOTAG, 6 March 2009), 18 September 2010, http://www.azi.md/ro/print-story/1644.

suffer infertility.[29] Also, because of their parents' selfishness, many children suffer. So, every year 650 children are abandoned.[30] According to UNICEF research, only eleven out of 650 children who are orphaned are biological orphans. The parents of the remaining 639 abandoned children are living somewhere.[31] Adolescents are increasingly vulnerable to risky practices in sexual behaviour and drug usage and to falling outside the law through petty crime. Five percent of youth aged fifteen to twenty-four report their first sexual experience as forced. Only fifty percent of adolescents with a health-related problem used medical services.[32]

The leadership of Moldavian society proposes their solutions to the challenges of society. In May 2009 there were five main political parties with representatives in our parliament. The Communist Party (PCRM),[33] which had governed the country from 2001 until 2009 saw the four opposition parties (PLDM, AMN, PL, PD)[34] as evil because they had the possibility of winning the election. Actually, evil was associated with all five of these parties.[35]

For the salvation of Moldavian society, the opposition parties saw the removal of the Communist Party from power at the elections on 5 April

---

29. O. G. Frolova, "Aborty v Moldove" [Abortion in Moldova], 27 October 2010, http://tawhid.narod.ru.

30. V. Sytkin, "Kogda govoryat" [When They Say], 22 January 2010, http://www.analytique.md/index.

31. "Abandonul copiilor in Republica Moldova" [Abandonment of Children in Moldova] (Guvernul Republicii Moldova, UNICEF, Chisinau, 2005), 16–17.

32. "Children of Moldova" (UNICEF, 1 January 2011), 11 February 2012, http://www.unicef.org/moldova/Children_of_MD_for_web.pdf.

33. During the eight years of being governed by the Communist Party, Moldova became the poorest country in Europe with the highest level of mass exodus of the workforce, consisting of more than one million people. As a result of this migration, many families were broken up and over 100,000 children have been living without one or both of their parents. Moldova became the country with the lowest pensions and salaries in Europe and with the worst medical system. As a result, the number of cases of tuberculosis and AIDS were doubled. The Communist Party has monopolized media and has banned access to opposition parties. Justice was subordinate to the Party. The external debt amounted to more than 4.5 billion dollars. "Interviu cu Mihai Ghimpu, presedintele PL" [Interview with Mihai Ghimpu, Chairman of PL], 16 May 2011, http://www.azi.md/ro/interview/8/1.

34. PLDM – Liberal Democratic Party of Moldova, AMN – Alliance Our Moldova, PL – Liberal Party, PD – Democratic Party.

35. "Comunistii ataca din nou: AIE respecta democtatia numai cand rezultatul le place" [Communists Again Attack AEI: They Respect Democracy Only When the Result is Convenient for Them], 12 June 2011, http://www.inprofunzime.md/stiri/politic/html.

2009. They promoted a new team of people from their parties, which, in their opinion, were the best-trained professionals.[36]

They were assured that only they were able to save Moldova. For example, the slogan of PLDM was "Moldova without poverty."[37] AMN promised the people to create 350,000 new jobs and that the average wage would be €500 per month. They also promised to increase the pension over €175 per month.[38]

People trusted the opposition parties and voted for them in the election on 5 April 2009. Four parties (PLDM, AMN, PL and PD) were able to create the Alliance for European Integration (AEI).[39] But the situation has not changed for the better during the last three years of AEI's governing. Moldova is still the poorest country in Europe.[40] Instead of creating new jobs, unemployment is increasing. Corruption is thriving in all spheres of Moldavian society. AEI is occupied with their own interests.[41] People are disappointed.[42]

The opposition parties and different organizations have used this situation for their own interests. Daria Bostan, chairman of the Female Trade Union, called for women to protest against government policy.[43] PCRM has made promises to correct the situation in Moldova and now calls for "changing

---

36. "Interviu cu Vlad Filat, presedintele PLDM" [Interview with Vlad Filat, Chairmanof PLDM], 15 May 2011, http://www.azi.md/ro/interview/4/1.

37. "Moldova fara saracie" [Moldova without poverty], 20 January 2011, http://pldm.md/index.php?option=com_content&view=category&layout=blog&id=73&Itemid=79.

38. "Interviu cu Serafim Urechean, presedintele AMN" [Interview with Serafim Urechean, Chairmanof AMN], http://www.azi.md/ro/interview/6/1 (12 May 2011).

39. "PLDM, PL, PD și AMN au semnat documentul de creare a coalitiei" [PLDM, PL, PD and AMN Have Signed the Document Creating the Coalition], 20 September 2009, http://m.protv.md/stiri/politic/pldm-pl-pd-i-amn-au-semnat-documentul-de-creare-a-coali-iei.html.

40. In the situation when almost all of the population is in deep poverty, there is a small group of very rich people. Among the millionaires are eleven members of Parliament. "Noul parlament are 11 milionari" [The New Parliament has Eleven Millionaires] (INFOTAG, 27 December 2010), 23 June 2011, http://www.azi.md/ro/print-story/15583.

41. Alex Oprunenco, "Zona de Liber Schimb Aprofundat și Cuprinzător dintre UE și R. Moldova: o trambulină spre modernizare sau o cale spre ruinare?" [Deep and Comprehensive Free Trade Zone between EU and Moldova: A Springboard for Modernization or a Path to Ruin?] (Centrul Analitic Independent "EXPERT-GRUP"), 25 May 2011, http://www.azi.md/ro/print-story/18256.

42. According to the survey, more than three-fourths of the population is dissatisfied with government activities. Of the total population 89 percent are not satisfied with their salaries, and 88 percent are not satisfied with their standard of living. ("Barometrul de Opinie Publică" [Public Opinion Barometer], 12 June 2011, http://www.azi.md/ro/print-story/18685.)

43. "Sindicalistele din Moldova anunță proteste pentru 8 martie" [Trade unions in Moldova Announced Protests on 8 March], (Info-Prim Neo 25 February 2011), 24 April 2011, http://www.azi.md/ro/print-story/16790.

the AEI regime" which, in their conviction, is the main evil for the country.[44] PCRM has a lot in common with the populist movement of nineteenth century Russia. Communists are convinced atheists; but in their minds, communist atheist ideology and Christian tradition freely coexist.[45] That's why members and leaders of the PCRM can be seen at the Lenin monument worshiping him[46] and at the Easter service in the Orthodox Church.[47]

The members of AEI consider themselves Orthodox believers, but at the same time they share a staunch materialistic vision. For AEI, the transformation of Moldova lay in a social rather than a religious transformation of society.[48]

1.3 Moldavian Church – Its Mission and Vision

First of all, for the purpose of this book, it is necessary to provide a picture of the Moldavian church, its mission and vision. For the purpose of identification of MECBC's vision and mission, a study of the periodicals published by MECBC from 2003 to the end of 2008 was undertaken, as well as a study of annual reports by MECBC for this period. The results of this research show the actual situation for a period of the six years.

The Moldavian Evangelical Christian Baptist Union (MECBU) is a union of 322 Churches,[49] sixty-five autonomous groups[50] and 194 affiliated

---

44. "Declaraţia PCRM" [PCRM declaration], 1 July 2011, http://www.pcrm.md/main/index_md.php.

45. Rozenblyum, *Tvorcheskie dnevniki Dostoevskogo*, 128.

46. "Voronin a depus flori la monumental lui Lenin" [Voronin Laid Flowers at the Monument of Lenin], 25 April 2011, http://forum.md/Themes/basarabia/322195.

47. "Mii de oameni au venit azi noaptea la catedrala metropolitan" [Thousands of People Came Last Night to the Metropolitan Cathedral], 26 May 2011, http://www.prime.md/ro/news/mii-de-oameni-au-venit-azi-noapte-la-catedrala-metropolitana-1004694/.

48. See "Interviu cu Vlad Filat, presedintele PLDM" [Interview with Vlad Filat, Chairmanof PLDM], 15 May 2011, http://www.azi.md/ro/interview/4/1 and "Interviu cu Mihai Ghimpu, presedintele PL" [Interview with Mihai Ghimpu, Chairmanof PL], 16 May 2011, http://www.azi.md/ro/interview/8/1.

49. Here a church means a group of believers who have an ordained pastor who can independently perform all kinds of ministries.

50. Autonomous groups are those churches that do not have a pastor, so periodically they invite a pastor from another church to officiate at some ministries such as the Lord's Supper.

branches,[51] present in nine regions of the Republic of Moldova, including the Transnistrian region.[52] In total the MECBU numbers 29,554 church members.[53] The majority of the inhabitants of Moldova are Orthodox Christians. They compose about 93 percent of the population, while the MECBU represents only 0.6 percent.

In the early 1990s, following the collapse of the Union of Soviet Socialist Republics (USSR), in Moldova, along with the proclamation of independence of the country, people received freedom of religion. These changes that occurred in society have contributed to some changes in the MECBC. If during USSR rule, church activities were confined only to the territory of the church, then with the coming of freedom arose the opportunity to have activities both in the church and outside it.

For the first time, came the opportunity to openly engage in evangelistic activities. Members of churches of the MECBU were active in taking the gospel message to people, using both personal and mass evangelism methods.[54] Their motivation was the understanding that people are unhappy without Christ. One could feel the love of believers towards unbelievers.[55] It is also necessary to note that society at that point in time, after a long time under atheist influence, was open to accepting Christ. For numerous people, spiritual values become more important than material ones. As a result of active evangelistic activities, churches grew significantly in number. To compare, in 1990 the MECBU had about 10,000 members in the churches, and 10 years later it numbered 20,000, despite the fact that during this period about 10,000 members of MECBC went abroad.[56] Many members of MECBC went on missionary work to Turkey, many as missionaries in different regions of Russia and Central Asia and mostly without any financial support.

---

51. An affiliated branch is a group of believers gathering during the week in their locality, but on Sundays, attending another church in which they are members.

52. The Transnistrian region is a breakaway territory of Moldova which is not recognized by any United Nations member states as an independent state, 1 December 2010, http://www.ambasadamoldova.cz/ru/respublika-moldova/o-respublike-moldova/geografia.

53. This is the data for December 2008. It was taken from the report of the Bishop MECBU.

54. Toivo Pilli, "Baptist History in Moldova," in *Dictionary of European Baptist Life and Thoughts*, edited by John Briggs (Milton Keynes: Paternoster, 2009), 337.

55. The author remembers very well the testimonies of people that the Christian attitude of love for them helped them to think about God.

56. Pilli, "Baptist History in Moldova," 337.

Also, a unique opportunity emerged, which allowed us to openly engage in social service. Until that time, USSR authorities had strictly prohibited any open social activities of the MECBU churches. In the early nineties prison ministries were begun among inmates and staff. Churches organized various children's social activities, such as children's day camps and assistance rendered to street children and those placed in orphanages. Some churches began to provide assistance for the rehabilitation of drug addicts and former prostitutes.[57] Believers collected clothing and food items for all of the above-mentioned needy people. Compassion and a desire to help people in need was the motivation for their social service.

Freedom allowed churches to begin various previously prohibited ministries in the churches themselves. For the first time, MECBC was able to organize Bible study groups and Sunday schools.[58] Seminars and conferences were held, aimed at uniting the members of MECBC through a common doctrine, in the centre of which were the teachings of Jesus Christ and His example of service.[59] Thus, a need emerged for the creation of a Bible college, which would prepare church leaders, missionaries in the countries of the former USSR, Sunday school teachers and Christian social workers. So in 1994, the College of Theology and Education (CTE) was founded. CTE is the first evangelical Christian theological school in Moldova. It began to train young people from Moldova, Ukraine and various countries of Central Asia.

But in the second half of the nineties growth ceased in all areas of the life and work of the MECBC. There were both internal and external causes. If people in the early nineties were hungry for spiritual values, then in later times people became more interested in material things. The change of values in society also affected many members of the MECBC. At that time, two external factors adversely affected the people in Moldova, including the believers. These were an economic crisis and loss of work for the majority of people on the one hand, and the opportunity to go abroad for work or to get permanent residence abroad on the other. Thus, at that time more than

---

57. N. Plicci, "Spasay vzyatykh na smerti" [Deliver Those Who are Being Taken Away to Death], *Svet Zhizni* 3, [Light of Life] (Sept.1995): 4.

58. V. Legcun, "Deschiderea Centrului Crestin pentru tineri" [Inauguration of a New Youth Centre], *Svet Zhizni* 1, (Jan. 1996): 15.

59. G. Serghienco, "Isskustvo Propovedi" [The Art of Preaching], *Svet Zhizni* 2 (July 1997): 9.

10,000 baptized adults with their children from MECBU churches left to live permanently in the United States.[60] Taking the country as a whole, to this day, about one million adults are living abroad either working or in search of work, while the population of Moldova numbers only 3.5 million people.[61] Among these people, there are also many Christians from MECBU churches. With the departure of numerous people from MECBU churches it has become harder to continue previously started ministries.

Today, the MECBU churches, though not as zealously as in the nineties, continue some of the ministries started dating back to as early as 1990. Also there are new emerging ministries. Most churches have Sunday schools. Many churches started organizing day-care and summer camps. In the MECBU seminars are held for youth, women and ministers.[62] The emphasis is still placed on preaching the teachings of Jesus Christ in the churches. CTE continues to train young ministers. From 1994 to 2010, the CTE has had 1,001 graduates. CTE graduates have been sent to serve in various countries, including Kazakhstan, Turkmenistan, Uzbekistan, Tajikistan, Azerbaijan, Georgia, Ukraine and remote regions of Russia.[63] However the number of students from MECBC has declined. Fewer young people want to devote their lives to the ministry.

Some of the evangelism methods have been changed in the churches. Thus, evangelistic activities through sports,[64] teaching of English and computer science were initiated.[65] Various clubs have been opened in churches, activities which promote acquaintance and fellowship with unbelievers.[66]

---

60. Pilli, "Baptist History in Moldova", 337.

61. See *Statistika* [Statistics], 15 December 2010, http://www.statistica.md/index.php?l=en.

62. O. Mocan, "O sluzhenii zhenschin" [About Women's Ministry], *Svet Zhizni* 3 (Sept. 1995): 12.

63. "Samoe mnogochislennoe pokolenie vypusknikov TPK" [The Most Numerous Generation of CTE Graduates], *Slovo Istiny* [Word of Truth], Cited hereafter as *Slovo Istiny* 3 (June 2003): 12.

64. Igor Mosneaga, "Misiune prin sport" [Missions through Sports], *Slovo Istiny* 3 (June 2003): 12.

65. See Valentina Stepaniuc, "Facultatea de studio biblic inductive in limba engleza" [The Department of Bible Study in English], *Slovo Istiny* 8 (Aug. 2008), 3; and Vasile Filat, "Tabara de limba engleza" [The Camp in English], *Slovo Istiny* 8 (Aug. 2008): 11.

66. Ion Burlacu, "Oportunitati pentru proclamarea evangheliei" [Possibilities for Proclamation of the Gospel], *Slovo Istiny* 5 (May 2008): 10.

Churches continue to be engaged in social service. The prison ministry has continued.[67] Due to the fact that Moldova is the poorest country in Europe, retired people and children have become particularly vulnerable. Therefore, some of the churches have organized charitable lunches for the elderly and for the children from disadvantaged families.[68] Unfortunately, the involvement of members of the church in social ministry has declined. Generally, this service involves small groups of Christians, and the rest do not care about it too much.

All these negative trends have affected the quality of life and mission of the MECBC. V. Ghiletchi[69] states that along with the increase in the number of churches in Moldova, unity has weakened among believers. He lists several reasons that led to the weakening of unity. The main reason is the shift of values taking place in society from love for other people to self-love. These changes are manifest in their actions and attitudes, which exhibit selfishness, vanity and the desire for enrichment in any way. Such attitudes affect the members of the MECBC.[70] They are less willing to serve each other and those outside the church. As a result of this overall decline, the number of converts and youth in the MECBC has decreased. For example, in 2007 2,005 people were converted in the MECBC, then a year later, only 1,372 people. The number of young people in general in the MECBC decreased from 4,036 people in 2007 to 3,419 in 2008.[71]

In the missionary resolution of the Euro-Asiatic Federation of Unions of the ECB (Evangelical Christian Baptists) the concern was expressed that "many churches are busy only with their internal issues, forgetting that people die right next to them." It contains a call "that all the members of the church: men and women, boys and girls, old men and old women, are to be

---

67. One of the results for this activity is described in an article which focuses on how Christ changed the life of Dima Spataru who had been sentenced to life in prison. See Alla Alexeeva, "Svet Bozhiy liubvi v temnitse" [Light of God's Love in Prison], *Slovo Istiny* 1 (Jan. 2004): 9.

68. Svetlana Nezhel'skaya, "Deti kotorym my mozhem pomoch" [Children Who We Can Help], *Slovo Istiny* 2 (Feb. 2007): 4.

69. V. Ghiletchi was a bishop of MECBU from 2001 to 2007.

70. V. Ghiletchi, "Obrashchenie glavnogo redaktora" [Chief Editor Speech], *Slovo Istiny* 7 (Oct. 2003), 1.

71. This data is from December 2008. It was taken from the report of the Bishop of the MECBU.

missionaries."[72] Ghiletchi also regrets to say that today there are too many Christians who like to "stay in the shade of the vineyard, rather than to bear fruit."[73]

Thus, the present situation in the MECBU churches suggests that, overall, its vision and mission are Christ-centred,[74] but there is a regression in all aspects. There is a need to improve the quality of life and mission. The study of Dostoevsky's theology is conducted from the perspective of a member of the MECBC. After studying its relevance for his society, we will look at the lessons which the MECBC can learn from Dostoevsky's theology.

1.4 Survey of Criticisms of Dostoevsky's Religious Views

In order to see the relevance of the research it is helpful to start with a survey of sources relating to Dostoevsky's religious beliefs. Much has already been written on the faith of Dostoevsky, and disputes about it continue. A characteristic feature of these debates is that along with the desire to understand the complex legacy of the writer, often the desire has been to define Dostoevsky as either one of "us" or as "foreign." Researchers often came from their personal viewpoints of acceptance or rejection of his beliefs. This was particularly marked at the point in the study of Dostoevsky's heritage related to criticism of him during his lifetime and evaluation of his religiosity in the beginning of the twentieth century.

Even as early as the 1880s, literary critics and philosophers – Westernists such as M. A. Antonovich and populists such as N. K. Mikhailovsky – spoke against Dostoevsky.[75] The first accused Dostoevsky of mysticism and asceticism, while the second called him cruel. Almost simultaneously, the religious

---

72. "Rezolyutsia missionerskoy konferentsii Evro-aziatskoy federatsii soyuzov EHB" [Resolution of the Missions Conference of the Euro-Asiatic Federation of Unions of the ECB], *Slovo Istiny*, Vol. 3 (June 2003), 5.

73. Rodica Ivtodi, "Membre in familia credintei" [Members of the Faith Family], *Slovo Istiny*, Vol. 5 (August 2003), 12.

74. Iosif Ton, "Cine suntem noi, baptistii?" [Who Are We, the Baptists?], *Slovo Istiny*, Vol. 9 (September 2003), 9.

75. See M. A. Antonovich, "Mistiko-asketicheskiy roman" [Mystical-Ascetic Novel] (Literatura: 2007), 10 January 2011, http://www.herzenlib.org/page21.php; and N. K. Mihaylovskiy, "Zhestokiy talent" [Cruel Talent] (June 2007), 10 January 2011, http://az.lib.ru/m/mihajlowskij_n_k/text_0042.shtml.

thinker K. N. Leontiev attempted to understand the faith of Dostoevsky. He compared his speech at the celebration of Pushkin with Orthodox dogmas and came to the conclusion that Dostoevsky had a "rosy-coloured Christianity."[76] From quite the opposite standpoint, the religious philosopher Vladimir Soloviev called Dostoevsky a true Christian, who believed in the realization of God's kingdom on earth.[77]

Such contradictory assessments continued to be present in the study of Dostoevsky's creative work. A. S. Voljsky claimed that Dostoevsky used a tremendous effort of will to force himself to believe.[78] In contrast also were those who found Dostoevsky to be the spiritual leader of Russia, her prophet who attained a deep understanding of the nature and the ways of Christianity in the world.[79]

The first Western European critic who drew the attention of the French in particular to Dostoevsky's work was E. M. de Vogue. He talked with deep conviction about the humanism, pity and compassion of Dostoevsky for disadvantaged people.[80]

Since 1910 there has been study of the religious outlook of Dostoevsky in relation to the analysis of his aesthetic principles.[81] In the period 1912–1921 Constance Garnett translated the novels of Dostoevsky and thus the United Kingdom came to know the great writer. At this time critical work by John Middleton Murry appeared. In "Dostoevsky: A Critical Study" (1916), Murry

---

76. See K. N. Leont'ev, *Nashi novye khristiane* [Our New Christians] (Moscow: Nauka, 1882).

77. See V. S. Soloviev, V. "Tri rechi v pam'yat' Dostoevskogo" [Three Speeches on Dostoevsky], 15 January 2011, http://www.vehi.net/soloviev/trirechi.html.

78. See A. S. Volzhlkiy, *F. M. Dostoevskiy. Zhizn' I propoved'* [F. M. Dostoevsky. Life and Sermon] (Moscow: 1906).

79. Those were V. V. Rozanov, D. S. Merejkovsky, N. Bulgakov and A. L. Volinsky. See V. V. Rozanov, *O Dostoevskom* [On Dostoevsky] (Sankt-Petersburg: Molodaya Gvardiya, 1894); D. S. Merezhkovskiy, *L. Tolstoy i Dostoevskiy* [L. Tolstoy and Dostoevsky] (Sankt-Petersburg: 1901-1903); S. N. Bulgakov, *Zhiznennyy podvig Dostoevskogo* [Life Deeds of Dostoevsky] (Moscow: 1908); and A. L. Volynskiy, *Dostoevskiy* [Dostoevsky] (Sankt-Petersburg: 1906).

80. See E. M. de Vogue, *Le roman russe* [Russian novel], 4th ed. (Paris: 1897), 203.

81. Here it is worth highlighting the works of A. L. Slonim, and V. I. Ivanov. See A. L. Slonimskiy, *F. M. Dostoevskiy: Tvorchestvo i Religiya* [F M. Dostoevsky: Creativity and Religion] (Sankt-Petersburg: 1915), and V. I. Ivanov, *Dostoevskiy i Roman Tragediya* [Dostoevsky and the Novel-Tragedy] (Moscow: Kniga, 1990).

presented Dostoevsky's work as a vindication of "human personality" against both positivistic science and the old Christian verities.[82]

Since 1920 interest in Dostoevsky has increased.[83] In 1922–1924 two collections of works of F. Dostoyevsky "Articles and Materials" under the editorship of A. S. Dolinin were published, in which the theme of the Christianity of Dostoevsky received substantial attention. They were articles by A. Askold, L. P. Krasavina and N. O. Lossky.[84] All of the above-mentioned thinkers sought to define a core of religious beliefs of the writer, placing him, some in the problem of freedom, some in the problem of evil, guilt and responsibility, immortality and paradise on earth, etc. At this time emerged studies of Dostoevsky's poetics, the chief representatives of which were L. P. Grossman and M. M. Bakhtin.[85] In connection with this the works of A. Z. Steinberg, B. M. Engelhardt and B. P. Vysheslavtsev appeared.[86] They analyzed how Dostoevsky's worldview determined the artistic characteristics of his work.

In the 1930s in Soviet Russia interest in the religious outlook of Dostoevsky died away. Outside Russia at this time two collections of books on Dostoevsky, published in Prague and edited by A. L. Bem also appeared.[87] They approached the topic of the Christianity of Dostoevsky through the lens of more

---

82. See G. Pattison and D. O. Thompson, "Introduction: Reading Dostoevsky Religiously," in G. Pattison and D. O. Thompson (eds.), *Dostoevsky and The Christian Tradition* (Cambridge: 2001), 13.

83. N. A. Berdyaev, G. A. Pokrovsky, V. L. Komarovich, L. Shestov, A. V. Lunacharskii wrote on his religious worldview. See N. A. Berdyaev, *Mirosozertsanie Dostoevskogo* [Worldview of Dostoevsky] (Moscow: Vysshaya Shkola, 1993); G. A. Pokrovskiy, *Muchenik bogoiskatel'stva* [Martyr in a Search for God] (Moscow: 1929); V. L. Komarovich, *Mirovaya garmoniya Dostoevskogo* [World Harmony of Dostoevsky] (Sankt-Petersburg: 1997); L. Shestov, *Dostoevskiy I Nitsshe: Filosofia tragedii* [Dostoevsky and Nietzsche: Philosophy of Tragedy] (Sankt-Petersburg: 1908); and A. V. Lunocharskiy, *Russkiy Faust* [Russian Faust] (Moscow: 1924).

84. See "F. M. Dostoevskiy: Materialy i isledovaniya" [F. M. Dostoevsky: Materials and Studies] in A. S. Dolinina, ed. (Leningrad: 1935).

85. See L. P. Grossman, *Tvorchestvo Dostoevskogo* [Creative Work of Dostoevsky] (Moscow: 1959); and M. M. Bakhtin, *Problemy poetiki Dostoevskogo* [Problems of Dostoevsky's Poetics] (Moscow: 1979).

86. A. Z. Shteynberg, *Sistema svobody F. M. Dostoevskogo* [System of Freedom of F. M. Dostoevsky] (Paris, 1980); V. M. Engel'gardt, *Ideologicheskiy roman Dostoevskogo* [Ideological Novel of F. M. Dostoevsky] (Sankt- Petersburg: 1924); and B. P. Vysheslavtsev, *Russkaya stikhiya u Dostoevskogo* [Russian Elements in Dostoevsky's Works] (Berlin, 1923).

87. In these collections were articles by I. I. Lapshin, R. V. Pletnev, V. V. Zenkovsky and A. L. Bem. See "O Dostoevskom: Sbornik statey" [On Dostoevsky: Collections of Articles], in A. L. Blem (ed.) (Prague: 1937).

philological issues, such as: the genesis of "Legends of the Grand Inquisitor" and the images of the starets[88] in Dostoevsky. At the same time, the magazine "Way" published articles by S. Gessen, L. Shestov, L. Frank, R. Pletnev.[89] In these articles, the global issues of good and evil, freedom and self-will once again came to the forefront. The role of the Bible and "The Gospel in Dostoevsky" were also discussed.

A very different kind of reception was developing in the German-speaking world. The reputable theologian Karl Barth "saw in Dostoevsky the supreme analyst of the forlornness of man without God, the novelist-theologian who had powerfully depicted all the horrible consequences of human estrangement from God." In an almost Calvinist manner, Barth's Dostoevsky reaffirmed the radical sovereignty of God. Dostoevsky's achievement, according to Eduard Thurneysen, was to call into question everything human in such a way and to such a degree that the only possible remaining answer is God.[90]

A study conducted by L. A. Zander in 1942 and published in English by the Student Christian Movement Press in 1948, drew several links between Dostoevsky and Bulgakov, who also reflected the influence of Dostoevsky. Zander saw Dostoevsky's understanding of human destiny as drawn from the imagery of the New Testament: becoming "the friend of the Bridegroom."[91]

Henri De Lubac in his "The Drama of Atheistic Humanism" (1943) presents Dostoevsky's work as the great modern antidote to Nietzschean nihilism. In de Lubac's view, Dostoevsky was the prophet who resisted the temptation of the "death of God" and dramatized the prospects for the resurrection of the soul through the spiritual overcoming of nihilism.[92]

The well-known German writer Stefan Zweig eloquently expressed his view: "At one and the same time [Dostoevsky] is the truest of believers and the most arrant atheist . . . He loves both the servant of God and the man

---

88. A starets is a respected elder in an Eastern Orthodox monastery.

89. See S. Gessen, *Tragediya dobra v Brat'yakh Karamazovykh* [Tragedy of Good in Brothers Karamazov] (Moscow: Kniga, 1990), L. Shestov, *Kirkegard I Dostoevskiy* [Kierkegaard and Dostoevsky] (Paris, 1935), L. Frank, *Dostoevskiy I krizis gumanizma* [Dostoevsky and the Crisis of Humanism] (Moscow: 1990); and P. V. Pletnev, *Dostoevskiy i Bibliya* [Dostoevsky and the Bible] (Moscow: 1938).

90. See *Dostoevsky and the Christian Tradition*, 15.

91. *Dostoevsky and the Christian Tradition*, 16.

92. *Dostoevsky and the Christian Tradition*, 17.

who denies God, both Alyosha and Ivan . . . In the very presence of God, Dostoevsky remains banished from the land of unity."[93]

From 1950 to the 1970s the majority of Soviet scholars of Dostoevsky's creative work preferred not to address the question of the religious views of the writer. A series of articles and monographs on the life and creative work of Dostoevsky appeared, but only some of them undertook the study of moral and religious issues. Among these one may mention Y. G. Kudryavtsev and Y. F. Karyakin.[94] At the same time in the works of V. E. Vetlovskaya and G. B. Ponomareva a tradition of studying the literary and cultural sources of Dostoevsky's novels developed, which was predominantly Christian in character.[95] In the 1950s N. O. Lossky, while in exile, issued a major work devoted to the study of the Christian worldview of Dostoevsky, where he announced that, for Dostoevsky the entire history of mankind took place in the struggle to reach the paradise of Christ.[96]

One interesting approach is to be found in the work of Stewart Sutherland. Sutherland sees Dostoevsky as both arguing for freedom and demonstrating its problems and limitations.[97] Sutherland's work provides insight into ways in which a religious reading cannot only admit but even require ambiguity or polyphony. A not dissimilar approach is provided in A. Boyce Gibson's "The Religion of Dostoevsky." This was one of the first religious readings of Dostoevsky in English to take on board the burden of Bakhtin's work.[98]

In the 1980's once again, literary critics and philosophers returned to the old argument of "for" and "against," in which researchers approached from

---

93. *Dostoevsky and the Christian Tradition*, 18.

94. See Y. G. Kudryavtsev, *Tri kruga Dostoevskogo* [Three Circles of Dostoevsky] (Moscow: Nauka, 1979); Y. F. Karyakin, *Dostoevsky: Vse – ditya* [Dostoevsky: All Are Children] (Moscow: Nauka, 1971).

95. See V. E. Vetlovskaya, *Tvorchestvo Dostoevskogo v svete literaturnykh I fol'klornykh parallekey. Stroitel'naya zhertva* [The Creative Work of Dostoevsky in Light of Literary and Folk Parallels] (Leningrad: Molodaya Gvardiya, 1978).

96. See N. O. Losskiy, *Dostoevskiy i ego khristianskoe moroponimanie* [Dostoevsky and His Christian World Outlook], (New York: 1953).

97. See G. Pattison and D. O. Thompson, "Introduction: Reading Dostoevsky Religiously," in G. Pattison and D. O. Thompson (eds.), *Dostoevsky and The Christian Tradition* (Cambridge: Cambridge University Press, 2001).

98. W. Boyce Gibson, *The Religion of Dostoevsky* (London: SCM Press, 1973).

different angles the analysis of the belief and unbelief of Dostoevsky.[99] In the past few years an interest has once again emerged on the theme of the Christianity of Dostoevsky.[100] In 1993, an international reading of "Dostoevsky and Modernity" took place in Staraya Russa, entitled "Dostoevsky and the Orthodox Culture," and in 1993 it was held under the theme "Dostoevsky as a Christian Writer."

One may conclude that the issue of faith in Dostoevsky's work has been investigated since the publication of his works right up to the present. In spite of this, there is still room for further research. A complete study of Dostoevsky on the subject of theology, which would not aim to classify Dostoevsky as "ours" or "not ours," but which would instead study Dostoevsky's living theology expressed in his life and works, has not been undertaken.

1.5 Convictional Theology

Dostoevsky was not a theologian and his books are not books of theology. His theology is not a collection of theological statements, but a "living way." It was shown in his daily life and in the lives of his characters. The focus of this book is primary theology (lived out convictions)[101]. To achieve this purpose, in the first part of the book I will use James Wm. McClendon's method

---

99. These are the articles of V. N. Belopolsky, V. A. Nikitin and G. Semenova. See V. N. Belopol'skiy, *Dostoevskiy i folosofskaya mysl' ego epokhi: Kontseptsiya cheloveka* [Dostoevsky and the Philosophical Thought of his Epoch: Concept of Man], (Rostov: 1987), V. A. Nikitin, *Dostoevskiy, pravoslavie i "Russkaya ideya"* [Dostoevsky, Orthodoxy and the "Russian Idea"], (Moscow: Nauka, 1989), G. Semenova, *Vysshaya ideya sushchestvovaniya u Dostoevskogo* [Higher Idea of Existence in Dostoevsky's Work], (Moscow: Nauka, 1989).

100. Pushkin House published the "Dostoevsky: Materials and Research" collection, containing articles by Y. F. Karyakin, G. S. Pomeranetz, B. N. Tarasov, Z. A. Mirkina, L. I. Saraskina, K. A. Stepanyan, I. B. Rodnyansky, A. M. Bulanova and G. B. Ponomareva. See *Dostoevskiy. Materialy i issledovaniya* [Dostoevsky: Materials and Research], (Moscow: Nauka, 2007).

101. The term was originally introduced by Parush R. Parushev in his plenary lecture at the "Theology for the Church: A Convictional Perspective on Community's Theological Discourse," IBTS Directors' Conference *The Dynamics of Primary and Secondary Theologies in Baptistic Communities* 24–28 August 2004, Prague, Czech Republic (forthcoming). Cf. Parush R. Parushev, "Theologie op een baptistenmanier" [Doing Theology in a Baptist Way], in Teun van der Leer, red., *Zo zijn onze manieren! In Gesprek over gemeentetheologie*, Baptistica Reeks (Series), Vol. 1 (Barneveld, Nederland: Unie van Baptisten Gemeenten in Nederland, September 2009, in Dutch), 15–16.

called "the biography as theology method."[102] McClendon proposed using biography as a way of doing theology. He was convinced that character[103] is based on convictions,[104] and theology has to do basically with convictions.[105] "A person's character is formed by the way he sees things, by his vision. It is shaped by the way he does things, by his style. It is coincident with his deepest and most dearly held beliefs, his convictions."[106] Therefore, theology and the ethics of character share common concerns about convictions, which can be found by investigating character through biography. The expression of theology must be discovered not in a systematic formulation of belief like creeds and formal statements of faith, but in the life experiences of people as revealed in their biographies.

The character we investigate in a biographical study is always character in community.[107] A person's convictions are formed in interaction with those of the community.[108] Those who belong to more than one convictional community form themselves and are formed by each community, though not without resultant conflicts in practice. The convictions can be changed.[109] A person's life may embody the convictions of the community, but in a new way; a person may share the vision of the community, but with new scope,

---

102. See James Wm. McClendon, Jr. *Biography as Theology* (Nashville, TN: Abingdon, 1974).

103. Character is the persistent qualities of selfhood. See James Wm. McClendon, Jr., *Ethics: Systematic Theology, Vol. 1* (Nashville, TN: Abingdon, 1986), 355. Character is both the cause and consequence of what we do. See James Wm. McClendon, Jr., *Biography as Theology*, 16.

104. Convictions are firm beliefs that guide the person. They do not change so easily, but if we change them, then the person changes as well. See James Wm. McClendon, Jr. and James M. Smith, *Understanding Convictions: Defusing Religious Relativism*, rev. ed. (Valley Forge, PA: Trinity Press International, 1994), 5.

105. According to James Wm. McClendon's definition, theology is "discovery, understanding, and transformation of the convictions of a convictional community, including the discovery and critical revision of their relation to one another and to whatever else there is". See James Wm. McClendon, Jr., *Ethics. Systematic Theology, Vol. 1*, 23.

106. James Wm. McClendon, Jr., *Biography as Theology*, 17.

107. McClendon, 170.

108. On the convictional perspective of a community of faith as offering epistemological groundings of a person's worldview, see Parush R. Parushev, "Convictional Perspectivism: A Constructive Proposal for a Theological Response to Postmodern Conditions," in John Corrie and Cathy Ross, eds., *Mission in Context: Explorations Inspired by Andrew Kirk* (Farnham, UK: Ashgate, 2012), 111–124.

109. McClendon, *Biography as Theology*, 18.

and his example of life may serve to disclose and to correct or enlarge the community's moral vision.[110]

Dostoevsky's biography was centred on his membership in Russian society during the nineteenth century. During his life he belonged to many communities who shared their convictions. Thus Dostoevsky's biography will be explored through his connection with the life of the communities in which his convictions were formed and expressed.

Dostoevsky expressed his convictions in his literature. To discover Dostoevsky's theology expressed in his literature, theological motifs[111] will be described and analysed in three of his novels. Theological motifs are evidence of an author's theology[112] and convictions as they are grounded in the Bible, in the life of Jesus Christ and in the author's religious experience.[113] The Bible narratives and the life of Jesus Christ inspired Dostoevsky to use theological motifs in his writing.

First, theological motifs of love, humility, and care were used by Dostoevsky to describe the relationship between people as they were in paradise, inspired by Genesis 1–2. Second, to show the distorted world after the fall (Gen 3), Dostoevsky used theological motifs of vanity, covetousness, gain, humiliation of others, committing crime for the sake of pleasure, indifference, pride, and inhumanity. He also used the following contrasts: contentment and envy,

---

110. McClendon, 22.

111. In a narrative, such as a novel, motifs are images, symbols, an idea, an object, a place, a statement or themes that are repeated throughout a piece of literature or across more than one piece of literature so as to form a pattern. Because they recur at different points in a narrative, motifs help to unify the text, particularly in cases where the narrative is fairly long. A motif need not necessarily be a primary theme of the piece of literature in which it appears, though it often is a dominant theme. Even when motifs are not the primary theme of a work, they still illuminate the primary themes of the work and direct the reader's attention toward them. Michael E. Travers, "Literary Motifs," http://bible.org/seriespage/literary-motifs (12 December 2010). The narrative motif is the vehicle by means of which the narrative theme is conveyed. James H. Grayson, *Myths and Legends from Korea: An Annotated Compendium of Ancient and Modern Materials* (New York; Abingdon: Routledge Curzon, 2000), 9.

112. Ivana Noble, being inspired by Paul Tillich's affirmation "that both theology and culture are in the ultimate concern" related to the "Ultimate Reality." See Ivana Noble, *Theological Interpretation of Culture in Post-Communist Context* (Farnham: Ashgate, 2010), 1–12.

113. On the convictional nature of moral reasoning, see Parush R. Parushev, "Convictions and the Shape of Moral Reasoning," in Parush R. Parushev, Ovidiu Creangă, Brian Brock, eds., *Ethical Thinking at the Crossroads of European Reasoning*, Occasional Publications Series, Vol. 7 (Prague, CZ: IBTS Publisher, 2007), 27–45.

modesty and vanity, charity and a desire to dominate, peacefulness and hatred, love and selfishness.

Third, Dostoevsky was convinced that even after the fall each person has an image of God and is able to love and to have compassion. In Dostoevsky's understanding, God gave free will to each person. The person can express his revolt against God, or recognize Him as God. He used theological motifs of love, compassion, and freedom to show the image of God within each person.

Fourth, the life, death, and resurrection of Jesus Christ inspired Dostoevsky. That is why he used theological motifs of faith in God and repentance as a way to start to live as Christ. Theological motifs of love, compassion, and care for people were an expression of faith in God and following the example of Jesus. Theological motifs are used by Dostoevsky to describe the virtues and vices that form the convictions of the main characters of his novels. All these theological motifs will be used to describe and analyze Dostoevsky's convictional theology expressed in his literature.

1.6 The Structure of the Study

This book divides logically into seven chapters. The first chapter is an introductory one. The goal of the first part of chapters 2–4 is to discover and analyze Dostoevsky's convictions as shown in his life. The biography as theology method has been used to achieve the goal. In terms of methodology, I evaluated Dostoevsky's life by building a narrative underlining the development and progression of events in the relevant socio-historical setting. Thus three chapters of this part will study three different periods of Dostoevsky's life, in which he held different convictions. Though the life of a person is one whole unit, it consists of different periods and parts. These periods may identify age, occupation, etc., depending on the type of research. Since our task is to study Dostoevsky's beliefs, it is easier to conduct research by looking at different periods of his life, which are characterized by common beliefs. Therefore, we will consider three periods: pre-Siberian (1821–1849), Siberian (1849–1859) and post-Siberian (1859–1881). For this task, the primary sources used were: F. M. Dostoevsky's memos and notebooks; *Diary of a Writer*; a collection of his letters; memoirs of his wife and daughters; and reminiscences of Dostoevsky's co-workers, acquaintances and friends. The importance of this part consists in presenting Dostoevsky's theology as expressed in his life.

The second part of chapters 2–4 investigates Dostoevsky's theology expressed in his literature. Three of Dostoevsky's novels: *The Poor Folk*, *The House of the Dead* and *The Brothers Karamazov* will be explored. The theological motifs in the books provide evidence of theology. The primary sources that were used in this part are the three novels. The second part of chapter 2 is the study of the first novel by Dostoevsky: *The Poor Folk*. There is unanimity among Dostoevsky's researchers that during the pre-Siberian period *The Poor Folk* was the most important novel by Dostoevsky. In chapter 3 there is an investigation of Dostoevsky's novel *The House of the Dead* which is the only novel of the Siberian period, though it was published two years after his return from Siberia, in 1861. In chapter 4 I investigate of *The Brothers Karamazov*. It is the last novel he wrote.

The goal of the investigation in chapter 5 is to unite as one whole the theology of Dostoevsky, discovered in his life and writings. This will seek to show if Dostoevsky's character is a holistic one or not. The goal of chapter 6 is to investigate the influence of Dostoevsky's theology on the society of his time and on a contemporary baptistic community. Because this research has been done by a member of the Moldavian Evangelical Christian Baptist Church, the goal of chapter 7 is to look at the lessons which can be learned from Dostoevsky's living theology by the MECBC today.

1.7 Conclusion

The central issue of this research is Dostoevsky's theology expressed in his life and literature and its relevance for the life and mission of the Moldavian Evangelical Christian Baptist Church (MECBC). The task undertaken here is to discover Dostoevsky's theology not in a systematic formulation of belief, but in his life-experiences as revealed in his biography. This method of examination has not been utilised before to study the theology of Dostoevsky.

CHAPTER 2

Pre-Siberian Period: The Quest

2.1 Introduction

The purpose of this chapter is to discover and analyse Dostoevsky's convictions as they were revealed in his life during the pre-Siberian period and to discover and analyse theological motifs expressed in *The Poor Folk*. To achieve this goal, it is necessary to first identify and analyse Dostoevsky's communities and their shared convictions; to identify and analyse Dostoevsky's own convictions; and to discover and analyse the influence of Dostoevsky's life on society. Second, theological motifs expressed in *The Poor Folk* will be identified and studied. The theological motifs discovered in these novels point to Dostoevsky's message for Russian society.

2.2 Dostoevsky's Convictions Shown in His Own Life During the Pre-Siberian Period

The purpose of the first part of this chapter is to identify and analyze Dostoevsky's convictions as expressed in the pre-Siberian (1821–1849)[1] period of his life. This encompasses his childhood, school and college years, and the beginning of his literary and political activities. Since some of the historical events in Russia during that period influenced the formation and revision of his convictions we will begin there; and since our method is "biography as

---

1. Siberian period: the time that F. M. Dostoevsky spent in hard labour in Siberian exile (*katorga*).

theology" we will explore Dostoevsky's *Letters*, *Diary of a Writer*, and notebooks; the memoirs of contemporaries, the writer's wife, his brother Andrei, and daughter Liubovi also serve as primary sources.

2.2.1 Under Family Influence (1821–1834)

The first of Dostoevsky's convictional communities was his parents' family. Home is the place where a person first interacts with the surrounding world. People, events and things may influence one to such an extent that even in early childhood some of the strongest impressions will shape various beliefs which will stay with a person for the rest of his or her life.

There were seven children in their family. The first child was Mikhail, Fyodor was second. Five more children followed him – Varenika, Andrei, Verochka, Nikolay, and the youngest of all was Alexandra.[2] Fyodor Mikhailovich was born in Moscow, on October 30, 1821, in Mariyn hospital, where his father worked as a physician.[3] He was only eight when his sister Lyubochka died. She lived only a few days.[4] Thus, early in his childhood, Dostoevsky knew the depth of grief that came into his family. Even as a child, he felt within himself the imperfection of the world.

There are many stories about Mikhail Andreevich (1788–1839), the father of Fyodor Mikhailovich, who was a severe man. He often caused unpleasantness in the family, where the writer had to grow up. Leonid Grossman shares this point of view in his biography of Dostoevsky.

> Mikhail Andreevich's character had little in common with his humane profession. According to several testimonies from the family, he was exceedingly irritable, extremely short-tempered and arrogant. He represented a stubborn and tireless type of worker, gloomy, performing his life duty, intolerant in his demands of others. His anger flashes were terrible. Nonetheless, he was appallingly stingy, and suffered from a heavy form of alcoholism.[5]

---

2. *F. M. Dostoevskiy v vospominaniyakh sovremennikov* [F. M. Dostoevsky in the Memoirs of Contemporaries] (Moscow: Hudozhestvennaya literatura, 1990), 29.

3. *F. M. Dostoevskiy v vospominaniyakh sovremennikov*, 31.

4. *F. M. Dostoevskiy v vospominaniyakh sovremennikov*, 36.

5. *Dostoevskiy* [Dostoevsky], (Moscow: Molodaya Gvardiya, 1962), 9.

In order to support this idea, he mentions Fyodor Mikhailovich's refusal to talk about his father, whenever asked. L. F. Dostoevskaya, the writer's daughter, confirms this standpoint. She portrayed her father's childhood in dark and dull colours.[6] Moreover, O. F. Miller has written that Fyodor Mikhailovich's father was sullen, nervous and a suspicious person.[7]

E. M. Rumyantseva shares Leonid Grossman's opinion that Mikhail Andreevich was a secluded and stingy person with a tough character. However, this stinginess, according to Rumyantseva, was a result of constant worries over the family's financial well-being. This is supported by the fact that he never hesitated to invest money in his children's education, despite regular complaints over financial difficulties. His sons studied in private schools and received a good education for their time, when studies in public schools would have cost much less. Rumyantseva believes that their father's constant reminders to his children about lack of money are not so much due to stinginess, as poverty.[8] Subsequently, there are no reasons to consider him as a monster or to believe that the life of Dostoevsky's family was completely nerve-racking and oppressive.

There is plenty of evidence to support the idea that the general tone of the Dostoevsky family life was a positive one. Andrei Mikhailovich, a younger brother of Fyodor Mikhailovich, agrees that their father was extremely demanding, impatient, and quick-tempered. Although he never physically abused children, his sons were afraid of him.[9] However, unlike L. F. Dostoevskaya, he also remembers their father's positive personal traits. He claims that while with his family, Mikhail Andreevich was always cheerful and kind, and used every opportunity to share useful information with his children.[10] He was also exceedingly careful with their morals, and especially with the oldest brothers, when they got older.[11]

In contrast to Fyodor Mikhailovich's father, who was a closed and a stingy person, his mother was the total opposite of her husband. Maria Fyodorovna

---

6. E. M. Rumyantseva, *Feodor Mikhaylovich Dostoevskiy* (Leningrad: Prosveshchenie, 1971), 6.

7. *F. M. Dostoevskiy v vospominaniyakh sovremennikov*, 191.

8. *Feodor Mikhaylovich Dostoevskiy*, 7.

9. *F. M. Dostoevskiy v vospominaniyakh sovremennikov*, 81–82.

10. *F. M. Dostoevskiy v vospominaniyakh sovremennikov*, 110.

11. *F. M. Dostoevskiy v vospominaniyakh sovremennikov*, 87.

(1800–1837) had a cheerful, light personality. She loved poetry and had wonderful literary abilities. She was deeply committed to her husband, children and family.[12]

Life in the family was very monotonous: pleasures and guests were very uncommon. The children spent the majority of their time under parental supervision, in a small government apartment. They played games like all children. According to Andrei's testimony, Fyodor was a very creative boy in starting games and was an obvious leader.[13] His cheerful personality, independent character and unusual sympathy were apparent even in his early childhood.

However, very rarely were the children able to get away from the hospital facilities. Every single day they saw sick and poor people coming to the hospital. Occasionally, without their father's awareness, Fyodor Mikhailovich was able to talk with patients. Out of these conversations, he would learn about the wider world.[14] The absolutism in Russia in the first part of the nineteenth century presented a late form of feudal state.[15] Economics and social relations were interconnected with the political structures of the country: autocracy, bureaucracy, state institutions.[16] Its main attribute was the unlimited power of the monarch. With the appearance of absolutism in Russia (in the first quarter of eighteenth century) this notion completely matched with the notion of autocracy.[17] In 1613, Russian people took a vow before Mikhail Romanov that the Romanov family would rule in an autocratic way, being responsible only to God.[18] This signifies that the context that was formed in the nineteenth century in Russia depended on emperors, who controlled the situation.

The poverty and illnesses which Dostoevsky met in the hospital were often the consequences of the tsar's despotism. Dostoevsky could hear and see from his childhood that a part of Russia society lived in slavery and that these people were unhappy.[19] A. Saveliev believes that compassion for the poor and

---

12. Rumyantseva, *Feodor Mikhaylovich Dostoevskiy*, 8.

13. *F. M. Dostoevskiy v vospominaniyakh sovremennikov*, 77.

14. *F. M. Dostoevskiy v vospominaniyakh sovremennikov*, 81–82.

15. N. P. Eroshkin, *Krepoctnicheskoe samoderzhavie i ego politicheskie instituty* [The Feudal Autocracy and Its Political Institutions] (Moscow: "Mysl,'" 1981), 24.

16. Eroshkin, 3.

17. N. P. Eroshkin, *Krepoctnicheskoe samoderzhavie i ego politicheskie instituty*, 24.

18. E. Radzinskiy, *Aleksandr II Zhizn' i Smert'* [Alexander II: His Life and Death] (Moscow: Izdatel'stvo AST, 2006), 81.

19. *F. M. Dostoevskiy v vospominaniyakh sovremennikov*, 82.

oppressed developed very early in Fyodor Mikhailovich in childhood, while living in his father's house in Moscow, at the hospital for poor people. Daily, Fyodor Mikhailovich would observe masses of poor people staying near the window, lying or sitting in the backyard of the hospital, waiting to be helped.[20]

Books had an enormous influence on the shaping of Dostoevsky's convictions. Love of reading was inculcated in the minds of the children in this family at an early stage. There was a family tradition to spend evenings in a dining room illuminated by two candles. This environment provided a good opportunity for the parents to read to their children. Careful attention was given to the most dramatic periods of Russian history. Two events and their consequences were dramatic for Russia. These were the Great Patriotic War of 1812 and the Decembrist revolt of 1825. The events of 1812 greatly influenced internal affairs. Seldom have external politics changed the inner life in Russia so drastically. The war was truly patriotic, a national war that awakened a new patriotism. It stirred up people's national consciousness and pushed it to a social revival. This became particularly noticeable in the army.[21] Noble youth nearly without exception were drafted into military service. Serving in the military they travelled abroad,[22] and got acquainted with German and French liberal ideas not previously heard in Russia.[23]K. N. Levin claimed that when the soldiers marched through Europe, they were impressed that in Western Europe, instead of the feudal system, new liberal social relations were formed. This fact greatly struck them.[24] They were able to witness other lifestyles, other political systems, different ways to manage a country and dissimilar conditions. A peasant for example could exist without being attached to the land and to his landlord. Military discipline could be sustained without physical punishment, which in Russia often meant death. People could talk and write about issues that were forbidden in Russia.[25] Back home there was slavery and the unrestrained arbitrariness of authorities. Soldiers started to

---

20. *F. M. Dostoevskiy v vospominaniyakh sovremennikov*, 166–167.

21. *Istoriya Rossii v XIX veke* [The History of Russia in the Nineteenth Century] (Sankt-Peterburg: Russkaya Skoropechatnya), 62.

22. *Istoriya Rossii v XIX veke*, 61–62.

23. *Istoriya Rossii v XIX veke*, 67.

24. *Istoriya Rossii v XIX veke*, 67.

25. S. V. Mironenko, *Samoderzhavie i Reformy: Politicheskaya bor'ba v Rossii v nachale XIX v.* [Autocracy and Reform: The Political Struggle in Russia in the Early Nineteenth Century] (Moscow: Nauka, 1989), 62.

sow the first seeds of revolt among the people.[26] Decembrist A. A. Bestuzhev remembers these soldiers' words: "We have shared our blood and now we are forced to work heavily at state labour. We have saved the motherland from a tyranny and now we are again tyrannized by landlords."[27] During this time the horrible consequences of the war were added to all the contradictions in society, to the chaos and poverty of the majority of the population. The country was ravaged by war, which caused titanic tension in the economy and enormous material and human losses.[28]

The reading of literature that Dostoevsky undertook was probably prompted by his parent's life experience, especially that of his father. He tried to prepare his children, in particular the boys, for a tough independent life, frequently reminding them of his own poverty. He wanted them to know that they would have to strike out on their own, since they did not have sufficient financial income and in the event of his death, all of them would become beggars.[29] The Great Patriotic War of 1812 and the Decembrist revolt of 1825 influenced the formation of Dostoevsky's patriotism and a desire for justice for Russian people.

Dostoevsky's parents' faith in God also influenced the formation of his convictions. His parents, especially his mother, were religious and took care of the children's religious education. From letters kept by Andrei Mikhailovich, we learn about his parents' faith and their relationships. Tenderness, love, longing for each other when separated, and other warm feelings can be sensed in these letters. Both father and mother, at the beginning of their letters, thank God. Yet, it is not a simple habit and custom, but a well-thought belief bound to a specific event: when their son Nikolay recovered from illness, his father rejoiced and thanked God for this miracle. Meanwhile discussing the negative consequences of never ending rains in a village, Mikhail Fyodorovich proclaims: "let it be according to God's will, let us fully rely on Him."[30] In other letter, he concludes one more time: "let it be according to God's pleasing

---

26. *Istoriya Rossii v XIX veke*, 67.

27. *Iz pisem i pokazaniy dekabristov* [From the Letters and Testimony of the *Decembrists*], ed. A. K. Borozdina (Sankt-Peterburg: 1906), 35–36.

28. Mironenko, *Samoderzhavie i Reformy. Politicheskaya bor'ba v Rossii v nachale XIX v.*, 9.

29. Rumyantseva, *Feodor Mikhaylovich Dostoevskiy*, 11.

30. *F. M. Dostoevsky v vospominaniyakh sovremennikov*, 99–101.

will."[31] One of Dostoevsky's first recollections as a three year-old boy was the daily evening prayer, "My hope is in You, O holy God, keep me under Your shelter." This was Fyodor Mikhailovich's favourite prayer and he used it during difficult moments of his life. It was one of the prayers that he prayed with his children, before going to sleep.[32] In 1873, Fyodor Mikhailovich wrote: "From an early age, in our family, we knew the gospel."[33] The younger brother of Fyodor Dostoevsky, Andrei, recalls in his memoirs, "Our parents were quite religious people. Especially our mother – every Sunday as well as on all the major religious feasts we would go to church for the day-hours service, and the day before that for the all-night service."[34]

Through different stages of life, Fyodor Mikhailovich differently assessed the nature of his childhood. In young adulthood, Dostoevsky did not consider his childhood as a "happy" one. However, as an older man, according to his wife, "he willingly recalled his cheerful and carefree childhood, and warm-heartedly spoke about mother."[35] At the end of the 1870s, Fyodor Mikhailovich shared with his brother Andrei his opinion about their parents: "You know, brother, after all, they were leading people . . . and presently they would be great leaders . . . As married people ourselves, fathers . . . it is something we can't attain, brother!"[36]

In 1831, Mikhail Andreevich purchased two small properties in Tula province near Darovoe and Cheremoshnu, villages with hundreds of fortress peasants.[37] The brightest of Dostoevsky's memories from late childhood are connected with these properties. The Dostoevsky family used to spend the summer there, without their father, and the children would have total freedom. Fyodor Mikhailovich was eleven when his parents bought this small estate. Their village house was a small one, and boys used to spend their time outside, in the fields, frequently among peasants. Various regular encounters

---

31. *F. M. Dostoevsky v vospominaniyakh sovremennikov*, 102.

32. N. O. Losskiy, *Bog i mirovoe zlo* [God and World Evil] (Moscow: Respublika, 1994), 36.

33. F. M. Dostoevsky, *Polnoe Sobranie Sochineniy v 30-i tomakh T. 21, Dnevnik Pisatelya za 1873g.,* [The Complete Works of Dostoevsky in 30 Volumes, Vol. 21, Diary of a Writer, 1873] (Leningrad: Nauka, 1980), 134. Cited hereafter as *Dnevnik Pisatelya*.

34. *F. M. Dostoevsky v vospominaniyakh sovremennikov*, 110.

35. A. G. Dostoevskaya, *Vospominaniya* [Reminiscence] (Moscow: Pravda, 1987), 94.

36. *F. M. Dostoevsky v vospominaniyakh sovremennikov*, 110.

37. Rumyanceva, *Feodor Mikhaylovich Dostoevsky*, 7.

with peasants and their lifestyle became lifelong memories for Dostoevsky.[38] During these years, he was very close to peasants, their lifestyle and the moral image of the simple Russian nation.[39] He enjoyed talking to them, leading horses with harrows and following the plough. He gladly tackled just about any assigned task.

A story is told of Dostoevsky, in which his sacrificial spirit is displayed in his attitude towards simple peasants who found themselves in need. Once, he happily carried a bucket of water from a village (15 kilometres away) for a peasant woman, who had accidentally spilled it, desiring to quench her child's thirst. In a village, Dostoevsky heard the stories about "martyrs and righteous people," and experienced kindness and peasants' sympathy that he remembered all his life.[40]

Fyodor Mikhailovich began his education fairly early; his mother taught him the Russian alphabet. She read the same book to all her children. The full name of this book is: "One hundred and four holy stories chosen from the Old and New Testament in favour of John Gibner's youth." The children loved this book. Andrei remembers: "I remember in the seventies talking with my brother Fyodor Mikhailovich about our childhood, and he mentioned this book; and what a joy it was for him to finally find this book and he kept it as something really sacred."[41]

Dostoevsky was especially fascinated by the book of Job, with its story about an innocent person who experienced great tribulations from God without complaint: the death of loved ones, ravaging of livestock, leprosy and poverty. Later he was healed, restored to financial well-being, became the father of a big family and "died, old and full of years." In 1875 Dostoevesky told his wife: "I read the book of Job and it brings me painful delight. I quit reading it and for hours walk in a room; almost crying . . . It is a strange thing, Anna, yet this book is one of the first ones to impress me, while I was still only an infant!"[42] The image of the Old-Testament sufferer Job and the images of martyrs became the foundation of Dostoevsky's understanding of

---

38. *Dnevnik Pisatelya*, 1877, 61.

39. *F. M. Dostoevskiy v vospominaniyakh sovremennikov*, 299.

40. Rumyantseva, *Feodor Mikhaylovich Dostoevsky*, 14.

41. *F. M. Dostoevskiy v vospominaniyakh sovremennikov*, 79.

42. Grossman, *Dostoevsky*, 15.

the tragic path and regeneration of the modern man. In the case of the child, the function of examples is to help him become aware of what he knows innately to be good.[43]

Education played a major role in the formation of Dostoevsky's convictions. It instilled in him love towards God's word and literature as such. Two teachers who had specialized in teenage studies were invited from the nearby University of Ekaterina to his home. It was in Moscow. One was a deacon, who taught God's law. He was gifted in oral communication and used to spend two-hour long lectures interpreting Holy Scripture.[44] The other teacher was Nikolay Ivanovich Sushard, who taught French.[45] His father also was concerned with the education of his children. He taught Latin, well known to him from Podol seminary and medical academy.[46] Soon after that, P. P. Semenov-Tyan-Shansky agrees with O. F. Miller in his memoirs, Fyodor Mikhailovich was an educated man. He claimed: "In his childhood, he had great training from his scientifically educated father, a Moscow military physician."[47]

In 1833 homeschooling was over for the older sons. Mikhail and Fyodor entered the Frenchman N. I. Drashusov's boarding school, and then during the fall of 1834 the brothers were transferred to the German Chermak's boarding school. D. Grigorovich says of this boarding school: "I have met numerous graduates of Chermak's boarding school, where Dostoevsky received his education; all of them impressed me with their remarkable literary training and knowledge."[48] They used to arrive home on Saturday afternoons and return to school on Monday mornings. Dostoevsky's study in these schools made stronger his love for literature.[49]

In boarding school, the brothers especially enjoyed oral communication classes, and leisure time was used to read books. Dostoevsky many times re-read a Russian history written by Karamazin,[50] and his narratives; Zhukovsky;

---

43. James P. Scanlan, *Dostoevsky the Thinker* (London: Cornell University Press, 2002), 91.

44. *F. M. Dostoevskiy v vospominaniyakh sovremennikov*, 80.

45. *F. M. Dostoevskiy v vospominaniyakh sovremennikov*, 81.

46. Grossman, *Dostoevsky*, 19.

47. *F. M. Dostoevskiy v vospominaniyakh sovremennikov*, 298.

48. *F. M. Dostoevskiy v vospominaniyakh sovremennikov*, 201.

49. *F. M. Dostoevskiy v vospominaniyakh sovremennikov*, 201.

50. Famous historiographer N. M. Karamzin helped him to settle a specific program, which could fit Nikolay I's character. Daily for two months he would come to the palace and share with Nikolay I personal views on the ruling tasks in Russia. *Kniga dlya chteniya po istorii*

and novels by W. Scott, Zagoskin, Lazhechnikov, Narezhny and Weltmann. Karamzin was a supporter of absolute autocracy. He tried to show that the problems of Alexander I's reign were bound to lead to a weakening of autocracy. Its restoration would mean revival and intensification of the state's power and strength in Russia.[51] Karamzin saw the role of the autocrat in a commitment to the interest and well-being of the country. "Committing himself to this service, the autocrat monarch has a right and must require total subordination from his employees, which would however lower them to the level of slaves and deprive them of personal freedom and patriotic feelings particularly."[52] This was Karamzin's heritage, which under Nikolay I's reign had to be implemented into the whole system of state management. Karamzin's Russian history helped Dostoevsky to become acquainted with the past of the Russian nation and stimulated patriotism in him.

Fyodor Mikhailovich began his conscious life when literary pieces were gaining supreme importance for shaping public opinion and consciousness in Russia. During the first half of the nineteenth century, Russian literature was mainly in the hands of the average nobility. Literature's noble origin had definitely influenced the forms and essence of its development. In terms of ideological content, noble literature reflected the worldview of its own class.[53] However, during Nikolay I's epoch the following writers appeared: Nedezhdin, Pogodin, Polevoi and Belinsky. More and more, literary figures become intellectuals outside of defined classes; to the same extent their ideology differed considerably.[54]

More and more writers tried to describe reality. A. S. Pushkin himself realized it and described the pale charm of Pskov's fields and forests. Both brothers could easily recite almost all of Pushkin's works.[55] Yet it was only Gogol who formed realistic aesthetics.[56] Gogol was a humorist. Laughter's

---

novogo vremeni. T. IV [A Book for Reading a History of Modern Time] (Moscow: Tipografiya T-va I. D. Sytina, 1914), 85.

51. *Kniga dlya chteniya po istorii novogo vremeni. T. IV*, 86.

52. *Kniga dlya chteniya po istorii novogo vremeni. T. IV*, 90.

53. *Istoriya Rossii v XIX veke*, 379.

54. *Russkoe obshhestvo 30-kh godov XIX v. Lyudi i idei*, [Russian Society of the Thirties of the Nineteenth Century: People and Ideas] (Moscow: Izdatel'stvo Moskovskogo universiteta, 1989), 46.

55. *Russkoe obshhestvo 30-kh godov XIX v. Lyudi i idei*, 82–85.

56. *Istoriya Rossii v XIX veke*, 431.

catharsis in Gogol's writings forced readers to look at modern reality in an alarmed, exciting and merry way.[57]

In 1836, in the darkest time of merciless censorship, a very bold composition in the "Telescope" magazine shocked society. It was the "Philosophical Letter" written by Peter Chadaev.[58] An aristocrat, a brilliant soldier who courageously fought against Napoleon, suddenly had spoken publicly. He wrote a composition, which exploded the obedient silence of the time.[59]

The censorship pressure was so heavy that no one expected writers to perform.[60] It was obvious that the censor did not even read a composition with a boring name "Philosophical Letter."[61] In a month's time, almost every home in Moscow spoke about Chadaev's article. The entire composition was an impossibly brave blow aimed at the whole official ideology. In his "Letter" Chadaev critiqued just about everything that the emperor considered holy.[62] He accused Russian Orthodoxy, writing that "true religiosity is upsettingly different from the stuffy environment in which we do live and most likely shall live."[63] "I did not learn to love my country with eyes closed, head bowed and mouth shut. I believe that a person can be useful to his country only if he sees it clearly. . ." – these are Chadaev's famous words.[64] The tsar declared Chadaev insane and placed him under house arrest.[65] A famous French writer (Kyustin) visited Chadaev and exclaimed: "What a glorious city Moscow is! Here you can find some historical absurdities . . . a gun, which never shot or a bell, which fell and never rings . . . However, a bell without a tongue is a symbol of a beloved native land."[66]

The second blow came in 1843, when Marquis Astolif de Kyustin's book *Russia in 1839* was published. Kyustin was a passionate follower of absolute monarchy. His father and grandfather were executed during the French

---

57. *Istoriya Rossii v XIX veke*, 435.

58. *Russkoe obshhestvo 30-kh godov XIX v. Lyubi i idei*, 35.

59. Radzinskiy, *Aleksandr II Zhizn' i Smert'*, 100.

60. *Kniga dlya chteniya po istorii novogo vremeni*, 104.

61. Radzinskiy, *Aleksandr II Zhizn' i Smert'*, 100.

62. *Russkoe obshhestvo 30-kh godov XIX v. Lyudi i idei*, 35.

63. Radzinskiy, *Aleksandr II Zhizn' i Smert'*, 101.

64. Radzinskiy, 101.

65. Radzinskiy, 102.

66. Radzinskiy, 104.

revolution. He willingly came to Russia, to be reassured once again of the advantages of an autocratic leadership style.[67]

According to V. Kirpotin, this was a time when "Russian literature became a megaphone for public and moral longings."[68] Dostoevsky turned out to be very open to new influences. Pushkin's influence was the strongest of all the literary influences experienced by Dostoevsky. "After all, through Pushkin we have reached contemporary issues, he was a beginning of what we have now," Dostoevsky wrote in one of his articles.[69] Pushkin was a poetry and harmony teacher. He taught ways to find the most harmonious and poetic things in the world around: in nature, history, society and especially in people. Human beings were the measure of Pushkin's world. Humanism was the highest manifestation of Pushkin's poetic and philosophical worldview.[70] V. Kirpotin considers that Pushkin promoted Dostoevsky's closeness with people. In his opinion, Pushkin, confirming a human value in each person, regardless of his orher position, really expressed closeness to people, not only to an uncomplaining and humiliated official, but to a peasant, or a rebellious one. "He, a spoiled man, son of a nobleman, got to know Pugachev and entered his soul, when nobody and nothing could enter before," Dostoevsky exclaimed in his "Winter Notes on Summer Impressions."[71]

Dostoevsky was sixteen when Pushkin was killed in a duel, Lermontov was exiled to the Caucasus, and Gogol moved abroad. Some of these and other events greatly influenced Dostoevsky: "When I was only about fifteen, I had some kind of fire in my soul that I believed in, regardless of the outcomes that did not bother me much . . ."[72]

At the same time, Dostoevsky lost his mother. Andrei remembers this time:

---

67. Markiz Astol'f de Kyuctin, *Nikolaevskaya Rossiya* [Nicholas' Russia] (Moscow: Izdatel'stvo politicheskoy literatury 1990), 5.

68. *Molodoy Dostoevsky* [The Young Dostoevsky] (Moscow: OGIZ, 1947), 58.

69. F. M. Dostoevsky, *Polnoe Sobranie Sochineniy v 30-i tomakh, T. 18, Stat'i i Zametri 1845-1861* [The Complete Works of Dostoevsky in 30 Volumes, Vol. 18, Articles and Notes, 1845–1861] (Leningrad: Nauka, 1978), 103. Cited hereafter as *Stat'i i Zametri*.

70. *Molodoy Dostoevsky*, 59.

71. F. M. Dostoevsky, *Polnoe Sobranie Sochineniy v 30-i tomakh, T. 5, Zimnie zametki o letnikh vpechatleniyakh* [The Complete Works of Dostoevsky in 30 Volumes, Vol. 5, Winter Notes on Summer Impression] (Leningrad: Nauka, 1973), 51–52.

72. F. M. Dostoevsky, *Polnoe Sobranie Sochineniy v 30-i tomakh, T. 29, Pis'ma* [The Complete Works of Dostoevsky in 30 Volumes, Vol. 29, Letters] (Leningrad: Nauka, 1986), 156. Cited hereafter as *Pis'ma*.

> This was the bitterest time in our childhood. We were prepared
> to lose our mother any time. Our family experienced pure shock
> and tremendous transformation when mother died. By the end
> of February 1837, doctors declared to father that their attempts
> were useless, and we should expect a tragic end. Father was
> destroyed by this news! I remember the night, before mother's
> death, on 26–27 February. Before her death, mother requested
> an icon of the Saviour and then she blessed us and father after-
> wards. We all sobbed.[73]

According to Grossman, their mother's death fully destroyed the family. Mikhail Andreevich tendered his resignation. Concerned about the well-being of the two oldest sons, Mikhail Andreevich sent them to the Academy of Engineers in Petersburg.[74]

Thus, the first sixteen years of the author's life could be considered a period of acquaintance with the surrounding world and shaping his first beliefs. We have enough evidence about the people and events that shaped Dostoevsky's attitudes while growing up. The formation of the later beliefs of Dostoevsky were influenced by love and parental education, books, education, Christian and Biblical characters. He fell in love not only with literature, but most especially with humans. One could see the manifestation of love and compassion of Dostoevsky towards simple and sick people. Most importantly, even in childhood, Dostoevsky formed a special attitude to the Biblical heroes, Christian martyrs and Christ. They became his role models. In *Diary of a Writer* in August 1880, Dostoevsky writes that he invited Christ into his soul, while in the family home.[75] This statement tells us that in the parental home, Dostoevsky had not only the knowledge of Christ, but something more. This means that his prayers, even those of a child, were not just ceremonial. He had a personal relationship with Christ. Christ could be sensed by Dostoevsky in his soul.

Dostoevsky, under family influence, became a creative leader, an independent character and a person who loved to communicate with people. He became a person who had concern and compassion for the poor, the sick and

---

73. *F. M. Dostoevskiy v vospominaniyakh sovremenikov*, 94.

74. Grossman, *Dostoevsky*, 28.

75. *Dnevnik Pisatelya*, August 1880, 152.

the oppressed. Dostoevsky treated each person kindly and had a sacrificial spirit toward people in need. He became stronger in his religious beliefs, and in his trust in God, as his love grew for reading God's word and for literature. His "living way" in theology held out promise for the future.

2.2.2 The Academy of Engineers (1834–1843)

This period begins with the author's first independent steps. Away from the family home, Dostoevsky faced injustice, lies, cruelty and pain. This was the reality of Russia, and it was a reality that helped to shape him.

The notion of "autocrat" during this time came together with the idea of "omnipotence." In 1839, French writer Marquis Astolif de Kyustin, after getting acquainted with Nikolay I and Russia, concludes: "for Russians, the monarch is god."[76] E. Radzinsky agrees with Kyustin, adding that he meant a pagan god, even though the autocracy was connected with Orthodoxy:

> Just as the Roman Caesar was a religious leader so is the Russian tsar, who took his title and became the head of the church. As Caesar was, so is the tsar, a pagan god. Soldiers responding to Nikolay I's greeting would cross themselves just like in front of an icon. Courtiers would not differ from other people and treated the tsar as a living god.[77]

Nikolay I managed the lives of his workers as it pleased him, allowing violence and lechery:

> Just like a squire managed the lives and desires of peasants, so was the tsar with his servants. He would pay attention. . . not only to young beauties at his palace – ladies and maids, but to girls he accidentally met while walking. If he liked someone during his walks or in the theatre, he would tell it to an adjutant on duty. And this girl would be under his control. If she had not been involved in any improper activities, then her husband (if she was married) or parents (if she wasn't married) would be told about the enormous honour, which they received. . . No one ever resisted the tsar's desires . . . In this strange country, to

---

76. Kyuctin, *Nikolaevskaya Rossiya*, 149.

77. Radzinskiy, *Aleksandr II Zhizn' i Smert'*, 63.

sleep with an emperor was considered as a great honour . . . for parents and even for husbands. . .[78]

People in the tsar's palace knew very well that the empress's maid, Varen'ka Nelidova, who lived in the winter palace, the most beautiful girl there, was the emperor's mistress.[79] The empress was aware of the fact, as was the whole of Petersburg, and it was "a very usual thing and order."[80]

According to Kyustin, Nikolay's I unpredictability could be read in his face:

Nikolay's face has a triple expression, yet none of it communicated his warm-hearted kindness. The most usual is an expression of strictness, the second is rather rare, but more suitable, an expression of solemnity, and finally the third one is an expression produced by his usual type. Yet, this casual, deceptive kind expression can't really impress, since it is just like the rest, an absolutely changing facial expression suddenly appears and in the same way disappears, without leaving even the slightest trace nor influencing a totally new expression. This is a full and quick change of background without any transition or a kind of mask, which can be put on or removed whenever willing. The emperor is always playing his role like a great actor. He has many masks yet lacks a real face and whenever looking for a living person, you only find an emperor.[81]

Using unlimited authority, the emperor could assign an impossible task and know that it would be done. In December 1837 when a fire destroyed the winter palace, the tsar ordered a huge palace built within one year. Amused Kyustin says of it:

In severe 25–30 below zero Celsius degrees, six thousand unknown martyrs, without any reinforcement, urged against their will by pure obedience, which is an inborn, violently vaccinated Russian virtue. They would be locked in palace rooms with temperature subsequently escalated to 30 above zero degrees Celsius

---

78. Radzinskiy, 75.
79. Radzinskiy, 74.
80. Radzinskiy, 75.
81. Kyuctin, *Nikolaevskaya Rossiya*, 107–108.

> due to the firebox that dried the sewers out. These wretched
> people, entering and exiting this palace of death, which due to
> their sacrifice would be changed into a palace of glory, glamour
> and pleasure, experienced a difference of temperature between
> fifty to sixty degrees. Labour in the Ural mines was way less dan-
> gerous for a person's life; meantime workers involved in building
> the tsar's palace were not criminals after all.[82]

The only goal of these countless victims was to satisfy the tsar's desires
and the return of the tsar's family to the restored palace on time.[83]

Nikolay I's independent nature considered every creature that did not
submit to his will as an evil example, like a soldier who rebelled against his
commander in the midst of the battle: disgrace falls on the army and the commander.[84] According to E. Radzinsky, the tsar's words "I do not need smart
fellows, but faithful servants" were a slogan for his empire.[85]

> In Russia, everything was done according to rules, all things
> were subordinated once and forever to accepted order. Military
> ideas corresponded in the best way to the ideas of order. A mili-
> tary person, who was used to fulfilling tasks rather than thinking
> about them and capable of teaching others, was considered as a
> talented leader. True abilities, knowledge and experience ceased
> to be the most important factors. All military people gradually
> occupy governmental jobs. Now all the officials wear uniforms.
> Even students are dressed in uniform.[86]

Seeing this situation, a question about injustice was raised by Dostoevsky,
which would accompany him throughout his life as he attempted to find an
answer. His behaviour during his studies in the Academy of Engineers will
demonstrate that he was against injustice.

Having arrived in Petersburg, Fyodor Mikhailovich was accepted in
the Academy of Engineers due to health issues; his brother was not. The

---

82. Kyuctin, 70.

83. Radzinskiy, *Aleksandr II Zhizn' i Smert'*, 85.

84. Kyuctin, *Nikolaevskaya Rossiya*, 95–96.

85. Radzinskiy, *Aleksandr II Zhizn' i Smert'*, 98.

86. Radzinskiy, 98.

brothers were separated, and their close friendship found expression in letters. According to A. Rizenkampf, the influence of Mikhail Mikhailovich on Fyodor Mikhailovich was enormous, and the closeness of their relationship was expressed in unchangeable friendship and fraternal love. They were, however, very different personalities.[87]

Fyodor Mikhailovich believed that his father's choice was unsuccessful. At the end of his life, he remembered: "Along with my brother we were escorted to Petersburg, to the Engineers Academy and it spoiled our future. I think it was his mistake."[88]

> Along with my brother, we were striving for a new life, dreaming badly about it . . . though, we both knew very well just about everything in regards to the math test, yet our dreams were all about poetry and poets. Brother wrote poetry, three poems a day, even on his way to different places, and I unstoppably used to write a novel from Venice life in my mind.[89]

On his way to the Academy, Fyodor Mikhailovich witnessed a cruel reality that existed in Russia then[90]:

---

87. *F. M. Dostoevskiy v vospominaniyakh sovremenikov*, 176.

88. *Pis'ma*, Vol. 29, 8 March 1869,23.

89. *Dnevnik Pisatelya*, 1876, 27.

90. Nikolay's arrival on the throne just like previous changes to the throne was accompanied by various peasant revolts raised by rumours about liberation in different places of Russia. In Spring 1826, in order to stop these revolts, a special manifesto was issued stating that peasants must undoubtedly fulfil all obligations and threatened strict punishment for disobedience. *Istoriya Rossii v XIX veke*, 236. In 1827 acceptance of serf peasants into boarding schools was prohibited. According to the school chart of 1828, children from families of lower classes were intended to enter a one-year program at parochial school, for merchants there existed a three-year program in district school, for children of nobleman and officials a seven-year program existed in the boarding school. *Rossiya: Entsiklopedicheskiy spravochnik* [Russia: Encyclopaedic Reference Book] (Moscow: Izdatel'skiy dom "Drofa", 1998), 130.

Nikolay realized the need to settle issues with serf peasants: Slave labour is wasteful and serf peasants became a "gunpowder cellar under the state." Radzinskiy, *Aleksandr II Zhizn' i Smert'*, 93.

Leaving the issue of serf peasants unsolved only aggravated the situation. The decline in prices for agricultural products, reinforcement of tax burden, cholera, poor harvests and hunger had weakened the solvency of the state's village, (*Kniga dlya chteniya po istorii novogo vremeni*, 127) and by 1836 there were arrears of 700,000 rubles. N. M. Druzhinin, *Gosudarstvennye krect'yane i reforma P. D. Kiseleva, t.1.* [State Peasants and Kiselyov's Reform] (Moscow-Leningrad: 1946), 3.

The gap between master and slave was enormous to the extent that a master considered himself as a person from another planet rather than part of the "simple" people (Kyuctin, *Nikolaevskaya Rossiya*, 301). Even though a new law forbade the sale of peasants without

> Somewhere in Tver province, near a big village, looking out of
> a window, he became a witness to an unusual road scene. After
> getting some refreshments at the station, one of the officials
> jumped into a three-horse carriage and started beating a car-
> riage driver very silently, calmly and even unflappably with his
> enormous fist. A shocked driver started beating the horses that
> began running madly out of physical pain.[91]

This scene of meaningless cruelty and innocent suffering stayed in Dostoevsky's memory for a lifetime.

After arriving at the Academy of Engineers, a collision of beliefs occurred. This was a pattern whenever he experienced local conditions. When experiencing cruel reality, he did not want to accept or follow local customs which perpetuated cruelty. He remained faithful to his beliefs, differentiating himself from others. He was angry with officials who used to rob soldiers and treat them cruelly. He knew officers who unjustifiably received rewards due to their relationships and connections. He witnessed the Academy's principal taking bribes from students' parents and paying more attention to students depending on the amount of the "payment."[92] He wrote to his father, "What a treachery! I was thunderstruck by this. We, who struggle for the last ruble, have to pay, while others, children of rich fathers, are accepted for free."[93]

D. Grigorovich, one of the closest of Dostoevsky's friends in the Academy, remembers: "The ability to test and humiliate freshmen was considered as a great heroism."[94] However, K. N. Trutovsky's testimony tells us that such

---

any land, many squires managed to avoid it. The greatest misery for peasants was a sale of the land, where they were born. Now, they were being sold with the piece of land that they were indissolubly bound to, which is the only good thing of a new law that forbade selling people without any land. Yet, many squires avoided this law by any means. Thus, they did not sell entire an estate with all the peasants, but only separate parts of an estate and a hundred, two hundred peasants apart. When the news about illegal sales reached officials, they would punish owners, yet it happened very rarely, since many people were interested in hiding these abuses (89). The main trait of the peasants' character was cunning just like the trait of their lives (176). Yet the moments when they get tired of cunning and rebelled against their masters became more frequent. Peasants' revolts increased: "Daily one can hear about new burning and murder of squires" (300).

91. Grossman, *Dostoevsky*, 28.
92. Rumyantseva, *Feodor Mikhaylovich Dostoevskiy*, 24.
93. *Pis'ma*, 4 February 1838, 236.
94. *F. M. Dostoevskiy v vospominaniyakh sovremennikov*, 193.

behaviour was unacceptable to Fyodor Mikhailovich. Trutovsky entered the Academy of Engineers in 1839, while Fyodor Mikhailovich was a sophomore. He remembered Dostoevsky very well, since he differed from others: "Seniors could easily rule over freshmen . . . I could draw pictures the best. Once, Fyodor Mikhailovich asked me to manage one task and as soon as I completed it, he became interested in my skills and started to defend me from tough bullies from the senior class."[95]

A. I. Saveliev who served as an officer in the Academy of Engineers, claims that while studying there, Dostoevsky was a very genuine man,[96] who could not dispense or handle flattery even though it could have saved him from various troubles and would have served to promote his well-being.[97]

During this time, Dostoevsky started reading the New Testament and praying, so that talking about God became a major interest. Saveliev testifies:

> Fyodor Mikhailovich was a very humble man; all of the necessary tasks and assignments he completed perfectly, yet he was very religious, having the lifestyle of a strict Orthodox Christian. You could see him reading the gospel and "Die Stunden der Andacht" (Prayer hours). After classes on God's Law by Poluektov, Fyodor Mikhailovich used to continue discussions with his law teacher. Thus his fellow colleagues have nicknamed him as a monk "Foti."[98]

From early childhood the New Testament was not simply a normal book. The gospel had entered deeply into his heart and he loved it. In Dostoevsky's letters from the Academy in the middle of 1840 God's name is often mentioned. In his letters to his beloved brother Mikhail, he elaborated upon the spirit of Christianity and the purpose of life. "Get to know nature, soul, God, love . . . It has got to be done through the heart, rather than the mind."[99]

Looking at Dostoevsky and comparing him with other Academy students, Saveliev came to an interesting conclusion:

---

95. *F. M. Dostoevskiy v vospominaniyakh sovremennikov*, 171.

96. *F. M. Dostoevskiy v vospominaniyakh sovremennikov*, 169.

97. *F. M. Dostoevskiy v vospominaniyakh sovremennikov*, 164.

98. *F. M. Dostoevskiy v vospominaniyakh sovremennikov*, 163.

99. *Pis'ma*, Vol. 28, 31 October 1838, 53.

> Usually youth used to change in four years, yet there were many young people, whose emotional characteristics never changed; in adolescence and late adulthood they remained unchanged. Fyodor Mikhailovich was such a person. In adolescence, he looked like an old man, just like in his adulthood years. He could not tolerate the customs, habits and worldviews of his peers.[100]

By that time, Fyodor Mikhailovich had his own firm beliefs which he treasured. He was honest, detested lying and flattery, defended young ones from the roughness of others and had compassion for the poor. Primarily, these beliefs did not allow him to take part in unacceptable events; therefore, Fyodor Mikhailovich had a secluded lifestyle. D. Grigorovich describes Dostoevsky's solitude:

> Back then, Fyodor Mikhailovich expressed his anti-social traits, he avoided participation in games, used to read books in a solitary place; soon he found one place and it became his favourite one: a deep corner in the fourth room with a window leading to Fontanka; he used to spend his recreation time there, alone, with a book.[101]

"Fyodor Mikhailovich had a few acquaintances and in general avoided them, feeling uncomfortable in the family homes," Rizenkampf recalls.[102]

Despite his seclusion, Dostoevsky had several friends, who were fascinated by his literary influence. These were Grigorovich, Beketov, Vitkovsky and Berezhitsky. K. A. Trutovsky remembers:

> Morally he (F.M.) was very different from his more or less light-headed peers. Always concentrated, spending his spare time thoughtfully, walking back and forth, without hearing or seeing events evolving around him. He was always kind and soft, but little did he find in common with his peers. There were only two persons, whom he talked to for a long time, discussing different issues. Such people were Berezhitsky and A.N. Beketov, I think.[103]

---

100. *F. M. Dostoevskiy v vospominaniyakh sovremennikov*, 165.
101. *F. M. Dostoevskiy v vospominaniyakh sovremennikov*, 200.
102. *F. M. Dostoevskiy v vospominaniyakh sovremennikov*, 180.
103. *F. M. Dostoevskiy v vospominaniyakh sovremennikov*, 172.

Grigorovich, comparing himself with Dostoevsky said: "By all means, Dostoevsky was more developed than I was; his knowledge was impressive."[104]

Second, during this time, he began his profound thinking about human beings. He recorded his first thoughts: "A human being is a mystery! It has to be revealed."[105] In his letter written to Karepin, Dostoevsky repeated: "My first goal and entertainment is to study people and life . . ."[106] V. I. Kirpotin thinks that the definition of "mystery of a human being" is not peculiar to Dostoevsky, but to his time, which meant that he cared about questions that concerned society. Dostoevsky, like other of his contemporaries, was eager to change Russian people and all of Russian society.[107]

In the beginning of the 1930s, in Moscow University, Belinsky, Stankevich, Lermontov, Gertsen, Aksakov and Buslaev studied almost simultaneously. They were destined to become prominent writers and public figures.[108] In Russia, during the 1930s and 1940s a noticeable revival of ideological societal life occurred. During this time, ideological movements like "Slavophilism" and "Westernism" appeared.[109] They reflected attempts to create concepts of the country's transformation.[110] Among progenitors of Slavophilia were: I.V. Kirievsky, A. S. Khomyakov, K. S. Aksakov, I. S. Aksakov and others. Their general philosophical concept included the following principles: Orthodoxy, autocracy and nationality.[111] However, these words sounded differently from the mouths of Slavophiles, i.e. they carried a rather progressive meaning.[112] Slavophiles claimed that every nation develops in its own way. They had a slogan: "The power of authority belongs to the tsar and power of opinion to the nation." Slavophiles considered that the tsar ought to gather Zemskie councils again and listen to their wishes.[113] The following historians belonged to the Westerners: T. N. Granovsky, K. D. Kavelin, S. M. Soloviev, and expert

---

104. *F. M. Dostoevskiy v vospominaniyakh sovremennikov*, 200.

105. *Pis'ma*, Vol. 28, 16 August 1839, 61.

106. *Pis'ma*, Vol. 28, 19 September 1844, 96.

107. *Molodoy Dostoevsky*, 37.

108. *Istoriya Rossii v XIX veke*, 454.

109. *Rossiya: Entsiklopedicheskiy spravochnik*, 132.

110. *Russroe obshhectvo 40-50-kh godov XIX v.* [Russian Society of the Forties and Fifties of the Nineteenth Century] (Moscow: Izd-vo Moskovskogo un-ta, 1989), 10.

111. *Istoriya Rossii v XIX veke*, 461.

112. *Istoriya Rossii v XIX veke*, 472.

113. *Rossiya: Entsiklopedicheskiy spravochnik*, 133.

in music and painting V. P. Botkin, V. G. Belinsky, A. I. Gertsen and N. P. Ogarev formed the left flank of Westernization. Those who associated with Westerners were the following writers: I. S. Turgenev, N. A. Nekrassov, A. F. Pisemskyi and M. E. Saltykov-Shedrin.[114] They believed in the unity of human civilization. They considered Western Europe as the head of civilization. Influenced by European literature and European life, and mainly by French socialist ideas, Westernization at the same time stayed in close contact with the recent Russian past, i.e. the social-political movement, which terminated on 14 December 1825.[115] Already thirty various clubs were organized, trying to continue the Decembrists' path. Sungurov and his brother Gurov invited students to their home to discuss the following issues: abuse from authorities, the tsar's despotism and the nation's poverty. They would delight in Polish heroism when they rebelled against the Russian government in 1830–1831.[116] This club did not exist for a long period of time. In 1832, the club's members were arrested, and Sungurov himself was exiled, while students were forced to enter military service and become soldiers.[117] Simultaneously, A. I. Gertsen started a youth club. The worldview of Gertsen and his friends started to develop early.[118] Gertsen possessed a "resistless hatred towards slavery and arbitrariness." He was only thirteen when the events of 14 December 1825 occurred, yet they greatly influenced him.[119] When asked about specific issues of Russian reality, Slavophiles, Westerners and early socialists unanimously acknowledged the urgency of Russian liberation, legality and the freedom of speech.[120]

During that time Dostoevsky had a considerable amount in common with both the Slavophiles and the Westerners. He shared the widely held conviction about the urgency of the country experiencing transformation. Like the Slavophiles he was patriotic, but he did not support autocracy and Orthodoxy as a solution for Russia. Like the Westerners, Dostoevsky was eager to see the universal unity of people. He was against abuse from the authorities, the

---

114. *Russroe obshhectvo 40-50-kh godov XIX v.*, 12–13.

115. *Russroe obshhectvo 40-50-kh godov XIX v.*, 13.

116. *Russroe obshhectvo 30-kh godov XIX v. Lyudi i idei*, 21.

117. *Istoriya Rossii v XIX veke*, 473.

118. *Istoriya Rossii v XIX veke*, 473.

119. *Istoriya Rossii v XIX veke*, 474.

120. *Istoriya Rossii v XIX veke*, 489.

tsar's despotism and the national poverty. In chapter 9 we will explore the influence of Dostoevsky on Slavophiles and Westerners.

Third, looking for answers, Dostoevsky immersed himself deeply in the world of fantasies. During this time, the dominant image for Dostoevsky was the "perfect world" in which love, humility and care were the motivation for people's relationships. His childhood beliefs were not adequate for the needed transformation of Russian society into a "perfect society." In one of his letters, he wrote: "I was such a big dreamer that I missed my youth . . . after finishing my duties, I used to run to my attic, dress in my robe, open Schiller's book and dream, suffer and love . . ."[121] However, he understood that it couldn't last long, and he wrote to his brother Mikhail: "The external world should be balanced with the inner one. Otherwise, with the absence of the external factors, the inner world will dangerously take over. Nerves and fantasies will occupy too much space in the essence of life. Any external phenomenon looks enormous and scary somehow. I start being afraid of life."[122]

But he continued to express his compassion for people in need. He never passed by a poor man without helping him, even though he needed support himself. Saveliev, whom students used to talk to about their joys and sorrows, is confident that external and internal events and the people of those times morally influenced Fyodor Mikhailovich.[123] He expressed his observations about Dostoevsky's compassion for the poor:

> The feelings of compassion remained in Fyodor Mikhailovich during his time of studies. They witnessed the life of poor peasants in a Staraya Kikenka village. The picture of terrifying poverty, absence of providence, poor clay ground and unemployment was unveiled. The main reason for this situation was a neighbouring wealthy property of Earl Orlov. Striking poverty, pitiful houses and masses of kids without good nutrition used to increase the level of compassion in young people's hearts towards peasants of Staraya Kikenka. Dostoevsky and Berezhesky

121. Rumyantseva, *Feodor Mikhaylovich Dostoevskiy*, 22.

122. *Pis'ma*, Vol. 28, Jan–Feb 1847, 137.

123. *F. M. Dostoevskiy v vospominaniyakh sovremennikov*, 169.

along with their friends used to do fund- raising for the needs of the poorest peasants.[124]

This was not a one-off event. When his brother Andrei became sick, Fyodor took care of him attentively by giving him medicines prescribed by a doctor.[125] Doctor Rizenkampf said of Dostoevsky: "Fyodor Mikhailovich had the type of personality that everyone enjoyed, yet these kinds of personalities were in need themselves. He had been robbed unmercifully, though due to his kindness and trust, he wouldn't want to get into details or rebuke servants that used his carelessness."[126]

O. Miller confirms that in 1842 Dostoevsky and Rizenkampf rented an apartment: "Living together with a doctor almost turned it into a constant source of new expenses. Every poor person who came to the doctor for a check-up was hosted by Dostoevsky as a dear guest. Frequently, he had an extreme lack of money."[127] "Next day the same picture: new loans with a barbarously high interest rate; in order to buy sugar, tea etc." added O. Miller.[128] Fyodor Mikhailovich writes in a letter to his brother in Revel: "Well, brother! You complain about your poverty. Not much to say, I am not rich either. Would you believe it that during performances in camps, I did not have any money, got sick with flu on my way home, was hungry and did not have even a penny to buy a cup of tea for my throat."[129]

During this time, his illness influenced him. There is no agreement about the date when Fyodor Mikhailovich had his first seizure, yet some of the witnesses say that it happened precisely during this difficult period of time. Grigorovich remembers: "Several times he had seizures. After such seizures, he used to be depressed for two or three days in a row."[130] Being a doctor, Rizenkampf explained in detail about the illness and its symptoms:

> First of all, he had a weak body, and his husky voice in addition to the throat glands swelling, as well as the ground type of

---

124. *F. M. Dostoevskiy v vospominaniyakh sovremennikov*, 166–167.

125. *F. M. Dostoevskiy v vospominaniyakh sovremennikov*, 124.

126. *F. M. Dostoevskiy v vospominaniyakh sovremennikov*, 189.

127. *F. M. Dostoevskiy v vospominaniyakh sovremennikov*, 189–190.

128. *F. M. Dostoevskiy v vospominaniyakh sovremennikov*, 191.

129. *Pis'ma*, Vol. 28, 9 August 1838, 49.

130. *F. M. Dostoevskiy v vospominaniyakh sovremennikov*, 207.

colour of his face, pointed towards a chronic disease that could
be fatal. Later, in other parts he had gland tumours, as well as
forming abscesses. In Siberia, he suffered from pains in his knee
bones. However, he endured such sufferings stoically and asked
for medical help only in extreme cases.[131]

He suffered from this disease for the rest of his life, which contributed to
loneliness on one hand and let him experience a feeling of being a part of
suffering people in society on other hand.

Love for literature allowed him to get acquainted with the new thinking
of distinguished authors on issues of interest to society. This is the reason
why Dostoevsky dug deeply into the world of literature and read and thought
so much. Reading literature also had a great influence on the formation of
his convictions.

According to V. Kirpotin, Dostoevsky thought about issues raised not only
by Russians but also by Western European life as well. Some of the contradictions that Western European life offered were of a rather complex nature by
contrast with domestic issues. The Feudal order in leading Western European
countries, such as in England and France, was over. The French Revolution at
the end of the eighteenth century inflicted an irreparable blow on feudalism.
Struggles for human rights, the future and happiness gained a completely new
type of nature during those times, a socialist ideal.[132]

Dostoevsky's letters and the memoirs of contemporaries reveal the level
and character of his knowledge of Western European literature. Passionate
and fascinated, he shared his impressions with his brother after reading
Homer, Shakespeare, Schiller, Servanis and Gete.[133]

Schiller's name was one of the Fyodor Mikhailovich Dostoevsky's earli-
est recollections. As a ten-year-old boy, he attended the play "Robber," with
Mochalov as the main actor. The play made a strong impression and Fyodor
Mikhailovich recalled this event in his mature years.[134] The fascination with
Schiller's writing talents occupied a huge place in Dostoevsky. Schiller's poetry
was a manifestation of human dignity in every person, thereby a worrying

---

131. *F. M. Dostoevskiy v vospominaniyakh sovremennikov*, 183.

132. Kirpotin, *Molodoy Dostoevskiy*, 98.

133. *Pis'ma*, Vol. 28, 1 January 1840, 66.

134. *Pis'ma*, Vol. 30, 18 August 1880, 211.

and rebellious challenge for equality. In conditions of a living protest against class hierarchy and serfdom's possession of souls, Schiller's humanism had a specifically attractive power.[135]

George Sand (full name Amandine Aurore Lucile Dupin) was welcomed by readers even more warmly than Schiller. According to Dostoevsky's testimony, as a sixteen-year-old boy, he read Sand's novel "L'Uscoque" for the first time. Years later in June 1876, in *Diary of a Writer* he remembered that after reading "L'Uscoque" he had a high fever all night long. He adored Sand, because she "preaches the beauty of compassion, patience and justice" and predicted a happier future of humanity.[136] George Sand's motifs were relevant for him, even during his last period of life.

Gogol too had a special influence on Fyodor Mikhailovich. By the time Dostoevsky left for Petersburg in 1837, Gogol was already a well-established writer.[137]

Yanovsky remembers:

> When he used to read "Dead Souls" nearly ever time after closing the book, he would exclaim: "What a great teacher for all Russians, especially for writers! What a desk book! You should read it daily, well at least one chapter a day, but read it."[138]

O. F. Miller supports this idea: "Out of all Russian authors, he particularly enjoyed reading Gogol and liked to memorize whole passages from "Dead Souls."[139] K. Trutovsky writes: "The clearest memories remained about the way he reflected on Gogol's writings. Fyodor Mikhailovich pushed me strongly towards development with his conversations, managing my reading and occupations."[140]

Dostoevsky claimed that Gogol was able to expose platitude with unbelievable confidence and openness. He also pictured a person's humiliation under the pressure of the rejected system of attitudes of the old reality.

---

135. Kirpotin, *Molodoy Dostoevskiy*, 103.

136. *Dnevnik Pisatelya*, 1876, 33.

137. Kirpotin, *Molodoy Dostoevskiy*, 83.

138. *F. M. Dostoevskiy v vospominaniyakh sovremennikov*, 238.

139. *F. M. Dostoevskiy v vospominaniyakh sovremennikov*, 187.

140. *F. M. Dostoevskiy v vospominaniyakh sovremennikov*, 173.

However, in the 1840s, Dostoevsky never came to hopeless conclusions out of Gogol's pictures.

> Dostoevsky until the end of his days considered that the core of all problems and contradictions in the sixties, seventies and eighties had their foundation in the forties. It is true to some extent. That is why he never got tired of repeating that Pushkin led Russian thinking people to topical contemporary issues and Gogol had asked them the deepest questions. In the beginning of his literary activity, Dostoevsky along with his most faithful contemporaries sought answers to tormented questions in the writings of the great Russian classics. That is where his fascination with Pushkin and especially Gogol comes from.[141]

In 1839, Dostoevsky lived in his own apartment, which was a permissible practice for senior classes. Occasionally, he lacked almost any funds and the only place that he could heat was his office.[142]

The next blow for Fyodor Mikhailovich was the death of his father. Lonely after the death of his wife along with his younger children at Darovoe, Mikhail Andreevich had a lot of difficult times and became aggressive. The characteristics of despotism and uncontrolled power became stronger as time passed. His over-bearing nature and cruel attitude towards peasants as well as alcoholism brought a tragedy. He was allegedly killed by his own peasants in 1839.[143] He was forty-six years old.[144] His granddaughter Lyubov Fyodorovna reported:

> In one of the summer days, he departed from Darovoe to Cheremoshna and never got back. He was found strangled with a pillow from the cab. The coachman disappeared along with the horses; some of the peasants from the village have disappeared as well . . . Some other serfs claimed that it was revenge: the old man treated the serfs very strictly. The more he drank, the more furious he became.[145]

---

141. *Molodoy Dostoevskiy*, 93.

142. Rumyantseva, *Feodor Mikhaylovich Dostoevskiy*, 29.

143. Rumyantseva, 8.

144. *F. M. Dostoevskiy v vospominaniyakh sovremennikov*, 116.

145. Grossman, *Dostoevsky*, 38.

According to Grossman, however, it is only speculation since there are no facts or witnesses and none of the investigation materials remained.[146] F. M. Dostoevsky had a hard time coping with his father's death. There is some suggestion that the news about his father's death brought on an epileptic seizure.[147] Even the apparent murder of his father did not stop Fyodor Mikhailovich from defending peasants.

After his father's death, Fyodor Mikhailovich read and studied a great deal. "I read in enormous amounts and reading affects me strangely," Dostoevsky writes to his brother. "Something that I read long ago, I read again and it seems like I make an extra effort, trying to clearly understand the essence, and as a result I extract the skill to create."[148]

His first attempt at an independently created piece of writing came in the beginning of the forties. Probably, *The Poor Folk* was started in the Academy. In 1843, after completing his studies, Dostoevsky enrolled in service under Petersburg's engineering team, as well as in the engineering mechanical drawing department. He still led a solitary lifestyle, full of passionate interest for literature only. He translated Balzac's novel *Eugenia Grande* as well as George Sand.[149]

During this time, Fyodor Mikhailovich remained a dreamer: "I was a big dreamer then."[150] However, according to Grossman, Dostoevskythe dreamer was Dostoevskythe writer already, who was still looking for his hero.[151] "The image of a daydreamer is one of the main ones in Dostoevsky's works in the forties." Nonetheless, the image of a daydreamer was tragic rather than humorous in Dostoevsky's works, as Belinsky saw it.[152] Rumyantseva says more on this subject:

> Dreaming was a manifestation of a critical attitude towards reality, dissatisfaction of the inner life. A person isolates himself, not willing to accept the world, living in an imaginary world

---

146. Grossman, 39.

147. Rumyantseva, *Feodor Mikhaylovich Dostoevskiy*, 8.

148. *Pis'ma*, Vol. 28, 24 March 1845, 106.

149. *F. M. Dostoevskiy v vospominaniyakh sovremennikov*, 206.

150. *Dnevnik Pisatelya*, 1877, 28.

151. Grossman, *Dostoevsky*, 43.

152. Rumyantseva, *Feodor Mikhaylovich Dostoevskiy*, 68.

rather than a real one. Even the selfishness and egocentrism of the dreamer could be explained: a person tries to find his or her own place in the common life of the people.[153]

Therefore, we have a good deal of information not only about the environment in the Academy where Fyodor Mikhailovich studied, but about his reactions. In this way, we can see some of his beliefs, which had already started to develop in the family home. On the one hand, he cared about the "uneducated simple person." At the same time, he adored Christ, and imitated him, yet he could not see in him solutions to the problems of a "small person." A happy person existed only in his dreams.

During his study in the Academy of Engineers, Dostoevsky became a person who did not accept injustice, lies, cruelty or pain. He was angry with people who treated other people cruelly. He was honest, detested lying and flattery, defended young ones from the roughness of other, and had compassion for the poor. He remained a person with a sacrificial spirit for the poor and sick and was interested in the problems of his society. He adored people who preached the beauty of compassion, patience and justice and appreciated friendship that grew over these years. He loved deep reading, trying to clearly understand its essence. In this period of Dostoevsky's life, he remained faithful to his early religious beliefs. He was accepted as a very religious and humble person and talking about God was a major interest. Dostoevsky thought deeply about the secret of human happiness and was a dreamer. His was not an academic theology.

2.2.3 Merging into Literary-Political Circles (1843–1849)

The third of Dostoevsky's communities was the literary-socialist community. Dostoevsky's literary and political views were formed in complicated historical conditions.[154] The government of Nikolay I tried to influence public thinking. Rumyantseva believes that it was interested in spreading false ideas

---

153. Rumyantseva, 22.

154. In 1840, a need to resort to an external loan occurred. The interest debts recorded in Nikolay's debit book by 1855 were 842 million rubles in silver. By the end of Alexander's I rule, they had increased by 634 million rubles in silver; non-interest debt by 1855 formed 3,563 million rubles in silver, which meant that the total amount of state's debt during Nikolay's I reign equalled to 1,198 million rubles in silver. These numbers tell that Russia kept on using extra funds just like during Alexander's I time; changes for better had not occurred. *Kniga dlya chteniya po istorii novogo vpemeni*, 128.

about humility, submissiveness, people's endurance, which were falsely reflected in its history, songs, traditions and stories. However, during this time, P. Kirevsky gathered songs, where the nation's rebellious character and love for freedom was displayed.[155]

In the fall of 1844, Dostoevsky resigned from the Army, wanting to make his living by writing. He wrote *The Poor Folk* and dreamt of great success. According to Grigorovich's instructions, he gave his first work to Nekrassov for his "Petersburg Collection." It greatly impressed Grigorovich, Nekrassov and Belinsky.[156] Grigorovich remembers: "From the very first page of *The Poor Folk*, I realized how far better Dostoevsky's creation was than mine. When I read *The Poor Folk* to Nekrassov, we both cried." Belinsky warmly welcomed Dostoevsky as one of the future great artists of Gogol's school. P. V. Annenkov writes of Belinsky's reaction: "Belinsky has shouted: Come here, I have news. I cannot get away from this manuscript for the second day in a row. This novel belongs to a new talent: what type of person he is and his thinking is unknown to me, yet his novel discovers such life mysteries and characters in Russia, which no one dreamed of before."[157] V. A. Sollogub after

---

The nobility had taken control of enormous land properties and had exploited peasant labour for two hundred years. They were used to serfdom as a social regime and did not think about its liquidation (138).

This terrible situation for peasants had naturally caused the abuse of the rights of serfs. Here and there in miscellaneous regions, peasant revolts appeared covering almost the entire central region of Russia. According to researchers, during Nikolay's reign about 674 cases of peasant rebellions were encountered. Each year, this number increased. In 1826 there were only eighty-five rebellions, but in 1845 there were about 207 cases of open disobedience to authorities (168).

Developing capitalism undermined the foundations of serfdom, intensifying class contradictions in the country. The complication of the political situation in late 1840s was mainly caused by poor harvests, epidemics, and other natural disasters. All these factors along with social oppression had weakened the country's economy and escalated the disastrous position of the working masses. The number of peasants' revolts grew in the country. For instance, in 1848, in twenty-seven provinces seventy rebellions occurred and many of them had to be suppressed by military forces. The intensification of the country's situation influenced ideological life in Russia in the late 1840s and promoted reinforcement of oppositional and revolutionary behaviour. V. V. Bogatov, *Osnovnye cherty mirovozzreniya vydayuschikhsya predstoviteley dvizheniya petrashevtsev* [The Main Features of World-famous Representatives of the Movement Petrashevists] (Moscow: Izd-vo Moskovskogo un-ta, 1958), 3.

155. Bogatov, 16.

156. *F. M. Dostoevskiy v vospominaniyakh sovremennikov*, 208.

157. *F. M. Dostoevskiy v vospominaniyakh sovremennikov*, 214.

reading a novel said: "Such an original talent is found, such simplicity and power that make me rejoice."[158]

In the 1840s, in Russia, many small political clubs sprang up.[159] A. P. Milyukov saw two reasons for this. They were the result of an unusual situation, which occurred in the mid forties in Europe and Russia. First, there were external events, and as a result people obtained new rights, yet at the same time a heavy sluggishness dominated in Russia. More than any other time, scientific and literary activity suffered, and censorship caused a sharp fear of books, while an oppressed social life did not show any signs of activity. Secondly, many liberal writings illegally entered the country from abroad. All these things affected the minds of intellectual youth. Steadily, in Petersburg, various political clubs were formed around young people who had common ideas.[160] All literary work was submitted to secret police supervision. In 1826, a merciless censorship law was issued, which made the existence and development of literature and publishing works in Russia impossible.[161] Just about anything that contained a shadow of "double meaning" or which could weaken loyalty to high authorities and laws would be ruthlessly blocked. Censorship was forbidden to be substituted with dots, so that the reader "would not be tempted to speculate about possible content of prohibited place." In the consciousness of Russian writers, the responsibility for printed words was placed neither before God nor a person's conscience, but before the emperor and the state. An author's right to hold a personal opinion that differed from state's opinion would be declared as "savagery and crime."[162] Gradually, Russian writers stopped dreaming about literature without censorship. Famous literary people worked as censors: a poet Tyutchev, writer Aksakov, Senkovsky and others. The tsar and the head of III Department became sovereign censors.[163] A. Nikitenko, a critique who was forced to work as a censor, wrote in his diary:

---

158. *F. M. Dostoevskiy v vospominaniyakh sovremennikov*, 223.

159. Rumyantseva, *Feodor Mikhaylovich Dostoevskiy*, 259.

160. Rumyantseva, 260.

161. *Kniga dlya chteniya po istorii novogo vremeni*, 100.

162. Radzinskiy, *Alekcandr II Zhizn' i Smert'*, 58.

163. Radzinskiy, 59.

> First of all, we compulsively tried to write and show our talent.
> However, we noticed it is not a joke and we are required to be
> inactive and keep silence; our talent and wit are destined to
> become numb and fester deep in our souls . . . any bright idea
> is a crime against public order, shortly, we were told that edu-
> cated people in our society are considered as creatures from a
> different nation; army discipline is regarded as the only begin-
> ning. Then, the entire young generation had suddenly become
> morally scanty.[164]

His diary is a vivid story of how Nikolay's time killed talent and energy in
a person and made one understand that the only appropriate behaviour was
to be silent and patient. The inevitable effect of a person's protest against this
oppressive public atmosphere became individualism and extreme egoism,
which brought tragedies and destroyed people's lives.[165]

Belinsky's club was one of the political clubs. Belinsky's positive feedback
on *The Poor Folk* drew him closer to Dostoevsky. Here Dostoevsky's "vice"
played its role. Being a proud[166] and ambitious man,[167] he was pleased to get
close to the famous literary critic, that being Belinsky. But this rapprochement would adversely affect Dostoevsky's change of convictions. Dostoevsky
was accepted in Belinsky's club. As a member of the club, he often attended
meetings and finally developed his social-humanistic ideals which Belinsky
spread. According to Rumyantseva, Dostoevsky's conversations with Belinsky
about common laws of development found a very lively response in him.
However, there was an issue that he constantly argued about with Belinsky – a
question about God.

> During our first days of acquaintance, Doestoevsky talked about
> Belinsky, clinging to me with all of his heart, he would try to

---

164. *Russkoe obshhectvo 30-kh godov XIX v. Lyudi i idei*, 24.

165. *Russkoe obshhectvo 30-kh godov XIX v. Lyudi i idei*, 23.

166. "And is it really so that I'm so great" – with shame I thought of myself in some sort
of shy delight. "Oh, do not laugh, then I never thought that I was great, but then – how can you
withstand it! Oh, I'll be worthy of praise, and what people, what people! That's where people
are, I will deserve it, I will try to be as brilliant as they, will be faithful. Oh, how frivolous I am,
and if only Belinsky knew what worthless, shameful things are in me! And they all say that
these writers are proud, ambitious." *Dnevnik Pisatelya*, January 1877.

167. *Pis'ma*, Vol. 28, 1 April 1846, 119.

convert me with the simple-hearted haste into his faith . . . I met him while he was a very passionate socialist, and he started with his beliefs in atheism.[168]

Yanovsky claimed that Fyodor Mikhailovich was well aware of written and spoken things on socialism, yet he did not sympathize with the teaching.[169] Kirpotin considers that in the forties Dostoevsky firmly kept the banner of social humanism[170] being under Belinsky's serious pressure.[171] He refers to the author's sayings in "Time":

In Belinsky's era, all other beliefs and views, except his views were not considered as noble and modern beliefs and convictions. Whoever did not notice in Pushkin, Gogol and Lermontov whatever Belinsky noticed, he would inevitably be considered as limited, retarded and even an anti-education person . . . His contradictions and transformation of opinions would appear inconsistent and opinion-changing only to those who were really limited during his epoch. For him and his students, i.e. for all of us more or less, these were moments of development, moments of longing for truth.[172]

Belinsky's positive attitude towards Dostoevsky finds a reciprocal reaction. He talked about Belinsky's club as of his own: "Our club is big enough."[173]

---

168. *Dnevnik Pisatelya*, 1873, 10.

P. P. Semenov-Tyan-Shansky described this club in his memoirs: "Dostoevsky would read from *The Poor Folk* and *Netochka Nezvanova* and would passionately express himself against the abuse of serfs. The fight with censorship issues was also discussed." The Debu brothers were also participants in the club. Despite their utter resentment, they could never think of achieving their ideals through revolutionary ways. "Senior Debu studied the history of the French revolution too well not to know that there were no means for revolution in Russia," P. P. Semenov-Tyan-Shansky notices, *Dnevnik Pisatelya*, 297.

169. *Dnevnik Pisatelya*, 241.

170. Kirpotin, *Molodoy Dostoevskiy*, 131.

171. Kirpotin, 132.

172. Kirpotin, 131.

173. *Pis'ma*, Vol. 28, 16 November 1845, 115.

Many memoirists, critics and literary historians of the 1840s pointed out Dostoevsky's like-mindedness with Belinsky. However, they had different opinions on one issue. It is thought that despite his closeness with Belinsky, Dostoevsky would never become an atheist and lose faith in Jesus Christ's divinity. Memoir-writers like Milyukov, Yanovsky, N. Strahov, O. Miller, V. I. Semevsky, P. N. Sakkulin, L. Grossman, and N. F. Belchikov, except Dolinin in his article

There are people like N. O. Lossky, who are confident that during times of extreme fascination with Belinsky's views, Dostoevsky had a warm feeling for the worship of Christ in his heart as the highest measure of goodness. "The loss" probably consisted in the fact that he denied the divinity of Christ and Holy Communion.[174]

However, according to Dolinin and Kirpotin, during this time Fyodor Mikhailovich not only grasped socialist convictions, but his Christian beliefs were shaken. They describe it as a time of "losing Christ."[175] Belinsky was a convinced atheist. He could not imagine transformation in Russia without forsaking Christianity. Dostoevsky used to say that both paid a lot of attention to Christ's personality. "The teachings of Christ, he (Belinsky)," Dostoevsky wrote, "as a socialist had to destroy, naming them as false and ignorant love towards mankind, and they are judged by modern science and economical beginnings; yet a bright image of Christ, which is morally unattainable and His miraculous beauty remained."[176] Initially, these conversations were unacceptable to Dostoevsky, especially whenever touching Christ' personally. "I am moved, when I look at him," Dostoevsky said of the critic's remarks, "whenever I mention the name of Christ, his face changes just like he wants to start crying."[177]

Kirpotin thinks that later Dostoevsky agreed that he had acquired Belinsky's views. "Then, I passionately accepted all of his teaching," categorically declares Dostoevsky.[178] In his letter to E. I. Totllben from Semipalatinsk on 24 March 1856, Dostoevsky wrote: ". . . I was rebuked in certain intentions . . . actions against the government . . . I believed in theories and utopian socialism."[179] This statement signifies that he was for utopian socialism. "We were polluted by the ideas of the former theoretical socialism!" later recalled

---

"Dostoevsky among Petrashevsky people," repeat this position as indisputable. Kirpotin, *Molodoy Dostoevskiy*, 152.

174. *Bog i mirovoe zlo*, 42.

175. *Dnevnik Pisatelya*, 1873, 9.

176. *Dnevnik Pisatelya*, 8.

177. *Dnevnik Pisatelya*, 9.

178. *Dnevnik Pisatelya*, 10.

179. *Pis'ma*, Vol. 28, 24 March 1856, 223.

Dostoevsky.[180] In Dostoevsky's notebook we find the following record, connected to *The Brothers Karamazov*:

> Rascals tried to poison me with an uneducated and astrological faith in God. These fools did not even dream of such power of denying God, which we find in the inquisitor in the previous chapter, and the whole novel itself answers the question. I believe in God not as fool (fanatic). Yet, these people tried to teach me and laugh off my underdevelopment. According to their foolish nature, they did not even dream of the great power of denying God, which I experienced. Is it they who are to teach me?![181]

In addition: "Even Europe did not have such power of atheistic expressions. Therefore, I do not believe in Christ like a little boy, because my hosanna has gone through the great forge of doubts."[182] These categorical records confirm that Dostoevsky had times in this period of his life when he used to deny God. Fyodor Mikhailovich in *Diary of a Writer* in 1880 supported the idea that he had forfeited Christ, when he became a European liberal.[183] It is just like Dostoevsky's correspondence in the 1840s, which showed no evidence of any interest in religious studies and traditions.[184] On the contrary, we can see the young writer's indifference to faith issues. All these arguments point out that after *The Poor Folk* came out Dostoevsky lost his faith in God and the deity of Christ, while being under the strong influence of Belinsky. Christ became for him only a good, ideal man. At this time, Christ was not the only example, but simply one of the best examples to be imitated. In a letter to his brother Dostoyevsky wrote about Homer, comparing him to Christ, "Homer may be parallel only to Christ, but not to Goethe. After all, in the Iliad, Homer gave to the ancient world organization of the spiritual and earthly life, quite in the same power as Christ to the new world."[185]

---

180. *Dnevnik Pisatelya*, 1873, 130.

181. *Neizdannyy Dostoevskiy Zapisnye knizhki i tetradi 1860– 1881 гг.* [Unpublished Dostoevsky Notebooks] (Moscow: Nauka, 1971), 667.

182. *Neizdannyy Dostoevskiy Zapisnye knizhki i tetradi 1860– 1881 гг.*, 667.

183. *Dnevnik Pisatelya*, 1880, 152.

184. Kirpotin, *Molodoy Dostoevsky*, 155.

185. *Pis'ma*, Vol, 28, 1 January 1847, 106.

Dostoyevsky for some time would continue to share the beliefs of Belinsky. Later, in 1871, he talked about atheism and Belinsky, and expressed this time his negative opinion of them:

> You had never known him, but I knew and saw, and now I fully comprehended. This man abused Christ in my presence with vulgar words, and yet he never could compare himself and all the philosophers of the world with Christ. He could not see how much in them was petty vanity, anger, impatience, irritability, meanness and, most importantly, pride. Cursing Christ, he never said to himself, "whom will we put in His place, can we by any chance propose ourselves, whereas we are so nasty. No, he had never thought about the fact that he was loathsome. He was pleased with himself to the highest degree, and this was a personal, foul, shameful stupidity.[186]

The success of *The Poor Folk* had affected Dostoevsky. He worked nervously and passionately, trying to shut the critic's mouth, and even outperform himself.[187] In all his writing Dostoevsky showed what man is like. The human being is contradictory: simultaneously good and evil. Human beings strive for happiness and pursuit of it often brings misfortune to others.

After 1847 Dostoevsky began his new period of exploration. He got closer to Petrashevsky's club, where he found people ready to defend the idea of justice.[188] Petrashevsky's club or society was very different in regard to the participants' worldviews. From 1846 to 1848 they would gather on Fridays at Petrashevsky's home. One of Petrashevsky's people, D. D. Ahsharumov wrote in his memoirs,

> "Once a week at Petrashevsky's we held our meetings that different people attended. This was an interesting kaleidoscope of various opinions on modern events, government laws, new literary pieces in diverse areas of knowledge; we read and discussed

---

186. *Pis'ma*, Vol. 28, 18 May 1871, 115.

187. Before his arrest in 1849, Dostoevsky wrote ten pieces, apart from sketches and unfinished writings: "The Double" and "Mr Prokharchin" (1846); "The Landlady" (1847); "A Weak Heart," "The Stranger-Woman," "A Jealous Husband," "An Honest Thief," "A Christmas Tree and a Wedding," and *White Nights* (1848); and *Netochka Nezvanova* (1849).

188. Rumyantseva, *Feodor Mikhaylovich Dostoevskiy*, 55.

our domestic news without any uneasiness. Occasionally, we would listen to a lecture from a specialist. Yastrzhembsky would lecture on political economy, Danilevsky on the Fury system,[189] at one meeting Dostoevsky read Belinsky's letter to Gogol."[190]

This letter was directed against the church.[191] Belchikov supports this witness: "Petrashevsky's society was not united and complete in its views. It gathered people of moderate views like D. D. Ahsharumov and those who had revolutionary positions such as N. A. Speshnev."[192] The best Russians in the 1840s, as many of Petrashevsky's people witness, experienced the process of inner "fermentation" and were perfectly aware of the necessity to establish relationships in society.[193] The common issue, to fight against serfdom, drew people of different views and directions together. In the worldview

---

189. The main thing in the teachings of the Fourier was the idea of socialism. This idea was a direct conclusion from the experience of revolutionary and post-revolutionary France of the eighteenth- to early nineteenth centuries. Since the political upheaval did not improve the situation of the people, thought the Utopians, a dissension from the heights of public buildings, leaving alone the political struggle was needed with radical reform of its foundation – the institute of property upon which all social and public relations of individuals, groups and classes were built. V. Vetlovskaya, *Roman F. M. Dostoevskogo "Bednye lyudi"* [Dostoyevsky's novel *Poor Folk*] (Leningrad: Hudozhestvennaya literatura, 1988), 25.

190. D. D. Akhshrumov, *Iz moikh vospominaniy 1849–1851 гг. [From My Memories 1849–1851]* (Sankt-Petersburg: 1905), 15.

191. Belinsky rebuked Gogol for his support of the Orthodox Church: "The preacher of the whip, apostle of ignorance, obscurantism and advocate of obscurantism and yagoism, eulogist of Tartar manners – what are you doing? Take a look under your feet, because you're standing over the abyss . . . You base your teaching on the Orthodox Church – that I can understand: it's always been the foundation of whip and pleaser of despotism, but why do you involve Christ here? What do you find in common between him and someone else, but especially the Orthodox Church? He first announced the doctrine of freedom to the people, that of equality and fraternity, and sealed this with his martyrdom, confirming the truth of his teachings. And it's only so long that it was saving people, until it got organized into a church and not taken as its foundation the principles of Orthodoxy. The church is a hierarchy, therefore an advocate of inequality, a flatterer of power, the enemy and persecutor of the brotherhood of people – and it continues to be so. But the meaning of Christ's teachings was discovered by a philosophical movement of the last century. And that's why someone like Voltaire, who used ridicule as his tool to put out fires of bigotry and ignorance in Europe, and he is of course, more the son of Christ, the flesh of his flesh and bone of his bones, rather than all of your priests, bishops, metropolitans and patriarchs, eastern and western" (V. Belinsky, *Pis'mo Belinskogo Gogoliu* [Belinsky's letter to Gogol], 25 December 2010. http://ru.wikisource.org/wiki/).

192. N. F. Bel'chikov, *Dostoevsky v processe petrashevcev* [Dostoevsky in Judicial Process of Petrashevists] (Moscow: Nauka, 1971), 7.

193. Bel'chikov, 9.

of "Petrashevsky's people," who philosophically headed the leading camp, liberalism and democracy were understood as synonyms.[194]

Dostoevsky attended Petrashevsky's meetings and was an active participant at Durov's club and Speshnev's club.[195] Malyukov describes Durov's club:

> This club included people attending Petrashevsky's place, yet who were not in a full agreement with his opinions, distributing books with revolutionary and socialistic content. They talked about issues, which could not be freely discussed. The biggest issue was the freedom of peasants, and during those evenings this matter was constantly discussed in attempts to find means to set peasants free. F. M. Dostoevsky believed only in a legal way of peasant's liberation rather than revolution. They also discussed the censorship issue.[196]

This description helps us understand what Fyodor Mikhailovich found in common with the members of clubs. Together with many others, he learned about socialists, though he was far from believing in a practical realization of plans. He agreed that the purpose of their teachings was a noble one but considered them to be honest dreamers. Dostoevsky suggested looking for sources of development of Russian society not in the research of Western socialists, but rather in the life of the historical formation of the Russian nation. Fyodor Mikhailovich would always speak against those actions, which in a way restricted people's freedom. He would especially speak negatively about abuse that lower classes and studying youth suffered from.[197] "On one hand, his love towards society but, on other a lack of acquaintances were the reason why he easily found a common language with Petrashevsky," Yanovsky claims.[198]

Dostoevsky explained his club visits with the following words: "I go to Petrashevsky, because I meet good people there that other people are not acquainted with."[199] However, there are some views that Dostoevsky himself

---

194. Bel'chikov, 9.

195. Bel'chikov, 8.

196. *F. M. Dostoevskiy v vospominaniyakh sovremenikov*, 262.

197. *F. M. Dostoevskiy v vospominaniyakh sovremenikov*, 264–265.

198. *F. M. Dostoevskiy v vospominaniyakh sovremenikov*, 244.

199. *F. M. Dostoevskiy v vospominaniyakh sovremenikov*, 245.

occasionally expressed himself against the former state regime, before the peasants' liberation, yet he had never been and never could be a rebel or conspirator.[200] P. P. Semenov-Tyan-Shansky admits that Dostoevsky "as a person he would experience resentment and even malice, whenever seeing violence over humiliated and insulted ones."[201]

The secret police kept on pressuring all freedom-loving, thinking individuals and movements. Therefore, ideological life was concentrated in close narrow clubs, where people had friendly relationships. It was hard for a police agent to become a part of these clubs.[202] The majority of participants of illegal anti-governmental clubs carried fiery patriotism, love, compassion to their own nation and hatred towards autocracy and serfdom.[203]

Dostoevsky's fascination with social-utopian ideas and, his participation in Petrashevsky's club resulted in catastrophe. The French revolution in 1848 scared the tsar and forced him to pay attention to the places of extreme freedom of thought in Russia. In Petersburg, Petrashevs became an object of investigation by the secret police. For thirteen months, agents of the Ministry of Internal Affairs kept a close eye on Petrashevsky's club, gathering information about participants, their political views and plans of activity. According to an investigation committee, F. M. Dostoevsky was included in the list of the most active members of the club as "one of the most important ones."[204] At night, on 23 April, thirty-four persons were arrested, including the founder, Mikhail Vasilyevich Butashevich-Petrashevsky.[205] Ten years later (in 1860), having returned from exile to Petersburg, he described this event in the album of his old friend's (A. P. Milyukov) daughter.[206] The arrests were made after a personal order from Tsar Nikolay I.[207]

This period of life was highlighted by Dostoevsky's recognition as a great writer, who cared about the problems of simple people. "A small person" had first place in his life. He cared for him, sympathized, helped by all possible

---

200. *F. M. Dostoevskiy v vospominaniyakh sovremenikov*, 246.

201. *F. M. Dostoevskiy v vospominaniyakh sovremenikov*, 301.

202. Vvoznyy, *Politicheskiy sysk i kruzhok Petrashevcev*, 10.

203. Vvoznyy, 11.

204. Bel'chikov, *Dostoevsky v processe petrashevcev*, 5.

205. Bel'chikov, 7.

206. Bel'chikov, 5.

207. Rumyantseva, *Feodor Mikhaylovich Dostoevskiy*, 83.

means, and yet could not see a solution to the problem, except the elimination of social inequality. When Belinsky convinced him to accept his socialistic beliefs, he agreed. Hence, this period became a period of "losing Christ." Belinsky's arguments turned out to be too strong for him, as Belinsky believed in human deliverance without Christ.[208] Obviously, "the loss of Christ," connected with "transformation into a European liberal,"[209] happened during friendly relationships with Belinsky, beginning in the summer of 1845 and continuing until the first part of 1846.

During this time, by contrast with the previous periods, it seems that Dostoevsky had little or no interest in religion and became largely indifferent to faith issues. He was angry with the government and the Orthodox Church for their injustice and oppression. He reached the stage where he denied God's existence. At the same time Dostoevsky dreamed of improving society, believing that all needs could possibly be met. Although some of his religious beliefs changed, he remained a person concerned for the poor, the oppressed and the sick. He craved justice and happiness for society. His love for literature was also evident, as it had been in the past; he worked passionately and nervously and was proud of his literary success.

2.2.4 Imprisonment (1849)

As it turned out, Dostoevsky's participation in political clubs was short-lived. Participation in Petrashevsky's club activities over three years and taking part in conversations about the strictness of censorship led to his spending eight months in Petrapavlosk fortress. In March 1849 he read Belinsky's letter to Gogol received from Moscow and given by Plesheev; he continued to read it at Durov's meetings and gave it to Monbelly to copy. He also listened to articles at Durov's place, was aware of a proposal to use lithography, and was a listener to "Soldier's conversation" at Speshnev's club.[210] Belinsky's letter to Gogol was an atheistic one, full of sharp attacks on the Russian Orthodox Church and Russian clergy.

P. P. Semenov-Tyan-Shansky claimed, "From the group of convicted ones, it was only Durov, except Petrashevsky who could be considered as

---

208. *Dnevnik Pisatelya*, 1873, 10–11,

209. *Dnevnik Pisatelya*, 1880, 152.

210. Bel'chikov, *Dostoevsky v processe petrashevcev*, 7.

a revolutionary person, who tried violently to undertake liberal reforms."[211] During interrogations on his relation to the socialistic movement, Dostoevsky answered:

> With all the sincerity I am telling you . . . my liberalism included only a simple desire to do all the best for my motherland, in an unstoppable desire to improve it. I had this developing desire as soon as I started to understand my own nature, yet it has never gone off limits . . . All I wanted is that all the voices be heard and all needs be possibly met.[212]

On 21 December 1849 Fyodor Mikhailovich along with others was driven to Semenov plaza, where they were sentenced to death by execution. This was the verdict of the general auditor:

> For participation in criminal activities, distribution of Belinsky's letter full of flippant expressions against the Orthodox Church and governing authorities, along with political attempts; distribution of compositions against the government through home lithography.[213]

During that time, the tsar and the Orthodox Church acted together. From the 1830s, the spiritual department (public prosecutor and Synod) became a real ministry. From 1835, the public prosecutor for spiritual department affairs had to be present at sessions of Departments of State Council and Ministerial Committee.[214] Consolidated by bureaucratic transformations, the Orthodox department in the 1840s and 1850s actuated their own administrative-police functions to an unusual degree, which was demonstrated in two directions: missionary activity and spiritual censorship.[215]

Militant intolerance of a church that dominated the Russian empire in the second quarter of the century had increased. People of other religions and religious dissenters became the main target for the State and Orthodox Church. Persecution of religious dissenters particularly increased after the

---

211. *F. M. Dostoevskiy v vospominaniyakh sovremenikov*, 302.

212. Rumyantseva, *Feodor Mikhaylovich Dostoevskiy*, 87.

213. *Pis'ma*, Vol. 28, March 1858, 383.

214. Eroshkin, *Krepostnicheskoe samoderzhavie i ego politicheskie instituty*, 130.

215. Eroshkin, 132.

highest command on 8 October 1835, which limited the civil rights of dissenters as representatives of "specially damaging sects."[216]

The sentenced ones experienced all the horror of "dead men," and just before the execution, the tsar changed the final sentence to exile "for four years, and then an ordinary person again".[217] In that moment one victim lost his mind[218] and some people believe that this was the moment when Dostoevsky lost his faith.[219] As we have demonstrated, however, the evidence suggests that this had happened quite a while before.

Even so, that moment of "execution" became a certain push when one could see his whole life in a single flash. Dostoevsky told A. E. Wrangell that "my whole life just stormed by in my mind vividly like in kaleidoscope, as quick as lightning."[220] He did not have a notion of a perpetrated crime, yet he reviewed his life repentantly:

> We Petrashevsky, stood on the scaffold, and we listened to the
> verdict without the slightest remorse. Without a doubt, I cannot

---

216. Eroshkin, 132. Jews were also limited in their rights. "Jews did not want to comply with common rules and become Christians. The tsar obliged Jews to pay taxes for wearing Jewish traditional caps and long coats as well as forbade the wearing of Jewish clothes. A special committee was created for the final correction of Jewish life and conversion to Christianity. Nikolay I considered a beloved army to be the best medicine. Previously, instead of serving in the army, Jews had to pay taxes, yet now they were to supply recruits to the army. The tsar believed that during military service, which lasted 25 years, Jews will certainly become Christians" (Radzinskiy, *Aleksandr II Zhizn' i Smert'*, 98).

Another punitive direction of the orthodox department was spiritual censorship. In the beginning of the nineteenth century, spiritual censorship was used only for censorship of church books. Spiritual censorship and interference in secular publishing affairs began in the 1820's and was sealed on 22 April 1828 by the "Charter of Spiritual Censorship." In the 1830s and 1840s, spiritual censorship was considered more captious than secular censorship. From 1828 to 1844, out of 2,659 manuscripts and books, spiritual censorship organs rejected 511 (i.e. 19 percent), and out of 6,904 writings presented for spiritual censorship in 1844 to 1855, 2,524 works were discarded (i.e. 36.6 percent). A. Kotovich, *Dukhovnaya cenzura v Rossii 1799–1855* [Spiritual Censorship in Russia 1799–1855] (Sankt-Petersburg: 1909), 595.

D. D. Ahsharumov's testimony about the priest's actions at Semenov plaza supports this statement: "Afterwards, a priest with a cross in his hand approached and stood before us saying: 'Today you will hear the equitable decision of your case – follow me!' The priest went to a scaffold – the same one, who escorted us – with the Gospel and the cross . . . Staying between us, he addressed with the following words: 'Brothers! You have to repent before dying . . . the Saviour forgives sins for the one who is repenting . . . I encourage you to confess your sins . . .'" (*F. M. Dostoevskiy v vospominaniyakh covremenikov*, 318–320).

217. *Pis'ma*, Vol. 28, March 1858, 383.

218. Rumyantseva, *Fjodor Mikhaylovich Dostoevskiy*, 90.

219. Grossman, *Dostoevskiy*, 17.

220. *F. M. Dostoevskiy v vospominaniyakh sovremenikov*, 345.

testify about everybody, but I think I will not be mistaken, saying that if, at the moment, if not everyone of us, then at least an overwhelming majority of us would consider it a dishonour to renounce their beliefs . . . The verdict of the death penalty by a firing squad, read to all of us previously, was not a joke, almost all the inmates were assured that we would be executed and rendered at least ten terrible, exceedingly terrible minutes awaiting death. In these last moments, some of us, instinctively went deep in ourselves and examined ourselves, checking such still young lives – some may be repented in other serious matters of theirs (of those that every human being keeps in secret on his conscience throughout life), but that cause for which we were condemned, those thoughts, those concepts that have owned our spirit – seemed to us not only not requiring repentance, but even something cleansing, martyrdom, for which we will be forgiven much.[221]

He expressed similar thoughts in a letter to his brother Mikhail, just a couple of hours after his return to the fortress:

As I look back on my past, I think how much wasted time I had, losing it in errors and mistakes, in inability to live; regardless that I cherished it, I have sinned many times against my heart and spirit, my heart full of sorrow. Life is a gift, life is happiness, and every minute could be a century of happiness. Now, changing my life, I am transformed into a new form. O, brother! I swear that I won't lose hope and will keep my spirit and heart in purity. I will change myself for better. This is my hope, my comfort![222]

These thoughts of Fyodor Mikhailovich brought a desire to read the Bible. Staying in the Petrapavlovsk fortress, in shackles, Dostoevsky began to show his interest in Christianity again. He read "Two Journeys to Holy places" and "Compositions of Saint Dimitry Rostovsky." He asked his brother to send

---

221. *Dnevnik Pisatelya*, 1873.
222. *Pis'ma*, Vol. 28, 22 December 1849, 161.

him "Notes of the Fatherland" and a Bible in French and the Slavic language.[223] His brother sent him the Bible, "Notes of the Fatherland" and Shakespeare. Many years afterward, Dostoevsky would tell A. U. Poretsky and Timofeeva that receiving that Bible in the fortress from his brother initiated his "spiritual regeneration."[224]

Fyodor Mikhailovich had never been depressed and comforted his brother at the moment of farewell, saying that "even in exile there are people, not beasts,"[225] and after liberation he "will have something to write about."[226] It seems as if he did not give careful consideration to the fact that was going to spend fours years in *The House of the Dead*, in chains, along with people cast away from society for horrible crimes. Maybe he thought about an attempt to find a humane line deeply hidden under ashes in the hearts of the worst criminals. He believed that this humane line still lived even in the most evil of men and lost outcasts.[227]Dostoevsky hoped to improve his life with the Bible's help. He began to show an increased interest in Christianity during this year.

2.3 Theological Motifs in *The Poor Folk*

The object of the second part of this chapter is to discover, describe and analyze theological motifs in *The Poor Folk*. The choice of this novel for research was made for two reasons. First, *The Poor Folk* was the first novel written by Dostoevsky. "Early in the winter [of 1845], suddenly, I began to write *The Poor Folk*, my first novel; I had never written anything."[228] Second, according to most researchers of Dostoevsky's literature, *The Poor Folk* was the most important novel of the writer during the pre-Siberian period.[229] This opinion was shared by Dostoevsky. Even at the end of his life Dostoevsky recalled with

---

223. *Pis'ma*, 161.

224. V. V. Timofeeva, *God raboty s znamenitym pisatelem* [A Year of Work with a Famous Writer] (Istor. Vest. II 1904), 531.

225. *Pis'ma*, Vol. 28, 22 December 1849, 161.

226. *Pis'ma*, 161.

227. *F. M. Dostoevskiy v vospominaniyakh sovremenikov*, 270.

228. *Dnevnik Pisatelya* (January 1877)

229. See V. Vetlovskaya, *Roman F. M. Dostoevskogo "Bednye Lyudi"* [The Novel *The Poor Folk* of F. M. Dostoevsky] (Leningrad: Hudozhestvennaya Literatura), 5; and Joseph Frank, *Dostoevsky: The Seeds of Revolt, 1821–1849* (Princeton, NJ: Princeton University Press, 1976), 137.

delight the time of writing *The Poor Folk*.[230] That means *The Poor Folk* shared the best message that Dostoevsky proclaimed in the pre-Siberian period.

The Poor Folk was cast in the form of an epistolary novel between two correspondents: poor copy-clerk Makar Alekseevich Devushkin and a distant relative he was taking care of, Varen'ka. Her full name is Varvara Alekseevna Dobroselova.[231]

The main challenge Dostoevsky faced was to reveal the mystery of the human being. He had a clear view of how human beings should be in an ideal world as it is described in Genesis 1–2. This is why at the beginning of his novel he depicted the ideal man. Dostoevsky felt more than others that the world in which we live is a distorted one and human beings have been marred. Thus, subsequently man is depicted in the novel as being corrupt, perverted and unfortunate. At the end of the novel, Dostoevsky showed that distorted relationships between people lead to tragedy.

Thus, the study of the theological motifs is going to be carried out in these two separate worlds: the ideal and the distorted. More precisely, the ideal human being and the distorted one.

2.3.1 The Perfect World

The novel begins with the characters' happy memories. There is not a precise reference to the times they were speaking about. Thus, Makar exclaimed: "How happy I was last night – how immeasurably, how impossibly happy!"[232] Varvara's memories were also joyous, carefree and warm: "We are like in a paradise in the room – it's clean and bright! . . . I felt so good . . ."[233]

These statements bring to mind the original state of the people in Paradise. In V. Vetlovskaya's opinion, there are two references entitled to such an interpretation. First, the main characters of the novel were close relatives. They had the same patronymics even though not being brother and sister. Such phrases as "my dear," "my angel," and "darling" also pointed to the celestial nature of the main characters. Second, the surroundings where the characters

---

230. *Dnevnik Pisatelya* (January 1877).

231. Dostoevsky used the old form of correspondence novel, which was used in French literature. It better expressed subtle emotions. This was how "Jacques" was written by George Sand. L. Grossman, *Dostoevskiy* (Moscow: Molodaya Gvardiya, 1965), 55.

232. *Bednye Lyudi*, 13.

233. *Bednye Lyudi*, 18.

were placed remind us of Paradise.[234] At the time when Dostoevsky had written the novel, for him the Bible was an authority which one should emulate.[235] Therefore, in the beginning of the novel, Dostoevsky gives a picture of Paradise that he draws from Genesis 1–2.

For Varvara, her childhood was a paradise. "My childhood was the happiest time of my life . . ."[236] The life of people in this ideal world was full of meaning.[237] People showed responsibility before other people and by doing so showed that they had freedom.[238] The description of the place she was born created an atmosphere of harmony, warmth and paradisiacal comfort:

> . . . the weather is clear and keen and bright; all the agricultural labour has come to an end; the great sheaves of corn are safely garnered in the byres and the birds are flying hither and thither in clamorous flocks; everything is so clear and joyful . . .; the pond covered over with ice as thin as paper, and a white steam rising from the surface, and birds flying overhead with cheerful cries. Next, as the sun rises, he throws his glittering beams everywhere, and melts the thin, glassy ice . . .; a peasant will pass the window in his cart bound for the forest to cut firewood, and the whole party will feel merry and contented together. What a wonderful childhood I had![239]

She continues, "Yes, truly I loved autumn-tide – the late autumn when the crops are garnered, and field work is ended, and the evening gatherings in the huts have begun, and everyone is awaiting winter."[240]

According to M. Gus, this picture recalls childhood memories, country observations and impressions of Dostoevsky.[241] But this is only by association.

For Varvara her childhood was a paradise, while for Makar paradise is related to his old apartment where he lived for almost twenty years:

---

234. Vetlovskaya, *Roman F. M. Dostoevskogo "Bednye Lyudi,"* 64–67.

235. *Dnevnik Pisatelya*, 1873, 134.

236. *Bednye Lyudi*, 27.

237. Losskiy, *Bog i mirovoe zlo*, 101.

238. Losskiy, 111.

239. *Bednye Lyudi*, 83.

240. *Bednye Lyudi*, 83.

241. M. Gus, *Idei i obrazy F. M. Dostoevskogo* [Ideas and Images of F. M. Dostoevsky], (Moscow: Hudozhestvennaya Literatura, 1962), 9.

> My old room was such a snug little place! True, its walls re-
> sembled those of any other room – I am not speaking of that; the
> point is that the recollection of them seems to haunt my mind
> with sadness. . . We used to live there so quietly – I and an old
> landlady who is now dead. How my heart aches to remember
> her for she was a good woman, and never overcharged for her
> rooms. . . . Oftentimes we shared the same candle and board.[242]

Life in the old apartment was modest, but no one felt the lack of anything, because it was full of common joy, love and care for each other:

> Also she had a granddaughter, Masha – a girl who was then a
> mere baby, but must now be a girl of thirteen. . . . Often of a long
> winter's evening we would first have tea at the big round table,
> and then betake ourselves to our work; the while that, to amuse
> the child and to keep her out of mischief, the old lady would set
> herself to tell stories. What stories they were! Though stories less
> suitable for a child than for a grown-up, educated person. . . .
> And then, as the story grew grimmer, the little child, our little
> bag of mischief, would grow thoughtful in proportion, and clasp
> her rosy cheeks in her tiny hands, and, hiding her face, press
> closer to the old landlady. Ah, how I loved to see her at those
> moments! As one gazed at her one would fail to notice how the
> candle was flickering, or how the storm was swishing the snow
> about the courtyard.[243]

Makar found the description of the paradisiacal life in the "book." He probably meant the Bible. "'Surely . . . we mortals who dwell in pain and sorrow might with reason envy the birds of heaven which know not either!' And my other thoughts were similar to these. In short, I gave myself up to fantastic comparison. A little book which I have says the same kind of thing in a variety of ways."[244] This shows that Dostoevsky wrote the novel drawing

---

242. Fyodor Dostoevsky, *Poor Folk*, trans. C. J. Hogarth (Urbana, IL: Project Gutenberg, 2000), from www.gutenberg.org/ebooks/2302; *Bednye Lyudi*, 20.

243. Dostoevsky, *Poor Folk*; *Bednye Lyudi*, 20.

244. *Bednye Lyudi*, 14.

his beliefs from the Bible, which clearly states that the world was perfect in the beginning (Genesis 1–2).

Vetlovskaya sees in these words a hint at a future paradisiacal life after death.[245] But nothing in this text points to the future. Makar's words are full of desire for the life described in the Bible. He had such a life in the past and wished to live it in the present. This picture is a look back into the past, but also a look ahead. This is Dostoevsky's desirable world, the creation of which he called people to in his speech at the Pushkin celebration.[246]

Being motivated by his conviction in the truth of Genes-s 1–2, Dostoevsky used love, humility, and care for other to show the relationship between human beings as children of God in a perfect world created by God. Theological motifs in the description of the past ideal life of the characters as love, humility and care for each other created an atmosphere of harmony, joy and happiness. Social relations were a consequence of the manifestations of the internal beliefs of people.

2.3.2 The Distorted World

At some point in the past, something disastrous happened which completely distorted the real world. Vetlovskaya understands these hints as a reference to the "fall" of man as it is described in Genesis 3.[247] Dostoevsky believed in the reality of the fall[248] and claimed that since then "the world has taken on a negative sense, and that out of lofty, refined spirituality has emerged a satire."[249] For Dostoevsky the word "satire" meant that even good intentions have a negative connotation. In the novel, he illustrated in detail the consequences of the fall as he will do in the story "The Dream of a Ridiculous Man."[250] Dostoevsky, in his description of the distorted world, was inspired by the same biblical narrative, Genesis 1–3. His characters missed the perfect world, comparing

---

245. Vetlovskaya, *Roman F. M. Dostoevskogo "Bednye Lyudi,"* 71–72.

246. *Dnevnik Pisatelya*, 1 August 1880.

247. Vetlovskaya, *Roman F. M. Dostoevskogo "Bednye Lyudi,"* 71–72. Here the expression "man" means "humanity." I will follow the way the Russian sources use the term.

248. Reinhard Lauth, *Filosofiya Dostoevskogo v sistematicheskom izlozhenii* [Dostoevsky's Philosophy in Systematic Presentation], (Moscow: Respublika, 1996), 279.

249. *Pis'ma*, Vol. 28, 9 August 1838, 50.

250. See F. M. Dostoevsky, *Polnoe Sobranie Sochineniy, Son Smeshnogo Cheloveka* [The Complete Works of Dostoevsky: The Dream of a Ridiculous Man], [CD-ROM] (Izdatel'stvo Adept, 2002).

their lives in the present with their lives in the past. Dostoevsky used contrasts of contentment and envy, modesty and vanity, charity and the desire to dominate, to illustrate the distorted man after the fall in comparison with the perfect world.[251] Both characters remembered well the transition from the "paradisiacal world" to the real, distorted and sick one.

Varvara drew the line between that time and this life when the family moved to the city. It was in the city that everyday life became more and more miserable. She was sharing how the lives of her parents had changed:

> Every day he grew more morose and discontented and irritable; every day his character kept changing for the worse. He had suffered an influx of debts, nor were his business affairs prospering. As for my mother, she was afraid even to say a word, or to weep aloud, for fear of still further angering him. . . . Yet this did not arise from any want of love for me on the part of my father, but rather from the fact that he was incapable of putting himself in my own and my mother's place. It came of a defect of character.[252]

According to Varvara, her father loved them, but with some strange love. This was a love which made them feel guilty about all the troubles and constantly afraid to speak. She thought the problem was not the result of their social situation (in other words, the father's debts), but a change in his character, an inner, deep problem associated with events in the past, as a result of which they had had to move to the city.

The second character, Makar, also saw a clear distinction between the "paradisiacal life" and the present one. In his case the turning point was the move from the old apartment to the one in which he was living at that moment: "Darkness is falling . . . My head and my back are aching, and even my thoughts seem to be in pain, so strangely do they occur. Yes, my heart is sad today, Varvara . . ."[253]

In this "new" life there were different, distorted values. Dostoevsky, surprisingly, showed in detail the manifestation of those negative inner changes in the characters' behaviour, which could be seen in their attitude towards

---

251. Vetlovskaya, *Roman F. M. Dostoevskogo "Bednye Lyudi,"* 199.

252. *Bednye Lyudi*, 28.

253. *Bednye Lyudi*, 21.

each other and towards other people. The world was distorted because people were distorted. In this distorted world nothing could be as before. Evil permeated everything.[254] There were no pure relationships, no pure love, no real relationships at all and therefore no joyous, happy life. Dostoevsky created this distorted yet real picture in *The Poor Folk*, using as theological motifs a set of contrasts. He used contrasts in all his novels to clearly show his message. What his characters were not able to see, Dostoevsky saw clearly.[255]

One of these is the contrast between contentment and envy. On the one hand, Makar is described as a satisfied person, thankful for his life. On the other hand, he was envious and unhappy. He characterised himself as being a modest person:

> Well, I am a burden upon no one. It is my own crust of bread that I eat; and though that crust is but a poor one, and sometimes actually a maggoty one, it has at least been earned, and therefore, is being put to a right and lawful use. What, therefore, ought I to do? I know that I can earn but little by my labours as a copyist; yet even of that little I am proud, for it has entailed work, and has wrung sweat from my brow.[256]

The modesty about which Makar talked was characteristic of him, but this was rather formal than natural. Social hierarchical relationships obliged those who were lower in status to be humble and contented. Makar himself confirmed this principle: ". . . I am a humble man, because I'm a little man."[257] Some other poor people like Pokrovsky and Gorshkov behaved the same way. Such forced modesty, imposed by the status of being poor, could not influence the character's behaviour.

What really characterized Makar was envy. He did not notice that he constantly compared himself to those above him in status, thus feeling his own inadequacy. Comparing himself with Rtaziaev, he concluded: "Well, who am I in front of him? Nobody. He is a man of reputation, whereas I – well, I do not exist at all."[258] This takes place as Devushkin accepted the lie of the

---

254. Losskiy, *Bog i mirovoe zlo*, 109.

255. Vetlovskaya, *Roman F. M. Dostoevskogo "Bednye Lyudi,"* 79.

256. Dostoevsky, *Poor Folk*; *Bednye Lyudi*, 47.

257. *Bednye Lyudi*, 47.

258. *Bednye Lyudi*, 51.

depraved world as the truth. It led him to sensual pleasure, not by means of truth but by lies and the feeling of sensual pleasure led him to envy.[259]

The world in which our characters lived elevated material things to the highest value. Wealth was associated with happiness, but poverty was seen as deficiency. Makar had the same opinion. He equated material wealth and happiness. He thought that Varvara was unhappy because of poverty. His words were full of annoyance, irritation and even anger because of the injustice of fate:

> In fact, it was interesting to be able to look so closely at a princess or a great lady. They were all very fine. At all events, I had never before seen such persons as I beheld in those carriages ... Then I thought of you. Ah, my own, my darling, it is often that I think of you and feel my heart sink. How is it that you are so unfortunate, Varvara? How is it that you are so much worse off than other people? In my eyes you are kind-hearted, beautiful, and clever – why, then, has such an evil fate fallen to your lot? How comes it that you are left desolate – you, so good a human being! While to others happiness comes without an invitation at all? ... Nevertheless, it is you, my darling, who ought to be riding in one of those carriages. Generals would have come seeking your favour, and, instead of being clad in a humble cotton dress, you would have been walking in silken and golden attire.[260]

Makar served as a copy-clerk. He envied the material success of people who had a higher status. The problem was not poverty and it was not in the hierarchy as Belinsky and Vetlovskaya maintained.[261] Makar especially envied writers:

> You should see how much money these fellows contrive to save! How much, for instance, does not Rataziaev lay by? A few days' writing, I am told, can earn him as much as three hundred rubles! Indeed, if a man be a writer of short stories or anything else that is interesting, he can sometimes pocket five hundred rubles,

---

259. Lauth, *Filosofiya Dostoevskogo v sistematicheskom izlozhenii*, 280.

260. Dostoevsky, *Poor Folk*; *Bednye Lyudi*, 86.

261. Vetlovskaya, *Roman F. M. Dostoevskogo "Bednye Lyudi,"* 83.

or a thousand, at a time! Think of it, Varvara! Rataziaev has by him a small manuscript of verses, and for it he is asking–what do you think? Seven thousand rubles! Why, one could buy a whole house for that sum! He has even refused five thousand for a manuscript, and on that occasion I reasoned with him, and advised him to accept the five thousand. But it was of no use.[262]

Rataziaev, who wrote poetry, was an example for him, an object of envious dreams: "What, do you think, is an idea that sometimes enters my head? In fact, what if I myself were to write something? How if suddenly a book was to make its appearance in the world bearing the title of 'The Poetical Works of Makar Devushkin?' What then, my angel?"[263]

Here all Rataziaev's real or invented virtues came. Since Ratazyaev was for him a living embodiment of the dream, Makar advocated him:[264] ". . . but he is my friend, and therefore, I must put in a word or two for him. Yes, he is a splendid writer. Again and again I assert that he writes very well."[265]

Comparing himself with people with a higher social position, Makar was dissatisfied with himself. He always seemed to be ashamed of something or even of himself.[266] Writing to Varvara about his new apartment, he tried to pick up every word so that the corner of the kitchen, where he lived, looked in her eyes like a real room: "I myself live in the kitchen – or rather, in a small room which forms part of the kitchen. The latter is a very large, bright, clean, cheerful apartment with three windows in it, and a partition-wall which, running outwards from the front wall, makes a sort of little den, a sort of extra room, for myself."[267]

He wanted Varvara to at least perceive him as he perceived himself in his dreams. Thus, he exaggerated his wealth and strong character:

> I shall be able to save money here, and to hoard it against the future. Already I have saved a little money as a beginning. Nor must you despise me because I am such an insignificant old

---

262. Dostoevsky, *Poor Folk*; *Bednye Lyudi*, 51–52.

263. *Bednye Lyudi*, 53.

264. Vetlovskaya, *Roman F. M. Dostoevskogo "Bednye Lyudi,"* 101.

265. *Bednye Lyudi*, 56.

266. Vetlovskaya, *Roman F. M. Dostoevskogo "Bednye Lyudi,"* 88.

267. *Bednye Lyudi*, 16.

fellow that a fly could break me with its wing. True, I am not a swashbuckler; but perhaps there may also abide in me the spirit which should pertain to every man who is at once resigned and sure of himself.[268]

Dreams were more important than truth, and when his dreams contradicted the truth, he gave a lie for the truth and vice versa. He was a poor man but wanted to look rich in Varvara's eyes, so Makar sold his uniform. With the money he received he bought candies and flowers for her, thus hiding his real condition. Makar did not want Varvara to know that in fact he had no money, so he accused Feodora of lying about the sale of the official uniform: "Tell her from me that she has not been speaking the truth. Yes, do not fail to give this mischief-maker my message. It is not the case that I have gone and sold a new uniform."[269]

Thus, in the contrast between contentment and envy, envy prevailed. It came out not in comparison with the past, "paradisiacal" life, but in comparison with those with a higher social status. Envy was a consequence of our characters' distorted understanding of the true values of life. His aim in life was not to be free among the free ones, equal among equals, cherished by close relatives but to exactly resemble "them," to have exactly the same things they had.[270] Thus, Makar appreciated material things and wealth by which he could achieve happiness. But as his dream could not yet come true, he envied all those who had climbed up higher on the social ladder and tried to copy their behaviour, so that at least in the eyes of someone he could be perceived as having a higher social position.

Another theological motif in the novel is **modesty and vanity**. They contrast with each other and come out simultaneously in the life of Makar. Makar thought he was a modest, humble man, although he loved to be praised: "You say, my darling, that I am kind and good, that I could not harm my fellowmen, that I have power to comprehend the goodness of God (as expressed in nature's handiwork) and so on. It may all be so, my dearest one – it may

---

268. Dostoevsky, *Poor Folk*; *Bednye Lyudi*, 17.

269. *Bednye Lyudi*, 25.

270. Frank, *Dostoevsk:. The Seeds of Revolt, 1821–1849*, 140.

all be exactly as you say. Indeed, I think that you are right."[271] But if one is humble, he does not speak of it.[272]

The need for praise and glory was a manifestation of vanity. This motif took many forms when speaking of him. On the one hand, Makar dwelt on himself. He was at the centre of his own reflections no matter what the subject of the conversation was. He did not miss the slightest occasion to be praised, and thus once again reasserted to Varvara's face his status of a man deserving to be respected: "It is a clever plan, is it not? And it was my own invention, too! Am I not cunning in such matters, Varvara? Still, it is pleasant to speak the truth sometimes."[273]

Yet in his mind, he thought that everybody around him underestimated him. Makar was not sure that his stirring speeches persuaded his companions that he was as worthy of respect as others who occupy a higher position in the hierarchy. Being a hypochondriac and wanting to satisfy the curiosity of others, he made many sacrifices, even ridiculous ones. L. Grossman considers that Makar genuinely sacrificed himself for the sake of others,[274] but mostly Devushkin's sacrifices were deliberately intended to impress and attract attention:

> But, somehow, I do not like having to go without tea, for everyone else here is respectable, and the fact makes me ashamed. After all, one drinks tea largely to please one's fellow men, Varvara, and to give oneself tone and an air of gentility (though, of myself, I care little about such things, for I am not a man of the finicking sort). . . .
>
> It is for other folk that one wears an overcoat and boots. In any case, therefore, I should have needed boots to maintain my name and reputation; to both of which my ragged footgear would otherwise have spelled ruin.[275]

In fact, no one was watching him. It was just his imagination. Both the idea that he was worse than others and his desire to be like anybody else were

---

271. *Bednye Lyudi*, 46.

272. Losskiy, *Bog i mirovoe zlo*, 182.

273. *Bednye Lyudi*, 17.

274. *Dostoevskiy*, 56.

275. Dostoevsky, *Poor Folk*; *Bednye Lyudi*, 17.

dictated by his wish to be superior to other people.[276] Furthermore, Makar was not even aware of his vanity,[277] considered himself to be a modest person and even viewed himself as an innocent victim of the created circumstances, when he said,

> The fact is that over-brooding proves the undoing of a man – his complete undoing. What has saved me is the fact that it is not for myself that I am grieving, that I am suffering, but for you. Nor would it matter to me in the least that I should have to walk through the bitter cold without an overcoat or boots . . . but the point is – what would people say, what would every envious and hostile tongue exclaim, when I was seen without an overcoat?[278]

So important to Devushkin were the opinions and views of others that he neglected charitable works including visits to the sick Varvara whom he had promised to take care of.

> Dear one, what would people say? I should have but to cross the courtyard for people to begin noticing us and asking themselves questions. Gossip and scandal would arise, and there would be read into the affair quite another meaning than the real one. No, little angel, it were better that I should see you tomorrow at Vespers. That will be the better plan, and less hurtful to us both.[279]

Fearing other people's opinions and views, Devushkin preferred correspondence to meetings. He lived next to Varvara and nothing got in their way to communicate openly except his hypochondria. Subconsciously, in fact, Devushkin himself did not want anyone to see him with Varvara. If she were standing a little higher on the social ladder, Devushkin would not feel the pressure of other people's opinions. He did not want to be close to those who had the same position as he in the social hierarchy. He aspired even more to equate himself with others after managing to get in their circle. He told Varvara about this with full enthusiasm and joy. "This is a long epistle that I am sending you, but the reason is that today I feel in good spirits after

---

276. Vetlovskaya, *Roman F. M. Dostoevskogo "Bednye Lyudi,"* 91.

277. Vetlovskaya, 79.

278. Dostoevsky, *Poor Folk*; *Bednye Lyudi*, 76.

279. Dostoevsky; *Bednye Lyudi*, 21.

dining at Rataziaev's. There I came across a novel which I hardly know how to describe to you."[280] As, finally, the dream of Makar became reality even though for a short time, he did not notice the negative features of his companions. He tended to idealise everything he saw. Instead of criticising their literature, in which nothing was true, he admired it. "What a splendid thing is literature, Varin'ka – what a splendid thing! This I learnt before I had known Rataziaev even for three days."[281] Varvara, being familiar with the literature and having read Rataziaev's novel concluded: "How is it that his compositions please you so much, Makar? I think them such rubbish!"[282]

Devushkin, being driven by vanity, had a high opinion of himself. His loftiness could be seen in his reaction to the books he had read. Finding out about Devushkin's passion for literature, Varvara gave him first one of the Pushkin's works, and then one by Nikolai Gogol. She wanted to introduce him to high literature. These were Pushkin's "Tales of Belkin" and "The Overcoat" by Gogol. Having read these works, Makar gave them a contradictory assessment. He liked Pushkin's work, but he was outraged by Gogol's. He wrote to Varvara about the Pushkin's work: ". . . if you were to ask my opinion of it, I should say that never before in my life I had read a book so splendid."[283]

The ambiguous reaction of Makar pointed to his motives. In Pushkin's narrative Makar saw the tragedy, taken from life, which could happen to anyone regardless of the position which he occupied in society.

> How natural, how natural! You should read the book for yourself. The thing is actually alive. Even I can see that; even I can realize that it is a picture cut from the very life around me. In it I see our own Theresa (to go no further) and the poor *tchinovnik* – who is just such a man as this Samson Vyrin, except for his surname of Gorshkov. The book describes just what might happen to ourselves – to myself in particular.[284]

Pushkin's work gave Makar the opportunity to denounce others, to feel superior to others. This is why he admired the book. According to Vetlovskaya,

---

280. *Bednye Lyudi*, 54.
281. *Bednye Lyudi*, 51.
282. *Bednye Lyudi*, 55.
283. *Bednye Lyudi*, 58.
284. Dostoevsky, *Poor Folk*; *Bednye Lyudi*, 59.

Devushkin saw in Pushkin's work only the edification addressed to people, like Dunyasha, who were worthy of these words: "Do not run away, do not plunge the poor father into sin and grief."[285] Therefore, he liked this book and used it to accuse Varvara when she wanted to get away from him: "Here you are wishing to go away and leave us; yet, be careful lest it would not be I who had to pay the penalty of your doing so. For you might ruin both yourself and me . . . Think better of it, Varin'ka, and pay no more heed to foolish advice and calumny, but read your book again, and read it with attention. It may do you much good."[286]

It is different with "The Overcoat" by Nikolai Gogol. In this work Makar saw a reproach in his position. Makar perceived Gogol's narrative about the titular counsellor Akaky Akakiyevich Bashmachkin as a story about himself, as a personal insult. He thought that Varvara purposefully gave him the story to humiliate him: "What a misfortune, my beloved, that you should have brought me to such a pass!"[287] The tragedy of Gogol's character is the tragedy of people with the same or even lower social position such as Makar. It could happen to Devushkin but not to the count. The count could not die from losing his coat. From Makar's perspective the main feature of Akaky Akakiyevich was his low social status, his poverty. For people like Devushkin, Akaki was a waning man. He saw himself a waning man, inferior to others and for him this was the worst thing that could occur.[288] But Makar did not want to associate himself with people with the same social status. Therefore, he praised himself and did not understand why Gogol never saw the positive features of Akaky Akakiyevich:

> I have now been thirty years in the public service, and have fulfilled my duties irreproachably, remained abstemious, and never been detected in any unbecoming behaviour. As a citizen, I may confess – I confess it freely – I have been guilty of certain shortcomings; yet those shortcomings have been combined with certain virtues. I am respected by my superiors . . . Of course, no one is free from minor faults . . . But in grave or in audacious

---

285. Vetlovskaya, *Roman F. M. Dostoevskogo "Bednye Lyudi,"* 113–114.

286. *Bednye Lyudi*, 59.

287. *Bednye Lyudi*, 61.

288. Vetlovskaya, *Roman F. M. Dostoevskogo "Bednye Lyudi,"* 115.

offences never have I been detected, nor in infringements of
regulations, nor in breaches of the public peace. No, never! This
you surely know, even as the author of your book must have
known it. Yes, he also must have known it when he sat down
to write. I had not expected this of you, my Varvara. I should
never have expected it.[289]

According to Gogol, Akaky ate and drank and dressed far worse than
the others.

What? In future I am not to go on living peacefully in my little
corner, poor though that corner is I am not to go on living, as
the proverb has it, without muddying the water, or hurting any
one, or forgetting the fear of the Lord God and of oneself? I am
not to see, forsooth, that no man does me an injury, or breaks
into my home – I am not to take care that all shall go well with
me, or that I have clothes to wear, or that my shoes do not require mending, or that I be given work to do, or that I possess
sufficient meat and drink? . . . Has it ever been my custom to
pry into other men's mouths, to see what is being put into them?
Have I ever been known to offend any one in that respect? No,
no, beloved! Why should I desire to insult other folks when they
are not molesting me?[290]

Vanity made Devushkin suspicious of everyone around him. He felt that
everything was against him:

Sometimes a man will hide himself away, and not show his face
abroad, for the mere reason that, though he has done nothing to
be ashamed of, he dreads the gossip and slandering which are
everywhere to be encountered. If his civic and family life has
to do with literature, everything will be printed and read and
laughed over and discussed.[291]

---

289. Dostoevsky, *Poor Folk*; *Bednye Lyudi*, 62.
290. Dostoevsky *Poor Folk*; *Bednye Lyudi*, 62.
291. Dostoevsky *Poor Folk*; *Bednye Lyudi*, 63.

Makar was outraged because he had been unmasked. He had been creating for a long time an image of himself as a man with a higher social position, deserving respect and honour and now the reality had been revealed. Makar considered that wealth was what makes people earn respect. He was dissatisfied with his social position, and this was the reason he reacted so badly to Gogol's work. But he was not against the hierarchy. Thus, he accepted the social order in which injustice, violence and indifference dominated. Therefore, he advocated for the authorities, who were criticized by Gogol as being indifferent towards Akaky's life. According to this character, the existing social order was the only possible one. Moreover, it had been arranged by God.[292] To be happy according to Devushkin one had to be in the higher hierarchical position.

> Our lots in life are apportioned by the Almighty according to our human deserts. To such a one He assigns a life in a general's epaulets or as a privy councillor – to such a one, I say, He assigns a life of command; whereas to another one, He allots only a life of unmurmuring toil and suffering. These things are calculated according to a man's capacity. One man may be capable of one thing, and another of another, and their several capacities are ordered by the Lord God himself.[293]

Devushkin did not understand that in this order of things, such a hierarchy was formed not out of brotherly love but of the desire to dominate and subjugate other people. Gogol described only the surface, the hierarchical system with unequal social relations requiring only power and obedience. There was no place for brotherly love. After all, when one had power but the other did not and must be in obedience, there could be no brotherhood.

As a whole, relations of that kind suited Makar, but he would prefer to have a higher social status. While he was poor, he suffered from a constant feeling of humiliation at the sight of others more fortunate than himself. Therefore, he refused to describe his neighbours in detail: "Do not think that I could write to you in a satirical vein, for I am too old to show my teeth to no purpose, and people would laugh at me, and quote our Russian proverb: "Who digs

---

292. Vetlovskaya, *Roman F. M. Dostoevskogo "Bednye Lyudi,"* 118.

293. Dostoevsky, *Poor Folk; Bednye Lyudi*, 61.

a pit for another one, the same shall fall into it himself."[294] Devushkin was convinced that the reality around him was satire.

The vanity of Makar led him to an open revolt against the existing order. For a moment he imagined not only being "among them," but also behaving like "them." Instead of obeying and accepting the situation, he rebelled against it. This rebellion was perceived by Devushkin as a failure: "Then I, my angel, went mad, I got lost and disappeared completely. . ."[295] He not only fell but he was thrown.[296] If Makar had not expressed his outrage publicly but had kept it secret, then nobody would have humiliated him. In such a hierarchy the form and not the content were important. Obedience and humility were not inner manifestations emanating from love and respect, but external forms only. Hence, Devushkin appreciated the form more than the appearance. Unlike Gogol's character, who was constantly thinking about his overcoat, Devushkin was concerned about a button. This responsibility for external appearances was dictated by the social order regardless of social position. All other concerns, however important they might be, were purely private matters and went beyond the needs and requirements of this hierarchical order.[297] A self-loving person is afraid to look ridiculous.[298]

Makar as well as Varvara blamed fate, or the "evil people" for all their troubles. But if all of them were "evil," then good people did not exist. There were just people. This shows how complex and distorted a human being can be. In the novel there is no clear answer to the question of who is to blame for the fact that people are evil. There are only hints. Vetlovskaya, Belinsky and others saw the problem in the unjust social order. That meant, if the social order were to be changed, the relationships between human beings would also be changed. Vetlovskaya cited the example of Gorshkov, who being poor behaved modestly, even humbly, but once he received an inheritance, did not even want to greet Rataziaev.[299] As we have already observed, humility and modesty were only external forms, and the desire to gain advantage over others lies deeply in each person. Dostoevsky showed how vanity, being

294. *Bednye Lyudi*, 21.

295. *Bednye Lyudi*, 66.

296. Vetlovskaya, *Roman F. M. Dostoevskogo "Bednye Lyudi,"* 131.

297. Vetlovskaya, 133.

298. Losskiy, *Bog i mirovoe zlo*, 183.

299. Vetlovskaya, *Roman F. M. Dostoevskogo "Bednye Lyudi,"* 95.

one of the theological motifs in this novel, was the inner factor promoting preservation of the hierarchical system, generating hypocrisy and formalism.

The contrast between the theological motifs of **charity and the desire to dominate** was also highlighted. Belinsky believed that the novel's characters, despite the terrible social conditions, retained within themselves this "infinite goodness."[300] Dostoevsky, however, showed that charity was caused by a desire to dominate. In the existing order of things, charity was based on honouring and censure principles. Anna Fedorovna's good deeds, Bykov's care for Varvara's mother or for Pokrovsky and his wife and son reflected the same approach: one was a benefactor, others accepted help. Benefactors dominated and were even critical of those who received help, were humble and were constantly forced to offer thanks.[301]

Makar behaved the same way in his relationship with Varvara. He chose for himself the role of benefactor, not an equal but a master. This enabled him to feel one step higher than Varvara or, to be more precise, positioned Varvara one step below himself. He built relationships using exactly the same rules which were used in building a hierarchical system. He helped, said that he loved, but primarily cared about himself and loved only himself. Devushkin was in extreme need of a person ranked below him.

Makar saw the manifestation of his love by taking care of Varvara. He repeatedly called her "dear" and "darling." For this reason Vetlovskaya calls the novel *The Poor Folk* a love story. According to her, it contains the love story of two poor people. But the motives of the characters were not "pure, high and fine at their sources."[302] The characters' love was distorted from the very beginning, even though they thought that they loved sincerely and disinterestedly. But this love was not pure love; it was impregnated with egoism and self-interest. Though he called Varvara "darling," she was not a friend for him and not a beloved woman. He loved her selfishly, as a master.

In relations between the characters, Makar first of all was Varvara's patron. He patronized, on the one hand, because Varvara needed protection; he helped because she was an orphan, weak and unprotected. But the greatest

---

300. V. G. Belinskiy, *Sobranie Sochineniy v 3 tomakh* [The Complete Works in Three Volumes] (Moscow: OGIZ, 1948), 10 November 2010, http://az.lib.ru/b/belinskij_w_g/text_0090.shtml.

301. Vetlovskaya, *Roman F. M. Dostoevskogo "Bednye Lyudi,"* 135.

302. Vetlovskaya, 135.

motive of caring for Devushkin was the desire to satisfy his own need to feel superior to someone, to be not only in obedience to someone, but also to have someone to control. In this respect, Devushkin was no worse than others; at least he offered pity and support for one who was in a more difficult position than he was.[303]

As protector and master, however, he expected submission and dared to rule Varvara. He was pleased when Varvara called him her benefactor. From beginning to end, the relations between the main characters were hierarchical relations. The first was a benefactor, the other accepted help and obeyed orders. Lossky states that often Dostoevsky considered lack of love to be evil,[304] in which case Devushkin was doing wrong, thinking he was doing good. Makar was allowed everything. Varvara was allowed only the things which did not offend the benefactor. For example, it was supposed that she could play jokes on the old man Pokrovsky but not on Makar. Any reproach in his address was regarded as ingratitude. That meant, while accepting the help and care of Devushkin, Varvara should be grateful to him for everything, letting him feel superior. Only she could be guilty, even when she was right, because their relationship was unequal. Vetlovskaya considered Varvara was guilty once and forever; her benefactor once and forever was right.[305] Therefore, she tried to thank Makar by all means, which said more about Makar's love for himself than for Varvara.[306]

Just as Devushkin felt uneasy when people with a higher position communicated with him, Varvara also felt uneasy because of his help and care. She understood that everything she received, she would have to pay back: "How many times have I told you that I stand in need of nothing, of absolutely nothing, as well as that I shall never be in a position to recompense you for all the kindly acts which you have loaded me? Why, for instance, have you sent me geraniums?"[307] Makar, however, did not expect special rewards from Varvara; he wanted only one thing – obedience. The novel began with this motive: "How happy I was last night – how immeasurably, how impossibly

---

303. Vetlovskaya, 136.

304. Losskiy, *Bog i mirovoe zlo*, 112.

305. Vetlovskaya, *Roman F. M. Dostoevskogo "Bednye Lyudi,"* 141.

306. Losskiy, *Bog i mirovoe zlo*, 182.

307. *Bednye Lyudi*, 17.

happy! That was because for once in your life you had relented so far as to obey my wishes."[308] He was glad that she had done what he wanted: "To the curtain, however, I had never given a thought. The fact is that when I moved the flowerpots, it looped itself up. There now"![309] But further, her intention showed that the desire of the benefactor for her became a duty: "Yes, I perceived that a corner of the curtain in your window had been looped."[310] Inflicting suffering out of an aspiration to show compassion is the feature of the human soul, mysterious and unexplainable, dissected here by Dostoevsky.[311]

Varvara also could not be ill, as this offended Makar because he had no means for her treatment. "On the other hand, in every letter I urge you to be more careful of yourself, and to wrap yourself warmly, and to avoid going out in bad weather, and to be in all things prudent. You go to disobey me!"[312] If it happened that she got ill, in order not to offend her benefactor Varvara told lies, hiding her illness: "For the love of God do not be anxious about me, my friend, my only benefactor . . . I am not really ill. I have merely caught a little cold. I caught it last night . . ."[313] But she had been very seriously ill for a month. Dostoevsky noticed that which Devushkin was to notice. The author went deep into the soul of the character,[314] to show the motivations for his actions.

Varvara was deprived of elementary rights. Her rights and duties were only those which brought pleasure and gratitude to Makar. It was impossible for her to invite Makar to visit her. "Moreover, how could I come and visit you frequently? How, I repeat?"[315] It was forbidden to her to cry. He replied: "Shame on you!"[316] Varvara also could not even dream in her sleep: "Also what kind of dreams and visions do you have! It is a shame my little

---

308. *Bednye Lyudi*, 13.

309. *Bednye Lyudi*, 14.

310. *Bednye Lyudi*, 19.

311. V. Rozanov, "Legenda o Velikom Inkvizitore [The Legend of the Great Inquisitor]," *F. M. Dostoevsky: Polnoe Sobranie Sochineniy* [The Complete Works of Dostoevsky] [CD-ROM] (Izdatel'stvo Adept, 2002).

312. Rozanov, "Legenda o Velikom Inkvizitore," 27.

313. Rozanov, 66.

314. V. Belinskiy, *Dostoevsky*, in *F. M. Dostoevsky: Polnoe Sobranie Sochineniy* [The Complete Works of Dostoevsky] [CD-ROM] (Izdatel'stvo Adept, 2002).

315. *Bednye Lyudi*, p. 67.

316. *Bednye Lyudi*, 68.

angel. You should not pay attention to them."[317] She could not even express her own opinion, for example, about Rataziaev's poetry: ". . . it is bad, dear and very bad! . . . for Rataziaev I will intercede . . ."[318] His aspiration to have a high position in society was tied together with the intention to protect it even from one who was close.[319]

Makar demanded gratitude from Varvara, even if it caused her pain. She was supposed to tell him in detail again and again what he already knew about how difficult her life was at Anna Fedorovna's and how Bukov abused her. That hurt Varvara, but gave pleasure to him, because thus she praised him; this way she expressed her gratitude to him for "rescue" from disasters. However, it strongly oppressed her because of such strange requirements from her benefactor:

> Also, you ask me to send you a continutation of my memoirs – to conclude them. But I know now how I contrived even to write as much of them as I did; and now I have not the strength to write further of my past, nor the desire to give it a single thought. Such recollections are terrible for me . . . My heart runs blood when ever I think of it . . . But all this you know.[320]

Having felt that he could lose Varvara, Makar, instead of building an equal relationship, multiplied his gifts. For him it was necessary that she did not leave him, but at the same time he did not want to build equal relations. Varvara needed pure and unconditional love. Devushkin considered himself superior, and considered that it was his duty to help. His gifts did not bring love but killed it. Once when Varvara expressed her wish to leave Makar and Feodora to earn her living, he invited Varvara to the theatre. Makar understood their relationship this way. Any dissatisfaction with fate meant for him a lack of good deeds. Varvara understood that such a relationship as Makar built did not differ from that built by Anna Fedorovna and Bykov. That was why she repeatedly expressed the desire to leave him. For Devushkin such desire meant ingratitude. Therefore, he used words like sin, shame and correction.

---

317. *Bednye Lyudi*, 56.

318. *Bednye Lyudi*, 56.

319. Lauth, *Filosofiya Dostoevskogo v sistematicheskom izlozhenii*, 280.

320. Dostoevsky, *Poor Folk*, 20 June.

"It is a sin, darling!"[321] Moreover, he saw in Varvara's desires revolt against God: ". . . do like I advise you and make an old man happy, be obedient to me. Then the Lord will award you, my darling, by all means He will do it."[322]

As for Makar the unique criterion of gratitude was receiving gifts; he could not understand Varvara's discontent. "What do not you have? We are so happy about you; you love us – so humbly live for yourself here."[323]

Makar's desire to dominate was evident from the beginning. He built relations in which only his opinion about things and their order was important. From Varvara he required only humility. Devushkin understood love as a virtue only for himself and as obedience for Varvara. Obedience must be expressed in an absolute refusal of her will on behalf of his. This explained Makar's indifference regarding Varvara's thoughts about the present and the future. Even in literature, at which she was very good, he did not ask for her opinion.[324]

Good deeds in the distorted world moved the benefactor to despotism, tyranny[325] and roughness, as evidenced in Anna Fedorovna's case, or tenderness and unselfconsciousness as in Makar's case, which did much good, but subjected the favoured person to slavery.[326] Thus, Makar demanded from Varvara love of this slavery as he considered absence of such love as ingratitude. Even in his first novel, Dostoevsky mentioned the theme of a person wishing to become God in the life of other people.[327] Devushkin gave flower pots, sweets, linen, a hat, and in exchange demanded full obedience: "Have a candy, sweetheart, and at each candy remember me."[328]

The logic of their relationship remained unclear to them because it was the inner part of them and conducted the characters to a tragic end. Dostoevsky understood that hierarchy was not the basis of such relations, but something deeper, which had deformed their understanding of true values. Such a distorted understanding also had generated a hierarchy. When somebody else

---

321. *Bednye Lyudi*, 58.

322. *Bednye Lyudi*, 60.

323. *Bednye Lyudi*, 56.

324. Vetlovskaya, *Roman F. M. Dostoevskogo "Bednye Lyudi,"* 148.

325. Lauth, *Filosofiya Dostoevskogo v sistematicheskom izlozhenii*, 280.

326. Vetlovskaya, *Roman F. M. Dostoevskogo "Bednye Lyudi,"* 148.

327. Vetlovskaya, 151.

328. *Bednye Lyudi*, 54.

did favours for Makar, he felt pain and humiliation. The scene when His Excellency did him a favour followed by Makar's reciprocal gratitude was the best example. Favour was perceived by Makar as a reproach: "I . . . burned, I burned in the hellfire! I was dying!"[329] However, he was not able to understand that Varvara felt the same when he was trying to protect her.

This constrained gratitude did not unite them because one, thanks to the help, rose to the heights, while the other was reduced to nothing. Instead of bringing two people closer to each other, these actions kept them away from each other.[330]

Gratitude toward the one to whom gratitude was rendered was always "gratitude" for being humiliated. The benefactor rejoiced that he had done a "good deed," at the same time also rejoicing to see someone's humility and misfortune. This was because another's humility in this case was the obvious proof of his own height. It could be seen very well in Makar's words after has helped Gorshkov with twenty kopecks: "It is a pity, it is a pity, and it is a pity, sweetheart! I have treated him kindly. He is a mislaid, confused person; he searches for protection, and so I have treated him kindly."[331]

Makar derived pleasure from an awareness of his own superiority over Gorshkov – an awareness of his own power over him. Thus, Devushkin was ready to offer his last kopecks to feel the pleasure of being the benefactor, and at the same time the receiver had a feeling of negligibility. Makar was sorry and loved Gorshkov only because he had appeared in a lower position than Makar. So, the virtues of one were in direct dependence on an absence of virtues in another. The pleasure of one depended on the misfortune of another.

Makar's love and pity were the means for satisfaction of his desire to achieve domination and power and came as a result of his vanity.[332] He was the benefactor and so first; second and lower in his eyes were those whom he helped. His part in the other's life, such as with Gorshkov or Varvara, was selfish; it was infected with egoism. Makar's love and mercy toward others were love only to himself.

---

329. *Bednye Lyudi*, 93.

330. *Bednye Lyudi*, 93.

331. *Bednye Lyudi*, 91.

332. Vetlovskaya, *Roman F. M. Dostoevskogo "Bednye Lyudi,"* 165.

This requirement for gratitude is alien to true love. True love not only makes people related, but equals: one has no more reason for gratitude than the other. In inequality there is no love. In unequal relations, when one is a benefactor and another must give thanks, there is no love.[333]

2.3.3 The Tragic End

The human being in *The Poor Folk*, as in Genesis, is a tragic, split creature, excluded from paradise.[334] Dostoevsky is convinced that the sinful relationship between people leads them to tragedy. Before meeting Makar, Varvara had experienced humiliation and pain from Anna Fedorovna and Bykov. She saw in Makar's desire to protect her the only hope of rescue for herself: "I am able to appreciate everything in my heart that you have made for me, having protected me from malicious people, from their persecution and hatred."[335] Varvara hoped Devushkin would rescue and protect her but as time passed he too began to disappoint her as he became more and more like her enemies. All his care oppressed and tormented her not less than when Anna Fedorovna's deceit and treachery had tormented her: "To what you have brought me, Makar! You think, truly that is nothing to me, that you so badly behave, you do not know yet, what I suffer because of you!"[336] Thinking to protect Varvara from treachery and insults, Makar involuntarily betrayed and constantly offended her.[337]

However, from such relations Makar became unhappy himself. Being a benefactor and patronizing Varvara, Devushkin suffered himself. He humiliated her and he humiliated himself. Because in the opinion of those who were above him on the scale of rank he was a poor man who needed their help, Makar felt humiliated when he was compelled to borrow money from other people. In the end of the novel, the characters appeared in identical positions: both hungry, both almost without a roof over their head, both undressed.[338]

Makar did not become a close and dear person to Varvara. He spent all his means and savings for Varvara. But what was the most important and

333. Vetlovskaya, 176.

334. William Leatherbarrow, *Fedor Dostoevsky* (Boston: Twayne Publishers, 1981), 36.

335. *Bednye Lyudi*, 21.

336. *Bednye Lyudi*, 80.

337. Vetlovskaya, *Roman F. M. Dostoevskogo "Bednye Lyudi"*, 170.

338. Vetlovskaya, 173.

most necessary and did not require any expense he could not offer her at all, because Varvara's greatest need was for a dear and near person.

Her constant and importunate requests to Makar to come were not heard by him: "What an unsociable person you are . . . And after all I am to you almost a close relative. You do not love me, Makar, and I sometimes feel very sad."[339] Varvara asked him to come, as a friend to rejoice together, to grieve and hope – together, to do it together instead of alone.[340] But they met with extreme precautions, preferring to see each other in the church: "Will you never come to see me? Occasionally, maybe only sometimes. We see each other only on Sundays at the sermon."[341]

Varvara repeatedly stated the requests to meet him, to come to her place: "Come to visit me, for God's sake, come today . . . you must come to us by all means today; yes it is better you would come round, you can always came to have dinner with us. Feodora cooks very well."[342] But for Makar the opinion of "the others" was more important than Varvara's wishes. Varvara was important to him but "they," who were on a step above in rank, were more relevant for him. Again there is obvious self-interest in the behaviour of the character.

Makar only ran to Varvara when she was definitively disappointed with him and decided to leave him for Bykov: "I come round to you, little angel, come round, by all means I would come round; I come to the doors of your house twice already. But this Bykov . . ."[343] Vetlovskaya considered that Makar, in the end of the novel, realized his error and found a way out, but it was too late to change anything. But, in Devushkin's actions can be seen despair. His vanity had led to despair. He was ready to make any changes that were necessary, but he did it only because he could not take care of her in any another way. Therefore, Devushkin remained the same.

The novel came to a tragic end. Varvara was not only disappointed with the "help" of Makar but put him below his worst enemy. She thought that Bykov could give her what Makar could not give her. Her leaving with Bykov also showed that she did not know how to make a good decision or how to

---

339. *Bednye Lyudi*, 55.

340. Vetlovskaya, *Roman F. M. Dostoevskogo "Bednye Lyudi"*, 174.

341. *Bednye Lyudi*, 55.

342. *Bednye Lyudi*, 68.

343. *Bednye Lyudi*, 101.

resolve this situation. Though Varvara is very weak, if life is to continue it will go in a circle for Varvara. It was clear that she could not expect anything good from Bykov, only humiliation, but for Varvara there was no alternative. She tried to convince herself of the correctness of her decision-making:

> If anyone could save me from this squalor, and restore to me my good name, and avert from me future poverty and want and misfortune, he is the man to do it. What else have I to look from the future? . . . Shall I go out into the world? Nay; I am worn to a shadow with grief, and become good for nothing. Sickly by nature, I should merely be a burden upon other folks. Of course this marriage will not bring me paradise, but what else does there remain, my friend – what else does there remain? What other choice is left?[344]

However, the problem was not so much the fact that the characters were poor, but that they were, first of all, alien each to the other and this predetermined the tragic end of their story. V. Maykov wrote: "It goes without saying that Makar's "love" should raise disgust in Varvara, which she constantly and persistently hid, maybe, and from herself."[345] However, not everybody took the same view. Joseph Frank came to the conclusion that Makar could not remain with Varvara because of their age difference. For this reason, he believed Varvara did not love him.[346] Frank, however, came to this opinion because he shared the point of view that the novel was social[347] and therefore believed that Makar sincerely loved Varvara. It is impossible to agree with such a conclusion. Varvara left Makar, not because he was faithful to her, but because this fidelity was selfish. She was pushed away not by real love but by egoistical love.

---

344. Dostoevsky, *Poor Folk*, 23 September.

345. A. Maykov, "Iz pis'ma k P. A. Viscovatomu" [From the Letter to P. A. Viscovatom], *F. M. Dostoevsky: Polnoe Sobranie Sochineniy* [The Complete Works of Dostoevsky] [CD-ROM] (Izdatel'stvo Adept, 2002).

346. Frank, *Dostoevsky: The Seeds of Revolt, 1821–1849*, 139.

347. Frank, 141.

Such deformed relations led to unhappiness. Dostoevsky used the theological motif of ***despair*** to create a picture of hopelessness and deadlock. Sin progresses so much in people that it leads to catastrophe.[348]

2.4 Conclusion

During his pre-Siberian period Dostoevsky was a part of two communities: family and socialist. Each of these communities shaped his convictions. His home environment prompted the formation of some of the writer's formative beliefs. It was his parent's serious attitude towards faith and images of biblical heroes, especially Job and Jesus, that found their place in the heart of Fyodor Mikhailovich. Dostoevsky's convictions in this early period were manifested in his love of reading of the Holy Scriptures, in prayer, in conversations about Christ, in compassion and help to the needy.

Encounters with poor sick people and later with poor peasants raised important questions that he tried to answer. Some writers deeply influenced Dostoevsky. Through their works he drew even closer to people. Fyodor Mikhailovich, author of *The Poor Folk* worried like many of his contemporaries about problems of social injustice and their elimination. He could not tolerate the fact that someone had to suffer all his or her life. In January 1876, in *A Diary of a Writer* Dostoevsky wrote:

> I could never understand the notion that only one-tenth of people should get higher education while the other nine-tenths of people should serve only as their material and means while themselves remaining in darkness. I do not wish to think and live in any other way than with the belief that all our ninety million Russians . . . will all someday be educated, humanized, and happy.[349]

Even though Dostoevsky valued Christ as a personality, this study has shown that he placed humanity, not Christ, in the centre of his life. His passionate desire to see the happiness of simple people led him to like-minded persons. He could not see Christ as "the Way" to simple people's happiness,

---

348. A. Bem, *Dostoevskiy* (Prague, 1938), 187.

349. Fyodor Dostoevsky, *A Writer's Diary*, trans. Kenneth Lantz (Evanston, IL: Northwestern University Press, 2009), 115.

because during this time, Fyodor Mikhailovich saw people's "problem" in the social arena. That is why his following of Belinsky led Dostoevsky to "losing Christ." While attending Petrashevsky's club after breaking up with Belinsky, Dostoevsky got to know Doctor D. Yanovsky, a deeply faithful and religious person, whom he spent many hours with talking about literature, art and religion.[350]

Arrest, imprisonment, a death verdict and the closeness of death were especially important moments in Dostoevsky's religious life. They were the beginning of his intense spiritual activity. Thus while staying in Petrapavlovsk fortress he longed for spiritual literature and Holy Scriptures. One can conclude that in the pre-Siberian period, Dostoevsky's convictions alternated between faith in Christ and atheism. But the dominant image of his life during this time was the 'perfect world' which he craved.

Dostoevsky's convictional theology was expressed in The Poor Folk. He is convinced that in the beginning people lived in harmony. To create a picture of paradise, Dostoevsky used the theological motifs of love, humility and care which came from Genesis 1–2. He believed that in the past people were happy. He believed in an initial paradise life when love, humility and care about each other were the motivation of people's life. Then people appreciated each other and built equal relations with each other. Dostoevsky uncritically accepted the biblical narrative of Genesis 1–11.

The Fall turned everything upside down. As a theological motif the statement was repeated showing how people suffer from the actions of their relatives and those who are close to them. Dostoevsky drew a picture of the initial accident that reversed the fate of humanity as a whole. The values of the people had changed. Life became "satire." From the first letters it was clear that the one who had turned all in this world was the devil at the Fall. Even the first letter began the eighth day. In seven days, the Lord created this world and symbolically Dostoevsky uses the figure eight to specify the disaster which happened in the universe at the Fall. To accept and admit this devil's world and his "order of things" as the norm would be the greatest misfortune and dishonour. But the form of the order, as Dostoevsky explained, was only a formal order; an image of order – only a visibility of order.[351]

---

350. *F. M. Dostoevsky v vospominaniyakh sovremenikov*, 312.

351. Vetlovskaya, *Roman F. M. Dostoevskogo "Bednye Lyudi,"* 199.

The world is deformed because evil is something inside the person. Therefore, the person builds unfair hierarchical systems that are seductive to many. To create this picture of being deformed by harm, Dostoevsky used as theological motifs contrasting conditions: contentment and envy; humility and vanity; charity and the desire to dominate. Thus, as he stated himself, it went deeper into showing how much the person was full of evil.

Everything in this world is sick and not good. Everything that was initially perfect has become mixed up with envy, vanity and the desire to dominate. In this sick world there are no truly kind people. There are those who would like to do well, but in their unawareness they do evil. Thus, everybody realizes evil when they feel it done to them, but people do not usually notice evil in their own promptings and actions. Meanwhile evil is in their disunity, in their hostility to all and to everyone, in the absence between them of valid relationships and brotherhood.[352]

Makar became a stranger to everybody, and everybody became a stranger to him. He was so impregnated by arrogance that he belonged to no one; he considered himself better than others.[353] All his "good intentions" were saturated by self-interest. To get his own profit, Makar made "good deeds" from everything that he had; he endowed everything. The vanity of Makar separated him from all other people and thus he could not be a brother to anybody. In his eyes he saw himself as better than others. This meant that he was infected by a general illness; but unfortunately, he did not understand this. Evil was the egoistical thought "first of all is me." He was content with himself on somebody else's account, and eventually, at the expense of other people. This was how all people living in this deformed world of Dostoevsky's looked to him.

What the characters in this novel did not get was unconditional love or simply, love; true suffering, true human advantage, instead of ambition: In other words, nothing that was not infected and not spoiled. Dostoevsky did not show an escape from humanity's problems. The novel came to a tragic end. The author only stated the problem, but he did not know a way out of it. He clearly understood that such a life leads people nowhere and makes a person unhappy, and life loses sense. His or her life comes to despair. Dostoevsky

---

352. Vetlovskaya, 185.
353. Vetlovskaya, 190.

showed here only that people are unhappy and need to return to the initial paradise of life. He pined for this life but did not know how to return to it. Volsky puts it this way: "Dostoevsky searches for an exit, the solutions to the painful questions, the horrors of life press on him, he doesn't know how to cope with them or where to search for salvation from evil and a lie."[354] The theological search was not, however, over for Dostoevsky.

Thus, during the pre-Siberian period, Dostoevsky's character was changed as well as his beliefs. Through this period, both in the time when he believed in Christ and when he turned away from Christ, he remained a person with compassion and a sacrificial spirit for the poor and sick, and was interested in society's issues. Dostoevsky hated injustice, lies and cruelty. He was a deeply thoughtful man. But if his thoughts were of spiritual things at the beginning of this period, then at the end of the period he was thinking more about the realm of social, material things. His humility changed into hate for the church and for authorities. Dostoevsky passionately enjoyed reading. In the beginning of this period, he enjoyed reading the gospel and history; later, he gave time to reading social and political literature. After the sentence, Dostoevsky took an interest in the Bible again. His theology was being formed through that experience.

---

354. Volskiy, *Feodor Mihaylovich Dostoevskiy* [Fedor Mihailovich Dostoevsky], (Moscow: Knizhnyy magazin D. P. Efimova, 1906), 23–24.

CHAPTER 3

The Siberian Period: The Regeneration of Convictions

3.1 Introduction

The purpose of this chapter is to discover and analyse Dostoevsky's convictions as they were revealed in his life during the Siberian period and to discover and analyse theological motifs expressed in *The House of the Dead*. To achieve this goal, it is necessary to first identify and analyse Dostoevsky's communities and their shared convictions; to identify and analyse Dostoevsky's own convictions; and to discover and analyse the influence of Dostoevsky's life on society. Second, theological motifs expressed in *The House of the Dead* will be identified and studied. The theological motifs discovered in these novels point to Dostoevsky's message for Russian society.

3.2 Dostoevsky's Convictions Shown in His Own Life During the Siberian Period

This chapter continues the investigation begun in the previous chapter, and concerns the next period of his life. The purpose of this chapter is to detect and analyze the convictions of Dostoevsky's Siberian years (1849–1859) in Petropavlovsk prison, his court trial, a four-year stay in penal servitude (*katorga*) and a six-year stay in exile in Siberia. Our primary sources are his *Letters*, *Diary of a Writer*, notebooks, memoirs of contemporaries, and memories of the writer's wife, his brother Andrei, and daughter Liubovi.

On the one hand this period was a difficult time for Dostoevsky, but on the other hand it was an important and formative part of his life. This was a period marked by the writer's encounter with simple people under severe conditions and a repeated acceptance of Christ in his soul. In August 1880, in a *Diary of Writer* Fyodor Mikhailovich wrote the following words that exposed the meaning of all these years spent in Siberia: "From people I accepted Christ in my soul, Christ Who I got to know as a child in my parental home and Who I had forfeited when I was transformed into a European liberal."[1]

3.2.1 On the Way to Siberia (1850)

On the night of 24–25 December, Dostoevsky was shackled and sent to Siberia. This was his first trip through Russia. In the Urals the temperature reached minus 40 degrees Celsius. On 9 January 1850, on the sixteenth day of the journey, Dostoevsky, Durov and Yastrzhembsky were dropped in Tobolsk and spent six days there expecting to be exiled to Omsk. They were put in a narrow, dark, cold and dirty room for people who had been arrested. Tough circumstances did not quench his fervor, which came from his childhood, to help a neighbour. Through a friendly talk Dostoevsky managed to stop Yastrzhembsky from committing suicide.[2]

There was one event in Tobolsk that stuck in his memory and impressed him greatly. Dostoevsky was met by the wives of the Decembrists. Fyodor Mikhailovich never forgot those four Siberian female activists who supported him in a time of need. They were P. E. Annenkova with her daughter, N. D. Fonvizina and G. A. Muravyeva. He received a New Testament as a blessing from them, and he never lost it.

> We have seen these great women, who willingly followed their husbands to Siberia, Dostoevsky remembers after a quarter of a century – Not being guilty, they endured just about everything that their husbands endured for twenty-five years. The visit lasted for an hour. They have blessed us on our new journey.[3]

---

1. *Dnevnik Pisatelya*, 1880, 152.
2. Grossman, *Dostoevsky*, 161.
3. Grossman, 161.

Dostoevsky also had a Bible that was sent by his brother to the fortress where he stayed. He took it to Siberia, but it was soon stolen, yet the New Testament received from the wives he treasured carefully and used constantly.[4] About 20 January, Dostoevsky and Durov were sent from Tobolsk to Omsk.[5] With his renewed love for reading God's word, he began to enjoy religion and finding his faith and trust in God as he traveled. He became more concerned for people in need. Dostoevsky was becoming able to deeply analyze his life and make decisions.

3.2.2 Katorga (1850–1854)

On 23 January 1850, they arrived in the Omsk fortress which was surrounded by moats and ramparts. "There were a lot of fleas, louse and cockroaches. There were empty plank beds. We had a common tub from evening until morning. Unbearable stuffiness. I was surrounded by a constant noise, swearing, shouts, and chain rattling. This was a hell, total darkness," remembers Dostoevsky.[6] But this was his community.

In *The House of the Dead*, and in his letters to his brother (22 February 22 1854) and Fonvizina, in the beginning of March of that same year, he wrote about his concerns in exile, his spiritual condition when leaving the place and the consequences following in his life. He had to experience "the fullness of revenge and persecution that people in exile live and breathe with towards the noble class."[7] "Yet, a constant act of self-concentration," he wrote to a brother, "that I practiced in order to run away from such bitter reality has brought its own fruits."[8] They encountered, as a second letter showed, "the strengthening of religious feeling,"[9] that almost faded "under the influence of doubts."[10] This was obviously what he meant by calling it as a "regeneration

---

4. *Dnevnik Pisatelya*, 1873, 12.

5. *F. M. Dostoevsky v vospominaniyakh sovremenikov*, 164.

6. F. M. Dostoevsky, *Polnoe Sobranie Sochineniy v 30-i tomakh, T. 4 Zapiski iz Mertvogo Doma* [The Complete Works of Dostoevsky in 30 Volumes, Vol. 5, *The House of the Dead.*] Cited hereafter as *Zapiski iz Mertvogo Doma* (Leningrad: Nauka, 1972),12.

7. *F. M. Dostoevsky v vospominaniyakh sovremenikov*, 279.

8. *Pis'ma*, Vol. 28, 30 January 1854, 166.

9. *Neizdannyy Dostoevsky Zapisnye knizhki i tetradi 1860–1881*, 667.

10. *Pis'ma*, Vol. 28, 20 February 1854, 175.

of convictions,"[11] in *Diary of a Writer*.[12] He reluctantly spoke about long deprivations in jail and bitterly remembered his estrangement from literature. However, he continued that by reading the Bible alone, he could understand the meaning of Christianity better and more deeply.[13]

Dostoevsky's life in prison is well known from the *The House of the Dead* in which he shared accounts of his life in exile using pseudonyms and describing former friends also in exile. In the secretly sent, more honest letter to his brother on 22 February 1854 the story is darker.

The work was hard. They had to pull down the huts, carry bricks, dig and knead clay. Sometimes, Petrashevs had an easier task "at alabaster."[14] Tokarzhevsky remembered the time in exile spent along with Dostoevsky:

> Working "at alabaster" pertained to the best and easiest jobs out of all that we were assigned to in Omsk fortress. We, as exiled convicts, were so-called "black workers" meaning that we did not know any craft work. "Alabaster" was ruled by the community of engineers, who as educated and cultured people could sympathize with politically exiled convicts and even favour them to some extent. Thus, we people from Poland and Russian writer Fyodor Dostoevsky would always be assigned to work "at alabaster."[15]

The head of penal servitude was indifferent to the fact that Dostoevsky was already a famous writer and that prior to his incarceration he had already written *The Poor Folk, White Nights, The Double* and *Netochka Nezvanova*.[16] Exiled convicts would be terribly punished; they were to run through "green" sticks. Sometimes the punishment would be split in two or three parts, since running through all the "sticks" could lead to inevitable death. When a punished, half-alive prisoner was escorted to the hospital, Dostoevsky was so

---

11. *Dnevnik Pisatelya*, 1873, 134.

12. *Dnevnik Pisatelya*, 134.

13. *F. M. Dostoevsky v vospominaniyakh sovremenikov*, 279.

14. *Zapiski iz Mertvogo Doma*, 177.

15. *F. M. Dostoevsky v vospominaniyakh sovremenikov*, 325.

16. *Dostoevsky v Omske* [Dostoevsky in Omsk] (Omsk: 1972), 5.

devastated that he would ask the medical assistants with a trembling voice: "Young people! Please save him . . . save the wretched one."[17]

There are two totally opposite opinions about the consequences of Dostoevsky's lonely imprisonment, the verdict at Semenov plaza and exile. Some people, relying on his words, claim that the horrible trial he experienced cured him of many defects, worked out his beliefs and observations of the surrounding world and revealed horizons and depths of the human soul that he as a writer had never seen before. Others say that his transition from one camp to another could be explained by the fact that his time in exile broke him morally and ruined his health.

In his novel *The House of the Dead*, Dostoevsky described his way of life in the characters and the destinies of the exiled convicts. In a reserved manner he told about their horrible crimes and shared his desire to reach the consciousness of the people.[18]

E. Rumyantseva considers that his rapprochement with people in exile served to transform his beliefs. Dostoevsky saw the whole measure of a person's sufferings, his defensiveness and lack of rights. He had always supported peasant liberation and defended those offended. He passionately desired social harmony, with a defined place for the nation.[19]

In the katorga, Dostoevsky was lonely. Often prisoners would not communicate with him, considering him a nobleman, a person from the other world. Even there, he wrote a composition, called "Siberian Copybook." There he recorded his thoughts, prison songs, proverbs, etc. "Siberian Copybook" became the main resource for writing *The House of the Dead*.

Based on the stories of soldiers, former alumni of Petersburg's Sea Cadet Body who served at Omsk prison, P. K. Martyanov describes the conditions of exiled convicts:

> Former brilliant Petrashevs looked like extremely sad people. In summer, dressed in common prisoner's garb consisting of a black and white jacket with a yellow ace on the back, and a soft cap without a peak. In winter, dressed in a short sheepskin coat with mitten and ear warmers, chained in rumbling shackles, they

17. *Zapiski iz Mertvogo Doma*, 150.

18. *F. M. Dostoevsky v vospominaniyakh sovremenikov*, 279.

19. Rumyanceva, *Feodor Mikhaylovich Dostoevsky*, 101.

did not differ from other prisoners. Only traces of education and good upbringing could not be erased, and this fact distinguished them from the mass of prisoners.[20]

Martyanov continues describing Dostoevsky's attitude towards other exiled convicts: "Exiled convicts did not like him,yet acknowledged his moral authority. They would look at him gloomily with hatred and silence. Recognizing this fact, he would avoid them as well, seldom talking to some of the prisoners whenever being unbearably sad."[21] Dostoevsky was struck by the hatred of prisoners towards condemned noblemen.[22] He survived the hostile attitude of the "black" mass of prisoners towards noblemen in a very difficult and grave way.[23] In a letter to his brother after release from katorga (30 January 30 – 22 February 1854) Dostoevsky described the social-psychological tragedy of his life in imprisonment:

> I became acquainted with exiles in Tobolsk and had to spend four years with them in Omsk. These people are rough, annoyed and angry. Hatred towards noblemen exceeds all possible limits and therefore we have encountered much hostility. The evil joy because of our grief was pictured on their faces. They would eat us alive, if allowed. However, think about it! Was our protection really a secure one, when we had to live, eat, drink and sleep with these people for several years, not having any opportunity to complain about countless insults? "You, noblemen, iron noses, pecked us to death. Previously you were our masters, tormenting our nation, and now worst of all you have become our brothers." This theme lasted for four years. 150 enemies never get tired of persecuting us, it was their joy, entertainment and occupation. The only way out for us was indifference, moral superiority, which they could understand, and respect our disobedience to their will. They would always acknowledge our superiority.[24]

---

20. *F. M. Dostoevsky v vospominaniyakh sovremennikov*, 336.

21. *F. M. Dostoevsky v vospominaniyakh sovremennikov*, 338.

22. *Zapiski iz Mertvogo Doma*, 165.

23. *F. M. Dostoevsky v vospominaniyakh sovremennikov*, 300.

24. *Pis'ma*, Vol. 28, 30 January 1854, 166.

In Fyodor Mikhailovich's words written to his brother after his return from the scaffold on 22 December 1849, Leonid Grossman sees doubts in his recent beliefs.[25] Dostoevsky would write: "Maybe we'll remember it one day . . . our youth and hopes that I have torn away with blood from my heart and buried them."[26] Yet, this was a process. Slowly, being in exile, Fyodor Mikhailovich would evaluate his fascination with his first ideas. During his fourth year in Omsk, he revised his whole life, strictly judging himself and radically reconstructing his earlier convictions. He wrote:

> Emotionally lonely, I revised my whole previous life, sorting just about every detail, meditating about my past, strictly judging myself. From time to time, I would even bless my fate, because it sent me this solitude, and without this solitude I would have never performed either this judgment over myself nor revised my earlier life.[27]

"It was difficult for me to share the story of the regeneration of my convictions," Dostoevsky wrote in 1873.[28] Grossman considers that he meant the transition from his utopian socialism of the 1840s to his reactionary beliefs after exile.[29] "Thoughts and convictions change. A human being changes as well," Dostoevsky wrote on 24 March 1856,[30] acknowledging with his usual sincerity that betrayed his previous convictions in the letter to Maikov in 1868.[31] He particularly experienced a new theme in exile, in his aloofness from people. He had to overcome it , not only as a convict of the second category, but as a writer of *The Poor Folk,* Grossman believed.[32]

The result of his meditations in exile was Dostoevsky's letter to the wife of one of the Decembrists, N. D. Fonvizina, after liberation from a prison:

> Let me tell you that I am a child of a century, a child of disbelief and doubts even until the coffin lid. It requires of me terrible

---

25. *Dostoevsky,* 173.

26. *Pis'ma,* Vol. 28, 22 December 1849, 161.

27. *Zapiski iz Mertvogo Doma,* 220.

28. *Dnevnik Pisatelya,* 1873, 134.

29. *Dostoevsky,* 174.

30. *Pis'ma,* Vol. 28, 24 March 1856, 223.

31. *F. M. Dostoevsky v vospominaniyakh sovremennikov,* 258.

32. *Dostoevsky,* 174.

torments to have this thirst to believe, which is stronger in my soul than any other opposite arguments.[33]

Tokarzhevsky recalls an event that communicated Dostoevsky's kind attitude towards animals while he was in penal servitude:

> Fyodor Mikhailovich loved animals, dispirited by the tragic fate of his favourite dog Kultyapka; he first found the presence of a dog in prison and treated it kindly. A dog would trustfully approach us. It was a very thin animal, with protruding bones through drenched and colourless wool. Obviously, it was a very exhausted and hungry dog, barely dragging its legs. When Dostoevsky caressed the dog, it started barking joyfully.[34]

In exile, Fyodor Mikhailovich's seizures occurred more frequently. According to Doctor Trotsky, epileptic seizures would shake Dostoevsky's nervous system.[35] During this time, he could not write anything and did not have a right to. However, he confessed to police magistrates that he would collect materials in his head for future writings.[36]

He became stronger in his faith by reading his Bible. Dostoevsky remained a person who had compassion for the sick and oppressed. He treated each person kindly and had a sacrificial spirit toward people in need. He was a humble and honest person and did not return evil for evil. Dostoevsky remained a person who did not accept injustice, lies, cruelty or pain. He had a desire to reach the consciousness of the people, and passionately desired social harmony.

3.2.3 Service in the Tsar's Army (1854–1859)

According to a court decision in February 1854 Dostoevsky was assigned to Semipalatinsk linear battalion as an ordinary soldier. In the fall of 1854 Dostoevsky's conditions got better. In November, A. E. Wrangell arrived in

---

33. *Pis'ma*, Vol. 28, 20 February 1854, 175.

34. *F. M. Dostoevsky v vospominaniyakh sovremennikov*, 327.

35. *F. M. Dostoevsky v vospominaniyakh sovremennikov*, 340.

36. *F. M. Dostoevsky v vospominaniyakh sovremennikov*, 344.

Semipalatinsk to serve as a member of the public prosecutor's control of government and criminal deals.[37]

In exile, Fyodor Mikhailovich did not complete any of his works, yet by this time he was already a famous writer within his own circle. This was why he became a friend of regional public prosecutor Wrangell, who was present in the winter of 1849, at the Petrashevs execution. Dostoevsky and Wrangell would discuss just about everything. According to Wrangell, Dostoevsky began telling the stories almost whispering, but once encouraged, his voice sounded louder and louder. During the moments of special emotions, almost choking, he would attract listeners with his passionate speech. He delightfully spoke about Christ, yet seldom attended church and disliked priests.[38] Dostoevsky continually disliked Russian priests[39] and did not attend church frequently until 1871.[40]

Wrangell also claimed that after time spent in exile, Dostoevsky's new position despite financial difficulties seemed like paradise to him, because of his relative freedom.[41] Fyodor Mikhailovich described this in the letter to his brother on 27 March 1854: "My health is fairly well, and during these two months many things got better; that's what it means to get out from tightness, stuffiness and heavy captivity."[42]

"All wretched, sickly and poor things hardened by fate would trigger his interest and participation," A. E. Wrangell commented, "his extremely impressive kindness was known to all of his close friends; Fyodor Mikhailovich's compassion towards people seemed as if it did not belong to this world."[43] Yet Dostoevsky could easily recognize his own negative traits. In a letter to his brother, he confessed: "I have a terrible defect: unlimited egocentrism and ambitions."[44]

Fyodor Mikhailovich's friendship with Wrangell offered him a chance to be in the highest class of society. On 1 October 1856, due to this acquaintance,

---

37. *F. M. Dostoevsky v vospominaniyakh sovremennikov*, 345.

38. *F. M. Dostoevsky v vospominaniyakh sovremennikov*, 358.

39. *Dnevnik Pisatelya*, 1877, 174.

40. Losskiy, *Bog i mirovoe zlo*, 45.

41. *F. M. Dostoevsky v vospominaniyakh sovremennikov*, 347.

42. *Pis'ma*, Vol. 28, 27 March 1854, 178.

43. *F. M. Dostoevsky v vospominaniyakh sovremennikov*, 353.

44. *Pis'ma*, Vol. 28, 1 April 1846, 119.

Dostoevsky who was an ordinary soldier became an officer. He had already gotten back his noble title.

Wrangell was a good friend to Dostoevsky in his passionately developing romance with Maria Dmitrievna Issaeva. "She appeared in the saddest period of my life and has resurrected my soul," remembered Dostoevsky.[45] On February 15, 1857 Dostoevsky married Maria, who was so strongly beloved by him, in a church in Kuznetsk. She was a widow. He fell in love with her from the very first glance, even though Maria Dmitrievna did not have an angelic nature, which was the reason for the later unhappiness of their marriage. According to Wrangell, Maria Dmitrievna was constantly ill, capricious and jealous.[46]

Dostoevsky found comfort in literary works and made his sketches for such pieces as "Uncle's Dream" and "The Village of Stepanchinkovo and Its Inhabitants," which were completed after the years in exile. He and his new wife settled in Semipalatinsk, and two years later Dostoevsky obtained retirement as a warrant officer. However, he was not immediately allowed to live in Saint Petersburg or Moscow but settled in Tver. Nonetheless, Dostoevsky soon obtained permission to move to the northern capital. In the second half of December 1859, exactly 10 years after his "execution" at Semenov plaza, he arrived in Saint Petersburg.

During these five years, he was known as someone who delightfully spoke about Christ, although he seldom attended church and he disliked Orthodox priests. Dostoevsky was known as a friendly and kind person, and this was evident in his growing compassion toward people who were poor and sick. During this period he learned to recognize his negative traits.

3.3 Theological Motifs in *The House of the Dead*

This novel was chosen for three reasons. First, though written in 1861, *The House of the Dead* reflected events from the Siberian period. Second, it was written in the form of a writer's personal diary, which described his life in penal servitude and revealing the feelings and conviction of the writer during

---

45. *Pis'ma*, Vol. 28, 9 November 1856, 240.

46. *F. M. Dostoevsky v vospominaniyakh sovremennikov*, 358.

this period.[47] Third, *The House of the Dead* is considered the second most influential of Dostoevsky's novels in that time period. *The Poor Folk* was at that time considered to be his most influential book.[48]

The House of the Dead was fully published in "Vremya" magazine in 1861.[49] The complete *The House of the Dead* consisted of twenty-two chapters, including the "Introduction." Dostoevsky's sketches reach the reader through the interposition of two frame narrators. The first is the presumed editor of the book, who appears in the Introduction and gives the impression of a curious and observant person. The second narrator is the nominal author of the sketches. He is a former landowner, Alexander Petrovich Goryanchikov, who had served a ten-year sentence for murdering his wife.

As stated in the first part of this chapter, Dostoevsky described what had been revealed to him about the "secret of man's happiness," while being in penal servitude.[50] Matters concerning the meaning of life, of the terrifying evil of life and of human happiness followed Dostoevsky to penal servitude. If in his first novel *The Poor Folk* he proved to everyone that man is depraved and even the good in man is permeated with evil, then in *The House of the Dead* Dostoevsky moved further. There is a development in his convictions which can be understood more fully by reference to the novel. During this time, Dostoevsky changed his beliefs. In the centre of Dostoevsky's set of beliefs is the life of Jesus Christ. The lives of convicts are examined in the light of Jesus's life.

3.3.1 The Sinfulness of Man

Dostoevsky had studied people and had come to his former conclusion that man was prone to evil. In order to reveal the picture of evil in man Dostoevsky used such theological motifs as **vanity, conceit, hatred, power struggle,** and

---

47. Makarov is convinced that the novel is the writer's diary in which he described his observations and beliefs. E. Markov, "Russkaya Rechi" [Russian Speech], in *Kriticheskie razbory "Zapisok iz Mernvogo Doma"* [Criticism of *The House of the Dead*], ed. V. Zelinskiy (Moscow: Tipografia Vil'de, 1907), 31.

48. See A. Milikov, "Svetoch" [The Torch], in *Kriticheskie razbory "Zapisok iz Mernvogo Doma,"* 7; E. Zarin, "Biblioteka dlya chteniya" [Library for Reading], in *Kriticheskie razbory "Zapisok iz Mernvogo Doma,"* 10; and E. Markov, "Russkaya Rechi," in *Kriticheskie razbory "Zapisok iz Mernvogo Doma,"* 28.

49. Milikov, "Svetoch," in *Kriticheskie razbory "Zapisok iz Mernvogo Doma,"* 1.

50. Volzhskiy, *Fyodoer Michailovich Dostoevsky: Zhizni i Propoved* (M. D. P. Efimov, 1906), 31.

committing evil for the sake of pleasure. As in the pre-Siberian period, Dostoevsky shows, in detail, the sinfulness of man as a result of the Fall. But he also is sure that there is only one ideal person, Jesus Christ, whose life that people have to follow. The evil is the attitude and actions of people that differ from the life of Jesus Christ that he saw in the gospel, an authority for him.

The motif of ***vanity*** was more easily noticeable than other motifs. From the very beginning of the novel it was patently obvious that "all were obsessed with how you were perceived by others."[51]

Goryanchikov gave an overall characteristic of the convicts serving their term in the colony: "I would actually say that these people, with the few exceptions of inexhaustibly-cheerful folk, and unanimously despised because of it, were sullen, envious, utterly conceited, boastful and squeamish and to the highest degree formalist."[52] Convicts, being vain, felt no need to repent.[53] They could not stand a rebuke for committing their crimes.[54] Reacting to this, convicts would turn to cursing.[55]

Speaking to the cruel convict Orlov, Goryanchikov "wanted to reach through to his conscience," to achieve some grounds for repentance. But Orlov's reaction amazed the author:

> He looked at me with a haughty and contemptuous air, as if I were a foolish little boy, to whom he did too much honour by conversing with him.
>
> I detected in his countenance a sort of compassion for me. After a moment's pause he laughed out loud, but without the least irony. I fancy he must, more than once, have laughed in the same manner, when my words returned to his memory.[56]

---

51. *Zapiski iz Mertvogo Doma*, 12.

52. *Zapiski iz Mertvogo Doma*, 12. Milikov considers that Dostoevsky led his reader into the suffering world which is a kind of real hell (Milikov, "Svetoch," in *Kriticheskie razbory "Zapisok iz Mernvogo Doma,"* 3).

53. Zarin, "Biblioteka dlya chteniya," 25.

54. Zarin, 21.

55. *Zapiski iz Mertvogo Doma*, 13.

56. Fyodor Dostoevsky, *The House of the Dead or Prison Life in Siberia: With an Introduction by Julius Bramont*, ed. Ernest Rhys (Urbana, IL: Project Gutenberg, 2011), www.gutenberg.org/ebooks/37536.

The vanity and arrogance of Orlov did not leave any room for repentance or admitting his own guilt in anything.[57]

Formalism, being the result of vanity, sometimes found its expression in outward lowliness. The convicts could say about themselves, "We are doomed people; we couldn't live in freedom and now we have to work hard in the colony." But Goryanchikov stated that these were only "the words."[58]

That calmness and lowliness that some of the inhabitants of the penal colony displayed while serving their term were deceitful. This behaviour was only the outward display of false humility. The example of the convict Petrov served as proof of such false humility. He humbled himself, observing the formalities, yet at some point exploded and was at the edge of murdering the Major. Only the appearance of another officer affected the positive outcome of this incident.

Vanity was also obvious in the desire of one of the convicts to be exalted over others. In this instance money played the most important role. With money a convict could buy items forbidden in the colony. Smoking pipes, for instance, were outlawed yet almost everyone smoked one.

Gazin, one of the convicts, was selling wine in the colony.[59] When he had money, he would put on new clothes, get intoxicated and roam together with a Polish violinist from one barrack to another, to show himself off before others.[60] Almost every convict who happened to have money acted in such a fashion, and the reason was conceit. They did heavy labour, saved money and then one day could spend everything to demonstrate their superiority.[61]

To earn the respect of all, some of the convicts, when celebrating their birthday, were willing to spend all their savings. Goryanchikov recounts,

> A convict, whose birthday was that day, would get up early in the morning, would place a candle before an icon and pray, after that would put his best clothes on and order his lunch, always to be served in solitude and very seldom inviting friends to share his meal with him. Then wine would come into the picture – the

57. Milikov, "Svetoch," in *Kriticheskie razbory "Zapisok iz Mernvogo Doma,"* 5.

58. *Zapiski iz Mertvogo Doma*, 13.

59. *Zapiski iz Mertvogo Doma*, 4.

60. *Zapiski iz Mertvogo Doma*, 32.

61. Zarin, "Biblioteka dlya chteniya," 25.

man of the day would get as drunk as a boiled owl, and undoubtedly would roam the barracks, staggering and stumbling, trying to show to everyone that he is drunk, that he is walking around and that by that fact he should be respected by others.[62]

Thus a convict was "sweating his guts out, sometimes several months in a row," only to guzzle away in one day all his earnings, but through this action to put himself above other convicts, to feel himself an aristocrat.

One of the most fearsome convicts, Gazin, who previously "loved to slaughter little children," even though outwardly he acted rationally, did not guzzle, but acted so out of "contempt for others, as if considering himself above all the others." Looking into his eyes, Goryanchikov concluded that "something arrogant and scornful and cruel was always in his eyes and in his smile."[63]

Isaiah Fomich, the only Jew in the colony, was a very vain person. Each Friday evening, he demonstratively observed his Sabbath. He knew that many convicts from different barracks gathered to watch him, so observing his rituals, he always played along to show himself off before others.[64] Goryanchikov remembered that instance in great detail:

He then began to pray. He read in a drawling voice, cried out, spat, and threw himself about with wild and comic gestures. All this was prescribed by the ceremonies of his religion. There was nothing laughable to strange in it, except the airs which Isaiah Fomitch gave himself before us in performing his ceremonies. Then he suddenly covered his head with both hands, and began to read with many sobs. His tears increased, and in his grief he almost lay down upon the book his head with the ark upon it, howling as he did so; but suddenly in the midst of his despondent sobs he burst into a laugh, and recited with a nasal twang a hymn of triumph, as if he were overcome by an excess of happiness.[65]

____

62. *Zapiski iz Mertvogo Doma*, 35.

63. *Zapiski iz Mertvogo Doma*, 41.

64. Zarin believes that vanity always has its external manifestation (Zarin, "Biblioteka dlya chteniya," 25).

65. Dostoevky, *House of the Dead*, ch. 10.

Coming from vanity a person might even overcome sufferings, to be in those sufferings superior to others. Isaiah Fomich was an example of such conceit. Being in the sauna with other convicts, he climbed to the highest bench, where the temperature was exceedingly high. The steam was so strong that even the sauna attendants, whom he paid to rub him could not stand such heat. But he endured, almost to the point of losing his consciousness, knowing that in this moment he was better than the rest.

Another theological motif was **hatred**. Hatred unfortunately was a characteristic trait of numerous convicts and workers of the colony. In the penal colony hate was directed at labour.[66] Labour was supposed to help convicts survive in the extreme conditions of the colony. But since labour "was not occupation, but duty," they generally viewed it with hate.[67]

Hatred, as a motif, was also displayed in convict relationships. "Forced common coexistence" was torture for many.[68] Rubbing shoulders with various convicts was not such an easy task:

> Look at them, at this rabble. One is from cantonists [cantonist – son of a soldier, obligated to serve in the military], another is from Circassians, the third is from dissidents, the fourth is an orthodox peasant, who left his family and children in his mother land, the fifth one is a Heeb, the seventh no one knows who, and all of them need to rub along no matter what, agree with each other, eat from the same bowl, sleep on the same plank bed.[69]

As a rule, many of the quarrels arose as the result of some tiny things and had hatred as the basis. Each morning, because there was only one scoop for washing, fights would start. Many wanted to wash themselves without staying in line.

Since in the same penal colony both commoners and nobles served their terms, a concealed and sometimes open hatred towards one another could be sensed. One of the convicts, Akim Akimich explained once to the author the reasons commoners hated nobles. "You are a different kind of people,

---

66. Milikov, "Svetoch," in *Kriticheskie razbory "Zapisok iz Mernvogo Doma,"* 4.

67. *Zapiski iz Mertvogo Doma*, 16.

68. Zarin, "Biblioteka dlya chteniya," 25.

69. *Zapiski iz Mertvogo Doma*, 28.

not like them, and secondly, they were always either from the pomeshchiks'
or from the soldiers' class."[70]

These words indicated that the nobles were perceived as the former lords
of the simple convicts. Hatred towards nobles was demonstrated by the fact
that simple convicts were now glad to see former nobles deprived of all their
rights in the penal colony, just as they were. They received pleasure every
time seeing one of the nobles undergoing suffering. They never wasted an
opportunity to humiliate, insult or even pick on a noble.[71]

Goryanchikov retold an incident that took place in the dining facility.
Gazin, one of the commoner convicts, being drunk and fueled by his hate
towards nobles, threw a large tray at them, which contained all the sliced
pieces of bread. Only a miracle saved them. It was amazing that none of the
convicts interceded and none protected them. Goryanchikov recalls,

> Despite the fact that murder or intentions of committing such
> would impose great nuisances to the entire colony – investi-
> gations, searches would start, discipline would be made more
> strict – and knowing that convicts tried the best they could not
> to get themselves in these extreme situations, despite all that,
> now everyone grew silent and the moment of waiting filled the
> facility. Not a single phrase "Help us!" was pronounced. Not
> a single shout directed at Gazin! That's how strong their ha-
> tred was towards us! They must have enjoyed our dangerous
> condition . . .[72]

The convicts mistreated the Poles who also came from noble backgrounds
with the same hatred shown to Russian nobles. In their turn, Poles did not
mask in their actions their disgust towards them. That was mutual hate. Akim
Akimich, also of noble descent, had chosen for himself a position like that
of the Poles. Mutual hatred also had its outward signs. As a rule, those were
quarrels, mocking and even fights. Thus, Akim Akimich serving the same
sauce to others would often get in fights.

---

70. *Zapiski iz Mertvogo Doma*, 28.

71. Markov, "Russkaya Rechi," in *Kriticheskie razbory "Zapisok iz Mernvogo Doma,"* ed.
V. Zelinskiy, 34–35.

72. *Zapiski iz Mertvogo Doma*, 42.

But hatred was not a part of the life of convicts only; it was also evident in the workers of the colony. Hatred was the foundation of the Major's conduct, one of the chief officers of the colony. He viewed all the convicts as his enemies. He had unlimited authority. Out of hatred towards convicts the Major came up with humiliating orders that all had to obey. He demanded that each convict sleep only on his right side and if during the night he saw anyone sleeping on his left side, then in the morning that person would be immediately punished.[73]

The hatred the Major had for the convicts fueled hatred in them for him. Many of the convicts were designing schemes to murder the Major or to harm him in some way. So, when the Major's favourite and much-loved poodle needed the veterinarian's attention, the veterinarian instead of treating the dog, wanting to get revenge on the Major, left the dog to die, saying it was not possible to do anything for the animal.

Hatred was also displayed in the relationships between the convicts of the same class.[74] Lomov, a convict of the commoners, out of hatred for another simple convict, Gavrilka, stabbed him with a knife. This was hatred concealed inside over a long period of time. Lomov was sent to the penal colony accused of a crime that in reality had been committed by Gavrilka. For a long time Lomov had stored up his hatred towards Gavrilka, until a trifling excuse came up and because of that he stabbed him.[75]

Covetousness also was used in the novel as a theological motif. Since people did not have much in the colony, one constantly sensed a need for material things, but Dostoevsky discovered that material things and money had become for many the highest value, and it was possible to see in the novel that people's actions were motivated by covetousness.[76]

Goryanchikov told of a young man, of the nobility, who cruelly killed his father out of covetousness because of his anticipated inheritance.

> This crime was not discovered until a month afterwards. During all this time the murderer, who meanwhile had informed the police of his father's disappearance, continued his debauches.

---

73. *Zapiski iz Mertvogo Doma*, 28.

74. Zarin, "Biblioteka dlya chteniya," 25.

75. *Zapiski iz Mertvogo Doma*, 183.

76. Milikov, "Svetoch," in *Kriticheskie razbory "Zapisok iz Mernvogo Doma,"* 4.

> At last, during his absence, the police discovered the old man's
> corpse in a drain. The gray head was severed from the trunk, but
> replaced in its original position. The body was entirely dressed.
> Beneath, as if by derision, the assassin had placed a cushion.[77]

Goryanchikov concluded that to kill your own father because of your inheritance and not to feel any guilt was something that could be committed only by "physical and moral deformity."[78]

The motif of gain was quite visible in the relationships existing between the convicts of the colony. They had no barriers keeping them from the desire to possess what belonged to others.[79] Goryanchikov said that "they stole anything from one another." On the very first day of his time in the colony one of the convicts "stole the Bible, the only book one was allowed to have in the penal colony." In order somehow to protect your belongings, many of the convicts "had a personal trunk with a lock to keep colony-owned things in." Dostoevsky also had a trunk like this, but those who obtained this trunk for him later stole from the same trunk that had "already issued colony-owned things." Theft permeated the convicts so deeply that when they stole something, they did not feel any guilt.[80]

Many of the denunciations also had gain as the motive. Convicts, putting up their things to a moneylender and getting money for it, would often report this to the senior subaltern officer, who would return the items to the previous owner. He would not give them back to the moneylender and would feel no remorse over it.

There were convicts in the colony like Petrov, "who were controlled by their mind until they wanted something."[81] Nothing could get in the way of their desires. They were ready to commit crimes of any kind to obtain what they wanted.[82] Once, Petrov started arguing with Antonov, a tall and exceptionally strong man, over some insignificant shred. Goryanchikov was amazed by the stubbornness of Petrov and his willingness to go all the way,

77. Dostoevsky, *House of the Dead*.

78. *Zapiski iz Mertvogo Doma*, 16.

79. Zarin, "Biblioteka dlya chteniya," 26.

80. *Zapiski iz Mertvogo Doma*, 18.

81. *Zapiski iz Mertvogo Doma*, 85.

82. Zarin, "Biblioteka dlya chteniya," 14.

even to commit murder because of something. Here were interwoven gain, spite and covetousness:

> Vasily Antonov . . . was yelling for a long time . . . Petrov grew pale all the sudden, his lips started jittering and became dark blue; he gasped for air. He got up from his place and slowly with his silent barefooted steps came to Antonov. All of a sudden everyone grew silent in the noisy and loud-mouthed barracks, one could hear a pin drop. Everyone waited for what was going to happen next . . . I thought, I won't have the time to walk to the doorstep as I will hear the scream of the slaughtered man. But the argument ended with nothing this time – Antonov, not waiting for Petrov to get close to him, silently and hastily threw the object of the argument to him.[83]

It was amazing that Petrov himself stole without having any qualms of conscience from his most kindred spirits.[84] It was Petrov who stole the Bible from Goryanchikov in the beginning of his term in the colony.

Covetousness served as the motivation for gambling. Each evening after the closing of the barracks some of the convicts played "'three leaves,' 'hill' and other games." Goryanchikov recalled that "each player would tip in front of him a load of copper money – all that he would have in his pockets – and would get up only having lost all of it or after having beaten his comrades in the game. The game would end late in the night, sometimes lasting till the dawn, till the moment when the barracks would be opened."[85]

Covetousness often ended in extortion. Some executioners extorted money from the relatives of the convict.[86] They offered to soften their strikes during punishment if their relative paid a modest amount of money. If the relatives were rich and they were able to pay the required sum, then the convict was lucky. If the relatives were poor and unable to pay, then the executioner would punish the convict in the cruelest way possible to intimidate other convicts.

---

83. *Zapiski iz Mertvogo Doma*, 85.

84. Zarin said that people such as Petrov were guided more by feelings than by reason (Zarin, "Biblioteka dlya chteniya," 17).

85. *Zapiski iz Mertvogo Doma*, 49.

86. Zarin, "Biblioteka dlya chteniya," 26.

In the novel Dostoevsky showed how conceit led men not only to ***self-exaltation***, but also to ***humiliation*** of others. Here, the desire to be the master over others, to dominate, served as a theological motif. As soon as a convict had money, he wanted to be put as master over others, to command. The subject of that could be their comrade, from the commoners.

Many of the convicts, arranging merrymakings with or without a reason, would hire a Polish violinist to accompany them. Out of conceit he had to visit all the barracks in an intoxicated state. The desire to rule was manifested in the fact that in front of others, he would periodically yell at the hired violinist, "You took the money, then play"![87]

When a convict who had lost in cards became a pauper, he was ready for any kind of work just to get money. Employers perceived themselves as lords and could command others with arrogance, as if they were servants. Almost every evening, once the colony was closed, everyone was engaged in forbidden activities. But to protect themselves in case of the sudden appearance of the commandants they would hire someone who was poorer than they to keep watch.

> He was usually hired by the gamblers for the entire night, paying 5 silver kopecks and his main responsibility was to be on watch the entire night. For the most part he froze 6 or 7 hours in the dark, in the mud room, at 30 below 0, listening for every knock, every ring, every step in the court.[88]

What was amazing was the sternness and ruthlessness of the hirers[89] who would continually yell to the serving convict, "You took the money, serve now"![90] Even though the commoners hated nobles when they had the opportunity to act as their former masters, they would do so, humiliating their own comrades.

Desire to take the place of God in the life of others is also present in this novel. The Major who slaughtered Luchiok continuously insisted that he was "tsar and god."[91] With that he showed that he was allowed to do anything, that

---

87. *Zapiski iz Mertvogo Doma*, 35.

88. *Zapiski iz Mertvogo Doma*, 49.

89. Zarin, "Biblioteka dlya chteniya," 28.

90. *Zapiski iz Mertvogo Doma*, 50.

91. *Zapiski iz Mertvogo Doma*, 90.

he was above everyone and that he could go unpunished for doing anything he wished.

The fear of punishment also served in the novel as a theological motif. "Each convict, no matter how courageous and insolent, would be afraid of everything in the colony" – concluded Goryanchikov. At times, from fear of punishment, convicts would commit a new crime to postpone the day of punishment. The novel told the story of a young man by the name of Dudov, who acted in this way:

> Horribly frightened, like the coward that he was, at the prospect of punishment, he threw himself, knife in hand, on to the officer of the guard, as he entered his dungeon on the eve of the day that he was to run the gauntlet through the men of his company. He quite understood that he was aggravating his offence, and that the duration of his punishment would be increased; but all he wanted was to postpone for some days, or at least some hours, a terrible moment. He was such a coward that he did not even wound the officer whom he attacked. He had indeed, only committed this assault in order to add a new crime to the last already against him, and thus defer the sentence.[92]

But it was not only the convicts who were afraid, so too were the colony personnel. Watching them, Goryanchikov came to conclusion that "they all look with some exaggeration at the convicts."[93] It was as if they were constantly afraid, expecting that the convicts every now and again would jump at someone with a knife."[94] The convicts noticed this fear of the colony's hired personnel as well, so they gained confidence, even though they wanted even more to gain trust and not to produce fear.

Also out of fear, invalids – "every barrack had one to watch the order" – had assumed the responsibility to go daily to the market to make purchases for the convicts.

What kinds of actions would people not resort to out of fear of punishment? Goryanchikov told of Alexander, a Kalmyk, who decided to be

---

92. Dostoevsky, *House of the Dead*, ch. 5.

93. *Zapiski iz Mertvogo Doma*, 30.

94. *Zapiski iz Mertvogo Doma*, 30.

baptized, to accept Christianity, thinking that becoming one of them he would not be punished.[95]

Committing crime for the sake of pleasure also served in the novel as a theological motif. Dostoevsky affirmed that there were some criminals who had committed their atrocious crimes for pleasure. Most often this would occur because the first crime they had committed had gone unpunished.[96] According to Goryanchikov even the simplest common man might turn out to be a serial killer, when the only motivation of his actions would be receiving pleasure. Goryanchikov explained this phenomenon:

> He is a peasant attached to the soil, a domestic serf, a shopkeeper, or a soldier. Suddenly he finds something give way within him; what he has hitherto suffered he can bear no longer, and he plunges his knife into the breast of his oppressor or his enemy. He then goes beyond all measure. He has killed his oppressor, his enemy. That can be understood – there was cause for that crime; but afterwards he does not assassinate his enemies alone, but the first person he happens to meet he kills for the pleasure of killing – for an abusive word, for a look, to make an equal number, or only because some one is standing in his way.[97]

Gazin, a Tatar, was just such a terrifying creature in the colony.[98] It seemed as if "nothing could be more fierce and monstrous than he." Goryanchikov, comparing him with the famous malefactor Kamenev whom he met in Tobolisk, concluded that even Kamenev yielded to Gazin in committing horrible evils. Of Gazin he wrote that "he previously liked to slaughter little children, solely out of pleasure – he would lead the child to some convenient place, first scare the child, torture the child and only having fully enjoyed the horror and quiver of the poor little victim, slaughter it quietly and with enjoyment."[99]

---

95. *Zapiski iz Mertvogo Doma*, 161.

96. Zarin said that the cruelty of the Russian people had been inherited from their ancestors (Zarin, "Biblioteka dlya chteniya," 10).

97. Dostoevsky, *House of the Dead*, ch. 9.

98. Milikov, "Svetoch," in *Kriticheskie razbory "Zapisok iz Mernvogo Doma,"* 5.

99. *Zapiski iz Mertvogo Doma*, 41.

The other such terrible convict was Luchika. It was said that he had murdered six people. Goryanchikov spoke in greater detail only about the murder of the Major.[100] Even though it might look from the first view that the motive of this murder was an insult, in reality Luchika enjoyed committing murders, similar to Gazin.

These serial murderers who kill for pleasure, according to the affirmation of Goryanchikov, "know that a horrible execution awaits them, but do not stop, until someone will stop them."

Goryanchikov also told of another person, Lieutenant Zcherebyatnikov, who fell into the depths of hell. He was an executioner. He liked, out of pleasure, to "swish and beat [convicts] with sticks".[101] Goryanchikov said that for him severely punishing a convict was a sort of art. He would continuously invent something new to intensify his pleasure when punishing convicts. Sometimes the Lieutenant could listen to all the pleadings of the convict with great attention prior to punishment. After that, as if out of sympathy, he promised to soften the punishment, raising the convict's hope. Yet this was nothing but a show invented by the Lieutenant.

> The procession went out, the drum rolled, the soldiers brandished their arms. "Flog him," Jerebiatnikof would roar from the bottom of his lungs, "Flog him! Burn him! Skin him alive! Harder! Harder! Give it harder to this orphan! Give it him, the rogue."
>
> The soldiers lay on the strokes with all their might on the back of the unhappy wretch, whose eyes dart fire, and who howls while Jerebiatnikof runs after him in front of the line, holding his sides with laughter – he puffs and blows so that he can scarcely hold himself upright.[102]

Goryanchikov showed that even though the Lieutenant was not one of the convicts, he would not yield to them in atrocities. He was one of the most malicious people of the kind who would derive joy and pleasure from causing the strongest pain and suffering to other people. Goryanchikov compared

---

100. *Zapiski iz Mertvogo Doma*, 82.

101. *Zapiski iz Mertvogo Doma*, 147.

102. Dostoevsky, *House of the Dead*.

such people to tigers "wanting to taste the blood." He came to the following conclusion:

> Those who have possessed unlimited power over the flesh, blood, and soul of their fellow-creatures, of their brethren according to the law of Christ, those who have possessed this power and who have been able to degrade with a supreme degradation, another being made in the image of God; these men are incapable of resisting their desires and their thirst for sensations. Tyranny is a habit capable of being developed, and at last becomes a disease.[103]

Goryanchikov wanted to attract the attention of those involved in the work in the penitentiary system, to let them know that such a system may create beasts such as the Lieutenant.[104] To be heard, Goryanchikov argued his position:

> I declare that the best man in the world can become hardened and brutified to such a point, that nothing will distinguish him from a wild beast. Blood and power intoxicate; they aid the development of callousness and debauchery; the mind then becomes capable of the most abnormal cruelty in the form of pleasure; the man and the citizen disappear for ever in the tyrant; and then a return to human dignity, repentance, moral resurrection, becomes almost impossible.[105]

This phenomenon harmed not only the individual,[106] but society as a whole:

> A society which looks upon such things with an indifferent eye, is already infected to the marrow. In a word, the right granted to a man to inflict corporal punihsment on his fellow-men, is one of the plague spots of our society. It is the means of annihilating all civic spirit. Such a right contains in germ the elements of inevitable, imminent decomposition.[107]

---

103. Dostoevsky, *House of the Dead*, ch. 3.
104. Zarin, "Biblioteka dlya chteniya," 12.
105. Dostoevsky, *House of the Dead*, ch. 3.
106. *Zapiski iz Mertvogo Doma*, 154.
107. Dostoevsky, *House of the Dead.*, ch. 3.

Goryanchikov affirmed that the capability of an executioner in the embryo was present in almost every person. Therefore, it was necessary not only to recognize one's own guilt and ancestral sin, but to totally unlearn it. Otherwise, without notice, man may slide down to the bottom. Goryanchikov told of an executioner, who once "wanted at first to punish the convict easily,"[108] but hearing him screaming and pleading for mercy, changed his mind and even added more than fifty strokes to his punishment. That was how the sense of domination manifested itself, and later out of impunity a sense of omnipotence came into play.[109] Goryanchikov summarized this problem with the following words: "It's hard even to imagine how greatly human nature can be distorted."[110]

3.3.2 Freedom

Despite the harsh conditions of the colony and the long terms that had to be served, Dostoevsky saw that man lived by his hopes for the future. Such theological motifs as longing for freedom and the desire to live showed that man as such is an optimist. Dostoevsky is convinced that God created humanity with free will. Even after the Fall, free will is present in men. That is why man is responsible before God and people for his behaviour. Dostoevsky, in *The Brothers Karamazov* will explain, in detail, his understanding of freedom.

Thus, **freedom** according to Dostoevsky was a theological motif.[111] Berdyaev said that "freedom is the heart of Dostoevsky's worldview."[112] In Dostoevsky's understanding, "man's true essence consists only in his freedom.'"[113] From the very first chapter, the longing for freedom was clearly visible in almost every convict. The atmosphere that prevailed in the penal colony was fundamentally different from that of the outside world. Goryanchikov said that "outside these gates a bright, free world existed, where people lived

---

108. *Zapiski iz Mertvogo Doma*, 155.

109. Milikov says that the novel forces the reader to think about the dark side of human heart (Milikov, "Svetoch," in *Kriticheskie razbory "Zapisok iz Mernvogo Doma,"* ed. V. Zelinskiy, 7).

110. *Zapiski iz Mertvogo Doma*, 157.

111. Lauth, *Filosofiya Dostoevskogo v sistematicheskom izlozhenii*, 108.

112. Berdyaev, *Mirosozertsanie Dostoevskogo*, 63.

113. V. V. Zenkovsky, "Dostoevsky's Religious and Philosophical Views," in *Dostoevsky. A Collection of Critical Essays*, ed. Rene Wellek (Englewood Cliffs: Prentice-Hall. Inc., 1962), 134.

just like everybody."[114] Therefore, many of the convicts, being driven by the longing for freedom, would always find some place in the colony to be alone and to dream, to make some plans for the future. The thought of approaching freedom was so inspiring to some that they resorted to strange pursuits:

> The favourite occupation of one of the convicts, during the moments of liberty left to him from his hard labour, was to count the palisades. There were fifteen hundred of them. He had counted them all, and knew them nearly by heart. Every one of them represented to him a day of confinement; but, counting them daily in this manner, he knew exactly the number of days he still had to pass in the prison. He was sincerely happy when he had finished one side of the hexagon; yet he had to wait for his liberation for many long years. But one learns patience in a prison.[115]

The longing for freedom was present in the convicts. Goryanchikov told of the elderly Old Ritualist (Russian *Starover*) that "there in him lurked a deep, incurable melancholy, which he tried to hide from everyone." Once Goryanchikov saw the old man weeping and praying: "Lord, do not leave me! Lord, strengthen me! My children are small, my dear children, never will we get to see each other"![116] He missed home and his family, and drew strength and patience from his prayers.[117]

Some of the actions of the convicts were dictated by as much conceit as the longing for freedom. Goryanchikov said that the feasts, partying and celebrations of birthdays on a grand scale were dictated on the one hand by the desire to show off and on the other hand by a thirst to feel as free men.

---

114. *Zapiski iz Mertvogo Doma*, 9.

115. Dostoevsky, *House of the Dead*, ch. 2.

116. *Zapiski iz Mertvogo Doma*, 34.

117. Milikov, "Svetoch," in *Kriticheskie razbory "Zapisok iz Mernvogo Doma,"* ed. V. Zelinskiy, 5. A longing for freedom also drove good, sincere people. Peaceful and calm Caucasian Nourra, who produced the warmest impressions, lived by a constant hope that one day he would return to the Caucasus. Goryanchikov was convinced that without this hope Nourra would have died. So did Aley, a kind and harmless young convict, pine for his own home. The motif of freedom was manifested in the worst criminals. Goryanchikov recalled that he met with those who were exiled for a twenty-year term, but even they had hoped for exemption. They could have easily said, "But wait, Lord willing, I will finish my time, and then . . ." (*Zapiski iz Mertvogo Doma*, 66).

At that point, a convict felt as if he were in control of the situation. By breaking the law, he acted as a free man, choosing himself what to do. Those who
managed to collect more money, being driven by a longing for freedom,
celebrated outside the colony, on the outskirts of the city, in someone's house:

> It sometimes happens that among the convicts there are admir-
> ers of the fair sex. For a sufficiently large sum of money they
> succeed, accompanied by a soldier whom they have corrupted,
> in getting secretly out of the fortress into a suburb instead of
> going to work. There in an apparently quiet house a banquet is
> held at which large sums of money are spent.[118]

Goryanchikov noticed that "a convict was so greedy towards money," but
since freedom for him was valued above money, he would be ready to part
with all his money, accumulated over many months.

Out of a desire to be free some were ready to escape, knowing that they
could be severely punished. Orlov, one of the most fearless convicts, calmly
endured all the punishment anticipating the time when he was going to get
out of the colony. The motif of freedom gave him the strength to endure all
the pain.[119] He said, "But now – it's over. I will endure the rest of the strokes,
and they will immediately send me with a shipment to Nerchinsk and I will
somehow get lost in the way! Only wish my back would heal up sooner"![120]
The other two convicts, Kulikov and A-v together with security guard Koller
made Orlov's dream came true and escaped the colony, to roam through
the woods, and be free. After a short time, they were caught and punished
very severely.

Goryanchikov himself repeatedly said that from the very beginning of
his time in the colony, he had developed a dream of freedom. His favourite
occupation was making plans, making some calculations as to when his years
in the colony would run out:

> I remember, too, that I was filled with a mighty longing for my
> resurrection from that grave which gave me strength to bear up,

---

118. Dostoevsky, *House of the Dead*, ch. 4.

119. Milikov, "Svetoch," in *Kriticheskie razbory "Zapisok iz Mernvogo Doma,"* ed. V.
Zelinskiy, 5.

120. *Zapiski iz Mertvogo Doma*, 48.

to wait, and to hope. And so I got to be hardened and enduring; I lived on expectation, I counted every passing day; if there were a thousand more of them to pass at the prison I found satisfaction in thinking that one of them was gone, and only nine hundred and ninety-nine to come.[121]

The motif of freedom was so strong in every convict that when they managed to implement something that would be a part of their life in freedom, no convict could hide his joy. This point was easy to observe during the preparation and celebration of Christmas.[122] In those days everyone was busy preparing for the holiday. Goryanchikov noted that "even the most humble and thrifty, all year round saving their kopecks, considered it their duty to dip into their pocket for such a day and celebrate it with the holiday table fitting the occasion."[123] Very few were interested in the significance of the holiday, but all tried to fulfill the rules and customs. All had a festive meal prepared, but no one ate until the priest would arrive. On this day, everyone tried to be more polite, even with strangers:

> . . . they behaved becomingly, possible much better than on ordinary days; neither quarrels nor insults were heard, every one understood that it was a great day, a great festival. The convicts went even to visit the other barracks in order to wish the inmates a happy Christmas; that day a sort of friendship seemed to exist between them all. . . . Several convicts whom I met wished me, with affability, a happy Christmas. I thanked them and returned their wishes. Some of them had never spoken to me before.[124]

A convict on this festive day felt as if he were "in contact with the entire world, that he was not a total outcast, not a totally lost man, not a cut off slice, and that the colony had the same things as in the rest of the world." Goryanchikov concluded that "they felt it, it was obvious." But in the evening,

---

121. Dostoevsky, *House of the Dead*, ch. 9.

122. Markov, "Russkaya Rechi," in *Kriticheskie razbory "Zapisok iz Mernvogo Doma,"* ed. V. Zelinskiy, 37.

123. *Zapiski iz Mertvogo Doma*, 104.

124. Dostoevsky, *House of the Dead*, ch. 11.

when the holiday celebration came to an end, came the sadness, longing. Everyone would see the holiday off, as if "being betrayed in some hope."[125]

Also, when the convicts could live like human beings, as in the outside world, they were filled with excessive joy. This joy could be seen in convicts during a theatrical performance. Having received permission from their superiors, the convicts tried to not make any trouble those days, fearing that their show would be cancelled. Long before the holidays, those who participated in the performance rehearsed their roles and sewed their costumes. During the theatrical performance, the barrack was full of convicts. All were childishly happy, because they had some sense of freedom.[126] For a short time they found themselves in another place where people acted of their own volition. Goryanchikov explained this joy of the convicts during the performances in a following way:

> Imagine the convict prison, chains, captivity, long years of confinementm of tsak-work, of monotonous life, falling away drop by drop like rain on an autmn day; imagine all this despair in presence of permission given to the convicts to amuse themselves, to breathe freely for an hour, to forget their nightmare, and to organise a play – and what a play! one that excited the envy and admiration of our town.[127]

Goryanchikov concluded that "only so little time was needed to let these poor people live in their own way, have fun like other human beings, live at least an hour without being on guard, and the men changed."[128]

Almost all of the convicts were ready to sacrifice much, even to become serious for some time, if in return they would get a bit of freedom.[129] It was said that when a horse by the name of Gnedko, that had long worked in the colony died, it was decided to buy another in its place. The Major entrusted the convicts to pick a horse. They were all delighted. Immediately

---

125. *Zapiski iz Mertvogo Doma*, 111.

126. Markov, "Russkaya Rechi," in *Kriticheskie razbory "Zapisok iz Mernvogo Doma,"* ed. V. Zelinskiy, 36–37.

127. Dostoevsky, *House of the Dead*, ch. 12.

128. *Zapiski iz Mertvogo Doma*, 130.

129. Pisarev, "Pogibshie i Pogibayuschie," in *Kriticheskie razbory "Zapisok iz Mernvogo Doma,"* ed. V. Zelinskiy, 74–75.

some experts surfaced among them, with expertise in this delicate matter, surrounded by a support group. Goryanchikov described in great detail with what seriousness all the convicts regarded this errand:

> Tsigans, Lesghians, professional horse-dealers, townsmen, came in to deal. The convicts were exceedingly eager about the matter as each fresh horse was brought up, and were as amused as children about it all. It seemed to tickle their fancy very much, that they had to buy a horse like free men, just as if it was for themselves and the money was to come out of their own pockets. Three horses were brought and taken away before purchase; the fourth was settled on. The horse-dealers seemed astonished and a little awed at the soldiers of the escort who watched the business.[130]

With the arrival of springtime, once again longing for freedom manifested itself with full force. Even the spring air, fresh air, was a reminder of freedom. This evoked despair in all the convicts, many of whom were at this time more irritable than usual. Oftentimes convicts argued and yelled at each other. But many also tried to find a comfortable place in the colony to look as far as possible into the steppe. Goryanchikov described this spring feeling: "The fetters are heavy in this time! . . . Apart from being warm, in the bright sun, when you hear and feel with all your soul, with all your being nature reviving around you with immense power, that makes it even harder to be in 'katorga' surrounded by guards and obeying the will of others."[131]

Goryanchikov did not hide his joy when he could work on the bank of the Irtysh River, because it was the only place where one could see the clean, clear distance and the uninhabited free steppe. This experience made a strong impression on him. In his story, freedom was one of the highest values:

> . . . while at the river-bank I could forget my miserable self as I sent my gaze over the immense desert space, just as a prisoner may when he looks at the world of freedom through the barred casement of his dungeon. Everything in that place was dear and gracious to my eyes; the sun shining in the infinite blue

---

130. Dostoevsky, *House of the Dead*, ch. 6.
131. *Zapiski iz Mertvogo Doma*, 173–174.

of heaven, the distant song of the Kirghiz that came from the opposite bank. Sometimes I would fix my sight for a long while upon the poor smoky cabin of some *baïgouch*; I would study the bluish smoke as it curled in the air, the Kirghiz woman busy with her two sheep . . . The things I saw were wild, savage, poverty-stricken; but they were free.[132]

The other spring event was also associated with earlier memories. Before Easter week, convicts were allowed to fast to prepare for the sacrament of communion, fasting and attending all the services. Goryanchikov liked the fasting week. They went to church every day, two or even three times. He admitted that he himself had not gone to church for a long time. He described in detail the worship services:

> The Lenten services, familiar to me from early childhood in my father's house, the solemn prayers, the prostrations – all stirred in me the fibres of the memory of things long, long past, and woke my earliest impressions to fresh life. Well do I remember how happy I was when at morn we went into God's house, treading the ground which had frozen in the night, under the escort of soldiers with loaded guns; the escort remained outside the church.[133]

This evidence also suggested the return of Goryanchikov to the church. Before this time, he had a period of being away from the church.

Lossky believed that every good or evil man seeks the perfect life.[134] On the one hand the convicts hated forced labour, but on the other it was well understood by them that without some occupation "man cannot live, he becomes corrupted, turns into a beast."[135] The motive of self-preservation was manifested in the desire of almost every convict to have some sort of "craft and occupation."[136] The author recalled how at night, especially in the winter, once the convicts were locked in the colony, all the barracks were

---

132. Dostoevsky, *House of the Dead*, ch. 5.
133. Dostoevsky, ch. 5.
134. Losskiy, *Bog i mirovoe zlo*, 143.
135. Losskiy, 16.
136. Losskiy, 16.

turned into workshops – "Many of the convicts entered the colony knowing nothing, but learned from others and then reentered the outside world
as skilled workmen. There were cobblers and shoemakers, and tailors, and
carpenters and locksmiths, and engravers, and goldsmiths."[137] About Akim
Akimich, a convict from the nobility, it was said that "he was a carpenter, a
shoemaker, a painter, a goldsmith, a machinist, and that all this he learned in
the colony."[138] Goryanchikov concluded that convicts were "guarded by work
from committing crimes: without work convicts would have eaten each other
like spiders in a jar."[139] Sometimes at night there could be sudden checks,
during the course of which they could take everything from you. But out
of the motive of self-preservation, after each search, the next day the night
production would resume in full measure.

Some crafts were not so positive and even risky. Many were in the colony for smuggling. These people could not find other occupation for themselves, except to smuggle wine into the colony. The author describes in detail
one smuggler:

> I knew in colony, one convict, of enormous external dimensions,
> but so gentle, quiet and humble, that it was impossible to imag-
> ine how he ended up in the colony. He was so gentle and easy
> to get along with that in all of his time in the colony he did not
> have a conflict with anyone. But he was from the western border,
> came for smuggling and, of course, could not restrain himself
> and started smuggling wine . . . Thanks to these individuals, the
> wine would never be exhausted in the colony.[140]

Even the fear of punishment did not stop the people from their occupations.[141] Of the smuggler Goryanchikov it was said that, despite his fear of the
whip and being oftentimes punished, he returned again and again to his occupation.[142] These crafts gave meaning and purpose in life. Purposeless work

---

137. Losskiy, 17.

138. Losskiy, 27.

139. Losskiy, 17.

140. Losskiy, 18.

141. Milikov, "Svetoch," in *Kriticheskie razbory "Zapisok iz Mernvogo Doma,"* ed. V.
Zelinskiy, 4.

142. *Zapiski iz Mertvogo Doma*, 18.

killed a man.[143] Self-preservation required a specific purpose.[144] Goryanchikov concluded that "if you would like to completely crush and destroy a man, to punish him with the most terrible punishment, so that the most terrible murderer would shudder from the penalty and would be frightened of it in advance, it would be worth only make the work absolutely futile and utterly meaningless."[145]

The motive of self-preservation manifested itself in the way seriously ill convicts who stayed in the hospital loved their treatments. Goryanchikov conveyed his observations: "The patients really loved to be treated, they carefully took the medicine and powders, but most of all they loved the external agents. Cupping glasses, leeches, poultices and blood-letting were greatly loved and trusted by the commoners, who took them willingly and with pleasure."[146]

Goryanchikov also understood that the work could "save him and strengthen his health." He resolved to "spend more time in the air, to get tired every day, to get used to carrying heavy weights." He worked in a shop or with alabaster or "carried bricks for constructions." He dragged these bricks for seventy miles. This way Goryanchikov felt an increase of energy and strength required to overcome all physical discomforts. He had a strong desire to not only survive, but also to stay healthy and strong. "I still wanted to live after the colony," said Goryanchikov.[147]

3.3.3 The Image of God in Each Person

Dostoevsky found in every person the capacity for good, however low they might be, and therefore in every criminal he looked for the image of God.[148] We can see here several theological motifs: *a manifestation of compassion, love and mercy.* According to Lossky, evil is never alone, but always appears

---

143. O. Miller, "Russkie Pisateli posle Gogolya," in *Kriticheskie razbory "Zapisok iz Mernvogo Doma,"* ed. V. Zelinskiy, 81.

144. Zarin, "Biblioteka dlya chteniya," 23.

145. *Zapiski iz Mertvogo Doma,* 20.

146. *Zapiski iz Mertvogo Doma,* 161.

147. *Zapiski iz Mertvogo Doma,* 178.

148. Milikov, "Svetoch," in *Kriticheskie razbory "Zapisok iz Mernvogo Doma,"* ed. V. Zelinskiy, 8.

alongside some small goodness.[149] His understanding that every person has God's image even after the Fall came from the Scripture.

Manifestation of compassion was common among the people living near the island who gave alms to the convicts out of pity. Everything received was divided equally, as, for example, when a tradesman with a beard having met convicts on the road gave them kopeks as alms. Goryanchikov recalled how once he received a kopek from a girl whose father died young in the hospital, while being under the court. "Having seen me, the girl blushed, whispered something to her mother, who immediately stopped, found a quarter of kopeck in the purse and gave that to the little girl. She came running to me . . . "Here, 'unfortunate,' take a kopek for Christ's sake,' and the girl returned to her mother very pleased."[150]

Akim Akimich, out of compassion, would stand up for each of the unjustly wronged convicts. He would even get into fights during his disputes, as he hated injustice. He sincerely "rebuked the convicts, sometimes reproached them for being thieves and seriously admonished them not to steal."[151] Akim Akimich was one of the few in the colony who were conscious of their guilt, and he himself committed the murder of the duke, who had burned his fortress.[152]

Even the Major, one of the most violent people in the colony, had a love object. He hated people, but he loved his poodle immensely. Goryanchikov noticed in detail the manifestation of these feelings in the Major when his poodle fell ill. He told them that "he loved the most his poodle Trezoroka and almost lost his mind from grief when Trezoroka fell ill. It was said that he wept over him as over his own son, tracked down the veterinarian and, as usual, almost got into a fight with him."[153] He once called the convict Zch. to himself and began to ask for forgiveness: "I offended you, I flogged you in vain, I know it. I repent! Do you understand that? I, I, and I – I repent"![154]

---

149. Losskiy, *Bog i mirovoe zlo*, 113.

150. *Zapiski iz Mertvogo Doma*, 19.

151. *Zapiski iz Mertvogo Doma*, 26.

152. Milikov, "Svetoch," in *Kriticheskie razbory "Zapisok iz Mernvogo Doma,"* ed. V. Zelinskiy, 5.

153. *Zapiski iz Mertvogo Doma*, 28.

154. *Zapiski iz Mertvogo Doma*, 217.

In that time when many made fun of the demented at the hospital, Goryanchikov was filled with compassion for them: "It was terribly difficult and hard to see these unfortunates. I've never been able to look dispassionately at the demented."[155]

Goryanchikov had a feeling of compassion even for the poor animals. In the colony there was a dog by the name of Squirrel. It was an unusual dog, in fact "someone ran over it with a cart, and its back was concaved inwards."[156] It also had festering eyes and its tail was almost hairless. Because of her unpleasant appearance, each convict who passed the dog considered it his duty to kick her with his boot. However, Goryanchikov spoke of himself: "From compassion I caressed her. And she could not meet me without a whimper. She would see me from afar and whimper, whine, with pain and tears."[157]

Some other convicts also manifested compassion for animals.[158] Once a steppe eagle lived for a while in the colony. It could not fly, as one of his legs was dislocated and its right wing was broken. In the beginning, everybody came to the far corner of the colony to have a look at the "beast" and then later almost everyone forgot about it. But Goryanchikov noticed that even though its visitors could not be seen, "every day one could see near him pieces of fresh meat and a pot with water."[159] Someone cared every day for the poor bird.

Love was also used as a theological motif. In these inhumane relations one could still meet people who would radiate the light of love. Nothing could take away the love for people from the elderly Old Ritualist. He was a deeply religious man, "about sixty years of age, small, gray-haired." He differed from the other convicts in that "something calm and quiet was in his eyes." He was sent to the colony for arson of Common Faith Church, as that church was involved in luring conservatives. The author described the old man with great pleasure,

> When one had lived some time by the side of this kind old man, one could not help asking the question, how could he have rebelled? I spoke to him several times about his faith. He gave up

---

155. *Zapiski iz Mertvogo Doma*, 159.
156. *Zapiski iz Mertvogo Doma*, 189.
157. *Zapiski iz Mertvogo Doma*, 190.
158. Zarin, "Biblioteka dlya chteniya," 20.
159. *Zapiski iz Mertvogo Doma*, 193.

none of his convictions, but in his answers I never noticed the slightest hatred; and yet he had destroyed a church, and was far from denying it. In his view, the offence he had committed and his martyrdom were things to be proud of.[160]

He was respected by all, even by the most vicious convicts. He was the only one they trusted with their money because they saw him as an honest man. But he never became conceited. Goryanchikov, describing the character of the old man wrote, "He was of an extremely communicative nature. He was cheerful, often laughed – not with that rude, cynical laughter of the convicts, but with a clear and quiet laughter, in which there was so much of the child's innocence, and the one that was particularly suitable for his gray hair."[161]

Sirotkin was another character about whom Goryanchikov spoke positively. He was considered "one of the most important military criminals." Being in despair at the office where he served, he wanted to commit suicide, but twice failed. At that time, his commander approached him and strongly criticized him. Then Sirotkin mechanically pointed the gun and shot him, for which he was sent to the penal colony. Goryanchikov spoke of him with warmth and respect because he simply loved people:

> His blue eyes, his clear complexion, his fair hair gave him a soft expression, which even his shaven crown did not destroy. . . . [He] neither drank nor played, and he scarcely ever quarrelled with the other convicts. . . . When he was not at work he wandered about the barracks; when every one else was occuppied, he remained with his arms by his sides; if any one joked with him, or laughed at him – which happened often enough – he turned on his heel without speaking and went elsewhere. If the pleasantry was too strong he blushed.[162]

Aley's brothers, who brutally murdered and robbed people in the Caucasus, showed love for their younger brother.[163] They, "usually dark and gloomy," were speaking to him almost as with a child, good-naturedly staring at each

---

160. Dostoevsky, *House of the Dead*, ch. 4.

161. *Zapiski iz Mertvogo Doma*, 34.

162. Dostoevsky, *House of the Dead*, ch. 4.

163. Milikov, "Svetoch," in *Kriticheskie razbory "Zapisok iz Mernvogo Doma,"* ed. V. Zelinskiy, 5.

other. From Aley himself, whom the author taught to read and write using the Bible, love and kindness radiated. Goryanchikov described him in great detail:

> Chaste as a young girl, everything that was foul, cynical, shameful, or unjust filled his fine black eyes with indignation, and made them finer than ever. . . He avoided quarrels and insults, and preserved all his dignity . . . Every one loved him, caressed him. At first he was only polite to me. . .[164]

Once, seeing sadness and longing in the eyes of Goryanchikov, Aley asked him a direct question for the first time, "What, that is very hard for you now?" He loved people and tried to support them, even though he himself needed their support:

> Ali often helped me in my work. In the barrack he did whatever he thought would be agreeable to me, and would save me trouble. In his attentions to me there was neither servility nor the hope of any advantage, but only a warm, cordial feeling, which he did not try to hide.[165]

That was how Aley showed his selfless love. Goryanchikov himself acknowledges that Aley loved him as much as he did his own brothers.

Convict Petrov, of whom it was said that he was "the most decisive, and least fearsome of all the convicts,"[166] who almost killed the Major and convict Vasily Antonov, could also love unselfishly.[167] Goryanchikov affirmed: "I'm sure that he even loved me and I was astonished by that. Did he consider me not a fully grown up, an incomplete man, did he feel towards me a special kind of compassion that instinctively every strong creature feels towards the other that is weak, recognizing me as such . . . I do not know."[168]

The manifestation of the unconditional love of Petrov towards Goryanchikov could be seen when the entire colony went to a Russian sauna. Since it was Goryanchikov's first visit to the sauna, he was not accustomed

---

164. Dostoevsky, *House of the Dead*, ch. 5.

165. Dostoevsky, ch. 5.

166. *Zapiski iz Mertvogo Doma*, 84.

167. Markov argues that Dostoevsky discovered God's spark even in the "fierce beast" (Markov, "Russkaya Rechi," in *Kriticheskie razbory "Zapisok iz Mernvogo Doma,"* ed. V. Zelinskiy, 32).

168. *Zapiski iz Mertvogo Doma*, 86.

to getting undressed quickly, given that he, like the rest of the convicts was wearing shackles. In the changing room it was as cold as on the street and you had to get undressed quickly and go to the bath, so as not to be taken ill. Without having to ask him, Petrov helped him to undress quickly. He swiftly unlaced his shoes for him and helped him remove the clothes from under the shackles, which was hard to do. Seeing that it was hard for Goryanchikov to walk in shackles without undergarments, Petrov led him by the hand as if he were a small child. He himself offered to wash him and even helped him to get back to the dressing room. Only then did Petrov return to the bath to steam and wash himself. All the assistance he rendered he did unselfishly and even with some joy.[169]

Compassion was also a theological motif in the novel. It is amazing how closely Dostoevsky studied people. He saw every act of compassion.

Nourra, whom Goryanchikov spoke as of an honest man, viewed with indignation the dirtiness and nastiness of the convict's life. He would be infuriated by theft, cheating and drunkenness. Yet even though he could not speak Russian, being a compassionate man,[170] he did as much as he could to support new convicts arriving in the colony. The author recalled how Nourra met him:

> Before I had been half-an-hour in the prison, he passed by my side and touched me gently on the shoulder, smiling at the same time with an innocent air. I did not at first understand what he meant, for he spoke Russian very badly; but soon afterwards he passed me again, and, with a friendly smile, again touched me on the shoulder. For three days running he repeated this strange proceeding. As I soon found out, he wanted to show me that he pitied me, and that he felt how painful the first moment of imprisonment must be. He wanted to testify his sympathy, to keep my spirits up, and to assure me of his good-will.[171]

Nobody sympathized with people like doctors in the colony. With what compassion they related to the convicts . . . It was said of them:

---

169. *Zapiski iz Mertvogo Doma*, 97.

170. Markov, "Russkaya Rechi," in *Kriticheskie razbory "Zapisok iz Mernvogo Doma,"* ed. V. Zelinskiy, 33.

171. Dostoevsky, *House of the Dead*, ch. 5.

> [They] never make between the prisoners the distinctions ob-
> served by other persons brought into direct relations with them.
> In this respect the common people can alone be compared with
> the doctors, for they never reproach a criminal with the crime
> that he has committed, whatever it may be. They forgive him in
> consideration of the sentence passed upon him . . . To the doctor
> the convicts have naturally recourse, above all when they are to
> undergo corporal punishment.[172]

Every convict received "affection" from the doctors, and "heard a kind word."[173]

3.3.4 Repentance – The Only Way to a Radical Life Change

Goryanchikov showed an example of growth for the better in all respects, despite the hardships and at times unbearable social conditions. This growth was used as a theological motif. Dostoevsky is sure that only God can help man to live as Jesus; but, for this, repentance before God is necessary.

Good, according to Goryanchikov, is in every person and can manifest itself in various acts, even in the most heinous criminals.[174] But for a person to be radically changed for the better he must change his convictions, and this must be preceded by repentance. He himself testified that he studied very seriously not only other convicts, but also himself:

> I remember, too, that though I had round me a hundred persons
> in like case, I felt myself more and more solitary, and though
> the solitude was awful I came to love it. Isolated thus among
> the convict-crowd I went over all my earlier life, analysing its
> events and thoughts minutely; I passed my former doings in
> review and sometimes was pitiless in condemnation of myself;
> sometimes I went so far as to be grateful to fate for the privi-
> lege of such loneliness, for only that could have caused me so
> severely to scructinise my past, so searchingly to examine its
> inner and outer life.[175]

---

172. Dostoevsky, ch. 5.

173. *Zapiski iz Mertvogo Doma*, 46.

174. Markov, "Russkaya Rechi," in *Kriticheskie razbory "Zapisok iz Mernvogo Doma,"* ed. V. Zelinskiy, 32.

175. Dostoevsky, *House of the Dead*, ch. 9.

The changes that occurred in his life, as a result of the revision of his own convictions, revived in him new hopes for a future life in freedom:

> What strong and strange new germs of hope came in those memorable hours up in my soul! I weighed and decided all sorts of issues, I entered into a compact with myself to avoid the errors of former years, and the rocks on which I had been wrecked; I laid down a programme for my future, and vowed that I would stick to it; I had a sort of blind and complete conviction that, once away from that place, I should be able to carry out everything I made my mind up to; I looked for my freedom with transports of eager desire; I wanted to try my strength in a renewed struggle with life.[176]

When Goryanchikov was released he exclaimed, "Yes, by God! Freedom, new life, resurrection from the dead . . . What a glorious moment"![177] Goryanchikov realized that his mission was to explore people, their behaviour and personalities. Sometimes, people like Akim Akimych did not understand his questions about convicts far and near. But Goryanchikov studied people, confronted them in real life, saw them day after day, in different circumstances.

He was not in some sort of privileged circumstances. Goryanchikov was in the same conditions as the other convicts. In the beginning of the novel he described everyday life:

> On the bunk I had three boards: it was all that made my place. On these benches placed in our cell alone existed about thirty people. In the winter we were locked in early, you had to wait four hours until everyone fell asleep. And before that – the noise, uproar, laughter, curses, the sound of chains, fumes and soot, shaved heads, branded faces, patchwork clothes, everything – berated, defamed . . .[178]

---

176. Dostoevsky, ch. 9.

177. *Zapiski iz Mertvogo Doma*, 232.

178. *Zapiski iz Mertvogo Doma*, 10. "The picture of 'the house of the dead' in which Dostoevsky led us was a real one" (Milikov, "Svetoch," in *Kriticheskie razbory "Zapisok iz Mernvogo Doma,"* ed. V. Zelinskiy, 2).

Moreover, it was hard for him to get used to life in the colony. He made some comparisons between the educated man and the commoner, who were in the same conditions in the colony:

> A common man sent to hard labour finds himself in kindred society . . . He loses his native place, his family; but his ordinary surroundings are much the same as before. A man of education, condemned by law to the same punishment as the common man, suffers incomparably more. He must stifle all his needs, all his habits, he must descend into a lower sphere, must breath another air. He is like a fish thrown upon the sand. The punishment he undergoes, equal for all criminals according to the law, is ten times more severe and more painful for him than for the common man. This is an incontestable truth, even if one thinks only of the material habits that have to be sacrificed.[179]

The hardest thing for Goryanchikov was the antipathy that the convicts displayed towards nobles. They would not allow them to be their friends or comrades. He even sometimes envied the simple convicts, who two hours after arriving in the colony, became as equal as everyone else. A simple convict "is understood by everyone and is known to all. Everyone regards him as one of them."[180] Not so with the nobles: "they will be hated for years, and the whole mass will look down upon them; they will not be understood, and more important – will not be trusted."[181] Although with time, many would become accustomed to having nobles around and would no longer hurt or humiliate them, a nobleman would never be one of them. Even those who loved them, as Petrov did, considered them their equal. Never was Goryanchikov so much offended as the day when bad food in the colony caused a riot. Everybody went into the yard and stood together, putting forward their claims to superiors. Goryanchikov went along with them, but they chased him away, as if he were a stranger.

Feelings of alienation from the people tormented Goryanchikov all four years he spent in the colony. He wanted to be received as one of them, but it

---

179. Dostoevsky, *House of the Dead*, Part I, ch. 5.
180. *Zapiski iz Mertvogo Doma*, 198.
181. *Zapiski iz Mertvogo Doma*, 198.

never happened. He concluded that "there is nothing worse than to live in the social environment that is not yours." It was hard to gain the confidence of the people, "earn their love," because they almost instinctively hated people from the nobility. Goryanchikov recalled that he "had to live nearly two years in the colony to get the good and the goodwill of some of the convicts." Finally, most of them grew to love him and recognized him as a good man.[182]

Goryanchikov did not change for the worse while in the penal colony. On the contrary, he was able to learn a lot about himself and many things about the men in the colony. Many of his actions and words suggest that despite the harsh conditions there, he was able to stand morally firm and not compromise. Goryanchikov could not accept the fact that you can "curse for fun and find amusement in it."[183]

His kindness and sacrificial spirit were not affected by ridicule. Some convicts often borrowed money from Goryanchikov, taking him for a stupid person who was uncomprehending of the cunningness of man. Although he knew their intentions very well, he remained kind and was always ready to lend them money.

The return of Goryanchikov to the Bible can be seen in his moral assessment of the actions of people. He had a negative attitude towards the girls, who came especially to flirt with the convicts in the workshops where they were taken to work. He said about one of them that she was "the naughtiest girl in the world."[184]

Also, Goryanchikov had his own attitude towards false denunciations which was quite distinct from that of the other convicts. While the rest of the convicts took false denunciations for granted,[185] without any indignation or resentment, Goryanchikov thought them to be utter filth.

He lived by the problems of people, of ordinary people, who continued to serve in the same miserable conditions of the penal colony. He was preoccupied with the idea of "the inequality of punishments for the same offence."[186] Goryanchikov understood that although two people may have committed

---

182. *Zapiski iz Mertvogo Doma*, 26.

183. *Zapiski iz Mertvogo Doma*, 25.

184. *Zapiski iz Mertvogo Doma*, 30.

185. Milikov, "Svetoch," in *Kriticheskie razbory "Zapisok iz Mernvogo Doma,"* ed. V. Zelinskiy, 4.

186. Milikov, 6.

the same murder, their circumstances, their motives could be different.[187] He explained,

> I reflected on the inequality of the punishments inflicted for the same crimes. . . . One has committed a murder for a trifle – for an onion. He has killed on the high-road a peasant who was passing and foundon him an onion, and nothing else. . . . Another criminal has killed a debauchee who was oppressing or dishonouring his wife, his sister, or his daughter. A third, a vagabond, half dead with hunger, pursued by a whole band of police, was defending his liberty, his life. . . the brigand who assassinates children for his amusement, for the pleasure of feeling their warm blood flow over his hands, of seeing them shudder . . . They will all alike be sent to hard labour; though the sentence will perhaps not be for the same number of years. But the variations in the punishment are not very numerous, whereas different kinds of crimes may be reckoned by thousands.[188]

Goryanchikov assisted needy convicts. He taught Aleya to read and write. He used the New Testament for this. While reading, Goryanchikov saw his interest in some passages of the New Testament and with his questions he tried to instill within Aleya love for Jesus. Thus, they read the Sermon on the Mount.[189]

Goryanchikov spoke openly about his regrets. For several years Sushilov, the convict, served him. For his work Goryanchikov paid him. But once he told him, "So, Sushilov, money you take, but you are not doing anything."[190] This statement offended Sushilov, because he served Goryanchikov from the heart and not for money. Then Goryanchikov had to find the strength to apologize and mend relations with the poor convict.

Having met A. in the colony, Goryanchikov concluded that if the bodily nature of man would not be kept internally by any norms or laws, then there would be no limit to its downfall. Of him he spoke as of a man who "was and became some piece of meat, with teeth and stomach, and with an

187. Zarin, "Biblioteka dlya chteniya," 12.

188. Dostoevsky, *House of the Dead*, Part I, ch. 4.

189. *Zapiski iz Mertvogo Doma*, 53–54.

190. *Zapiski iz Mertvogo Doma*, 61.

unquenchable thirst for the coarsest, the most brutal corporal pleasures." For the satisfaction in one of the least of these pleasures, he "was capable to kill cold-bloodedly, slaughter, and in other words do anything just making sure that everything would be hidden." Goryanchikov understood that restraint from moral degradation could only come from inside a man. Therefore, for himself, he decided "that above all one should act directly as the inner feeling and conscience tell."[191]

Goryanchikov argued that in the colony he had his first "encounter with the common people." He became as simple as they were, he knew their habits and customs as such, though did not share them in essence. Although he acknowledged that in the first year he did not notice much, but then, looking at the people, he began to notice, even among his hated convicts some good people that could think and feel "despite the hideous crust covering them from the outside."[192]

For Goryanchikov, even in the colony the feeling of compassion for the "less fortunate" was one of the highest values.[193] He enthusiastically recalled the wives of the Decembrists, who gave him the gospel, while he was still in Tobolsk. About them he said they were the ones "who also suffered in exile, and counted time by decades and who have long been accustomed to see a brother in any misfortunate."[194] He also remembered the poor widow Anastasia Ivanovna, who lived in the same town where the colony was located. She saw his mission in helping the exiles, convicts and all those who needed compassion and caring.

Goryanchikov, describing the case in his early life as a convict when Petrov stole his Bible, recalled with regret the loss, "I was sorry for my Bible."[195] He also missed reading books. Being from the nobility it was twice as hard for him to be in the colony. First, he had to get used to different living conditions. In the penal colony all slept on the benches made of three boards. In the barracks were bedbugs and fleas all of which reached an enormous size. His story about his stay in hospital even painted a darker picture of the life

---

191. *Zapiski iz Mertvogo Doma*, 63.

192. *Zapiski iz Mertvogo Doma*, 179.

193. Milikov, "Svetoch," in *Kriticheskie razbory "Zapisok iz Mernvogo Doma,"* ed. V. Zelinskiy, 8.

194. *Zapiski iz Mertvogo Doma*, 67.

195. *Zapiski iz Mertvogo Doma*, 86.

of a convict. The hospital was dirty, convicts suffering from different diseases were lying next to him, some were even mentally ill.[196] Conditions were so severe that one could easily contract an eye disease which was widespread in the Omsk province.

Goryanchikov out of compassion helped the needy patients.[197] Being in the same hospital, he shared his tea with convicts punished by beating or flogging,

> The soldier who had just come in was twenty-three years of age . . . His back, uncovered down to the waist, had been seriously beaten, and his body now trembled with fever beneath the damp sheet with which his back was covered. For about an hour and a half he did nothing but walk backwards and forwards in the room. I looked at his face: he seemed to be thinking of nothing; his eyes had a strange expression, at once wild and timid . . . I fancied I saw him looking attentively at my hot tea . . . I invited him to have some; he turned towards me without saying a word, and taking the cup, swallowed the tea at one gulp, without putting sugar in it.[198]

He remained impartial, fair and honest in the colony as much as in the outside world. He called doctors who took bribes in order to assist the sick, the apostates of the case and wolves in sheep's skin. Nothing, no reference to the medium could justify their actions, especially if they had lost their humanity. Because "benevolence, affection, brotherly compassion to the sick sometimes is in greater demand than all the drugs."[199] Goryanchikov stated:

> It is time to stop these apathetic lamentations on the circumstances surrounding us. There may be truth in the lament, but a cunning rogue who knows how to take care of himself never fails to blame the circumstances around him when he wishes his faults to be forgiven – above all, if he writes or speaks with eloquence.[200]

---

196. *Zapiski iz Mertvogo Doma*, 136.

197. Pisarev, "Pogibshie i Pogibayuschie" in *Kriticheskie razbory "Zapisok iz Mernvogo Doma,"* ed. V. Zelinskiy, 76–77.

198. Dostoevsky, *House of the Dead*, Part II, ch. 1.

199. *Zapiski iz Mertvogo Doma*, 142.

200. Dostoevsky, *House of the Dead*, Part II, ch. 2.

Out of compassion for convicts, Goryanchikov showed his misunderstanding of the system of punishment, when application of the laws has no logic. He saw a double punishment in that the chambers of the hospital closed for the night and the convicts had to use the toilet they had in their chamber, even though there was a bathroom down the corridor and there was a sentry near each door.[201] He also could not find any explanation as to why the shackles were not removed from the terminally ill, especially for those suffering from phthisic.[202]

3.4 Conclusion

Years of exile intensified Dostoevsky's search for true religion. The beliefs from his existing firm morality beginning helped Dostoevsky survive tough times in exile in the midst of common lawlessness and chaos. After a period of time in exile, staying in Omsk and expecting to be sent to Semipalatinsk to serve in the military forces, Dostoevsky wrote a remarkable letter to N. D. Fonvizina, one of the Decembrist's wives, who had presented him with a New Testament back in the beginning of his time in exile. He shared his personal struggles and the deep nature of his religious struggles:

> What great torments it takes to have this thirst to believe, which is much stronger in my soul now, Dostoevsky writes. However, God sends me these minutes sometimes, when I am perfectly calm, and I love these moments, because I know that I am loved, and exactly during these moments I embrace the symbol of faith, which is clear and holy. This symbol is a very simple one, here it is: to believe that there is no one better, deeper, more attractive, reasonable, courageous and perfect than Christ is, and with a jealous love I am saying that it can't be any other way. If someone would have told me that Christ is outside the truth and truth is outside Christ, then I would better stay with Christ rather than with truth.[203]

---

201. D. Pisarev, "Pogibshie i Pogibayuschie," in *Kriticheskie razbory "Zapisok iz Mernvogo Doma,"* ed. V. Zelinskiy, 48.

202. *Zapiski iz Mertvogo Doma,* 139.

203. *Pis'ma,* Vol. 28, 20 February, 1854, 175.

In the katorga, beliefs and convictions were formed that led Dostoevsky to harsh disputes with socialists and passionate opposition to everything that oppresses a human being.[204]

E. Rumyantseva concludes that Dostoevsky remained faithful to the beliefs of his youth. He remained a humanist. On one occasion he said that if there was something which was experienced by heart, it could not be mistaken. Such "not mistaken things" were the dreams of his youth.[205] However, Dostoevsky's humanism was a Christian humanism that viewed even the worst person as God's image.[206]

Having examined the novel The House of the Dead, this chapter has identified, described and analyzed several theological motifs, which taken together form the main themes of this novel.

Dostoevsky, exploring the people in the colony and reflecting on his own experiences there, concluded that man is complicated. Man is so complicated that he is simultaneously capable of being evil and good. Vanity, conceit, hatred, covetousness, a desire to dominate, fear, cruelty in committing crimes for pleasure, all show how low a person can fall. Dostoevsky used real-world examples to show how evil can expand and give birth to other sorts of vices. With his examples he warned that once evil turns a man into a beast, then he will commit crimes for pleasure.

But man is also able to show sympathy, love and compassion. He does it sincerely, if rarely. Dostoevsky said that Aleya was loved and caressed by all.

---

204. Kirpotin, *Molodoy Dostoevsky*, 154.

205. Pumyanceva, *Fjodor Mikhaylovich Dostoevsky*, 102.

206. S. L. Frank, *O Dostoevskom* [About Dostoevsky] (Moscow: n. p., 1990), 391–397. Dostoevsky is far removed from optimistic humanism, an idealization of a person. Humanity's essence according to Dostoevsky is totally opposed to the "reasonable person" of the enlightenment, and the "beautiful soul" of romanticism. Dostoevsky believed that evil, blindness, chaotic nature and disharmony are not only typical of humanity, but in some sense connected with a human being's essence. The irrational depth of the human spirit, which cannot fit into any form of goodness or reason, is the source of all evil, and has a chaotic, blind and rebellious character. However, according to Dostoevsky, *this is the area* where a person is able to meet God and join in the rational powers of goodness, love and spiritual enlightenment. This beginning leads to the only way to God. Any other rational, secure and less problematic way doesn't exist. It is truly "a narrow way," surrounded from all sides by sin, madness and evil. It is probable Dostoevsky thought that spiritual enlightenment and possession of the gifts of grace is impossible without experiencing sin and evil. He offers a remarkably honest acknowledgment of gospel truth, which states that in heaven there is much more joy about one repentant sinner rather than over ninety-nine righteous persons. This is a perfect description of Dostoevsky's *humanism*, which has a way out from the crisis of previous humanism.

This means that the convicts were able to love in a way that was selfless, pure, fresh, meek and beautiful.[207] Dostoevsky found that everyone has the ability to do good. Even the most brutal murderer was able to learn to love someone.

But unlike the first novel, Dostoevsky now understood how people could dramatically change for the better; that goodness could overcome evil in man, even if in the past that man was the worst offender. For that to happen man needed to repent. Repentance changes a person's convictions about other men, and then his life will be totally different. After repentance, for example, Luchika became somewhat humble. Therefore, looking at him in the penal colony, none of the convicts could have believed that someone like Luchika had committed so many murders.

Fortunately, men's longing for freedom and their aspiration to live testify that each person has an optimistic desire for a better life. The precise nature of that "better life" may change, but the desire in itself conveys so much. Man is given freedom of choice; he is given the opportunity to change his life. Some like Luchika or Goryanchikov himself took advantage of that and in his personal life, Dostoevsky showed that no matter how strongly social factors influence us, it is our choice to do good or evil. Consequently, man is responsible for his good or evil deeds.

One can agree with the statement of Leo Tolstoy on *The House of the Dead* in his letter to N. N. Strahov following the death of Dostoevsky, "I do not know a better book out of the modern literature . . . it's not the tone, but the point of view, amazing – sincere, natural and Christian."[208] It is a theology which has a focus on the possibilities of freedom of choice and of spiritual change which is portrayed here.

Thereby, Dostoevsky's convictions after his time in exile gained new tones. The fascination with utopian socialism came to an end for Dostoevsky. Religious beliefs were strengthened. Beliefs in the usefulness of anti-government activity expressed in Petrashevsky's club had faded. The revolutionary West ceased to captivate his imagination. Beliefs about the Russian way of development that, according to Dostoevsky, depended on the peasant values

---

207. D. I. Pisarev, "Pogibshie i Pogibayuschshie" in *Kriticheskie razbory "Zapisok iz Mernvogo Doma,"* ed. V. Zelinskiy, 71.

208. O. Miller, "Russkie Pisateli posle Gogolya" in *Kriticheskie razbory "Zapisok iz Mernvogo Doma,"* ed. Zelinskiy, 86.

of a righteous, sinless life, full of love towards a neighbour as Christ's example affirms, were strengthened.[209] From this time on Christ became the centre of his convictions, even though this walk of faith would be through thorns and would involve many doubts.

---

209. Rumyanceva, *Fjodor Mikhailovich Dostoevsky*, 102.

CHAPTER 4

Post-Siberian Period: Self Sacrifice

4.1 Introduction

The purpose of this chapter is to discover and analyse Dostoevsky's convictions as they were revealed in his life during the post-Siberian period and to discover and analyse theological motifs expressed in *The Brothers Karamazov*. To achieve this goal, it is necessary to first identify and analyse Dostoevsky's communities and their shared convictions; to identify and analyse Dostoevsky's own convictions; and to discover and analyse the influence of Dostoevsky's life on society. Second, theological motifs expressed in *The Brothers Karamazov* will be identified and studied. The theological motifs discovered in these novels point to Dostoevsky's message for Russian society.

4.2 Dostoevsky's Convictions Shown in His Own Life During the Post-Siberian Period

To detect and analyze Dostoevsky's convictions from his return from exile (1859–1881) until his death (1859–1881), our primary sources are the *Letters* of Dostoevsky, the *Diary of a Writer*, a notebook, and memoirs of contemporaries, as well as memories of his wife and daughter. This was a time in which Dostoevsky had to endure bad convulsions which caused him severe physical problems. In the spiritual realm, his life encounters with simple people in Siberia and soldiers during his military service had provided him with an expansion of life experiences. All these events produced an essential transformation in Fyodor Mikhailovich's views. He understood the defects of socialism as an attempt to improve mankind internally by using the external tools of a new social system. The image of Christ that he had previously loved took precedence in his life. The thirst for social justice stayed alive in him. Yet he searched for tools for its realization in spiritual areas rather than an external formation of society. Love for Russia and the Russian people, which along with Christian ideas, were always typical for Dostoevsky, had a leading place in his worldview and activities. He dreamed about "the nations' reconciliation" with Russian help.[1]

4.2.1 Arrival in Petersburg (1859–1863)

Arriving in Petersburg in December 1859, Dostoevsky committed himself to literary and social activity. He became a member of the "Assistance Society for Writers and Scholars in Need," participating in literary readings and amateur performances.[2] He wanted to announce his new conviction, established after years in Siberia, and *de facto* started to manage the political magazine "Time." He was closely watched by the police and therefore since he could not become the official editor, his brother, Mikhail Mikhailovich, became sole editor.[3]

According to Rumyantseva, in the foundation of this magazine there was an idea of a nationalist trend "pochvennichestva," i.e. closer and better relationships between intellectuals and simple people.[4] Dostoevsky objected to the inclusion of democrats and Slavophiles in the "grounding" position. In his opinion, revolutionary democrats rejected the existence of any folk, since they did not understand the meaning of "closeness with people." Moscow Slavophiles in "The Day" newspaper who belonged to the pre-Peter period could not be approved either.

> There were enough lies and cheatings in pre-Peter Russia, especially in the Moscow period, Dostoevsky writes. Lying in public relations, with a mixture of motives: domination, although with external humility, slavery, etc. Lies in religion that possibly did not state outright disbelief, yet possessed a hidden apathy or hypocrisy. Falsehood in family relationships that humiliated a

---

1. Losskiy, *Bog i mirovoe zlo*, 19.
2. Rumyantseva, *Feodor Mikhaylovich Dostoevsky*, 115.
3. Rumyantseva, 116.
4. Rumyantseva, 116.

woman to the role of an animal, who would be considered as a thing rather than personality . . . In pre-Peter, Muscovite Russia there were a lot of Asian things, eastern laziness, pretence and life . . . According to this Moscow ideal, Slavophiles want to reconstruct Russia . . . For them, all small improvements and developments that took place since Peter, would come to naught.[5]

Strahov recalled talking to Dostoevsky about revolution; he passionately quoted words from the New Testament: "For all those who take up the sword shall perish by the sword."[6]

The first major piece written by Dostoevsky after his years in exile was published in the beginning of 1861 in the first edition of "Time." This work was called "The Unpleasant Predicament" with Ivan Petrovich being the main character, who experienced events from the author's life. Dostoevsky preached the idea of forgiveness and suffering instead of the active fight against social injustice.

Roughly at the same time, his literary work The House of the Dead came into being. In The House of the Dead, Dostoevsky expressly described his life in the Siberian jail. The novel also reflected the impressions of things experienced and seen by Dostoevsky in Omsk, Siberia, in penal servitude, where he spent four years having been convicted in the case of Petrashevists. Immediately, in the first letter sent out from jail to his brother Michael, Dostoyevsky wrote, "In general, the time for me is not lost. If I have not learned a lot about Russia, then at least I have learned more than most people know about the Russian people."

The House of the Dead will be examined in greater detail in the second part, since through it Dostoevsky proclaimed his new thoughts about humans.

In 1862, the situation in Russia was very alarming. Student movements developed. N. Strakhov remembered, "Students planned meetings, had their own budget, library, published magazines and books, and judged their own folks. Many students were arrested, taken to court, and sentenced to jail. Universities were closed.[7] E. Radzinskiy writes that because of Alexander's

---

5. Rumyantseva, 122.

6. Losskiy, *Bog i mirovoe zlo*, 52.

7. Rumyantseva, *Feodor Mikhailovich Dostoevsky*, 129.

reforms, young people received some freedoms that they did not have during the reign of Nikolai I.

> Alexander II softened censorship. He gave the people an opportunity to express themselves. He gave more rights to the universities and permitted the young people to travel abroad. And now, according to some reports, students began to gather together for "meetings." During these meetings they dare to criticize the Manifesto and quote one "evil" line from Nekrasov's poem: "Stop rejoicing!" – *Muse* told me. It is time to move forward. People are free but are they really happy?"[8]

The first leaflet from this movement (Russian *proklamatsyia*) in Russia was printed in 1861. Before that Hertsen's publishing house produced some illegally printed publications. Then they were even printed in St. Petersburg.[9] Significant student riots began to take place in major universities in St. Petersburg, Moscow and Kharkov. Students fought with police, university administrations and reactionary professors. They began to publish handwritten student newspapers and pamphlets, and organized student gatherings.[10]

After the suppression of the Polish rebellion of 1863–1864 and the attempt to murder the tsar by D. V. Karakozov on 4 April 1866, Alexander II agreed to tighten security.[11] The reforms were still underway, but they were not implemented methodically and systematically. One could especially notice the change after the death of 21-year-old Nikolai, the oldest son of the Emperor.[12]

Eleven years had passed since the reign of Nikolai I. These years gave birth to a new generation, which dreamed of a rapid revolution. According to E. Radzinskiy, these were "writers that had no talent, students that did not manage to graduate, lawyers without court trials, actors with no abilities, and scientists without science. They were people with great ambitions but with no talent whatsoever."[13] They denied all values of the past and saw revolution as the only way that would lead to the nation's prosperity.

---

8. Radzinskiy, *Aleksandr II Zhizn' i Smert*, 165.

9. Radzinskiy, 165.

10. Radzinskiy, 165.

11. Radzinskiy, 220.

12. Radzinskiy, 204–207.

13. Radzinskiy, 215.

During this time the youth tended to promote a vast number of forbidden books and ideas. The most radical young people despised the past generation of liberals, and even the radical Russian hero of the past Alexander Herzen. With hatred to the older generation youngsters called them "compromisers," "important gentlemen, who under the cover of their brilliant minds and revolutionary slogans were unable to get rid of the old order." The older generation believed in reforms, yet the only belief that can exist is the hope of the revolution, which will soon, without any doubt, break out in Russia. What is needed is just one external push. The murder of the tsar can become the catalyst of the revolution.[14]

Such faith went through the minds and hearts of the participants in the revolutionary movement of the second half of the nineteenth century. In 1876 the "Populists" (Russian *narodniki*) decided to form their own political party, "Land and Will."

The charter of the "Land and Will" should contain all the best ideas of Russian radicals, that all land should be given to peasants, and that the reign of the tsar should be abolished. Russia must follow the socialist path in its own way, by avoiding capitalism, through peasant communes. But the charter also had something new – the right of political assassination.[15]

Kravhinsky, Figner, Morozov and Tikhomirov, "Populists" and future terrorists, joined the organization.[16]

The liberal opposition came to life simultaneously with the heightening of the activity of revolutionaries. K. D. Kavelin and B. N. Chicherin, professors of history, were the most prominent representatives of the Russian liberal movement. The most liberal magazine, "European Herald," was published beginning in 1866. Russian liberals defended the evolutionary way of development of society. They were in favour of realistic demands unlike the utopian programs of the revolutionaries. They tried to obtain more rights

---

14. Radzinskiy, 214.
15. Radzinskiy, 310.
16. Radzinskiy, 310.

over local governing bodies (Russian *zemstva*) and wanted to include their representatives in the State Council.[17]

In the summer of 1862, Dostoevsky made his first trip abroad.[18] His Western European impressions were not pleasant, intensifying his doubts about the correctness of Western civilization. In the fall of 1862, his feelings were reflected in announcements about subscriptions to the magazine "Time," where Westerners were being heavily criticized.[19] In the summer of 1863, Dostoevsky once again travelled abroad. Before his departure, the magazine "Time" was closed because of N. Strahov's article "Fatal question."[20] This article was misinterpreted as supportive of the Polish defense in 1863.[21]

During this trip, Dostoevsky met Appolinariya Prokofievna Suslova, who had left the country earlier. Dostoevsky's romance with Suslova was tempestuous, nerve-wracking and short. "I still love her, very much," Dostoevsky wrote to Suslova's sister, after several years, "yet, I do not like to love her. She doesn't deserve this love. I feel pity about her, because I foresee that she will be eternally unhappy. She won't find a friend or happiness. The one who requires so much, without having any responsibilities will never find happiness."[22] This affair with Suslova took place while his wife was seriously ill.

The Polish rebellion in January 1863 turned Dostoevsky against Western civilization even more and directed his attention to the role of Catholicism and what he saw as its negative development. Dostoevsky's turn to the Orthodox Church began not because of the positive values he saw in this Church, but because of the revulsion he felt towards Catholicism.

In 1864 Mikhail Mikhailovich Dostoevsky received a license to issue a new magazine "Epoch." Again, Fyodor Mikhailovich was one of the employees of the magazine and in the same year he wrote *Notes from Underground*. Due to censorship much of the positive message in this work was either lost or greatly reduced. Dostoevsky wrote to his brother on this matter: "These censors are pigs, because they missed all the places where I mocked and blasphemed, yet removed and forbade my conclusion of our necessity in faith and Christ. Are

---

17. *Rossiya: Entsiklopedicheskiy spravochnik*, 142.

18. *Rossiya: Entsiklopedicheskiy spravochnik*, 131.

19. Losskiy, *Bog i mirovoe zlo*, 53.

20. Rumyantseva, *Fjodor Mikhaylovich Dostoevsky*, 135.

21. Losskiy, *Bog i mirovoe zlo*, 52.

22. Losskiy, 137.

these censors against the government?"[23] For this reason, Leo Shestov realized that Dostoevsky got depressed and upset about all "great and beautiful" things until the end of his life.[24]

Many literary critics name this piece as a prologue to a mature novelistic creativity. From that time on his genius would finally grow to maturity and find expression in great writings with religious themes. Dostoevsky focused on the life of Christ. He adored Jesus's image as an example to follow and grew strong in his faith. His thirst for social justice was vibrant in his life with his compassion for the sick and oppressed being evident. Dostoevsky matured into a writer with strong a Christian message.

4.2.2 Significant Losses (1863–1866)

1863–1864 marked a very difficult period in Dostoevsky's life. Mikhail Mikhailovich was ill, while Fyodor Mikhailovich found himself beside the bed of his dying wife in Moscow. Magazine activities were abandoned.[25] In 1864, Dostoevsky's wife, Maria Fyodorovna died. On July 22, his brother Mikhail also passed away due to disease.[26] It was a heavy blow for Fyodor Mikhailovich, and all of the problems of "Epoch" fell on his shoulders. In February of 1865, the magazine was closed.

In the summer of 1865 Dostoevsky left for the West. He could not resist gambling, losing much money, and as a result ending up in an extremely difficult financial situation. His Siberian friend A. E. Wrangell as well as Turgenev rescued him by sending some funds.

There is evidence that during this time Dostoevsky was seen as a contradictory and controversial person. On the one hand Dostoevsky sacrificed everything for the benefit of others; on the other hand, he impetuously gave into gambling, losing everything. It is one thing to be out of money because of helping others, and another thing to be out of money by playing roulette, which could be viewed as another of his sins. Infatuation with roulette gambling drove him to negative actions. O. Miller wrote about the attitude of Dostoevsky regarding money:

23. *Pis'ma,* Vol. 28, 26 March 1872.

24. *Dostoevsky i Nicshhe: Filocofiya tragedii* [Dostoevsky and Nietzsche: Philosophy of the Tragedy] (Berlin: 1922), 87.

25. Rumyantseva, *Feodor Mikhaylovich Dostoevsky,* 138.

26. Rumyantseva, 142.

> In November 1843 Dostoevsky received from his guardian from
> Moscow, 1000 rubles and instantly lost them all playing billiards;
> so, he had, therefore, to borrow 300 rubles from a lender on the
> condition of exorbitant interest, and moreover, to ask his sister's
> husband to send 150 rubles. Two months later, he was down to
> only 100 rubles, and in the same evening this money also was
> spent on the game of dominoes.[27]

Being a proud person, Dostoevsky made numerous attempts to enrich himself, played and lost at roulette many times, and reached a state of humiliation. All these forms of evil, created by an irritated pride, were recognized by Dostoevsky in his *Notes from Underground*, where he portrayed the underground man. At the end of *Notes from Underground* he spoke on behalf of his character, "I felt ashamed all the time I was writing this story – so, this is not literature, this is corrective punishment."[28] To his brother Michael, he wrote that the story "will come out as something strong and sincere and the testimony will be true."[29]

During this trip to the West he found an idea for *Crime and Punishment*.[30]

> In the Russian democratic press of the sixties criminal issues,
> proceedings, punishments were heavily discussed. Publicists-
> democrats would seek to prove that crimes in society are gen-
> erated by poverty, emotional retardation, i.e. consequences of
> social oppression. Dostoevsky agreed with them, yet his novel
> did not become a work about murder and a morally ill per-
> son, but about a passionate writer's views on serious issues that
> bothered his contemporaries. Raskolnikov is pushed to commit
> a crime not as so much by necessity, but because of an idea.[31]

---

27. Losskiy, *Bog i mirovoe zlo*, 27.

28. F. M. Dostoevsky, *Polnoe Sobranie Sochineniy v 30-i tomakh, T. 5, Zapiski iz Podpolie* [The Complete Works of Dostoevsky in 30 Volumes, Vol. 5, *Notes from Underground*] (Leningrad: Nauka, 1973), Chapter X.

29. *Pis'ma*, Vol. 28, 19 June 1863.

30. Rumyantseva, *Feodor Mikhaylovich Dostoevsky*, 147.

31. Dostoevskaya, *Vospominaniya*, 149.

According to Rumyantseva, Raskolnikov illustrated a type of "new people," like Chernyshevsky, who organized people into exclusive personalities and "material" things.[32]

> Dostoevsky's hero with his polemical concentration against revolutionary democracy should be viewed not as an artistic picture of a certain social group but rather an honest image mixed up in his own thoughts, influenced by various circumstances. The critical historic epoch of the 1860s with a breakdown of the old serf moral principles, the development of bourgeois individualism, and the self-affirmation of personality has frequently caused the unstable segment of youth to commit errors and fluctuations in ideas. Rodion Raskolnikov has presented this in the novel.[33]

In his notebook, Fyodor Mikhailovich mentioned a number of ideas regarding his novel: "The idea of a novel. The Orthodox outlook; what is the meaning of Orthodoxy? There is no happiness in comfort, happiness comes through suffering. A human being is not born for happiness. A person earns his happiness and earns it through suffering."[34]

Yet again, the same problem occurred – another lack of funds. Dostoevsky, who was without money, signed a one-sided agreement with a Stellovsk publisher. According to the agreement, Dostoevsky must complete a new novel by November 1, 1866 for the upcoming volume of his compositions. If he did not fulfill this condition, he would lose ownership of all of his works for nine years. However, he could not write anything. A month prior to deadline, according to friendly advice, he hired a stenographer and in twenty-eight days he dictated the novel *The Gambler*, since Dostoevsky knew a gambler's psychology and tactics very well. The idea of the novel is an all-consuming passion for gambling. After a short period of time, Fyodor Mikhailovich asked the typist, Anna Grigorievna Snitkina, to marry him.

During this period of time, he continued to remain a person who had compassion for the sick and oppressed, but he also was a contradictory personality. He sacrificed everything for the benefit of others; yet he gave in to

---

32. Dostoevskaya, 152.

33. Dostoevskaya, 154.

34. Losskiy, *Bog i mirovoe zlo*, 55.

gambling, losing everything. In spite of all that transpired, Dostoevsky was a proud person. The living of "Christ's Way" did not seem, for him, to be following a way of humility.

4.2.3 Success and Acknowledgement (1867–1881)

On February 15, 1867 Anna Grigorievna became his wife. This was truly a happy marriage. In 1866, Dostoevsky dictated his immortal novel *Crime and Punishment* to his new typist and completed it in the following year. Anna Grigorievna recalled: "Once, during the first weeks of our marriage, Fyodor Mikhailovich escorted me to the courtyard of one house, and showed me a stone, where Raskolnikov had hidden the stolen possessions of an old woman."[35] *Crime and Punishment* is a novel with the moral that the worse punishment happens in a person's soul rather than happening in prison or somewhere else after committing a crime.

From 1867 until 1871 the writer, along with his new wife, spent a lot of time abroad, rarely coming to Russia, in an attempt to escape creditors. They occasionally lived in various cities such as Dresden, Berlin, Basel, Geneva and Florence. On the way to Geneva, they stopped at night in Basel to see a painting, about which Dostoevsky had heard. This painting, by Hans Holbein, portrayed Jesus Christ, who had undergone inhuman torture, had already been removed from the cross and his body had been made subject to decay. His swollen face was covered with bleeding wounds, and his appearance was terrible. This artwork produced an overwhelming impression on Fyodor Mikhailovich, and he stood as if startled in front of it. Anna Grigorievna recalled,

> I was no longer able to look at the painting: it produced too heavy an impression, especially in my morbid state, and I went to other halls. When I returned after fifteen–twenty minutes, I found Fyodor Mikhailovich continuing to stand before the painting, as if chained to it. In his agitated face I saw the same frightened expression, which I had already witnessed in the first minutes of an attack of epilepsy. I quietly took my husband's arm, led him into another room and sat him down on the bench

---

35. A. G. Dostoevskaya, *Vospominaniya* (Moscow: Pravda, 1987), 204.

at any moment expecting the onset of a seizure. Fortunately, this did not happen; Fyodor Mikhailovich gradually calmed down and when he was leaving the museum, insisted once again to go to look at the painting that amazed him so much.[36]

This note written by his wife captured only the outward commotion, while the deep impulses found embodiment later in the novel *The Idiot*.[37]

In 1868, in Geneva a daughter Sofia was born. His wife writes:

> Fyodor Mikhailovich turned out to be a very gentle father; he would certainly be present when we bathed our daughter, helping me greatly, wrapping our daughter in a warm blanket, carrying her in his hands, abandoning all other businesses, running to see her whenever he heard her voice. He would stay for hours beside her bed, singing songs and talking to her.[38]

Unfortunately, this happiness did not last long. In the third month of her life, his daughter was taken ill with a lung inflammation and soon died. "Deeply shocked and saddened because of her death," Dostoevskaya wrote, "I was terrible afraid for my poor husband: his desperation was tempestuous, he cried and wept as a woman, standing beside a cold body of his favourite girl, warmly kissing her face and hands."[39]

For the first time Dostoevsky opened his heart fully, complaining to his wife about his destiny, which had followed him his entire life,

> Looking back, he told me about his sad lonely adolescence following the death of his beloved mother, remembered the taunts of his fellow writers in his literary career, who first recognized his talent and then cruelly offended him. He remembered about the penal colony, and about how much he suffered in four years of stay in it. He talked about his dreams to find in his marriage with Maria Dmitrievna the so desired family bliss, which alas, did not come true . . . And now, when this "great and unique

---

36. Dostoevskaya, 204.

37. F. M. Dostoevsky, *Polnoe Sobranie Sochineniy, Idiot* [The Complete Works of Dostoevsky, *The Idiot*], [CD-ROM] (Izdatel'stvo Adept, 2002).

38. Dostoevsky, *Polnoe Sobranie Sochineniy, Idiot*, 14.

39. Dostoevsky, 16.

> human happiness to have one's own child visited him," and he
> had the opportunity to recognize and appreciate this happiness,
> the evil fate did not spare him and took away from him such a
> dearly loved creature.[40]

Anna Grigorievna wrote that Dostoevsky never before, nor afterwards, told her of this bitter resentment that he had to endure in his life.

Only by the end of 1871 after paying off all debts was he able to return to Petersburg. On the way, Dostoevsky completed his great novel The Idiot, which was published in "Russian News" in 1868.

Here is what Dostoevsky wrote about the idea of this work:

> The main idea of a novel is to portray a positive person. There is
> nothing more complicated in this world than portraying such a
> person, especially nowadays. All writers, not necessarily domes-
> tic ones, even European authors, who tried to portray a positive
> image of a person, would always fail since the problem is huge. A
> positive image is an ideal, which is neither ours nor something
> which belongs to civilized Europe. There is only one positive
> image in the world – Christ, an extraordinary phenomenon,
> infinitely amazing person, and a true miracle.[41]

Dostoevsky tried to portray Christ's image in Prince Myshkin.

All Russia worked on the "production" of an ideal image. In Russia, the populist movement spread and developed. In the historical process, populists were looking to fulfill their ideas of moral ideals. P. Lavrov writes: ". . . the very process of destroying the immoral lifestyle and consciousness of the fight for the sake of development includes the element of goodness and fairness."[42] According to Rumyantseva, in *The Idiot* Dostoevsky actively rejected the Western bourgeois world, criticized socialists for their bourgeois views and found a way out in Christianity.[43] D. H. Lawrence could not separate the

---

40. Dostoevsky, 16.
41. *Pis'ma,* Vol. 28, 1 January 1868, 246.
42. Rumyantseva, *Feodor Mikhaylovich Dostoevsky,* 165.
43. Rumyantseva, 166.

writer from his creations, and interpreted Myshkin and others as biographical evidence of Dostoevsky's life.[44]

In 1866, life in Russia, which Dostoevsky closely followed from Dresden, was full of new longings and events. The time of "ideal production" had come to an end. A period of broad practical activity unfolded by populists began.[45]

A year and a half after Sonia's death, a second daughter Lyubovi was born. "With the baby's arrival happiness came back to our family,"[46] claimed Dostoevskaya. After several years of living together, Dostoevsky would often say to his wife that they "became one soul." He wrote to her: "We became one body and one soul."[47] In his family, Dostoevsky found and realized his ideal of love towards one another, unity of life and a readiness to sacrifice himself for others. Yet, his need to perform ideal goodness was not to be entirely satisfied in his family life. From his youth, he had been fascinated by an absolute perfection not only in personal and family life, but in the public realm also. All "great and beautiful" things bothered him deeply; he sought for perfect kindness, without the presence of egotism or any kind of evil. In other words, he looked for the kindness which could be found only in God's Kingdom.[48]

In 1871, Dostoevsky wrote his novel *The Devils*, where "devils" are anarchists, whose ideas started to spread in Russian reality. The motif of universal rebellion was taken to the limits of cruelty in *The Devils*.[49] According to Rumyantseva, *The Idiot* and *The Devils* were connected to the author's idea about an extraordinary human personality, which could not find his place in society. Despite the common idea in both novels, his main characters were not only different but opposites: one righteous, the other evil. Just like shade and light, they contrasted and complemented each other.[50]

In July 1871, Dostoevsky returned to Russia. One could notice in him a marked change of character. He had overcome many of the passions that

---

44. Peter Kaye, *Dostoevsky and English Modernism 1900–1930* (UK: Cambridge University Press, 1999), 25.

45. Kaye, *Dostoevsky and English Modernism 1900–1930*, 174.

46. Dostoevskaya, *Vospominaniya*, 209.

47. *Pis'ma*, Vol. 29, 24 July 1876, 112.

48. *Dnevnik Pisatelya*, 1876, 104.

49. R. Y. Kleyman, *Skvoznye motivy tvorchestva Dostoevsky* [Cross-Cutting Theme of Dostoevsky] (Kishinev: "Shtiinca," 1985), 32.

50. *Feodor Mikhaylovich Dostoevsky*, 176.

tormented him, had become somewhat spiritually enlightened, and was calmer and softer. Religious issues presented to him even greater interest than before. He returned having made the decision to speak directly on stirring religious themes, ignoring the fear of being misunderstood. Dostoevsky's friends noticed the change that had taken place in him. So Strakhov points out,

> He started continuously shifting the conversation to religious themes. Moreover, he had changed in his manner of speech, which exhibited greater softness and at times he would assume complete meekness. Even his facial features bore a trace of this sentiment, and a gentle smile appeared on his lips . . . The best Christian feelings, apparently, lived in him, those feelings that were more and more clearly expressed in his writings. In such a state he returned from abroad.[51]

It is hard to define someone's prayer life since it is a personal manifestation of the internal religious life. However, after he married Anna Grigorievna, we have many evidences of Dostoevsky's prayer life. He wrote to her: "At night, in tears I prayed about you."[52] When their first baby was almost due, Dostoevsky prayed all night long. Before the birth of their son Fyodor, he prayed all day and night long.[53] A two-year old daughter Lyubov broke her hand and experienced some complications later that required a surgery. "Anna, let us pray, and ask for God's help, may the Lord help us!" A. Dostoevskaya remembered, "we kneeled and never prayed so passionately as in these minutes."[54]

He diligently attended church at this time. This is what the widow of a priest recalls. She often met Dostoevsky in Znamenskaia church, "He would always come to the morning service or mid-day service. He used to come before us all and leave after everyone would leave. And he would always kneel in a corner, by the door, behind the right pillar, so as to not be overly visible. And he would always be on his knees and pray with tears. Sometimes

---

51. F. M. Dostoevsky, *Polnoe Sobranie Sochineniy* [The Complete Works of Dostoevsky] [CD-ROM] (Izdatel'stvo Adept, 2002).

52. *Pis'ma*, Vol. 28, 8 May1867, 188.

53. Dostoevskaya, *Vospominaniya*, 144.

54. Dostoevskaya, 144.

during whole services he would kneel on his knees and would not get up a single time."[55]

In 1873, Prince Meshersky, owner of the conservative magazine "The Citizen," invited Dostoevsky to become an editor of his publication. Fyodor Mikhailovich, who had missed the public life for a long time, gladly accepted the offer. For the first time on the pages of this magazine we can see the author dealing with many issues that were in Diary of a Writer and that he continued to write about until the end of his life. This was not simply a description of his life, but a look at the events of those years; a description of Russian and foreign realities from his point of view; his specific thoughts and what he called thoughts "without any cause." He would occasionally publish his short stories, such as "A Gentle Creature" or "A Little Boy at Christ's Christmas Tree." Once, working in the printing house with a corrector of "The Citizen" Varvara Vasilyevna Timofeeva, Dostoevsky asked her what she thought about the gospel. She answered that she saw the meaning of the gospel in the realization of Christ's teaching on earth and in our life and consciousness. "Is that all?" Dostoevsky continued. "No, this earthly life is only a step to the other world," she answered and Fyodor Mikhailovich could only raise his hands and agree with her.[56] In April 1874 Dostoevsky left "The Citizen" magazine; the parting was unhappy.

After 1872 Dostoevsky's family spent each summer in a small town, Staraya Russa, in Novgorod province. In this place, Dostoevsky would rest from his restless Petersburg life. Later, he bought a house here. One of Dostoevsky's friends was extremely surprised to see the famous writer strolling through town looking for his cow. Fyodor Mikhailovich wanted to have fresh milk for his children. In Staraya Russa, he wrote many chapters of *The Brothers Karamazov* and fully completed the novel *A Raw Youth*, in which Arkadiy Dolgorukiy was a main character, a landlord's son born out of marriage to a peasant woman who dreamed about getting rich. With the help of Makar Dolgorukiy, his father's servant who lived according to Christian law, he realized much. Makar Dolgorukiy said:

> Go and give your treasures to the poor and become a servant . . .
> Only then, will you be truly rich; for not by bread or valuable

---

55. *Istoricheskiy Vestnik, T. 2,* [Historical Journal] (Sankt-Petersburg: 1904), 541.
56. *Istoricheskiy Vestnik,* 526.

clothes, nor by pride or envy alone shall a man live happily, yet by countless love. You won't gain a small amount of wealth, not a hundred thousand, not even a million, but the whole world![57]

In one of his early statements about *A Raw Youth*, Dostoevsky said: "Decadence is the main and obvious idea of a novel . . . nobody thinks about the future."[58]

In the 1870s Dostoevsky was at the peak of his talent and would frequently be invited to various charity evenings and meetings, where he read fragments from his pieces and Pushkin's poems, since he valued Pushkin above all other poets. He became a recognized and widely popular writer. He was elected as an associate member of the Academy of Science and Art in the department of Russian language and literature.

Dostoevsky particularly loved children. A. Dostoevskaya said: "I have never seen a person in my life, who would be as capable as my husband in understanding children's ideas and getting them involved and interested in his dialogues. During these hours, Fyodor Mikhailovich would become a child himself."[59] Talking about the long family voyage to Kursk province during the summer of 1877, Dostoevskaya said:

> I was impressed with my husband's ability to calm a child down: whenever someone out of the three children would get capricious, Fyodor Mikhailovich would approach and take the capricious child to his place and as a result the child would immediately become peaceful. My husband has a special skill to talk to children, interest a child, build trust in such a way that in a moment a child becomes happy and obedient. It is his eternal love for little children, which helped and showed him how to act in certain circumstances or situations.[60]

---

57. F. M. Dostoevsky, *Polnoe Sobranie Sochineniy v 30-i tomakh, T. 13, Podrostok* [The Complete Works of Dostoevsky in 30 Volumes, Vol. 13, *The Raw Youth*] (Leningrad: Nauka, 1975), 311.

58. *Neizdannyy Dostoevsky Zapisnye knizhki i tetradi 1860–1881*, 366.

59. Dostoevskaya, *Vospominaniya*, 293.

60. Dostoevskaya, 336.

Whenever it was time for the children to go to sleep, Fyodor Mikhailovich would come to them, bless them and read his favourite prayer from childhood.[61]

In 1877, the Dostoevsky family moved to their last house in the life of Fyodor Mikhailovich. This house was located at the corner of Kuznechny lane and Yamskaya Street – Kuznechny Lane, 5. In this house, he wrote his greatest work, *The Brothers Karamazov*, a novel which was the conclusion of Dostoevsky's literary life. It was the product of extensive thinking on various issues. Numerous ideas, characters and episodes of the novel were built upon previous works or appeared in his literary imagination long before its completion. Dolinin names this book a "Russian Bible," because this book contains all human weaknesses, advantages and values; and all major thoughts on atheism and religion, parents and children, wealth and poverty. This book, it was considered, teaches us how to live.

Fyodor Mikhailovich until the end of his days related to the poor and sick in a very compassionate way:

> Having heard about the poverty of one widow, who remained with three children 11, 7 and 5 years of age after her husband's death, Dostoevsky out of pity hired her as a servant with all of her children . . . Fedosya with tears in her eyes shared with me, while I was still a bride, about Fyodor Mikhailovich's kindness. According to her, at nights whenever hearing a child coughing or crying, he would come to him or her and cover with a blanket, calm him orher down, or at least wake their mother up.[62]

Experiencing financial difficulties, he still provided monthly support to his brother's family after Mikhail's death. Dostoevsky cared about his stepson Pavel Isaev, even when he sold parts of his stepfather's library.

Dostoevsky always helped beggars: "It happened once," his wife said, "when my husband did not have enough money with him and some beggars stayed near our house, that he invited them to come in and there he gave them alms."[63]

61. Dostoevskaya, 196.
62. Dostoevskaya, 78.
63. Dostoevskaya, 220.

He tried not to render evil for evil but forgave his offenders. In 1879, a drunken peasant knocked Dostoevsky down on the street and he fell bleeding. In the police station, Fyodor Mikhailovich asked the officer to set his offender free, because he forgave him. However, this case had already been sent for the court's investigation sessions. Dostoevsky addressed the judge asking him not to subject his offender to punishment, since he had forgiven him. The judge considered Dostoevsky's request, yet still fined the peasant for public misconduct sixteen rubles or four days of arrest. Dostoevsky waited for his offender and gave him sixteen rubles to pay the fine.[64]

Defending Dostoevsky from the slander of N. N. Strahov, his wife claimed that Fyodor Mikhailovich was a man of unlimited kindness. He expressed it not only towards people he was close to, but to all he had sympathized with, because of their unhappiness, failure or troubles. There was no need to ask him, he always helped first.

> Having influential friends, my husband used their influence in order to help others. He placed many old people in elderly homes, children to orphanages and helped losers to find their place in society. He had to read and correct many other writings, listen to honest confessions and offer advice on very personal issues. He did not regret about his time or his strength, trying to help his neighbour. He helped financially; in cases when he lacked funds, he would sign bills and had to later pay them off. Sometimes, Fyodor Mikhailovich's kindness contradicted family interests, and often I would get upset about his unlimited kindness, yet I could not help but delight seeing him rejoice whenever having opportunity to help others.[65]

Dostoevsky sympathized with children especially, whenever hearing about their oppression.[66] Dostoevsky cared about his children's future. After completion of *The Brothers Karamazov*, he wanted to buy a property. Fyodor Mikhailovich wrote: "Here, I dream about a comfortable future and buying a

---

64. Dostoevskaya, 354.
65. Dostoevskaya, 421.
66. *Dnevnik Pisatelya*, 1877, 182–187.

property. Would you believe it, I am almost obsessed with this idea. I worry about my children and their future."[67]

In the spring of 1878, when Dostoyevsky started to work on his novel *The Brothers Karamazov*, his beloved son, Alyosha, whom he loved greatly, suddenly died. His father's grief knew no bounds. To find some solace, Dostoevsky, on the advice of Anna, drove to the Optina desert monastery, which he had planned to visit before. On this trip Dostoevsky was accompanied by his young friend, V. S. Soloviev, a former regular visitor at the Dostoevsky's house. Shortly before the sad event, the same spring, during Lent, Soloviev had given lectures on God and manhood and Dostoevsky was his constant listener. Dostoevsky and Soloviev spent two days in Optina. During their visit, the famous starets (elder) Ambrose was still alive, who became famous among the people for his gifts of understanding providence and of miracles. Dostoevsky saw him three times: once in the crowd, with others, and twice alone. Conversations with Starets Ambrose made a deep, spiritual impression on Dostoevsky.[68]

Anna Grigorievna recalled in her memoirs,

> When Fyodor Mikhailovich told the starets about the misfortune that had happened to him and about my excessive expression or mourning, the old man asked him whether I was a believer or not, and when Fyodor Mikhailovich replied affirmatively, asked him to give me his blessing, and the words which later in the novel, Starets Zosima would say to the saddened mother. From the stories of Dostoevsky, one could clearly see how much a foreseer of hearts and the future was respected by all starets.[69]

By the end of his life, Dostoevsky became a spiritual leader for many people. Daily, he received letters from all over Russia, and welcomed visitors who sought his advice, edification or instructions. This kind of activity was similar to the public ministry of an "elder" in a monastery, just like elder Ambrose, whom he met in the Optina desert or Father Zosima he created in *The Brothers Karamazov*.[70]

---

67. *Pis'ma*, Vol. 30, 16 August 1879, 113.
68. Dostoevskaya, *Vospominaniya*, 233.
69. Dostoevskaya, 233.
70. Losskiy, *Bog i mirovoe zlo*, 19.

Dostoevsky tried to find time for everyone and a right word. This was what he wrote to a student of higher women's courses,

> Your letter is warm and sincere; you indeed are really suffering and cannot help but suffer. But why should you be discouraged? You're not the only one who lost faith, but then you saved yourself. You had your faith in Christ destroyed, you write. But how can you not ask yourself first and foremost the question: who are these people who reject Christ as Savior? That is not what I'm saying, that they are good or bad, but do they know Christ themselves, in essence? Believe me, no – because, having learned at least a little, you see an unusual, but not simple, being similar to all the good and the best people . . . I know a lot of deniers, who came with all of their being to Christ at the end. But these aspired for truth not falsely, and he who is looking, at the end will find.[71]

And in another letter, to a lady who complained of her dualism, he wrote,

> Why do you write about your duality? Is it not the most common trait among people . . . not quite, however, ordinary . . . Would you mind not being so developed, would it be limited, you would be less conscientious, and would not have this duality. On the contrary, you would be a subject of great self-conceit. Still, this duality is a great torture. My dear, respected, do you believe in Christ and in His promises? If you believe, than you need to completely surrender yourself to Him, and the suffering from this duality will be strongly softened and you will get the outcome of the soul, which is the main thing.[72]

Dostoevsky's dreams and thoughts about universal happiness that he was fond of all his life reached their brightest expressions during his speech about Pushkin, on 8 June 1880, six months prior to his death. At the end of his speech, he confidently spoke:

---

71. *Pis'ma,* Vol. 30, 15 January, 1880, 340.

72. *Pis'ma,* Vol. 30, 11 April, 1880, 342.

A future Russian generation will realize that to become a truly Russian person means to contribute to the final reconciliation of European contradictions, to indicate a solution to the European issue in one's own Russian humanistic and unifying soul, welcome all our brothers with brotherly love and lastly announce a final agreement of all nations according to the gospel law of Christ.[73]

It is the mission of the Russian nation to implement "The Russian idea," which he defined, on the most abstract level, as a universal panhuman unification. He fervently believed that the matchless qualities of the Russian people gave them the capacity to deliver other people from evil and lead the world to a kind of harmony and unity.

By the end of 1879, doctors examined Dostoevsky and noticed that his lung disease was progressing rapidly. He was advised to avoid physical activities and emotional stress. On 26 January 1881 Dostoevsky worked at night and accidentally dropped a pen. Trying to pick it up, he moved a heavy bookshelf. This physical activity caused throat bleeding and led to a sharp intensification of the disease. Bleeding would occasionally stop only to start all over again. Dostoevsky spent his last days in a very peaceful way, as a true Christian, thinking about God. A. Dostoevskaya remembered his words:

Anna, please immediately invite a priest, I want to confess my sins and receive communion! Fyodor Mikhailovich warmly welcomed a priest, confessed his sins and received communion. When the priest was gone, along with the children I entered his office with the acceptance of holy mysteries to congratulate him. He blessed the children and me, asking us to live in peace and love and care for one another. When the children left the office, he thanked me for the happiness I have given him, and asked me to forgive him of any wrongdoing from his side.[74]

In the morning of 28 January, Dostoevsky said to his wife: "I will die today," and asked her to give him the New Testament, presented by the wives of Decembrists in Tobolsk, which he had retained in exile and afterwards.

---

73. *Dnevnik Pisatelya*, 1880, 148.

74. Dostoevskaya, *Vospominaniya*, 394.

A. Dostoevskaya remembered that Fyodor Mikhailovich opened the New Testament and asked her to read it. It was the Gospel of Matthew, chapter 3, verse 14: "But John tried to prevent him saying: 'I have a need to be baptized by You, and do You come to me?' But Jesus answering said to him: 'Let it be so; for in this way it is fitting for us to fulfill all righteousness.'" Dostoevsky looked at his wife and said: "Did you hear it, 'let it be so,' which means I will die."[75] That very day, at 8:38 p.m. Dostoevsky passed away. Thousands of people came to say a last "good-bye" to the great writer. At the funeral, young people tried to bring shackles to Dostoevsky's grave, as a sign that he had suffered for his political beliefs.

Thus, during the last period of his life Dostoevsky tried to follow Christ's image in sacrificial help to people in need. This happened as he became mature in his faith. He related to the poor and sick in a very compassionate way. He overcame many of the passions that tormented him and became somewhat spiritually enlightened, calmer, and softer. Religious issues presented to him an even greater interest than before. He returned from Siberia with a predetermined decision to speak directly on stirring religious themes, ignoring the fear of being misunderstood. In contrast to his outspoken spirit for social injustices, Dostoevsky was a gentle father. He sympathized with children, especially when hearing about their oppression. He became a spiritual leader for many people and had a dream for universal happiness.

4.3 Theological Motifs in *The Brothers Karamazov*

This chapter has much in common with the previous two chapters in terms of theological motifs, but uses *The Brothers Karamazov* as the primary source, for two reasons. First, because it was written in Dostoevsky's post-Siberian period and, second, because of the unanimous opinion among scholars that it is the synthesis of Dostoevsky's literary activity.[76] *The Brothers Karamazov* is his last known work. It was first published in parts in the journal "Russian Herald" *(Russky Vestnik)* in 1879–1880. The story is narrated by a witness,

---

75. Dostoevskaya, 228.

76. Grossman, *Dostoevskiy*, 558, and A. P. Vlaskin, *Ideologicheskiy kontekst v romane F. M. Dostoevskogo* [Ideological Context in Dostoevsky's Novel], (Chelyabinsk: "Chelyabinskiy rabochiy", 1987), 5.

telling the story of the Karamazov family,[77] with Alexei Karamazov as the main character.[78]

After penal servitude, Dostoevsky decided to serve the country as a writer and publicist through literary works and nonfiction articles.[79] He was already near the end of his creative path.[80] He had endured much since the "regeneration of his convictions." As noted in Part I of Chapter 4, Dostoevsky's life was full of suffering yet in spite of everything, he wanted to question the meaning of human life, sharing with others all he could discover about humanity through his works.

In his first novel, *The Poor Folk*, Dostoevsky demonstrated how the human being is corrupt, and how even the good in us is permeated with evil. In *The House of the Dead*, he went on to show how even the most hardened criminals have the capacity for goodness, and then in his last work, *The Brothers Karamazov*, he proclaimed the secret of man's happiness. This secret lies in resolving the issue of faith in God and in following the example of Christ's life.

The Brothers Karamazov can be divided roughly into several parts, according to the major theological themes. As in his other works, Dostoevsky reiterated the theme of corruption of human nature, yet maintained that people are capable of doing good: they love, they display compassion. But in corrupted humanity, goodness is manifested only from time to time.

Achieving happiness calls for a willingness to do good all the time; this is only possible by believing in God and immortality, when the life of Christ will be an example to follow. But the path from disbelief to accepting faith is difficult. It is full of doubts. The main theme is acceptance or not of a world created by God.

4.3.1 The Sinfulness of Man

Evil manifested itself differently in the characters of the novel. The picture of evil in the novel consisted of theological motifs, such as: ***covetousness, indifference, pride, vengeance, controversy and inhumanity.*** As in *The Poor People* and *The House of the Dead*, Dostoevsky shows, in detail, the evil in

---

77. *Brat'ya Karamazovy*, 15.

78. *Brat'ya Karamazovy*, 5.

79. Losskiy, *Bog i mirovoe zlo*, 19.

80. Volzhskiy, *Fyodoer Michailovich Dostoevsky. Zhizni i Propoved*, 31.

each man as a result of the Fall. ***Covetousness*** as a theological motif occurs several times in the actions of the characters. To begin with, covetousness appears as a desire for gain and a passion for acquisition. The author does this by having all the characters hide their intentions by resorting to lies.[81] One such example is the marriage of Fyodor Pavlovich Karamazov to Adelaida Ivanovna Miusovna. They each had their own interests. Adelaida Ivanovna agreed to marry Fyodor Pavlovich Karamazov and to run away from home.[82] Fyodor Pavlovich Karamazov invented a cunning plan of marrying Adelaida Ivanovna from the "rich and noble family of nobles – Miusovy" – to acquire her property. Not only did he want to acquire her property but there was no mutual love whatsoever. He was "eager to arrange his career." Fyodor Pavlovich wanted to "cling" to a good family to take the entire dowry. Therefore, as soon as Adelaida Ivanovna got a dowry from her parents, Fyodor Pavlovich took away all her money, up to 25,000 rubles, and no one else saw the money ever again. Even the village and a house in the city, which she received as dowry, he "tried his very best" to re-register in his name.[83] The attitude of mercenary is a consequence of disbelief, while true Christianity advocates sacrifice for the sake of others.[84]

Another example is when his eldest son, Mitya, came to receive his inheritance left by his mother and he gave him only a small amount of money, sending money in small amounts to prevent his son knowing exactly how much he had received and then claiming that he had sent his son even more than his due and that Mitya was indebted to him. Thus, because of greed, Fyodor Pavlovich resorted to hypocrisy and deception.[85] Conceit gives birth to struggle, even among those most closely tied together.[86]

---

81. Lauth, *Filosofiya Dostoevskogo v sistematicheskom izlozhenii*, 280.

82. *Brat'ya Karamazovy*, 8.

83. *Brat'ya Karamazovy*, 8.

84. Kudryavtsev, *Tri Kruga Dostoevskogo*, 270.

85. *Brat'ya Karamazovy*, 11.

86. Lauth, *Filosofiya Dostoevskogo v sistematicheskom izlozhenii*, 280. Another example showed the same greed for money. This time his other sons suffered from his selfish actions. In order not to spend money on raising his sons, Fyodor Pavlovich entrusted his sons, Ivan and Alexey, to be brought up by a general's wife, a distant relative (*Brat'ya Karamazovy*, 13). Still, he had no rest, worrying that his sons may ask for the inheritance that was due to them. The author said that Fyodor Pavlovich "was afraid about it his whole life" (*Brat'ya Karamazovy*, 15).

Covetousness in the life of Fyodor Pavlovich was a manifestation of selfishness and egotism.[87] That allowed him to be insensitive to the needs of loved ones. When his son Dimitry needed money, Fyodor Pavlovich, instead of helping him, hid away three thousand rubles in order to make a bid for the sympathy of Grushenika. He put his own interests above the needs of his son, and again resorted to hypocrisy and lies. So no one would interfere in the exercise of his covetousness, he deceived his son, Ivan, and sent him to Tchermashnya, allegedly with an important task.[88]

Out of greed, Fyodor Pavlovich resorted to "generosity." After Dimitry beat him up, he did not report this to police. But he was prompted to such an "honourable" deed not by forgiveness or love for his son. He had his own interest, even in this difficult situation. Fyodor Pavlovich followed the advice of Ivan and used this incident to get the sympathy of Grushenika. The logic of Ivan, who was an egotist, was simple. He advised that if Fyodor Pavlovich reported it to the police, then Grushenika would have compassion on Dimitry, but if not, then she would have sympathy for him. Fyodor Pavlovitch liked the advice of Ivan.[89]

Ivan Fyodorovich was also a selfish person. Even Fyodor Pavlovich understood Ivan's plans, which were essentially selfish:

> That's something that Ivan is afraid of and he is guarding me
> to make sure that I will not get married, and for that he pushes
> Mitika, so that he would marry Grushka: in this way he both
> wants to save me from Grushka (as if I would give him money,
> if I'll marry Grushka!), on the other hand, if Mitka marries
> Grushka, then Ivan will get a rich bride, that's his plan! Your
> Ivan is a real rascal![90]

The other character in the novel, Rakitin, did everything out of covetousness. He persuaded Alyosha to go to Grushenika to get the twenty-five rubles promised by Grushenika and the champagne. He too wanted to see

---

87. Richard Curle, *Characters of Dostoevsky* (New York: Russell & Russell, 1966), 190.

88. *Brat'ya Karamazovy*, 106.

89. *Brat'ya Karamazovy*, 150.

90. *Brat'ya Karamazovy*, 149.

"the downfall of the righteous," but also out of selfishness.[91] Rakitin wanted to marry Madame Khokhlakova to buy himself a "house made of stone in St. Petersburg."[92]

Grushenika's Polish fiancé along with his Polish friend fraudulently won two hundred rubles from Dimitry in a card game. Out of greed and driven by lies, they substituted the cards,[93] once again illustrating how conceit can lead a woman or a man to indifference even towards people who are the closest to them.

Indifference, because of the Fall arising out of selfishness, also serves as a theological motif in the novel. Fyodor Pavlovich, after the death of his first wife, treated his three-year-old son Dimitry with indifference. He even forgot about his existence.[94] The author said that when Peter Miusov told him that he took Mitya to be with him, Fyodor Pavlovich, "for some time did not understand what child was discussed, and even seemed surprised that he had a small child somewhere in the house."[95] When his second wife Sofya Ivanovna died, Fyodor Pavlovich reacted in the same indifferent way to his sons Ivan and Alyosha.[96] Out of indifference, Fyodor Pavlovich had never gone to the grave of his ex-wife Sophia Ivanovna, and was not even able to point out the grave where she was buried to Alyosha.[97] The indifference of Fyodor Pavlovich had selfishness at the centre of it, as it was never directed toward himself. This signifies his excessive self-love. According to James Scanlan, the regress of Fyodor Pavlovich from his moral standards took place because of selfishness.[98]

Pride is another evil manifesting itself in the characters of the novel as a theological motif. Losskiy says that "pride is the source of countless distortions of the soul, and it invariably leads to disaster, because all individuals are of equal value before God."[99] Pride manifested itself first as overly high

---

91. *Brat'ya Karamazovy*, 299. The same opinion is shared by Dneprov (Dneprov, *Idei, Strasti, Postupki*, 209).

92. *Brat'ya Karamazovy*, 497.

93. *Brat'ya Karamazovy*, 365.

94. *Brat'ya Karamazovy*, 9.

95. *Brat'ya Karamazovy*, 10.

96. *Brat'ya Karamazovy*, 13.

97. *Brat'ya Karamazovy*, 20.

98. James P. Scanlan, *Dostoevsky the Thinker* (New York: Cornell University Press, 2002), 83.

99. Losskiy, *Bog i mirovoe zlo*, 169.

view of himself in the actions of Ivan. When he was a university student, his benefactor, Yefim Petrovitch died. It was very difficult for Ivan to study and to provide for himself, but out of pride, the author mentioned, he would not want to ask his father for help.[100] Peter Miusov also spoke of the pride of Ivan, immediately after meeting him.[101] Ivan did not want to humble himself, but out of pride chose rebellion.[102] Ivan's pride led him to hate his father. Ivan, in a conversation with Alyosha, openly recognized that he hated his father. For this reason, he did not even want to dine with him.[103]

Out of pride, Fyodor Pavlovich wanted to lift himself above others at a meeting in Starets Zosima's cell. But since he valued his own negative qualities, he proudly spoke of himself as a liar.[104]

Sometimes pride manifested itself very strangely, as strange as love. But such love pushes people away from each other.[105] So Katerina Ivanovna loved Dimitry, according to Ivan, "to continually contemplate her heroic act of loyalty and reproach him for infidelity." He concluded that her action was dictated by her pride.[106]

Often evil led to retribution and revenge rears its head as a further theological motif. Some characters chose to return evil in response to those who inflicted harm on them when the opportunity arose to do so.[107] Thus Ivan, an educated, fairly well-known man, who came to live for a time with his father who had ignored him his whole life and did not give a kopek for his life or education, surprised everyone. Revenge was not immediately obvious, but the ostentatious attitude of Ivan towards his father was visible to the naked eye.[108] Ivan concealed his intentions, and disguised himself as a peacemaker, "mediator and conciliator between the father and the elder brother Dimitry Fyodorovich, who then started a big brawl, and even filed a formal claim

---

100. *Brat'ya Karamazovy*, 14.

101. *Brat'ya Karamazovy*, 16.

102. Vlaskin, *Ideologicheskiy kontekst v romane F. M. Dostoevskogo*, 19.

103. *Brat'ya Karamazovy*, 200.

104. *Brat'ya Karamazovy*, 36.

105. Losskiy, *Bog i mirovoe zlo*, 196.

106. *Brat'ya Karamazovy*, 164.

107. Revenge is committing evil in return for inflicted evil.

108. *Brat'ya Karamazovy*, 16.

against his father."[109] Alyosha was suspicious "that Ivan is busy with something, something inner and important, that he follows some purpose, which can be very difficult to attain."[110] Vengeance was also reflected in the hidden joy, when the "enemy" suffered or was humiliated in the eyes of others. When in the starets' cell, Fyodor Pavlovich acted as a jester, and Ivan, who could have stopped him, "was now sitting absolutely motionless in his chair, lowering his eyes and, apparently, with some inquisitive curiosity expected, what is all of this going to end with?" In this way he took revenge on his father.[111]

If Dimitry openly expressed his hatred for his father, through his words and actions, then Ivan hid it all. He coldly calculated his moves. He hid his hatred from his father and Dimitry, though words of anger and hatred burst out of him before Alyosha. Moreover, from these words one could see that he would be glad if Dimitry were to kill their father. This way he would get revenge on his father and get rid of the competition for Katerina. Even Fyodor Pavlovich saw more of a threat in him than in Dimitry.[112]

Dimitry also saved his resentment toward his father and waited for the right moment to avenge himself. In his confession to Alyosha, Dimitry said that he had something somewhere in his heart the crime was ready. He admitted that he "is in full control" whether or not to stop the conceived crime. Although Dimitry understood that what he conceived was evil, he intended to carry out his plan. Therefore, he asked Alyosha not to pray for him, because he was a scoundrel.[113]

Revenge, like greed, motivated people to act with hypocrisy, to look "virtuous" on the outside. Grushenika recognized that she did not lead a lecherous life not out of her virtue, but so that when she would meet her offender, she would to be able to tell a scoundrel everything that she had in her heart. She did this even though for her these were five years of torture.[114] But all these five years people thought of her as of an honest woman.

Even children suffered vengeance in the novel. So Ilyiusha out of a desire to protect the good name of his father longed for the moment when he would

---

109. *Brat'ya Karamazovy*, 16.

110. *Brat'ya Karamazovy*, 28.

111. *Brat'ya Karamazovy*, 38.

112. *Brat'ya Karamazovy*, 124.

113. *Brat'ya Karamazovy*, 136.

114. *Brat'ya Karamazovy*, 365.

be able to get revenge on his father's offender. He not only did not want to forgive Dimitry for the open humiliation of his father, but also strictly asked his father not to forgive the offender under any circumstances. Moreover, he himself, despite being a child, built a plan for revenge. He was ready to go to any lengths just to repay in full his father's offender. Built-up anger in him was reflected in his aggressive relations with other children. This anger and revenge affected him. He himself suffered from this, so he behaved reservedly, cried and dreamed of revenge.[115]

Revenge might be a manifestation of an offence that a man kept from his childhood and throughout life. Smerdyakov, in his candid conversation with Maria Kondratievna, expressed words that indicate the internal grievance concealed from his childhood about his birth from Smerdyashaya. His resentment grew into hatred. He was even willing to commit a crime:

> I would be able to do so much more, I would know even much
> more, if it would not be my lot from the time of my childhood.
> I would kill in a duel with a pistol that person, who would say
> to me that I am a scoundrel, because I did not have a father and
> came from Smerdyashaya, and in Moscow they poked this in my
> face, from there due to Grigory Vasilevich it spread further . . .
> I hate all of Russia . . .[116]

Revenge, if carried out, took the form of a carefully planned crime. Smerdyakov in conversation with Ivan openly said that something terrible would happen and pointed to the death of Fyodor Pavlovich. He revealed his plan and all the benefits that Ivan himself would receive from the death of their father. Despite some objections from Ivan, one feels more a kind of a passive acceptance of what was proposed.[117] Smerdyakov began to implement his plan. He purposely fell down the stairs in the cellar, and said to Fyodor Pavlovich, that certainly Grushenika would come to him, and that he would open the door, once he heard a knock.[118] In this situation Ivan and

---

115. *Brat'ya Karamazovy*, 178–182.

116. *Brat'ya Karamazovy*, 193.

117. *Brat'ya Karamazovy*, 234–235.

118. *Brat'ya Karamazovy*, 242.

Smerdyakov agree on the statement "if there is no God, then all things are permissible."[119] Thus Ivan's idea "helped" Smerdyakov to become a murderer.[120]

Out of vengeance, another character of the novel, Katerina Ivanovna, bore false witness in the court against Dimitry.[121] Hatred without forgiveness creates in man a sense of revenge. Thus Dimitry, being in a desperate condition, hoped for a miracle of God that Alyosha would be able to persuade his father to give him three thousand rubles so he could return them to Katerina. In Dimitry a constant hatred toward his father was ever present and he was afraid that this hatred could lead him to committing a crime. He confessed this to Alyosha.[122]

For Dostoevsky evil was the acts of men, in which good and evil were intermingled. He was able to convey this picture very well in his first novel *The Poor Folk*, where even the good was impregnated by evil.[123] The problem of inconsistency and the duality of man are shown in this novel. Dostoevsky's characters could do completely contradictory things.

The contradiction could be seen in the life of Fyodor Pavlovich. Being in Starets Zosima's cell, Fyodor Pavlovich made certain hypocritical gestures and at the same time quoted Scripture. The author said that at some point Fyodor Pavlovich fell down on his knees and said, referring to the starets, "Teacher, what must I do to inherit eternal life?"[124] It was more likely formal rather than true piety. The behaviour of Fyodor Pavlovich in the starets' cell was contrary to all customs. The author told of former visitors to the cells and their behaviour:

> In this same cell, for maybe forty or even fifty years, even in times of former starets, visitors would gather, but always with the deepest reverence. Almost everyone entering the cell understood that they were being shown a great mercy. Many plunged to their knees and did not rise during the entire visit. Many of the "high status" persons and the most learned, some of the free-thinking,

---

119. Vlaskin, *Ideologicheskiy kontekst v romane F. M. Dostoevskogo*, 64.

120. Vlaskin, 65.

121. *Brat'ya Karamazovy*, 584.

122. *Brat'ya Karamazovy*, 106.

123. *Bednye Lyudy*, 87.

124. *Brat'ya Karamazovy*, 39.

even those who came out of curiosity, or for any other reason, entering the cell with others or getting a private audience, chose as their foremost duty to act in deepest respect and sensitivity in the time of audience, so that much money was not used here, but only love and mercy on the one hand, and on the other repentance and desire to resolve some difficult questions of the soul, or a difficult moment in the life of one's own heart.[125]

The author thus showed that the buffoonery of Fyodor Pavlovich was beyond the scope of appropriate behaviour in the cell. The behaviour of Fyodor Pavlovich was unusual when being a cold-blooded, proud, self-serving, selfish man he learned of the death of his first wife Adelaida Ivanovna. Suddenly, he burst into tears like a little child. The author said that "in most cases people, even the villains are much more naive and simple-hearted than we think about them being."[126] Fyodor Pavlovich liked to be hypocritical almost all the time, to play some role. The author affirmed that "this trait is common to very many people, even the very smart ones."[127]

Dimitry was a peculiar character; he had a constant internal struggle. He loved Grushenika and wanted to start a new life with her. But in the beginning, Dimitry considered it necessary to repay Ekaterina Ivanovna without fail. Since he had no money, he was even ready to commit a crime to do this. He said,

> ... it is better to even kill and rob someone, but to return the debt to Katya. I would rather appear a murderer and a thief that robbed and murdered a person, and be sent to Siberia in front of all the people, than if Kate would be able to rightfully say that I cheated on her and stole her money and using her money ran away to start a virtuous life with Grushenika! This I cannot let happen![128]

With this it seemed he himself decided who deserved a good, honest attitude, and who was worthy of punishment. Step by step, Dimitry came close

---

125. *Brat'ya Karamazovy*, 37.

126. *Brat'ya Karamazovy*, 9.

127. *Brat'ya Karamazovy*, 10.

128. *Brat'ya Karamazovy*, 311.

to the execution of his evil plan. So, not finding Grushenika home, running out of the house in despair, Dimitry grabbed a knife from the table. He saw his father as guilty in everything, although he had no clear plan to kill him, yet he wanted him to die.[129] Dimitry was willing to use violence not only in regard to his father, but also to anyone who interfered with the implementation of his plan. So he stabbed Grigory, who tried to stop him. He choked Fenya until she told him where Grushenika had gone.[130] But twenty minutes later, Dimitry regretted the fact that he shed blood.[131] Both composure and self-pity were present at the same time in the actions of Dimitry.

This contradiction in Dimitry was especially noticeable as soon as he got the money. Instead of repaying the debt for which he was ready to commit a crime, he began to spend money on champagne just to impress Grushenika.[132] Dimitry saw this kind of contradiction in himself: "I love life, I adore life too much, too much that I became to a point of detestation . . . Why then am I pleased with myself? I mean I am a scoundrel, but am pleased with myself."[133] He was tormented by this contradiction in himself. Loving life, at one point, on the road to Mokroe, Dimitry wanted to stop and shoot himself to put an end to it.[134] Dimitry's prayer was a recognition of his contradiction:

> Lord, take me in all my iniquity, but do not judge me. Skip me past Thy trials . . . Do not judge, because I am condemning myself, do not judge because I love Thee, O Lord! Disgusting I am, but I love Thee: be Thou wilt send me hell, there I shall love Thee and from below I shall scream, I love Thee forever and ever . . . but let me love Thee here . . . and here to love, just five hours before Thy hot rays . . . For I love foremost. I will come swiftly, will fall down before her, you're right, that you went past me . . . Farewell and forget your sacrifice, do not disturb yourself ever![135]

---

129. *Brat'ya Karamazovy*, 331.
130. *Brat'ya Karamazovy*, 334.
131. *Brat'ya Karamazovy*, 336.
132. *Brat'ya Karamazovy*, 334.
133. *Brat'ya Karamazovy*, 334.
134. *Brat'ya Karamazovy*, 348.
135. *Brat'ya Karamazovy*, 350.

Hatred and peacefulness over the same occasion were manifested in Dimitry. To win in the competition with his father for the heart of Grushenika, Dimitry was ready to do anything. He hated his father also because of this rivalry. But, strangely, when the officer appeared on the horizon – the first love of Grushenika, and thus also his rival – Dimitry was calm, he did not feel any jealousy, any hatred.[136]

Dimitry, according to his explanation, was a scoundrel with calculations in view. He purposefully did not spend all the money taken from Katerina; he had some to send to Moscow so he could at least return some portion. In this case, according to him, he was a scoundrel, but not a thief. If he spent the entire amount at once, he would have been a scoundrel and a thief, or more precisely an extreme scoundrel.[137] He was so tormented by the money, taken and not returned, that Dimitry acknowledged that it was not only hard for him to live, but also he could not die a scoundrel. This was the greatest reason why he had not committed suicide.[138]

The essence of the internal contradiction of Dimitry was on the one hand the love for God, and on the other hand the following of "the demon."[139] With ease he returned 4,500 rubles to Katerina Ivanovna in order to save his father and at another time just as easily used three thousand rubles given by Katerina to send them to Agafiya Ivanovna in Moscow. He spent them with Grushenika simply because "he could not resist, being like an animal."[140] Dimitry described this internal contradiction as follows:

> I cannot bear, moreover, that sometimes even the person with a lofty heart and mind begins with the ideal of the Madonna and ends with the ideal of Sodom. Even more frightening is the one who already, with the ideal of Sodom in his soul, does not deny the ideal of the Madonna, and his heart burns away, as in his teenage years. No, man is broad, even too wide, I would have him narrowed. The devil knows what, what's all that! What

---

136. *Brat'ya Karamazovy*, 347.

137. *Brat'ya Karamazovy*, 416.

138. *Brat'ya Karamazovy*, 418.

139. *Brat'ya Karamazovy*, 93. "Individuals, who have acted contrary to the law of love, know that what they have done is wrong and repent having done it" (Scanlan, *Dostoevsky the Thinker*, 92).

140. *Brat'ya Karamazovy*, 104.

appears to the mind a shame, to the heart is a complete beauty. Is there beauty in Sodom? Believe, that in Sodom it is for the vast majority of people – did you know this secret, or not? The fearful thing is that the beauty is not only fearsome, but also a mysterious thing. Here the devil is fighting with God, and the battlefield is the hearts of men.[141]

Alyosha took note of the inconsistency in Grushenika as well. On the one hand she had her baby eyes shining, on the other hand her unnatural conversation was full of evil.[142] She said one thing, and afterwards abandoned her promises. That is how she behaved in a conversation with Katerina Ivanovna, when Grushenika twice waived her words, humiliating her.[143]

Another story is told of a contradiction in Grushenika. In her were present conflicting desires to fool around and to pray to God. So she, being in Mokroe, admitted those desires to fool around. At the same time, Grushenika wanted to pray to God and ask for forgiveness.[144] She noted this contradiction, not only in herself, but also in Dimitry.[145] She understood that in Dimitry lived both brutality and nobility. They suffered themselves from this duality of nature. Therefore, Grushenika wanted to radically change her life and Dimitry's. She wanted Dimitry to take her far away, there where they would be honest and kind. She even saw this in her night dreams. Dimitry shared the desire of Grushenika.[146]

At the same time both ***love and selfishness*** were manifested in man. Selfishness is the natural display of man's sinfulness.[147] Kolya Krasotkin, a teenager of fourteen years, was too controversial. He was very ambitious, but also very fond of his mother.[148] He found the strength to forgive Ilyusha for the fact that he stabbed him with a knife.[149]

---

141. *Brat'ya Karamazovy*, 94.

142. *Brat'ya Karamazovy*, 130.

143. *Brat'ya Karamazovy*, 132–133.

144. *Brat'ya Karamazovy*, 373.

145. Dneprov, *Idei, Strasti, Postupki*, 215.

146. *Brat'ya Karamazovy*, 374.

147. Losskiy, *Bog i mirovoe zlo*, 101.

148. *Brat'ya Karamazovy*, 434.

149. *Brat'ya Karamazovy*, 436.

Katerina Ivanovna was yet another controversial personality.[150] She cared about Ilyusha when he was ill and spent her money on doctors. She resorted to lies and gave bribes to the doctor so that he would prove that Dimitry had committed a crime of passion, and thus save him from punishment.[151] But then in the court Katerina Ivanovna, getting revenge on Dimitry, testified against him very calmly, prudently. Her testimony played the major role in the jury's decision.[152] She continued to be led by concealed pride.[153]

Contradiction in actions comes from a misunderstanding of good and evil. This in turn derives from the fact that a person has no absolute authority. When there is no absolute authority, the authority could become the view of anyone. So Dostoevsky showed in the example of Lisa how she, not having absolute authority, took evil for good. Lisa craved sin, lewdness, evil in general. She admitted that she loved those who commit crime. But Alyosha told her directly that her problem was reading bad books that had distorted her understanding of what good is. These appalling books became an authority for her. Evil penetrated into her to such a degree that even in her dreams Lisa saw demons trying to grab her and only by crossing herself was she able to drive them away.[154] In one of the books read by Lisa the story was told of a brutal murder and of the indifference of the killer. What was interesting was that Lisa sometimes wanted to take the place of the murderer. Ivan also negatively affected her. He approved of her idea of murder. But according to Alyosha, Ivan was sick, so that was why he believed so. His disease was the lack of faith.[155] The European books and the teaching of Ivan led Lisa to crime, to misfortune.[156]

Evil unstopped then takes the form of inhumanity. **Inhumanity** appeared as a theological motif of the characters' behaviour and at the same time as a consequence of unbelief.

The inhumanity of Fyodor Pavlovich followed from his belief in complete domination over others. He regarded himself as the master of his second

---

150. Curle, *Characters of Dostoevsky*, 217.

151. *Brat'ya Karamazovy*, 486.

152. *Brat'ya Karamazovy*, 584.

153. Vlaskin, *Ideologicheskiy kontekst v romane F. M. Dostoevskogo*, 18.

154. *Brat'ya Karamazovy*, 491.

155. *Brat'ya Karamazovy*, 493.

156. Vlaskin, *Ideologicheskiy kontekst v romane F. M. Dostoevskogo*, 14.

wife Sophia Ivanovna, who was a poor, unhappy sixteen-year-old orphan. He deprived her of the most elementary rights. He humiliated her in the most perverse ways. The author told us that "in his house, in the presence of his wife, Fyodor Pavlovich would gather lewd women, and held orgies."[157] Fyodor Pavlovich had no limit in his debauchery. Dostoevsky told us that over time, "he started to love not only doing ugly sexual things with women but progressed to even more disgusting forms."[158] Nor did he stop at this. Fyodor Pavlovich abused poor, mute, homeless Lizaveta Smerdyashaya. This woman, according to the author, was quiet, not greedy; all that she received from others she gave to people passing by. She was the direct opposite of Fyodor Pavlovich, but he, out of his impudence, abused her and left her pregnant to die in labour,[159] literally killed with cruelty.[160]

Ivan recognized that each person is inclined to evil. Inherent evil in man is called "*karamazovschina.*"[161] In his conversation with Alyosha, he said, "In every man, of course, hides a beast, the beast of anger, the beast of voluptuous loss of control over the screams of the tormented victim, the beast without restraints, unchained, the beast acquired in the depravity of diseases, gout, liver malfunctions, and so on."[162]

4.3.2 The Image of God in Every Person

As in *The House of the Dead*, Dostoevsky also found in every person the capacity for good. In this novel he showed that no matter how angry the person might be, the image of Christ is still there. Father Passiy was convinced that even "rebels who renounced Christianity and are in rebellion against Him in their being are of the same image of Christ's essence."[163] Lossky affirms that in Dostoevsky's works, the image of God in man can never be destroyed by sin, even at the lowest degree on his downfall.[164]

---

157. *Brat'ya Karamazovy*, 12.

158. *Brat'ya Karamazovy*, 20.

159. *Brat'ya Karamazovy*, 85–87.

160. Vlaskin, *Ideologicheskiy kontekst v romane F. M. Dostoevskogo*, 13.

161. Vlaskin, 8.

162. *Brat'ya Karamazovy*, 208. Curle considers that the tragedy of Ivan lies in the dualism of his nature (Curle, *Characters of Dostoevsky*, 198).

163. *Brat'ya Karamazovy*, 147.

164. Losskiy, *Bog i mirovoe zlo*, 121.

Dostoevsky's characters were able to love, to show care and compassion. Theological motifs of **love, compassion and care** are the expression of people's goodness.

Everyone likes it when someone loves them or cares about them. Even regarding the worst people, good makes its own impact. Fyodor Pavlovich was a man full of evil, but when someone truly loved and cared about him, he simply shuddered. Thus, the relationship of Grigory to Fyodor Pavlovich produced in his soul a certain kind of "spiritual fear and moral shaking." A display of humility can be seen in the service of Grigory.[165] Fyodor Pavlovich wanted to have next to him a person like Grigory, who would have the following characteristics:

> So that besides, nearby perhaps though not in the room, would be such a man – faithful, firm, absolutely not like him, not corrupt, who even seeing all the debauchery and knowing all the secrets, but still out of loyalty would overlook it all, not resist, and most importantly, not blame and not threaten him with anything, and in case of need, would defend him.[166]

The same feelings arose in Fyodor Pavlovich upon the arrival of Alyosha. The author spoke about the impact of the father of Alyosha in the following way: "Alyosha pierced his heart with the fact that he lived, saw it all and yet did not condemn. More so, he brought with him an unprecedented thing: a complete absence of contempt for him, the old man; on the contrary, unfailing tenderness and absolutely natural straightforward affection for him, who deserved it so little."[167]

Despite all the negative qualities of Fyodor Pavlovich and Smerdyakov, sometimes one could see in them a manifestation of good. So, it was said that Fyodor Pavlovich loved Alyosha. Also, Fyodor Pavlovich, once he learned about the illness of Smerdyakov, began to take care of him out of compassion.[168] Smerdyakov in turn manifested himself several times as an honest man. He even returned the money he found to Fyodor Pavlovich.[169]

---

165. Vlaskin, *Ideologicheskiy kontekst v romane F. M. Dostoevskogo*, 59.

166. *Brat'ya Karamazovy*, 82.

167. *Brat'ya Karamazovy*, 82.

168. *Brat'ya Karamazovy*, 108.

169. *Brat'ya Karamazovy*, 110.

Some people showed their kindness not only to their loved ones, but simply to all those who were in need.[170] In the very beginning of the novel, compassion was shown by strangers and not by close relatives. So Grigory, the servant of Fyodor Pavlovich cared first about Mitya and later about Ivan and Alyosha. In this is the revelation of his love.[171]

After that, the children were taken care of by a distant relative of Yefim Petrovich Polenov, trustee of Ivan and Alyosha. He "personally and especially liked" Alyosha, so that he cared about him as of a member of his family.[172] He was the antithesis of Fyodor Pavlovich. Of his selflessness, kindness and love, the author writes,

> And if these young men owed to anyone their upbringing and education for their entire life, then it was precisely to Yefim Petrovich, a most noble and humane man, such as are difficult to find. He kept the thousands for the babies left by the general's wife untouched, so that by the time of their adulthood the amounts with compounded interest increased to two thousand each. He brought them up using his own money, and certainly had spent much more than a thousand on each of them.[173]

Even in Dimitry we can see generosity showed to a loved person. Simply the chance to sit next to Grushenika made him content and he sacrificed the money which he needed so badly to return to Katya for the joy of spending time with her. Dostoevsky affirmed that "if any peasant man would ask him in those moments for money, he would have immediately pulled out his entire sheaf and would have started giving out to the right and to the left with no account."[174] Dimitry worried about Grushenika. Not wanting to implicate her in his problems he told his investigators and prosecutors that she was an innocent Christian soul bright as light and that out of love for him she was ready to sacrifice herself and to share his punishment.[175]

---

170. "Knowledge of the law of love is innate in human beings, a 'gift' of the Creator." That is why Dostoevsky affirmed that a person must feel the need to love his neighbour (Scanlan, *Dostoevsky the Thinker*, 88).

171. Vlaskin, *Ideologicheskiy kontekst v romane F. M. Dostoevskogo*, 59.

172. *Brat'ya Karamazovy*, 14.

173. *Brat'ya Karamazovy*, 14.

174. *Brat'ya Karamazovy*, 358.

175. *Brat'ya Karamazovy*, 393.

Love manifested itself in the family relations of spouses. Grigory Kutuzov, the servant of Fyodor Pavlovich, was a man honest and faithful, despite his position. He loved his wife, Martha.[176]

Children showed love and compassion to each other. For the love of Ilyusha, Kolya found the dog Zchuchika, for whom Ilyusha blamed himself, thinking that he killed it. The fact was that the last time, when Ilyusha saw it, he had given it bread with a pin inside. Kolya led Zhuchika to Ilyusha to please him and reassure him that the dog was all right.[177] Kolya was so fond of Ilyusha, that he taught Zchuchika different tricks to please him. He even brought a small real cannon, which Ilyusha wanted to see so much.[178]

Love even stopped some people from committing suicide. Dimitry was saved from suicide by the confidence that he loved someone else in the world:

> That's the broom, a scarf there, a shirt I have, now it is possible to twist them into a rope, and help in addition, why be a burden on the earth, and dishonour it with my presence! And now I hear you coming, Lord, it just came down on me suddenly – But there is a person whom I love, there he is, here's that man, my dear brother, whom I love more than anything in the world – the only one whom I love! And so I loved you, so much at that moment I loved, that I thought, "Now I'll throw myself in his embrace!"[179]

Special acts of kindness were shown by Alyosha Karamazov and Starets Zosima. They both just loved people, because at the heart of their love was faith in God, belief in immortality and the example of Christ's love.

Alyosha simply loved people and did so selflessly.[180] On his youthful love it was said,

> But he loved the people: it seemed that he lived all his life believing in people, and yet nobody ever thought he was either a simple or naive person. There was something in him that spoke and impressed on others that he does not want to be the judge

---

176. *Brat'ya Karamazovy*, 81.

177. *Brat'ya Karamazovy*, 454.

178. *Brat'ya Karamazovy*, 460.

179. *Brat'ya Karamazovy*, 134.

180. *Brat'ya Karamazovy*, 17.

of people, that he does not want to take upon himself the right to accuse and would not condemn in any circumstances.[181]

The sincere, friendly attitude towards people that Alyosha exercised brought love even on the part of Ivan[182] and his father:

> Since childhood he had loved to go into a corner and read books, and yet, his companions loved him so much that he could absolutely be called everyone's favourite in all his time spent in school . . . Grievances he never remembered. It would be common that an hour after the insult, he would respond to the offender or would speak to him with such a clear and trustful look, as if nothing had happened between them at all. It was not that he had accidentally forgotten or intentionally forgiven an insult, but simply did not consider it an insult, and it strongly captivated and conquered the hearts of children.[183]

In turn, Alyosha was loved by all from early childhood. Lisa loved Alyosha.[184] Dimitry loved Alyosha and was ready to open up and confess in front of him.[185] He referred to Alyosha as an angel.[186] Alyosha was loved even by the colony guards, where Dimitry was detained.[187]

Alyosha's philanthropy could also be seen in his generosity. There was no selfishness in him, but on the contrary, he was one of those "be it that suddenly even huge capital would get in his hands, it would not become difficult for him to give it at first demand, or use it for a good thing, or maybe even give to a slicker, if such would ask for it."[188] Being generous himself, others also showed generosity to him. Thus, those with whom he was familiar showed care for him. Peter Miusov said about Alyosha, "That may be the only person in the world, whom you will leave alone and without money in an unfamiliar

---

181. *Brat'ya Karamazovy*, 17.

182. Dneprov, *Idei, Strasti, Postupki*, 220.

183. *Brat'ya Karamazovy*, 18.

184. *Brat'ya Karamazovy*, 159.

185. Dneprov, *Idei, Strasti, Postupki*, 225. In this way, in *Crime and Punishment*, Sonya turned out to be the only person to whom Rasskolnikov felt confident to share the fearful mystery of murder (Dneprov, 227).

186. *Brat'ya Karamazovy*, 92.

187. *Brat'ya Karamazovy*, 496.

188. *Brat'ya Karamazovy*, 19.

area of the city with one million inhabitants, who would never die of hunger and cold, because he would be instantly fed, immediately arranged."[189]

Alyosha especially loved the monastic Starets Zosima, "to whom he was bound with the first hot love of his unquenchable heart."[190]

Starets Zosima loved all people, even the most sinful of them. Out of love for Alyosha, he allowed him to live in his own cell. Even though the starets himself was ill, he was living with the needs and problems of people. Out of love for the people, the starets prayed for the healing of the sick. He accepted people with their problems, and they came out after a conversation with him full of joy and happiness.[191]

A sense of contentment and gratitude could be seen in the attitudes and actions of Starets Zosima. The author, describing Starets Zosima's cell, emphasized that "objects and furniture were rough, cheap, and only the most necessary."[192] Zosima did not claim credit for the miracles he performed. When a monk was visiting Zosima he was surprised to see the healing of Lisa and he praised Starets Zosima. To this praise he modestly replied that God healed her.[193]

The sincere feeling of Starets Zosima for the other servants of the monastery can be seen in his blessings for them at each of their meetings. The author noted that this ceremony was performed with them with a deep sense, not as a mere ritual.[194] The starets, out of love and respect even for Fyodor Pavlovich, told him the truth about his problem: "Do not give way to drunkenness and verbal intemperance, nor indulge in lust, and especially in the adoration of money, and close your drinking houses. If you cannot close down all of them than at least two or three. And most importantly, most importantly do not lie."[195] Next, the starets showed the consequences of such a state. He argued that a man who is not respectful of anyone "ceases to love, and a man not having love indulges himself in entertainment and is given to passions and

---

189. *Brat'ya Karamazovy*, 19.

190. *Brat'ya Karamazovy*, 17.

191. *Brat'ya Karamazovy*, 26.

192. *Brat'ya Karamazovy*, 35.

193. *Brat'ya Karamazovy*, 48.

194. *Brat'ya Karamazovy*, 34.

195. *Brat'ya Karamazovy*, 39.

coarse lewdness and decays quite fast to bestiality in his vices, all of that from continual lying to others and himself."[196]

Zosima received everybody who came to him with their problems. He healed the possessed women and gave them peace of mind. Those who were grieving for the loss of loved ones, he consoled with the words of Scripture and examples from the life of the holy fathers. He also gave advice on the restoration of family relationships. The starets advised a woman who buried her three-year old son to return to her husband. He therefore wanted to help a woman regain the meaning of life. Convincing words about life after death and that her son was now among the angels and was praying for her provided consolation for the woman after her son's death.[197]

Father Zosima shared a love of active love. He gave the following definitions:

> Love in dreams desires quick action, rapid satisfaction and such that all would look at it. It is a fact that men will even give their lives, so that something will not last long, but be soon done, as if on stage, and so that all would look and praise. But active love is work and endurance, and for some it is perhaps, the real science . . . The main thing is, run away from falsehood, all lies, lies to yourself in particular. Watch your lies – be aware of them every hour, every minute. Flee from being disgustful too, whether directed at others or at yourself – what you felt inside yourself as vile, just by the fact that you noticed this, will in itself be clear. Run away from fear too, even though fear is only a consequence of all lies. Do not be afraid ever of your own cowardice in achieving love – do not be overly frightened even by your bad deeds.[198]

The idea of sacrifice for Christ's sake was not clear to everyone and not everyone shared it. So Smerdyakov did not understand the feat of a soldier who died at the hands of Muslims, refusing to renounce Christ. He believed it was necessary for the soldier to renounce Christ and save his life.[199] His belief, according to Alyosha, "was not the Russian faith." Smerdyakov believed

---

196. *Brat'ya Karamazovy*, 39.
197. *Brat'ya Karamazovy*, 41–44.
198. *Brat'ya Karamazovy*, 51.
199. *Brat'ya Karamazovy*, 111.

that if we abandon Christ, then we would be punished by God as those who never were Christians. In this he attributed blame to the parents who did not believe in Christ. Non-Christians, in his view, would not be punished severely by God. Hence, his hint that having renounced Christ one may commit any crime and feel confident that there would not be a severe punishment.[200]

Alyosha, like the starets, in a very inoffensive form indicated to his brother Dimitry his bad deeds. For example, when he spoke about the conflict that occurred between Katerina Ivanovna and Grushenika, Dimitry even laughed at this story. But Alyosha pointed out to him that the cause of the conflict was Dimitry himself. This led to Dimitry's realization of his guilt. The words, "Your brother is a scoundrel!" was Dimitry's answer.[201] In caring for Alyosha and his feelings towards his brother, Dimitry was motivated by love. Saying goodbye to his brother, Alyosha cried, knowing what awaited him.[202] Even at the time of the recognition of Ivan's hatred towards Alyosha, Alyosha loved his brother and took care of him. Seeing that Ivan was ill, Alyosha supported him, laid him on the couch and prayed for him and his brother Dimitry.[203]

Out of love for his brother Dimitry and in obedience to Starets Zosimus, Alyosha suffered humiliation in the home of Nikolai Ilyich Snigiriov, the former headquarters captain who was humiliated in front of his son by Dimitry Karamazov.[204]

Alyosha was not only ready to fulfill someone's request, be it of the starets or Katerina Ivanovna. He also pondered sometimes for hours or even over-night how to execute instructions so not to offend or humiliate anyone.[205]

As was predicted by the elder Zosima, Alyosha lived with other people's problems. When Ilyusha, who once bit his finger till it bled, was very sick, he did not leave him but was even able to collect all the boys to please Ilyusha. Alyosha spoke with the boys on equal terms for which he was also respected and loved. Even Kolya, an ambitious teenager, though socializing only a little with Alyosha, loved him. Alyosha stood up for an unknown boy of six at whom other boys were throwing stones. He also did not answer evil for

---

200. *Brat'ya Karamazovy*, 114.

201. *Brat'ya Karamazovy*, 136.

202. *Brat'ya Karamazovy*, 503.

203. *Brat'ya Karamazovy*, 553.

204. *Brat'ya Karamazovy*, 172–174.

205. *Brat'ya Karamazovy*, 186.

evil. When this same boy bit his finger and threw stones at him, instead of returning kind for kind, Alyosha searched himself for guilt, realizing that he might in some way have wronged the boy, and decided to find him and learn what was wrong.[206]

Alyosha worried about his brothers and their father. He said to Lisa, "My brothers are ruining themselves, and so is our father. And they ruin the others along with themselves."[207] Alyosha was so worried and he loved his family so much that he even wept.[208] He did not want them killing each other but they were not willing to listen to him though they loved him.

Alyosha lived with the problems and joys of other people and when Kolya finally came to Ilyusha, he communicated with him in the freezing cold dressed in light clothing. Filled with joy that Kolya came to Ilyusha who needed his forgiveness, Alyosha did not notice the cold. He humbled himself so much that he could listen for a long time, even to those who were much younger than he. Alyosha even treated Kolya's talk about the ideas of socialism seriously. He listened and without pride expressed his opinion.[209]

With this attitude he won so much respect that Kolya acknowledged that he was ready to learn from him.[210] So Alyosha became an example to follow.[211]

4.3.3 Faith in God

The happiness of man depends on a proper understanding of **belief and disbelief** in God; the two key theological motifs of the novel are these two ideas.

Disbelief in God leads to misfortune. Smerdyakov came up with an alibi in order to escape punishment for the murder of Fyodor Pavlovich and spent two days pretending that he had epileptic seizures.[212] As Smerdyakov was a man of "the lowest nature and a coward," he was able so carefully to plan and carry out the murder in cold blood.[213] He was prompted by greed and revenge, at the basis of which was his disbelief in God.

---

206. *Brat'ya Karamazovy*, 153.

207. *Brat'ya Karamazovy*, 189.

208. *Brat'ya Karamazovy*, 134.

209. *Brat'ya Karamazovy*, 462.

210. *Brat'ya Karamazovy*, 453.

211. Curle, *Characters of Dostoevsky*, 205.

212. *Brat'ya Karamazovy*, 387.

213. *Brat'ya Karamazovy*, 402.

Disbelief in God is a way to permissiveness.[214] Smerdyakov had confessed the planning and implementing of the murder of Fyodor Pavlovich to Ivan. After this confession, Ivan knew that the murder was to take place, but did nothing to stop the crime. Smerdyakov himself told of the benefits for Ivan if Fyodor were to be murdered. In this case, he would receive the third part of the inheritance, and if Dimitry committed murder, he would receive half of the inheritance.[215] Aware of his involvement in the murder of his own father, Ivan almost went crazy. He twice saw the devil appearing to him and talking about the crime, faith and disbelief in God's paradise.[216] In Ivan the strongest fight of faith and unbelief took place. In one and the same moment, a man might "view such depths of belief and unbelief" that one more step and this would be all.[217]

To destroy all, it was necessary to destroy the idea of God in man, the devil told Ivan. He said,

> From this one must begin . . . Once mankind uniformly re-nounces God, then by itself it will fall, to the former view of life, more importantly, to the old morality, and there will come new things. People will unite to take from life all that it can give, what is needed for happiness and joy in this world alone. Man will be exalted in the spirit of divine, titanic pride and the man-god will appear . . . Love will satisfy only the moments of life, but the realization of its instantaneous nature will increase the fire so much as it previously blurred in the hopes of life after death and infinite love.[218]

The same idea, shared by Dostoevsky is repeated – where there is no faith in God, everything is permitted.[219] The devil continues,

> But as God and immortality do not exist, the new man is allowed to become a man-god, may he even be the only one in the whole world, and, of course, with a new rank, with a light heart to skip

---

214. Dneprov, *Idei, Strasti, Postupki*, 245.

215. *Brat'ya Karamazovy*, 513.

216. *Brat'ya Karamazovy*, 537.

217. *Brat'ya Karamazovy*, 545.

218. *Brat'ya Karamazovy*, 548.

219. Gibson, *The Religion of Dostoevsky*, 185.

> all the old moral barriers of a former slave man, if wanted. For
> God there are no laws! . . . Everything is permitted.[220]

Grigory testified in court that Smerdyakov was an atheist, and that he had been taught "godlessness by Fyodor Pavlovich and his elder son, Ivan."[221] Ivan was an atheist. Alyosha speaks of this with confidence.[222] Even Dimitry did not understand how his brothers Ivan and Rakitin, being atheists, hoped to be virtuous without God.[223]

Without solving the question of faith, a person suffers. For Ivan, the question of belief in immortality was directly connected with love. According to him, the only thing that makes a person love another person is the belief in immortality. If you kill in a man the "belief in immortality, he will immediately run out from not only love, but also of every living force to continue life in the world."[224] From this he deduced that,

> For each individual who believes neither in God nor in his own
> immortality, the moral law of nature must change quickly to
> completely contrast with the former, religious law, and that self-
> ishness, even to the point of evil, should not only be allowed to
> man, but also to be considered necessary, the most reasonable
> and noble outcome in his state.[225]

Ivan had not decided yet about the matter of faith; that is why he was so tormented. This lack of faith was his sorrow because it required a solution.[226]

Ivan realized that for three months from the date of his meeting with Alyosha, that Alyosha had been waiting for him to share just one life story which referred to his faith in God. Therefore, at a frank meeting, Ivan affirmed that he believed in God, but did not accept God's created world.[227] However it

---

220. *Brat'ya Karamazovy*, 548.

221. *Brat'ya Karamazovy*, 561.

222. *Brat'ya Karamazovy*, 28.

223. *Brat'ya Karamazovy*, 499.

224. *Brat'ya Karamazovy*, 61.

225. *Brat'ya Karamazovy*, 61.

226. *Brat'ya Karamazovy*, 61.

227. His rejection of God's peace indicates his disbelief (Gibson, *The Religion of Dostoevsky*, 171).

seemed that he doubted the existence of God, since he repeated the thought, "if there were no God, one would have to invent Him."[228]

An unbeliever cannot understand sacrificial love. Ivan could not understand how to love one's neighbour. In his opinion, "to love a man, it is necessary that he would hide himself, and almost as soon as he shows his face, the love is gone." According to him, no one can love as Christ, because He was God, but people are not. Alyosha said that in the opinion of the starets, "the human face often prevents people more inexperienced in love from loving."[229] Smerdyakov, an unbeliever, refused to believe in creation of the universe by God, according to the book of Genesis. He did not forgive insults. Thus, the author pointed out that he would remember for a lifetime the hurtful words of Grigory, his foster father who had raised him. The author also affirmed that Smerdyakov liked no one and behaved arrogantly.[230]

Also, Dostoevsky showed the struggle of belief and disbelief in man. He was interested in moments of struggle between good and evil in man and in the reevaluation of values.[231] Dimitry, "an explosive, uneducated man, who commited lewd and brutal acts, found the courage to confess and repent, even in these actions."[232]

People who do not believe in God sometimes show signs of religion, or their actions at least testify to it. Fyodor Pavlovich, for example, was "not a religious person." One day, however, after Alyosha visited the grave of his mother, his father gave a thousand rubles for "the remembrance of the soul" of his first wife.[233] Also the surprising thing was Fyodor Pavlovich's fear of hell. Fyodor Pavlovich was afraid of punishment but did not want to live a godly life. Several times he asked Alyosha whether there were any hooks in hell by which he would be captured by demons. He must surely know the answer to this question, because in his logic, if there is no ceiling in hell, so there are no hooks, and this means that there will be no punishment. Such a response would suit him well because he could live immorally.[234]

---

228. *Brat'ya Karamazovy*, 202.

229. *Brat'ya Karamazovy*, 203.

230. *Brat'ya Karamazovy*, 108.

231. Losskiy, *Bog i mirovoe zlo*, 201.

232. *Brat'ya Karamazovy*, 65.

233. *Brat'ya Karamazovy*, 21.

234. *Brat'ya Karamazovy*, 22.

Belief in God was in the centre of the convictions of the positive characters, such as Grigory, Alyosha, and Starets Zosima. Each of them had his own thorny path passing through doubts to faith in God.

The beliefs and behaviour of Grigory were influenced by the book of Job, and also the sermons of Father Isaac the Syrian. Grigory loved people and not only humanity as a whole, but some people in particular. For example, despite the fact that his and Marfa's child died just two weeks from birth, he treated other children, such as Dimitry, Ivan and Alyosha Karamazov, with love and care. He also took care of Smerdyakov. Grigory loved his wife and was an exemplary husband. He was also well respected and obeyed his master, Fyodor Pavlovich.[235]

Ivan's assertion that he did not accept God's world, served as a temptation for Alyosha. This became especially noticeable on the day Starets Zosima died. Prior to this, Alyosha was certain that some great explicit miracle would happen on the death of the starets. But instead of a life-size miracle, the old man suddenly started to produce some "bodily smell." In this case, many ill-wishers gathered to see "the righteous fall," though nowhere was it stated that it should be like this. Alyosha, confident of the righteousness of the starets, became so sorrowful that he questioned the justice of God.[236]

It was a painful, excruciating time for Alyosha because of the fact that all the love of Alyosha, "all and everything" was focused on his beloved elder. At this point Alyosha had some contradiction in his heart. On the one hand, he continued to love God, but on the other hand, he did not accept God's world. He saw a kind of injustice in everything that happened. It was his rebellion against God. So he ate sausage, and was ready to drink vodka, and even agreed to go to Grushenika.

But during a meeting with Grushenika something happened. His attitude towards her, his forgiveness, calling her a sincere sister, seeing in her a loving soul, Alyosha admitted that she had restored his soul. He helped Grushenika forgive the offender and then everything bad that she went through in these five years and renounce all the plans that she stored up to get vengeance on her offender. She admitted to Alyosha, "Why had you, cherub, not come before? All my life, I waited for someone like you, knew that someone would come

---

235. *Brat'ya Karamazovy*, 82–84.

236. Vlaskin, *Ideologicheskiy kontekst v romane F. M. Dostoevskogo*, 20.

and forgive me. Believe that someone would love me, nasty person, and not only for my shame!"[237]

The final change took place in Alyosha when he returned to the monastery and knelt to pray. At this moment, hearing the words of monk Paissy, who was reading a story about the miracle at Cana, God responded to his questions. In these words from the Gospel, he saw parallels with the words of the starets and what happened in the house at Grushenika. This was a miracle. It was as if the scales fell from his eyes, and everything became so clear. Realizing this truth, he fell on his face, wept and kissed the ground. At this point, he "just wanted to forgive everyone and everything and to ask for forgiveness." He vowed to love all. The author said that "he fell on the ground as a weak boy, but stood up firm for life." Alyosha knew that "someone visited his soul in that hour."[238] At that moment was amalgamated the aspiration to believe and aspiration to live for others.[239] Alyosha was a realist, believing in miracles.[240] Belief in the existence of God and immortality gave Alyosha the strength to live: "I want to live for immortality, and do not accept half compromise."[241] So he went to the monastery. "It seemed strange for Alyosha and even impossible to live as before."[242]

Alyosha lived with the hope that the kingdom of God would come when people "will love each other, and there will be neither rich, nor poor, neither exalted nor humbled, but all would be like children of God."[243] Alyosha believed in God and in immortality. Ivan did not believe in the existence of God or of immortality. Fyodor Pavlovich was on Ivan's side.[244]

Dostoevsky was convinced that believing in life after death, a person can come to love people for real. Starets Zosima was sure of the afterlife. Moreover, he now felt like he was at the threshold of death for each remaining day of

---

237. *Brat'ya Karamazovy*, 278–304.

238. *Brat'ya Karamazovy*, 305–308.

239. Vlaskin, *Ideologicheskiy kontekst v romane F. M. Dostoevskogo*, 22.

240. *Brat'ya Karamazovy*, 23.

241. *Brat'ya Karamazovy*, 24.

242. *Brat'ya Karamazovy*, 24.

243. *Brat'ya Karamazovy*, 28.

244. *Brat'ya Karamazovy*, 117.

his life, as the earth already was in contact with a new, infinite unknown, but near the hereafter.[245]

Thus he could comfort the mourners whose relatives died. Once the landowner Khokhlakova admitted in the presence of all, confessing to the starets that he doubted the afterlife. This uncertainty gave her over to fear and therefore she could not be happy. Starets agreed that such a state of disbelief in the afterlife killed a man, but he also found practical advice for her. He agreed that it was impossible to prove life after death but argued that it was possible to verify its existence. The elder explained how this could happen:

> The experience of active of love. Try to love your neighbours actively and tirelessly. As you prosper in love, you will be sure of the existence of God and in the immortality of your soul. If you reach a full self-sacrifice in love for your neighbour, then there is no doubt that you will believe, and no doubt will be able to enter into your soul. It has been tested, it is for sure.[246]

When people came to the starets with misconceptions about faith, he could expose them and at the same time gave a correct understanding of the issue. So when a woman who had not received any news from her son throughout the year went to the elder on the advice of others to pray for his repose, the old man scolded her, pointing out that her son was alive, and in the case of the living it was right to pray for their health.[247]

The author claimed that God forgives all sin if a person sincerely repents. Starets Zosima believed in the forgiveness of sins, even of the greatest of sins. So he suggested a way out of the state of condemnation for a woman who had wanted her husband's death, when he was sick. He died, and she condemned herself. The elder advised,

> Do not be afraid, never be afraid and do not be sad. Just see that repentance does not grow thin in you – and God will forgive all. And there is nothing that can be on earth which the Lord would not forgive to the truly repentant. Yes, and man cannot quite commit such a great sin that would have exhausted the

---

245. *Brat'ya Karamazovy*, 250.

246. *Brat'ya Karamazovy*, 49.

247. *Brat'ya Karamazovy*, 45.

infinite love of God. Can there be a sin that would exceed God's love? Worry only about perpetual repentance and cast fear away altogether. Believe that God loves you in the way that you do not even comprehend, and even with your sin He loves you. One who repents causes more joy in heaven than even ten righteous, as said a long time ago. Go on and fear not. Do not worry about people; do not get angry for offences. Forgive in your heart even the dead, whatever they insulted you with, be truly reconciled with them. If you repent, then you love. And if you love, you are already God's . . .[248]

There is no perfect man; all people need the forgiveness of sins. Of himself Zosima said that he was a sinner.[249] So the necessity of repentance was shown in the novel. Change is impossible without repentance. Dimitry believed in his own sinfulness and in the sanctity of Christ. Comparing himself with Katerina Ivanovna, he concluded that he was "a million times more insignificant a soul than she is." Hence, he concluded that she was worthy of Ivan, who cunningly fell in love with her.[250] Dimitry condemned himself and his vile behaviour and was ready to give up his bride and accept Grushenika's terms – marry her and allow her to do anything she wanted.[251] Alyosha very seriously listened to the confession of his brother Dimitry, and felt the suffering of this controversy. He gave tips for the reconciliation of Dimitry and Katerina Ivanovna. Alyosha believed that she would understand.[252]

Dimitry admitted that he was the meanest scoundrel. Not because he killed, because he did not commit the murder of his father, but because he wanted to kill. For this reason, he was ready to suffer and be purified by suffering.[253] Lossky argues that "suffering, according to Dostoevsky, has not only repayment, but also a healing sense: it encourages people to think better, to purify and to seek new ways of life."[254]

---

248. *Brat'ya Karamazovy*, 45–46.

249. *Brat'ya Karamazovy*, 46.

250. *Brat'ya Karamazovy*, 102.

251. *Brat'ya Karamazovy*, 104.

252. *Brat'ya Karamazovy*, 104.

253. *Brat'ya Karamazovy*, 430.

254. Losskiy, *Bog i mirovoe zlo*, 181.

Dimitry started feeling shame and saw Gregory's blood where he had been beaten. He admitted that this blood tormented his heart all night.[255] On the road to Mokroe, Dimitry decided to shoot himself at dawn, but after meeting Grushenika, he wanted to live.[256] He strongly wanted Grigory, whom he had beaten, to survive. Dimitry prayed to God about it:

> God, revive the defeated down by the fence! Pass this terrible cup from me! After all, you did the wonders, O Lord, for these same sinners, like me! Well, what if the old man is alive? Oh, then the rest of the shame I will destroy, I will return the stolen money, I'll give it back, . . . There will not remain any of the shame except in my heart forever! But no, no, oh impossible dream of a coward! Oh, damnation![257]

Dimitry candidly acknowledged his guilt in the beating of Grigory and the hatred he had for his father. Also he pled guilty to being jealous of Grushenika over his father, and believed that his father owed him more money, but he did not admit guilt in the murder of his father.[258] Dimitry was convinced that God witnessed all that had happened, so he called on God to be his witness, when he talked about the signs that only Smerdyakov and "the heaven" knew about.[259]

When the prosecutor told Dimitry that Grigory was alive "his face lit up." He thanked God that his prayer was heard, although he recognized that he was sinful and wicked.[260] The news raised Dimitry up in an instant, as he thought that he killed Grigory who looked after him in his childhood.[261]

Grushenika also came to need repentance. She was aware that she had tortured Dimitry out of spite and thus she became aware that she was guilty. She admitted her wrongdoing and asked for his forgiveness. At the time of Dimitry's arrest, she claimed to the prosecutor that she was to blame for the fact that Dimitry had committed a crime. She was ready to accept a penalty

---

255. *Brat'ya Karamazovy*, 389.

256. *Brat'ya Karamazovy*, 386.

257. *Brat'ya Karamazovy*, 371.

258. *Brat'ya Karamazovy*, 391.

259. *Brat'ya Karamazovy*, 401.

260. *Brat'ya Karamazovy*, 388.

261. *Brat'ya Karamazovy*, 389.

with him, even to death.[262] Grushenika saw herself as guilty of all the wrongs and was even willing to go along with Dimitry to the penal colony.[263] Dimitry wanted to live after he heard from Grushenika that she would be with him all his life.[264]

Starets Zosima was sure that punishment did not correct the offender and society did not become more secure because of it, as the root of the evil remained. He compared it with a plant; if it was cut and the twigs were taken away, in their place will grow new ones. The only solution the starets saw to end crime was in the changes that Christ makes in a person. He stated,

> If what protects the society even in our time can remedy the criminal himself and turn him into another man reborn, then this is solely the law of Christ, embedded in the understanding of one's own conscience. Only having realized the guilt, as a son of Christ's society, that is the church, he is conscious of his guilt before the society itself, that is, before the church.[265]

Starets shared the position of Ivan, which claimed that the only court should be a church court, when the state became a church. Zosima would like society to become a Christian society, but this would be in the future, because "only before the church can a modern criminal be capable of admitting his guilt, rather than before the state."[266] He believed that such a time would come in the future, perhaps in the end times, but it would come. In contrast to Rome, which wanted to turn the church into the state, Starets Zosima saw the mission of Russian Orthodoxy was to turn all the earth and society into a church. Even Scripture was quoted: "From the East the Star shall shine."[267]

4.3.4 Rebellion against God

In the parable the "Grand Inquisitor" Dostoevsky posed the problem of the society of his time. Lossky understands the poem as a criticism of the Catholic

---

262. *Brat'ya Karamazovy*, 372.

263. *Brat'ya* Karamazovy, 577.

264. *Brat'ya Karamazovy*, 429.

265. *Brat'ya Karamazovy*, 56.

266. *Brat'ya Karamazovy*, 56.

267. *Brat'ya Karamazovy*, 58.

Church.[268] Rozanov shares the same view, as the Catholic Church decided to arrange the destiny of mankind, taking advantage of the weakness of man.[269] But as Dostoevsky saw flaws in the Orthodox Church,[270] or rather one should say that the author criticizes Christianity which shares the views of socialists.[271] Also, the parable reveals the essence of the souls of some Russian people, like Ivan, and their relationship to God.[272] In the parable, the teaching of Christ was presented by its antipode, the Grand Inquisitor (a Roman Catholic cardinal), pretending to be a disciple of Christ. Christ put a great value on man, believing that he would prefer an orientation to "be," rather than "to have."[273] He loved people and did everything in the name of love. Christ was most concerned with the freedom of man, his spirituality and the unity of all people.[274] He expected a voluntary union, not one based on coercion.[275]

The Grand Inquisitor once was with Christ, and then he left Christ.[276] He did not believe in immortality, and therefore did not allow for the existence of absolute good.[277] He believed that man is by nature focused on "having." He is convinced that man is weak and therefore freedom is not necessary for him. Moreover, it is burdensome for humans. That is why the Grand Inquisitor tried to prove Christ was wrong by setting three questions in front of Him.

The essence of the first question was the "bread and freedom." Antichrist believed that, above all, people of the earth need bread. The best thing you can do for the people therefore was to feed them. According to the Inquisitor, the person lives just by bread and is not thinking about freedom. For the sake of

---

268. Losskiy, *Bog i mirovoe zlo*, 220. Gibson concludes that Dostoevsky showed the confrontation between Christ and the Catholic and Protestant churches, as the Catholic church was offering people unity without freedom, and the Protestant church freedom without unity (Gibson, *The Religion of Dostoevsky*, 187).

269. Rozanov, "Legenda o Velikom Inkvizitore."

270. Losskiy, *Bog i mirovoe zlo*, 221.

271. Rozanov, "Legenda o Velikom Inkvizitore."

272. "Russian socialist-atheist rejecting the idea of the Divine good raises to absolute heights some relative value and comes to excessive limits of consecutiveness" (Losskiy, *Bog i mirovoe zlo*, 221).

273. Kudryavtsev, *Tri Kruga Dostoevskogo*, 302.

274. *Brat'ya Karamazovy*, 212.

275. Gibson, *The Religion of Dostoevsky*, 183.

276. Rozanov sees a parallel between the rebellion of Lucifer and that of the Great Inquisitor. The position he argues with is that evil comes from a religious person.

277. Losskiy, *Bog i mirovoe zlo*, 124.

quenching material thirst, people will give all their spiritual things because they are weak. Those who would follow Christ, are very few: "thousands, tens of thousands." But the bread will be followed by millions. The Inquisitor considered that Christ did not think about these millions of the weak.[278]

Christ knew the key to human freedom, and therefore rejected the path of the Antichrist, the way of the Inquisitor. He did not want to deprive a person of liberty in exchange for "bread." He proceeded from the thesis, "not by bread alone shall a man live."[279]

Gus sees a similarity between the Inquisitor's words and the teaching of European Socialists. He cites what Dostoevsky said before the students, "The current socialism in Europe, and everywhere here, everywhere eliminates Christ and works primarily for having bread."[280]

According to Rozanov, the first question presents the rebellion of all earthly things in man against all heavenly things in him. Such a person will laugh at his former saints as unnecessary people, and will bow down before the new benefactors.[281] But Christ himself chose the path of voluntary suffering for the sake of others, and thus set an example for people. Thus for Dostoevsky, suffering was associated with the universal human responsibility for sin and lead to purification and to sacrificial life for the benefit of others.[282]

The second question was to whom shall we give our worship?[283] The Inquisitor believed that it is necessary to take away man's freedom, to force men to bow before Him. This can be done on the basis of three powerful forces: "There are three forces on the earth which alone may forever defeat and capture the conscience of these feeble rebels for their happiness; those forces are: the miracle, the mystery, and the authority."

But Jesus did not want to take advantage of the three forces and did not force men to bow before Him. He did not want to take away their right to freedom. He would not make a secret of the meaning of human life, would not appease the conscience of the people and did not want to deprive them of responsibility for their actions. He did not want an imposed faith and slavish

---

278. *Brat'ya Karamazovy*, 213.

279. Kudryavtsev, *Tri Kruga Dostoevskogo*, 302.

280. Gus, *Idei, I obrazy F. M. Dostoevskogo*, 452.

281. Rozanov, "The Legend of the Great Inquisitor."

282. Scanlan, *Dostoevsky the Thinker*, 116.

283. Kudryavtsev, *Tri Kruga Dostoevskogo*, 303.

love. This is why He did not take the Grand Inquisitor's solutions offered to Him in the second question. But pure love can only be the free manifestation of the personality.[284]

The third question was about the need of people for worldwide unity. This need flows out as a consequence of the weakness of people. For a more rapid establishment of unity Christ was invited by the Inquisitor to resort to force, to the sword of Caesar.[285] Having power over people, the Inquisitor manipulates them.[286]

But Christ rejected the sword and did not want to impose unity by force. Christ did not accept the Grand Inquisitor's version of the three questions. He simply withdrew.

The essence of the mysteries of the Inquisitor, in addition to concealing the meaning of life was still as follows, "We are not with you, and with him, that's our secret! We have long ceased to be with you and with him the last eight centuries."[287] The mystery lies in the fact that for a long time now the Inquisitor was not with Christ and was with Antichrist, although he covered up his own affairs with the authority of Christ. He used lies to lead people to lies.[288]

With the Inquisitor the line between righteousness and sinfulness were erased. Anything is sinful that is without permission. Righteous things are all that are permitted. "We shall allow or forbid them to live with their wives and mistresses, to have or not have children . . ."[289]

Christ radiated the light, and He went with a "quiet smile." The Inquisitor was gloomy. Christ believed in the temporality of inquisition. Reality did not make Him change His mind. He had not changed His convictions, His view of man. Silently having listened to the Inquisitor, He also silently kissed him. He said therefore, that he was sorry for the deluded man. With His behaviour, He gave the Inquisitor an example of the way out showing the height of the person.

---

284. Losskiy, *Bog i mirovoe zlo*, 113.

285. Kudryavtsev, *Tri Kruga Dostoevskogo*, 305.

286. Vlaskin, *Ideologicheskiy kontekst v romane F. M. Dostoevskogo*, 40.

287. *Brat'ya Karamazovy*, 215.

288. Vlaskin, *Ideologicheskiy kontekst v romane F. M. Dostoevskogo*, 39.

289. *Brat'ya Karamazovy*, 216.

Rozanov believes that Dostoevsky shared the view that European Christianity, sharing socialist views, turned the words of Jesus upside-down, "Seek first his kingdom and his righteousness, and all these things will be given to you as well" (Matt 6:33). They were so immersed in earthly affairs that they had lost the ultimate meaning of life.[290] Dostoevsky believed that in the West, "the state overcame the church completely. The church was destroyed and finally found reincarnation as the state."[291]

The Grand Inquisitor's understanding of man was the same as Ivan's.[292] Ivan, like the Grand Inquisitor, saw the major error of Christ in His high appreciation of man. He believed that not only man but God as well was weak.[293] He did not believe in the possibility of the development of society with love towards people. Therefore, he recognized deception, lies, "everything is permitted" as the means of arranging a temporary life. He wanted one thing, so that on the road to perdition the people would be happy, not knowing the essence of life.

Ivan denied the divine structure of the world. In his reflections on God, Ivan completed the Grand Inquisitor's claims to Christ with his own. Ivan admitted the existence of God and produced a bill for Him. This can account for the fact that the Almighty was willing to pay a high price for harmony. This price is human suffering in the process of achieving harmony. Ivan developed the idea of the incompatibility of God and suffering mankind and of the just God with unrequited crime.[294]

Ivan used as an argument against Christ the suffering of pure and innocent children. The tears of a child spoke of the imperfection of the world. Ivan could not accept the idea that children suffer for the sins of adults. No one can forgive torturers. The person was left to live but was not authorized to live for he did not suffer. Whoever died because of the torture could no longer forgive, although he was the only one who had the right to pardon. Hence, compensation is not possible in any harmony.[295] Alyosha directly

---

290. Rozanov, "The Legend of the Great Inquisitor."

291. *Dnevnik Pisatelya* (August 1880).

292. Kudryavtsev, *Tri Kruga Dostoevskogo*, 313.

293. Losskiy, *Bog i mirovoe zlo*, 110.

294. Rozanov, "The Legend of the Great Inquisitor."

295. Rozanov believes that the suffering of children is only the outward manifestation of the original sin.

labeled Ivan's rants a rebellion. Ivan immediately raised the question of costs and disbursements of harmony. Ivan doubted the omnipotence of God, who allowed this.[296]

Evil penetrated into this world so deeply that some people started to have doubts that the world was created by an almighty and good God.[297] Some people, seeing the evil in the world, came to atheism.[298]

Ivan went further than the Inquisitor. He not only did not believe in man but also denied God, even if God loved man. Harmony in this case also is the road. In fact, Ivan denied not only the world that God created, but God in general, including the God that is within man. He denied morality and proclaimed the principle that "everything is permitted." He came to even greater controversy. For the tears of a child he denied God who creates harmony. But he came to the principle of "everything is permitted," entailing a flood of tears and blood. As the Inquisitor, Ivan did not believe in harmony, coming from the low nature of man. Paradoxically, Ivan believed man to be weak but not himself. If he would include himself in the number of the weak, he would have to recognize the limitations of his mind and the wisdom of God.[299] Considering himself wiser than God, he could not forgive sinners and so rejected God's harmony.[300]

Christ did not use words to argue with the Inquisitor. With both words and deeds Alyosha and Zosima contradicted the inquisition. From the standpoint of Alyosha, Christ won. Alyosha understood that Ivan thought as the Inquisitor thought. Therefore, he said that with this kind of understanding of the world order one cannot live. When Ivan stated that he would not give up the thesis that "all is permitted," Alyosha kissed him. Alyosha repeated the act of Christ. The tragedy of Ivan is in bringing together rejection of "the peace of God" and total permissiveness in an "ungodly world."[301]

---

296. *Brat'ya Karamazovy*, 217.

297. Losskiy, *Bog i mirovoe zlo*, 109.

298. Losskiy, 110.

299. Rozanov, "The Legend of the Great Inquisitor."

300. Gibson, *The Religion of Dostoevsky*, 180.

301. His position on the one hand does not let God be a part of his life, and on the other he can view with indifference the sufferings of others and any manifestation of evil. Exactly this destroys his person (Vlaskin, *Ideologicheskiy kontekst v romane F. M. Dostoevskogo*, 32).

Zosima did not listen to Ivan and his legend. He did not argue with Ivan directly. He argued with him with his life. His life was the same kind of kisses that were in Christ and Alyosha. The story "Russian Monk" from the novel is his answer. Zosima also saw flaws in man and in humanity. Zosima called people to resolve conflicts with love. He called covenant people to be morally responsible. In spite of everything, "The human race does not accept its prophets and beats them, but people love their martyrs and honour those whom they tortured." It is difficult, but people must act.[302]

Zosima did not resort to intimidation of people with hell. Suffering over that which you can no longer love: that is what hell was to Zosima. The main thing for Zosima was internal punishment. Zosima understood God as the inner part of everyone. He produced a bill not to the Almighty, but to himself. Everyone should blame himself.

Dostoevsky using his parable of the Grand Inquisitor hinted, and in the example of Zosima and Alyosha showed, that the only solution for people was in Orthodox Christianity, which offered both freedom and unity. Although he had a radical understanding of Orthodoxy,[303] Dostoevsky was convinced that evil came from socialist ideas prevalent in society, such as denying God, which could destroy the world. Gus concludes that Dostoevsky's parable "had to prove that Catholicism, in alliance with atheism and revolutionary socialism will create hell on earth."[304]

4.3.5 Christ-Like Living of Life

Alyosha and Starets Zosima had a specific mission: *to live like Christ.* For the elder Zosima his aim in life was to fulfill the covenant of God on this earth. "This was his happiness."[305] Zosima is a Dostoevsky's representation of a true saint.[306] The mission of the elder was more concentrated within the monastery and to the people who visited it. The mission of Alyosha focused more on

---

302. Kudryavtsev, *Tri Kruga Dostoevskogo*, 318.

303. Gibson, *The Religion of Dostoevsky*, 187.

304. Gus, *Idei, I obrazy F. M. Dostoevskogo*, 448.

305. *Brat'ya Karamazovy*, 48. Dostoevsky warned that even children like Krasotkin are already fully corrupted by convictions (Scanlan, *Dostoevsky the Thinker*, 85).

306. Losskiy, *Bog i mirovoe zlo*, 191.

life outside the monastery, although he lived in a monastery. Dostoevsky's Christianity is an active Christianity.[307]

First, the relationship of love between people helped to remove their erroneous beliefs. Grushenika long planned her revenge. She had stored it up for five years after an officer disgraced her and all those years longed for her moment to arrive. Only after meeting Alyosha, who treated her with forgiveness, was her heart changed when she responded to genuine love and forgave her abuser, not holding any more ill will against him. The whole desire for vengeance went away in a moment.[308]

The open, honest, arrogant attitude of Alyosha to Kolya produced its fruit during their first conversation. Since the behaviour of Kolya was influenced by some ideas of socialism, he understood that there was also something behind the attitude and behaviour of Alyosha and was right about it. Therefore, he spoke to Alyosha about faith in God, although he was trying to prove that you can love people without faith in God, citing the example of Voltaire.

According to Kolya Voltaire loved people, to which Alyosha modestly replied, "Voltaire did not believe in God, but it seems he loved humanity also very little." From this we may deduce that Alyosha was convinced that true love could only be in the believer in God. Alyosha also indicated to Kolya that over time a person could change his convictions.[309]

Curle sees a lot in common between Mishkin and Alyosha.[310] But they are different in that Mishkin is "innocent," with no evil in his soul, while Alyosha realizes in himself the presence of "Karamazov's nature."[311] So he is portrayed as a mere mortal, who is a believer and can serve as an example for each and everyone. Alyosha helped Kolya not to live like everyone else, because most people have distorted values. The distorted nature of Kolya was visible at the time when he mocked and insulted the doctor who came to see Ilyusha.[312] According to Alyosha, the source of pride for Kolya, from which he was afraid to appear ridiculous and thus hurt others, was a demon, the devil. This was a common problem of mankind, so Alyosha calls Kolya to

---

307. Gibson, *The Religion of Dostoevsky*, 186.

308. *Brat'ya Karamazovy*, 287–304.

309. *Brat'ya Karamazovy*, 467.

310. Curle, *Characters of Dostoevsky*, 205.

311. Dneprov, *Idei, Strasti, Postupki*, 211.

312. *Brat'ya Karamazovy*, 472.

be "not like everyone else" even if only he would be different. According to Kolya, these words of Alyosha served as a consolation for him.[313]

Second, Alexei and Starets Zosima listened to people with an open mind and gave them advice on their needs. If people came to the starets in the monastery with their problems, needs and griefs, then the advice and assistance of Alyosha was increasingly needed outside the monastery as well. Katerina Ivanovna needed the advice of Alyosha, and Lisa missed fellowshipping with him.[314]

Dimitry needed Alyosha for a frank talk, to confess and open his soul, his own experiences. In his confession to Alyosha, Dimitry pointed out some contradictions in himself. About these contradictions, Dimitry already told the "angel from the sky." This indicated his confession to God. At the same time, Dimitry felt the need for confession before Alyosha. Therefore, seeing Alyosha, Dimitry called him "an angel on earth." Alyosha was needed by everyone except Smerdyakov. Even Katerina Ivanovna waited for him to learn the truth.[315]

Starets Zosima, being sure of the usefulness of open and sincere confessions, used to gather all the monastic brethren in the evenings at these meetings. Although some of his detractors objected to such innovations, the old man continued to collect the brothers in his cell. "Usually in the evening, after the service, daily, at bedtime, the monastic brotherhood would flood the elder's cell, and each out loud confesses to him his sins of the day, sinful dreams, thoughts, temptations, even quarrels among themselves, if they occurred."[316]

In his dying speech, Starets Zosima called his monastic brothers to love each other. Similarly, he urged them to love God's people and proceeded to explain to them how to achieve this love. First, in his opinion, the monks should not consider themselves holier than the lay people, but rather see themselves as sinners, worse than the entire world's people. Second, realizing their sinfulness, the monks must understand that they bore the guilt of every person living on earth. Starets argued that such consciousness "is the

---

313. *Brat'ya Karamazovy*, 470.

314. *Brat'ya Karamazovy*, 48–49.

315. *Brat'ya Karamazovy*, 127.

316. *Brat'ya Karamazovy*, 137.

crown of the monastic path and of every man on earth." Only then, he said, the human heart would be touched and would be capable to love the world.[317]

Further, the elder, like the Apostle Paul, gave short but important tips and cautions to his brothers. They felt love, compassion, caring[318] and a firm conviction of that which he advised:

> Everyone watches one's heart, everyone confesses to yourself relentlessly. Do not be afraid of your sins, even having realized them, just repent of them, but do not put conditions on God. Again, I say – do not be proud. Do not be proud before the small; do not be proud before the great. Do not hate and reject those who are defamatory, abusing you or slandering you. Do not hate atheists, teachers of evil, materialists – love not only the good, because in all of them there is much good, especially of those who are in our time. Remember them in prayer . . . God's people must love, do not allow the flock to be taken by the strangers, because if you fall asleep in the laziness and disgust of your pride, and most of all dishonest gain, they will come from all countries and take from you your flock. Interpret the gospel to the people unceasingly . . . Do not extort . . . Do not love silver and gold, do not keep it . . . Believe and hold the banner. Highly exalt it . . .[319]

The old monk Ferapont, an opponent of Starets Zasima's teaching, considered the most important thing in the monastic ministry to be fasting. Everything else – concern for people, compassion – he thought to be superfluous innovations.[320]

Alyosha was one of the few characters of the novel whom everyone needed, and who almost all believed and trusted. Grushenika also asked only Alyosha for advice.[321] Even Mrs Khokhlakova always looked forward to meeting with Alyosha. She dreamed of Alyosha marrying her daughter Lisa. She was ready to entrust Lisa only to him. She also opened up her secrets before Alyosha in

---

317. *Brat'ya Karamazovy*, 140.
318. Vlaskin, *Ideologicheskiy kontekst v romane F. M. Dostoevskogo*, 77.
319. *Brat'ya Karamazovy*, 141.
320. *Brat'ya Karamazovy*, 146.
321. *Brat'ya Karamazovy*, 475.

hopes of receiving his advice. She told him about the men who frequented her and even offered to marry them.[322] Alyosha was amazingly able to listen to his companion, even if the other person was a chatterbox, such as Mrs Khokhlakova.[323] Dimitry also eagerly awaited Alyosha to pour out his soul. Dimitry admitted to Alyosha that during the past two months, he felt like a new person, a resurrected person. He clearly saw his mission was to help people even in prison to revive. He stated,

> And what is it to me that in the mines I will be twenty years knocking out ore with a hammer – I'm not afraid of it at all. The other thing I'm scared of now – that the resurrected man not depart from me! One can find there in the mines, under the ground, near him, in the same convict, the murderer, the human heart, to meet him, because there can one live, and love and suffer! You can, you can take care of him and over the years bring up, finally, from the dark den to the light, the already high soul, pained consciousness, to revive the angel, to resurrect a hero! And there are, in fact, hundreds of them, and we are all to blame for them . . . Oh yes, we'll be in chains, there will be no freedom, but there, in our great sorrow, we will be resurrected again in joy, without which man cannot live, but to God be the glory, for God gives joy.[324]

He was sure that it was because of his belief in God that he did not kill his father and was to blame for the evil which he did in his life. Because he believed in God, he loved God. Dimitry wanted to live, even in the mines.[325] In recognition by Dostoevsky's characters of guilt on behalf of all, Dostoevsky showed his conviction in the universal nature of sin.[326]

The mission of the characters still consists in declaring the future of universal brotherhood. In order to create a universal harmony one thing common to all is needed.[327] Dostoevsky was convinced that this thing should be

---

322. *Brat'ya Karamazovy*, 482.

323. *Brat'ya Karamazovy*, 486.

324. *Brat'ya Karamazovy*, 498.

325. *Brat'ya Karamazovy*, 499.

326. Scanlan, *Dostoevsky the Thinker*, 106.

327. Losskiy, *Bog i mirovoe zlo*, 112.

the transformation of society in Christ. The means of achieving this purpose consisted not in a revolution, but in the truth of Christ.[328] Zosima embraced the idea of the future of the fraternal association of people in Christ, when the servant and his master would have a fraternal relationship. He believed that such a merger would happen; it would be in Russia and the Russian people would go further. He affirmed:

> Without servants the world cannot be, but act so that if you have a servant, your servant would be freer in spirit than if he was not a servant. And why can I not be a servant to my servant, so that he would even see it, and already, without any pride on my part . . . Why would my servant not be to me as a close relative, so that I would accept him, finally, in my family and rejoice in this? Even now still this is doable, but will serve as a platform for the future the already magnificent union of men, when the servants will not seek for themselves masters and when men will not turn those like them into servants, as it is now, but rather, with all one's might wish to become oneself a servant to all according to the gospel.[329]

For Starets Zosima the problem of people is not in the social sphere, but in the spiritual. People may say that they are free, but they are slaves to the acquisition of necessities. The rich have solitude and spiritual suicide and the poor have jealousy and murder. Zosima concluded, "Instead of freedom they fell into slavery, and instead of serving brotherly love and human unity they fell on the contrary, in isolation and seclusion."[330]

According to Zosima, the problem of poor people is in their depravity, from small children to the elderly: drunkenness, vice, indecent words. He asked his brothers to teach them the truth, because they still believed deep down in their soul and often repented and cried. They could return to God. Worse, in his opinion, was the case with the superiors, who "want to pursue science with only their minds, but without Christ." Rejecting Christ, they rejected also His teachings about sin and crime.[331]

---

328. *Dnevnik Pisatelya*, June 1876.

329. *Brat'ya Karamazovy*, 271.

330. *Brat'ya Karamazovy*, 268.

331. *Brat'ya Karamazovy*, 269.

The call to total responsibility is nothing other than following Christ who took all responsibility upon himself.[332]

Third, the characters predicted the developments in the lives of the interlocutors. Starets Zosima helped Alyosha to understand that his mission was beyond the walls of the monastery. The people out there were more in need than those within the walls of the monastery. His place was among the members of his family in whom there was no peace. He needed to serve them and pray for them. Starets, even on his deathbed gave a command to Alyosha to leave the monastery immediately after his death. Zosima charged Alyosha,

> I bless you for the great obedience in the world. Much more you will wander. And you shall get married. All will have to be overcome, once again to endure. A lot of labour there will be. But in you I have no doubt, therefore I send you. With you is Christ. Save Him [keep Him and He will keep you], and He shall save thee. You will see a great woe and in this woe you will be happy. Here's the covenant – in sorrow seek happiness. Work, work tirelessly. Remember my words . . .[333]

Even while dying, the old man insisted that Alyosha should leave the monastery, as his mission lay in the world. Alyosha must bring morality to this perverted world.[334]

Another example of the starets predicting fate was in a strange symbolic bowing of the elder to Dimitry. Starets Zosima bowed to Dimitry as he testified, foreseeing in him the future. He saw in his eyes the future suffering for which Dimitry prepared himself. Therefore, the old man sent Alyosha to find his brother to warn him of something terrible.

The elder not only saw the fate of Dimitry but also the future life of Alyosha in the world. Starets Zosima spoke of Dimitry quoting the Gospel of John, and also predicted the life of Alyosha:

> Unless a grain of wheat falls into the ground and dies, it abides alone: but if it dies, it brings forth much fruit. Remember these things. And you, Alyosha, many times I silently blessed you in

---

332. Scanlan, *Dostoevsky the Thinker*, 109.

333. *Brat'ya Karamazovy*, 67.

334. Kudryavtsev, *Tri Kruga Dostoevskogo*, 268.

my life for your face, know now . . . I think of you this way –
you will leave these walls now, and in the world will endure as a
monk. Many enemies you will have, but the enemies themselves
will love you. Many misfortunes will bring you your life, but
you will be happy in them, and life will be blessed, and you will
compel others to bless – which is most important.[335]

Fourth, the characters attributed great importance to prayer and reading
of the Scriptures. Alyosha thought very highly of the importance of prayer.
He prayed for a long time, praising and glorifying God and asking to be
pleasing to Him.[336]

The attitude of Starets Zosima to the Scriptures was amazing. He admired
the book, "My God, what a book this is and what lessons it contains! What a
book is the Scripture, what a miracle, and what a force given with it to men!"[337]
Dostoevsky was clearly fascinated when speaking of the Bible.[338]

The word that was sown in his child's soul back in his parents' house, in
combination with a visit to the temple brought forth its fruit. He admitted
that even then "the first time in his life he meaningfully took the first seed
of God's word in his soul." Especially then being an eight-year old, he was
astonished by the story of the life of Job. Job's life was similar to Dostoevsky's
life. He was taught to read by using the book "One Hundred and Four Sacred
Stories of the Old and New Testament." In the story of Job, he discovered for
himself a little mystery of innocent suffering. He describes it this way,

The mystery here is that fact of the earth passing by and the
eternal truth, touched here together. Before the earthly truth
are committed acts of the eternal truth. Then the Creator, as
in the first days of creation, ending each day of praise, "Seeing
that it was good" looks at Job and again boasts of the creation
of His own. And Job, praising the Lord, serves not only Him,
but will serve all of the creation in generations, because he was
intended for that.[339]

---

335. *Brat'ya Karamazovy,* 244.
336. *Brat'ya Karamazovy,* 138.
337. *Brat'ya Karamazovy,* 250.
338. See Part I.
339. *Brat'ya Karamazovy,* 250.

He admired how God restored Job. God gave him new wealth, new children and the joy of life. In Job's "old sorrow of the great mystery of human life he moves slowly into the quiet joy of emotion" and thus became again a happy man.[340] All the above-mentioned coincides exactly with events from the life of Dostoevsky.[341]

In his last instructions to his brothers elder Zosima encouraged them to read and if necessary to interpret the Scriptures to people. Do not worry about its content, the main thing was to perform their ministry of sowing the Word. He explained the power of the Word, "You just need a small seed, a tiny one, cast it into the soul of a commoner, and it will not die, it will live in his soul all his life, lurking in him in the darkness, among the stench of his sins as a bright spot, as a great reminder. You do not need to have to interpret a lot and to teach, he will understand it easily."[342]

The main thing that the starets emphasized was to read Bible stories to children. He enumerated in detail the stories of the Old and New Testaments pointing to the practical teachings contained in each of them. Consequently, he believed that the transfer of words must be accompanied by examples. He encouraged them to have just one hour a week to read Bible stories to children. It was better to conduct these meetings with the priest at a home in a friendly atmosphere. Pay attention to how these stories for children were read:

> And it's not the same as building mansions for this matter, but simply to accept them in your log house. Do not fear, for they will not they make a mess of your house, for you only gather them for an hour. Expand the named book and start reading it without the wisdom of words, and without arrogance, without elevation of oneself over them, but tenderly and gently, being glad that you read to them and that they listen to you and understand you. Loving much these words, only occasionally stop and explain something otherwise incomprehensible to the commoner. Do not worry, all will understand you, everything will be understood by the orthodox heart![343]

---

340. *Brat'ya Karamazovy*, 250.

341. See Part I.

342. *Brat'ya Karamazovy*, 251.

343. *Brat'ya Karamazovy*, 250.

The elder agreed that the people would perish without the word of God, because it was wanted by every soul. Only the word of God can convert "atheists who broke away from their native land." He noticed that the whole creation rendered glory to God:

> Every blade of grass, every insect, ant, golden bee, all know their way to a surprise, since not having minds to show the mystery of God, constantly make it themselves . . . for all creation and all creatures, every leaf is fixed to the word of God and sings glory to God, cries to Christ, and to itself committing the mystery of its sinless existence.[344]

Fifth, the characters suffered, seeing how people were blinded by sin. Alyosha cried when he was unable to help though he saw how one person humiliated another. So it was in a meeting with Dimitry. He began to cry because Dimitry, after beating and cursing his father, could easily joke. He did not understand the seriousness of the act as Alyosha understands it.[345]

Alyosha looked with pain at the young people caught in nets of atheism. The novel showed one of the problems of Russian society to be the spread of socialist, atheistic and revolutionary ideas.[346] Even Kolya Krasotkin, not yet fourteen years old, picked up these ideas. Kolya argued that the "Christian faith has served only the rich and noble to hold in chains the lower class."[347] Alyosha was very sad about the fact that in Russia even teenagers such as Kolya, who had not yet begun to live, were already perverted.[348] Kolya admitted to Alyosha that he was a scoundrel because all his life he could not get rid of his selfish ambitions and dastardly autocracy. Alyosha explained to him that the problem lay in his corrupted nature.[349]

Sixth, the characters helped people to understand correctly the essence of repentance, which led to a complete change of life. In order for man to return

---

344. *Brat'ya Karamazovy*, 252.

345. *Brat'ya Karamazovy*, 134.

346. Gus, *Idei, I obrazy F. M. Dostoevskogo*, 465.

347. *Brat'ya Karamazovy*, 467.

348. Dostoevsky warned that even children like Krasotkin are already fully corrupted by convictions (Scanlan, *Dostoevsky the Thinker*, 85).

349. *Brat'ya Karamazovy*, 469.

to his good origins, he needed outside assistance.[350] A spiritual turnaround has external manifestations. Such a turn could be seen in Grushenika. According to Alyosha, "her face was as if even more attractive," and showed "some sort of immutable humbleness and irrevocable commitment"; "one could see not a trace of the former volatility, in the previously proud eyes now shined some softness, although they occasionally blazed with some sinister glow."[351] These changes were also visible in her care and compassion for old Maximov during his illness.[352] Grushenika, the day before the trial of Dimitry, admitted to Alyosha that she was very worried about the outcome of the trial.[353]

The story of the repentance of Markel, brother of Starets Zosima, clearly indicates a complete change of life. The circumstances of his life and his illness had not changed, but the result of repentance led him to find true happiness. He described it this way: "My mother, my joy, I'm full of fun, do not cry from grief, because I myself want to be guilty before them. I do not know how to interpret this to you, because I do not know how to love them. I suppose I have sinned before all, but all will forgive me; that's paradise. Am I now not in heaven?"[354]

In the story of Starets Zosima is a description of his repentance. Despite the fact that he had known God and revered the word of God from childhood, it was his time in the Cadet Corps, where for eight years while under a new impression he muted his childhood experiences, though he had not forgotten anything. At this time, he recognized that he had "adopted so many new habits and even opinions that he was transformed into almost a savage, cruel and absurd creature." He carried the Bible with him, but scarcely read it. Selfishness, pride, and anger here served as the motives for many attitudes and behaviours. He insulted an innocent man and challenged him to a duel, hiding the real reason. In fact, he imagined that this man stole his bride, which was not the case. For no reason he severely beat Aphanasy, who had faithfully served him, in his face.

---

350. Kudryavtsev, *Tri Kruga Dostoevskogo*, 182.

351. *Brat'ya Karamazovy*, 474–475.

352. *Brat'ya Karamazovy*, 475.

353. *Brat'ya Karamazovy*, 478.

354. *Brat'ya Karamazovy*, 248.

But that evening he felt something "shameful and low in his heart." The reason for his shame was this beating of Aphanasy. In just that moment he remembered the words of his brother Markel, who after his repentance had appealed, "Dear Mother, my blood, indeed every one is guilty before all, only people do not know that and if they would it would be heaven here!" He wondered, "why did the other person, the same as him, the image and likeness of God, serve him?" He cried. Then the whole truth of what he intended to do opened before him – to kill a man. The first thing he did was to go to Aphanasy and asked for forgiveness, falling prostrate before him. Then, going to the duel, he gave his opponent an opportunity to shoot, threw down his revolver and begged his opponent for forgiveness, admitting his villainy. Some began to criticize him, but he paid no attention. Repentance changed his view of everything:

> Sirs, look round at the gifts of God: clear sky, clean air, sweet grass, birds, nature is beautiful and sinless, and we, only we the godless ones and stupid, do not understand that life is paradise, for if we would want to understand and see the beauty all around us, we would immediately embrace and weep . . .[355]

Repentance also led the old man to proclaim God's truth to others. People gathered in different houses and he explained the whole truth to them about how "man was behind all the blame." "But how would people understand and know when the world has so long been the other way out, and when the lie of lies was believed to be the truth, and demanded the same lies from others"?[356] Starets Zosima told the story of a mysterious visitor who had passed through all the stages of human degradation. Michael, being young and sinful, decided to take revenge on a woman because she chose another. At night, he secretly went to see her, killed her and arranged everything in such a way so that suspicion would fall on the servant. In the beginning, he felt no remorse, but afterwards, when he was married and had children, he could not even love his own children. Moreover, even at night he saw the innocent dead servant whom he had accused of murder in his dreams. He did not have a single moment of peace.

---

355. *Brat'ya Karamazovy*, 251–256.
356. *Brat'ya Karamazovy*, 257.

Hearing the testimony of Zosima, Michael started having long and complicated internal struggles. He desperately wanted liberation from his inner conviction but was afraid to harm his wife and children. Yet he dared to confess it to all on his birthday, fifteen years after the crime. Many did not believe him. But he got inner liberation even though he was very ill. Through sufferings he rose to a new life, and that is the heart of the novel. About his state Michael says:

> God has taken pity on me and is calling me to Himself. I know that I am dying, but I feel joy and peace after so many years. I instantly felt paradise in my soul, just fulfilled what was necessary. Now I dare to love my children and kiss them. Nobody believes me, and nobody believed it, neither my wife, nor the judges, not even my children. God's grace I see in this for my children. I will die, and my name will be spotless for them. And now I apprehend God, my heart rejoices as in paradise . . . I fulfilled my duty . . .[357]

Thus, from the teachings of Starets Zosima one can paint a portrait of a Christian. A Christian constantly has the image of Christ before him, not to get lost, and has a consistent prayer life; he loves people even in their sins and he loves all of God's creation. He is always taking care not to be a stumbling block to anyone and ready to suffer even for a crime he did not commit but for which is still indirectly responsible. He is cheerful, and he does not judge anyone, and he believes in the existence of hell and eternal spiritual torment.[358]

Dostoevsky believed that the moral regeneration of society is possible if only righteous men possess the above-mentioned qualities and have overcame in themselves their evil origins.[359]

4.4 Conclusion

This was the most fruitful period in the life of the great writer. He always expressed compassionate feelings for people, especially for the poor and

---

357. *Brat'ya Karamazovy*, 266.

358. *Brat'ya Karamazovy*, 272–277.

359. Dneprov, *Idei, Strasti, Postupki*, 200.

the oppressed. He saw people's problems as spiritual rather than social. Dostoevsky was confident that the need was internal rather than external. Finally, he was able to connect to Christ, who became the centre of his life and who connected everything with "humanity." The image of Christ, who sacrificed Himself for others, was the centre of Dostoevsky's convictions.

Elena Andreevna Shtakenshneider's testimony is part of the evidence for my statement. She remembered Dostoevsky's arguments with another writer D. V. Averkiev. Dostoevsky shared his fundamental idea, which seems strange, paradoxical and utopian to a shallow mind: "To realize one's own existence, and be able to say: I exist! – is a great gift, Dostoevsky said, but to say: I do not exist, and to sacrifice oneself having this authority is even a greater gift." Averkiev could not remain silent anymore and exclaimed: "Surely, this is a great gift, but none have it, and the only One Who has it, is God Himself." Dostoevsky objected. According to Shtakenshneider, Averkiev "kept on saying that there is no one except Christ Who has sacrificed Himself for others. Yet, He has done it without any pain because He was God." However, for Dostoevsky, Christ was not only God, but also a human being who had endured great pain since it was His calling. This earthly, unifying beginning of Christianity was the most essential thing for Dostoevsky.[360] For Dostoevsky, then, there was an absolute moral good for humanity: it was the condition of perfect adherence to the law of love, or in other words loving another to the point of a Christlike giving of oneself to them unreservedly. According to Dostoevsky, "Christ's Way"[361] is the only way that people should accept to find real happiness. This is the way of love, suffering, deprivation and sacrifice for one's neighbour's sake.

Thus, after examining the novel *The Brothers Karamazov,* many theological motifs jointly identified from the main themes of this novel have been described and analyzed. In the novel *The Brothers Karamazov* Dostoevsky set out all the results he had come to in his research on man. This novel answers the main question of his youth, "What is the meaning of life?" At the end of his life, he concluded that the meaning of life is to have an active faith in God which will reverberate in constant love for people, just as in the life of Christ.

---

360. *F. M. Dostoevsky v vospominaniyakh sovremennikov,* 20.
361. Christ-centred living theology.

But Dostoevsky understood that it is not so easy for a person to come to faith in God and to accept His world order. This was especially true in a time when everywhere in Russian there were pronounced urges to give people happiness while bypassing God. Therefore, in the novel the writer, as deeply as possible, showed the sinfulness of man. Each individual was depicted by Dostoevsky in detail, was probed deeply, to the sinews of his heart.[362] Man, according to the novels of Dostoevsky, is permeated with evil. Evil has many forms and manifests itself in all aspects of life. Evil can take the form of permissiveness.

Dostoevsky also did not forget that in every person is the image of God. No matter how low we may fall, we can always hope for a better and happier life. Thus in the novel were intertwined such theological motifs as love, compassion and care. If an unbeliever can at times do good, then even more so doing good is and should be the most important thing in the life of a believer. This is possible only through true repentance, which fundamentally changes the belief of man and his behaviour.

The mission of the Christian is to live like Christ. Dostoevsky said, "Perhaps the only love of the Russian people is Christ."[363] People's problems, their joys and sorrows should bother him. Only in this way can one install universal harmony on earth. To do this, a person needs to feel personally responsible before every other person. Dostoevsky wrote, "The recognition of the human person and his freedom, and consequently his responsibility is one of the most basic ideas of Christianity."[364] Dostoevsky was convinced that people will choose brotherhood and unification with Christ. His theological conviction was that the only salvation from *"karamazovschina"* (human sinful nature) was through the preaching of love and humility.[365]

---

362. Losskiy, *Bog i mirivoe zlo*, 171.

363. *Dnevnik Pisatelya*, 1873.

364. *Dnevnik Pisatelya*, 1876.

365. Vlaskin, *Ideologicheskiy kontekst v romane F. M. Dostoevskogo*, 79.

CHAPTER 5

Dostoevsky's Theology

5.1 Introduction

This is the principal chapter where we address the question we set out to answer: What is the theology of Dostoevsky expressed in his life and literature? A synthesis of Dostoevsky's life and writings will be undertaken, using analytical and critical methods.

5.2 Synthesis of His Life and Writings

Following our exploration of Dostoevsky's life and writings, the next step is to unite these into one whole theology of Dostoevsky. To accomplish this, we propose an assessment of the similarities and differences in his life and works, beginning with the question of how the similarities and differences arise.

5.2.1 Scripture

From the time of Dostoevsky's childhood, the Scripture had authority and influence on people.[1] The New Testament is a book which contains the great story of Jesus and other characters, the lives of whom are worthy to be followed.[2] This is evident in Dostoevsky's admiration and imitation of

---

1. *Dnevnik Pisatelya*, 1873, 134.
2. Rumyantseva, *Feodor Mikhaylovich Dostoevsky*, 14.

Jesus's life story and other biblical characters.[3] He also frequently read Bible stories,[4] and shared them with others.[5]

The gospel also had authority and influence in the childhood of Starets Zosima who repeated it almost word for word, just like Dostoevsky.[6] We see that the words of Starets Zosima are almost identical to Dostoevsky's words in the *Diary of a Writer* which he wrote about himself.[7]

During the second half of the pre-Siberian period, Dostoevsky changed his understanding of the Scripture. The Bible became for him an interesting book, but it lacked the ultimate authority he had once seen it to possess. This belief is evident in the priority Dostoevsky gave to socialist and atheistic books throughout that period.[8]

During the Siberian period, Dostoevsky viewed the Scripture as the word of God. This means that it has authority and the ability to influence people.[9] This belief was evidenced in Dostoevsky's own life. The gospel helped him "to better understand Christianity."[10] He also shared gospel stories with others, treating them as the word of God.[11] In the life of Goryanchikov in *The House of the Dead* one can see an attitude similar to the story of Christ.[12]

According to Dostoevsky, the Scripture is the ultimate truth.[13] This is evidenced by his frequent quotations of the gospel and his use of it as an ultimate truth in giving advice to people.[14] When asked by a mother which book he would recommend for her son, Dostoevsky promptly answered:

---

3. Grossman, *Dostoevsky*, 15.

4. *Dnevnik Pisatelya*, 1873, 134.

5. *F. M. Dostoevskiy v vospominaniyakh sovremennikov*, 79.

6. *Brat'ya Karamazovy*, 249. Also, the starets Zosima said that he had been taught to read by the book "One Hundred Four Holy Stories Chosen from Old and New Testament in Favour of John Gibner's Youth" (*Brat'ya Karamazovy*, 250).

7. *Brat'ya Karamazovy*, 249.

8. *Pis'ma*, Vol. 28, 24 March 1856, 223.

9. *Dnevnik Pisatelya*, 1873, 134.

10. *Dnevnik Pisatelya*, 1873, 134.

11. *F. M. Dostoevskiy v vospominaniyakh sovremennikov*, 79.

12. *Zapiski iz Mertvogo Doma*, 53–54.

13. *Dnevnik Pisatelya*, 1873, 134.

14. *Pis'ma*, Vol. 30, 19 December 1880.

"the gospel." The same conviction is seen in the life of Starets Zosima in *The Brothers Karamazov* in his advice to monks to obey the gospel.[15]

The Bible is also an influential Book. Its stories influenced people to repent and revealed to them the meaning of life. This is seen in the life of Alyosha[16] and Raskolnikov.[17] The gospel is God's word which is not changeable.[18] But in Dostoevsky's understanding, it needs to be rightly interpreted.[19]

5.2.2 Christ

From the time of Dostoevsky's childhood, one may notice some rudiments of his **understanding of Christ**. Christ, in his understanding, is a living personality.[20] Such an understanding of Christ is based on two pieces of evidence. First, there were Dostoevsky's own words in the *Diary of a Writer* in 1880. He recalled the moment from his childhood when he accepted Christ into his soul.[21] Dostoevsky's expression "accepted Christ in the soul" means that Christ occupies a central place in a person's life. Second, the practice of prayer which he took seriously since childhood, is evidence of his understanding of Christ as a living personality.[22]

For Dostoevsky, Christ was also Lord and the source of good.[23] He was one who shared the good by His mercy[24] to those who asked Him in prayer.[25] This is clearly demonstrated by Dostoevsky's specific requests in his prayers.[26]

---

15. *Brat'ya Karamazovy*, 137.

16. *Brat'ya Karamazovy*, 305–308.

17. F. M. Dostoevsky, *Polnoe Sobranie Sochineniy, Prestuplenie i Nakazanie* [The Complete Works of Dostoevsky, *Crime and Punishment*], [CD-ROM] (Izdatel'stvo Adept, 2002).

18. *Brat'ya Karamazovy*, 14.

19. *Brat'ya Karamazovy*, 147.

20. From early childhood, he positively accepted Christ in his soul (*Dnevnik Pisatelya*, 1880, 152). This is not just the testimony of a small child, because he spoke of it in later life.

21. *Dnevnik Pisatelya*, 1880, 152. Long before he wrote any novels there was a strong similarity between these witnesses and the story of starets Zosima in *The Brothers Karamazov*. Zosima, telling about his childhood memories, said he was only eight years old when he was first visited by some touch of the Spirit and at that time the word of God was sown in his heart (*Brat'ya Karamazovy*, 250).

22. Losskiy, *Bog i mirovoe zlo*, 36.

23. *Pis'ma*, Vol. 28, 23 July 1837, 38.

24. *Pis'ma*, Vol. 28, 8 October 1837, 41.

25. *Pis'ma*, Vol. 28, 3 December 1837, 44.

26. *Pis'ma*, Vol. 28, 8 October 1837, 41.

Similar requests are seen in the prayers of Makar and Varvara, the characters of *The Poor Folk*.[27]

In Dostoevsky's understanding, Christ as a human being lived a hard but perfect life in the first century. In Dostoevsky's mind, His life was the best example for mankind and one which ought to be followed. The way in which Dostoevsky's attitude toward Christ affected his behaviour was indicated by numerous examples given in the first part of this study. His behaviour in school along with his compassion and assistance to the needy all stemmed from his desire to imitate Christ and other Biblical characters.[28]

In the end of the pre-Siberian period, Dostoevsky changed his understanding of Christ. For him, **Christ** was no longer a living personality in the present, nor was He to be the Lord of one's life. This period was associated with Dostoevsky's "loss of Christ."[29] Lossky considered the expression "loss of Christ" to mean that Jesus was no longer considered to be a divine person by Dostoevsky.[30] Dostoevsky himself said that at that time he accepted the atheistic view of Belinsky,[31] meaning that he rejected Christ as a living personality.

But according to Dostoevsky, Christ was a human being[32] who lived in the first century.[33] He continued to view Christ as one who had lived an ideal life.[34] But Christ was merely one of many great men who have lived on earth, like Homer.[35]

---

27. *Bednye Lyudi*, 30–35.

28. *Bednye Lyudi*, 169.

29. *Bednye Lyudi*, 169.

30. Lossky, *Bog i mirovoe zlo*, 40.

31. *Dnevnik Pisatelya*, 1873, 10.

32. *Dnevnik Pisatelya*, 1873, 9.

33. From 1846 all the way to the penal colony there is no discussion of any problems of Christian content in his letters (*Dnevnik Pisatelya*, February 1841, 77) and any mention of God is only in passing in such stereotypical phrases as "for God's sake" (*Pis'ma*, December 1842, 80), "God knows" (*Pis'ma*, August 1844, 93), and "God forbid" (Losskiy, *Bog i mirovoe zlo*, 39). Comparing his life with his novel *The Poor Folk* and other works of this period, we notice many similarities. As in his life and his works of this period, almost nothing is said about God (*Bednye Lyudi*, 55). Also the works of this period have not discussed any problems with the Christian worldview (Losskiy, *Bog i mirovoe zlo*, 39).

34. Lauth, *Filosofiya Dostoevskogo v sistematicheskom izlozhenii*, 328.

35. *Pis'ma*, Vol. 30, 1 January 1880, 63.

The key words of Dostoevsky's ***understanding of Christ*** during the Siberian period can be found in his description of Christ in the letter to Fonvizina. Dostoevsky stated, "there is no one better, deeper, more attractive, reasonable, courageous and perfect than Christ."[36] Laut saw in this description the similarities with the Orthodox understanding of beauty, which points to the divinity and humanity of Christ. The beauty of Christ according to Orthodox understanding is first a reflection of the external, divine light of Christ as evident during the Transfiguration of Christ and after His Resurrection.[37] Second, Laut affirmed that it also refers to the internal beauty of Christ which consists of his virtues.[38] Laut also referred to Dostoevsky's letter to his niece Sofia Ivanova. Dostoevsky wrote that "neither Russia nor civilized Europe was able to produce an ideal person because there is only one positively beautiful person. This is Christ."[39] This image of Christ as "the only beautiful person" was dominant in the life of Dostoevsky during the Siberian period. A similar understanding of Christ is evident in the life of Aley and Goryanchikov in *The House of the Dead.*[40]

Dostoevsky's understanding of Christ during his post-Siberian period became clearer and deeper. Vladimir Soloviev, who knew Dostoevsky well, stated that for Dostoevsky, Christ was not only a personality of the past; Christ was God-Man.[41] Christ was the embodied Logos. Dostoevsky quoted the words of the Apostle John, "the Word became flesh" (John 1:14) and commented that all virtues of heaven and earth found their source in the embodied Logos. Iustin, scholar of Dostoevsky, held that the Apostle John's words contain the whole gospel. Humanity's only hope for knowing eternal reality was to be found in the fullness of Christ.[42] Dostoevsky stated that in

---

36. *Pis'ma*, Vol. 28, 20 February 1854, 175.

37. Lauth, *Filosofiya Dostoevskogo v sistematicheskom izlozhenii*, 328.

38. *Pis'ma*, Vol. 28, 20 February 1854, 175.

39. *Pis'ma*, 175.

40. *Zapiski iz Mertvogo Doma*, 643.

41. Reverent Iustin, *Dostoevsky o Evrope I slav'anstve* [Dostoevsky about Europe and the Slavs] (Moscow, Sretensky monastyr', 2001), 10 January 2011, http://www.pravoslavie.ru/sretmon/izdatel/justinpopovic-dostoevskij.htm.

42. Reverent Iustin.

Christ humanity not only realized its ideal, it found its essential dimension: "Christ is the reflection of God to the earth."[43]

Lossky was sure that for Dostoevsky, Christ was God. He came to this conclusion based on Dostoevsky's participation in communion within the Orthodox Church, since before the sacrament the pre-communion prayer is uttered, "Lord, I believe, and I confess that Thou art truly the Christ, the Son of the living God . . ."[44]

Dostoevsky paid attention to the human nature of the God-Man. For him, Christ was the only ideal,[45] the only one to fully overcome his personality, his "ego," and through this He sacrificed Himself entirely for everyone.[46] According to Dostoevsky, Christ's life was not made easier because of His omnipotent divinity. Quite the contrary, Dostoevsky was sure that Christ, by His human strength alone, accomplished His mission and made humanity free.[47]

5.2.3 Man

During the pre-Siberian period, Dostoevsky gave special emphasis to the **understanding of man's nature.**[48] He was sure that man was created perfect. For him, the original inner being of man contained no evil. This image of the first perfect community will be the dominant image in his life during the pre-Siberian period.

The Fall changed the first community. After the Fall, man became imperfect and unhappy.[49] Man is good and evil simultaneously.[50] The question

---

43. M. Dostoevsky, *Polnoe Sobranie Sochineniy, Iz zapisnoy tetradi, 1860-1865gg.* [The Complete Works of Dostoevsky, From his Notebooks, 1860–1865] [CD-ROM] (Izdatel'stvo Adept, 2002).

44. Losskiy, *Bog i mirovoe zlo*, 69.

45. *Dnevnik Pisatelya*, 1880, 153. "People were not able to create another high image to people."

46. M. Dostoevsky, *Polnoe Sobranie Sochineniy, Iz zapisnoy tetradi, 1860-1865gg.* [The Complete Works of Dostoevsky, From his Notebooks, 1860–1865] [CD-ROM] (Izdatel'stvo Adept, 2002).

47. Lauth, *Filosofiya Dostoevskogo v sistematicheskom izlozhenii*, 331.

48. *Pis'ma*, Vol. 28, 19 August 1839, 62.

49. *Pis'ma*, Vol. 28, 9 August 1838, 50.

50. In *The Poor Folk*, both Makar and Bikov were good and bad at the same time. The good was no longer good, since it was steeped with evil. It could also be seen in "Mister Prokharchin" where evil in relation to man are the men of his social layer, not the exploiters. See F. M. Dostoevsky, *Polnoe Sobranie Sochineniy, Gospodin Procharchin* [The Complete Works of Dostoevsky, Mister Procharchin], [CD-ROM] (Izdatel'stvo Adept, 2002).

of the origin of good and evil was basically left open by Dostoevsky during pre-Siberian period. Man is complex and contradictory. Evil is in man[51] and from him it is spread throughout society.[52] Especially noticeable is the manifestation of evil in the hierarchical system, where it took the form of humiliation, domination, vanity and egoism.[53]

At the end of the pre-Siberian period, Dostoevsky's **understanding of man** remained the same as in the first part of his pre-Siberian period. Man is complex, contradictory and unhappy. But throughout this time, his view of the source of man's unhappiness shifted. He came to see man as unhappy not because of the evil inside of him but because of the social injustice taking place around him.[54] Man was corrupted because of hierarchical structures. This understanding of man's problem was totally opposite from Dostoevsky's views from the first part of this period.

During his Siberian period, Dostoevsky retained his understanding of man as controversial and corrupted. Throughout his letters he described the anger and hatred of the convicts he encountered. When he looked at a man he compared him with his dominant image of Christ.[55]

In his novel *The House of the Dead* as well as in other Siberian stories, Dostoevsky deepened the idea of the complexity of man. The division between good and bad people did not occur on the basis of social grounds. A rich person, according to Dostoevsky, is not necessarily good.[56]

Man is so complicated that he can simultaneously be both good and evil. As in *The Poor Folk*, the goodness in man can be impregnated with evil. Just as he described the sinfulness of people he encountered in Siberia in his letters, so also conceit, hatred, greed, fear, cruelty and desire to dominate are portrayed by the characters of his novel *The House of the Dead*. He stated

---

51. Dostoevsky wrote about it to his brother in 1838. He said that "the atmosphere of the human soul consists of merging of heaven and earth." Dostoevsky thought then that "the world took on a negative value" (*Pis'ma*, Vol. 28, 9 August 1839, 62).

52. Kirpotin, *Molodoy Dostoevskiy*, 131.

53. See F. M. Dostoevsky, *Polnoe Sobranie Sochineniy, Netochka Nezvanova* [The Complete Works of Dostoevsky, Netochka Nezvanova], [CD-ROM] (Izdatel'stvo Adept, 2002). The contradiction of the man is so strong that in "The Double" the writer showed a bifurcated man with opposite qualities. See F. M. Dostoevsky, *Polnoe Sobranie Sochineniy, Dvoynik* [The Complete Works of Dostoevsky, The Double], [CD-ROM] (Izdatel'stvo Adept, 2002).

54. Kirpotin, *Molodoy Dostoevskiy*, 131.

55. Kirpotin, 16.

56. Kirpotin, 26.

that people can fall down and reach the state of beasts.[57] Evil can progress and give birth to other evils.[58]

But unlike the first period in which Dostoevsky could not see anything but good in a person, he discovered something new for himself about man. He found that every human being has within him the image of God.[59] The image here is something which is a part of human nature at the time of his creation.[60] This means that sometimes even the most brutal men can perform an act of goodness that would be free from evil. That is, sometimes he can sincerely, without greed and selfishness, start to love someone or something[61] although this does not happen often. The image of God is universal. It is present in every person always. Therefore, it is present even in the greatest sinner.

According to Dostoevsky during the post-Siberian period, **man** has an immortal soul.[62] He derived this belief from his conviction in the truth of God's reality. Dostoevsky stated that the immortality of the soul is as equally logical and natural as God's existence.[63] Since Christ is God-Man, man is immortal.[64] From this Dostoevsky held that it was logical to conclude also that the resurrection of man is real. He stated, "I and Soloviev believe in the real, literal, personal resurrection, and that it will be fulfilled on earth."[65] Ten years earlier he wrote to his niece, "Dear Sonya, do you not believe in the continuation of life and, more importantly, the progressive and the infinite, consciousness and the common merger of all? Let us be worthy of the best of both worlds, and of the resurrection."[66]

---

57. Zarin, "Biblioteka dlya chteniya," in *Kriticheskie razbory "Zapisok iz Mernvogo Doma,"* ed. V. Zelinskiy, 10.

58. *Zapiski iz Mertvogo Doma*, 154.

59. *Zapiski iz Mertvogo Doma*, 193.

60. Millkov, "Svetoch," in *Kriticheskie razbory "Zapisok iz Mernvogo Doma,"* ed. V. Zelinskiy, 8.

61. *Zapiski iz Mertvogo Doma*, 217.

62. *Dnevnik Pisatelya*, 1876. "There is only one supreme idea on earth, and that is – the idea of the immortality of the human soul, for all the other "supreme" ideas of life, which a person may live, only stem out of it."

63. *Dnevnik Pisatelya*, 1876.

64. Reverent Iustin, *Dostoevsky o Evrope I slav'anstve* [Dostoevsky about Europe and the Slavs], (Moscow: Sretensky monastyr', 2001), 10 January 2011, http://www.pravoslavie.ru/sretmon/izdatel/justinpopovic-dostoevskij.htm.

65. *Pis'ma*, Vol. 28, 24 March 1878.

66. *Pis'ma*, Vol. 28, 29 March 1868.

Dostoevsky remained sure that man is evil. His eyes looked with increasing fierceness at man. Man inspired by evil. In the *Diary of a Writer* Dostoevsky wrote, "Evil lurks in the person more deeply than is usually assumed."[67] Evil has many forms and manifests itself in all aspects of human life and influence on others, causing them pain and suffering. The same truth can be seen in such characters as Fyodor Pavlovich Karamazov, Smerdyakov and Ivan from the novel *The Brothers Karamazov*." Evil is so progressive in the lives of these characters that it led them to tragedy. One went insane, another was killed and a third committed both murder and suicide.

Dostoevsky did not subscribe to the theory of the influence of one's societal environment. He did not agree with the statement "if society will be arranged properly, once and for all the crimes will disappear, because they will not have anything left to protest, and all in one moment will become righteous."[68] "In no model of society," he wrote, "will you escape the evil . . . the human soul remains the same . . . abnormality and sin comes from it on their own."[69]

Man, according to Dostoevsky, is a free being. Nothing compels him to commit evil deeds. If a person deviates from the path of goodness and embarks on the path of evil, he suffers and has no right to shift the blame onto others, on the way in which he lives or on God, as if God had poorly created the world.[70] The problem is people and that they give priority to the material rather than the spiritual. The purpose of the Grand Inquisitor was purely earthly and spiritless. It was opposed by Christ with His love and freedom.[71]

The separation of good and evil was not done by the writer on social premises. There were good and bad dukes, generals and landlords. The commoners were the same way. The princes were both Myshkin and Valkovsky. Raskolnikov, Razumikhin and Marmeladova had basically one and the same medium in which to live but their paths were different.

Dostoevsky also remained true to the conviction that in every man there is an image of God. Having the image of God, man at any time can use his

---

67. Losskiy, *Bog i mirovoe zlo*, 171.

68. F. M. Dostoevsky, *Polnoe Sobranie Sochineniy, Prestuplenie i Nakazanie* [The Complete Works of Dostoevsky, *Crime and Punishment*], [CD-ROM] (Izdatel'stvo Adept, 2002).

69. *Dnevnik Pisatelya*, July 1887.

70. Losskiy, *Bog i mirovoe zlo*, 111.

71. *Brat'ya Karamazovy*, 212–227.

free will for the achievement of perfection. That is why man has high value.[72] We find this same truth in the novel *The Brothers Karamazov*. Even Fyodor Pavlovich was able to love and show care.[73]

Dostoevsky also continued to share the view that man is contradictory. In man there is a constant struggle between good and evil. Dostoevsky expressed this in the words of Dimitry Karamazov: "The devil is fighting with God, and the battlefield is the hearts of men."[74] Therefore, he was convinced that man is contradictory. Man, created in the image of God, became deeply distorted because of the fall. Thus, in the fallen man are present simultaneously the seeds of both good and evil.

Man as a free human being can walk in a hostile and indifferent way or he can entirely embrace the world by his love. The latter is the will of God.[75] In regard to human nature, Dostoevsky believed that man is God-centred but because of his freewill man oftentimes becomes devil-centred. Dostoevsky understood that man is continually coming nearer to either God or to the Devil.[76]

5.2.4 Redemption

During the first half of his pre-Siberian period, Dostoevsky, being dominated by the image of the "original perfect society," longed for ***man's redemption***. For him, redemption was the process of making man as happy as he was in the beginning. Dostoevsky's deep desire for redemption is evident in his aspiration to unravel the secret of man's happiness[77] and in his attitude of love and compassion for people.[78] It is also seen in his dreams,[79] and this was as the result of his inability to discover the way of redemption. Dostoevsky held that man is not able to redeem himself. Evil triumphs over good. Therefore, the

---

72. Losskiy, *Bog i mirovoe zlo*, 121.

73. *Brat'ya Karamazovy*, 82.

74. *Brat'ya Karamazovy*, 94.

75. Losskiy, *Bog i mirovoe zlo*, 111.

76. Reverent Iustin, *Dostoevsky o Evrope I slav'anstve* [Dostoevsky about Europe and the Slavs] (Moscow: Sretensky monastyr', 2001), 10 January 2011, http://www.pravoslavie.ru/sretmon/izdatel/justinpopovic-dostoevskij.htm.

77. Reverent Iustin, *Dostoevsky o Evrope I slav'anstve.*

78. *F. M. Dostoevskiy v vospominaniyakh sovremennikov*, 166–167.

79. *Pis'ma*, Vol. 28, January–February 1847, 137.

redemption of man can be possible only in dreams.[80] His idea of dreaming and fantasy as an attempt to rise above dull reality is disclosed in *White Nights*.[81]

At the end of the pre-Siberian period, Dostoevsky saw the **redemption** of man in the social dimension. Because of this, he shared his beliefs within a variety of political circles. According to his view, the main problem of people is the hierarchical system in which one class is oppressed by another. Redemption is found in the deliverance from the oppressive class by a sub-stitutionary political system.[82] In order to achieve this goal, any means can be used, even violence.[83]

Throughout the Siberian period, Dostoevsky saw *the redemption* of man not as a result of changes within the social environment, but throughout a man's life in accordance with the dominant image, the transformation of man to be as "beautiful as Christ," to have Christ's virtues. In Dostoevsky's under-standing, redemption is a long process which starts with faith in Christ and repentance.[84] Faith means regeneration of beliefs. Repentance, according to Dostoevsky, is man's regret of his sin and firm decision to abhor it. It involves a painful process, but the result has the external evidence of devotion to Christ. Thus, the process of man turning into a beast is stopped.[85] The result of repentance is the person's free decision to refuse the egoistic way of life.

The process and result of repentance can be seen in the life of Dostoevsky and in the lives of Goryanchikov and Aley, two characters in his work *The House of the Dead*.

According to Dostoevsky during the post-Siberian period, people can by **redeemed** only by Christ. Redemption is a long process of transformation of a man's life into Christ's way. The first meaning of Christ's death is the forgiveness of sins. To receive forgiveness man needs faith and repentance.

---

80. *Dnevnik Pisatelya*, 1877, 28.

81. The entire *White Nights* speaks about that (F. M. Dostoevsky, *Polnoe Sobranie Sochineniy, Belye Nochi* [The Complete Works of Dostoevsky, White Nights], [CD-ROM] (Izdatel'stvo Adept, 2002)).

82. Lauth, *Filosofiya Dostoevskogo v sistematicheskom izlozhenii*, 268.

83. Lauth, 270.

84. *Pis'ma*, Vol. 28, 20 February 1854, 175.

85. *Zapiski iz Mertvogo Doma*, 87–90.

As Starets Zosima said: "Be careful that repentance will not fall into decline, because God will forgive you."[86]

In Dostoevsky's understanding, there is solidarity of sin and crimes.[87] Man has to recognize the common guilt and suffer a just punishment even for those sins which he committed because he became guilty before he recognized his free will and moral responsibility.[88]

The second meaning of Christ's life and death, according to Dostoevsky, was the perfect example of love which was evident in His complete dedication to God's will.[89] For Dostoevsky, redemption is not only the forgiveness of sins. It is also a radical change in human "existence" affecting man's entire perception of life and life itself.[90]

The goal of redemption is kenosis. According to Dostoevsky, after Christ's embodiment as the ideal man, it was clear that the highest development of man is to come to an understanding that the highest goal of his personality is to annihilate his "ego," to give himself as a whole to everyone. For Dostoevsky, this is the greatest happiness.[91] This is Christ's paradise.[92]

5.2.5 The Church

According to Dostoevsky, the Orthodox Church is the true church. His **understanding of the church** is radical. Orthodoxy, according to Dostoevsky, had not forgotten Christ. It called all people, without exceptions, to unity. In the Orthodox Church, according to Dostoevsky, the external, or the rituals, were of little importance. The first is he who serves, not the one who is being

---

86. *Brat'ya Karamazovy*, 45.

87. *Brat'ya Karamazovy*, 285–286.

88. Lauth, *Filosofiya Dostoevskogo v sistematicheskom izlozhenii*, 403.

89. *Dnevnik Pisatelya*, 1873. A man, according to Dostoevsky, having gotten to know Christ, must live like Christ. Dostoevsky wrote in a letter to N. Lyubimov of the starets Zosima, "If we succeed, I will do a good thing: I will make one admit that a pure, perfect Christian is not abstract thing, but real, figurative, potential, personally sensed" (*Pis'ma*, Vol. 28, 8 July 1866).

90. Millard J. Erickson, *Christianskoe bogoslovie* [Christian Theology], (Sankt-Petersburg: Biblia dlya vseh, 1999), 761.

91. Losskiy, *Bog i mirovoe zlo*, 94.

92. M. Dostoevsky, *Polnoe Sobranie Sochineniy, Iz zapisnoy tetradi, 1860-1865gg.* [The Complete Works of Dostoevsky, From his Notebooks, 1860–1865] [CD-ROM] (Izdatel'stvo Adept, 2002).

served. In this regard Orthodoxy is not exactly identified with the existing Orthodox Church. He himself seldom went to church until 1871.[93]

For Dostoevsky, **the mission of the Church** was to resolve the contradictions existing in society and to create a harmony of interests leading to freedom, equality and fraternity. Also, the mission of the Church in Dostoevsky's understanding was the rise of spirituality in man.

The means of the mission of the Church is love: to love people by the example of Christ, regardless of circumstances.[94] This way one could create a perfect society. Seeing the example of love, Dostoevsky held that others would follow with their actions, and when the whole of Russia would become "Orthodox," it would need to carry this "Orthodoxy" into the rest of the world, creating universal happiness.[95]

In the 1860s Dostoevsky wrote, "All consists in the truth and rectitude of motivation, in love. Love is the foundation of motivation, a pledge of its durability. Love conquers cities. Without it, one can take nothing and no one will, except by force, but there are things that are impossible to take with force.[96] Love is more understandable than anything, more than all sorts of tricks and diplomatic niceties."[97] In his last novel, this is expressed by Zosima, almost word for word.[98]

The images of some of his characters are called to confirm Dostoevsky's views on the strength of Orthodoxy. For example, Mishkin was an example of gentleness. In any situation, he was balanced, kind and courteous. Independent in thought, self-critical to the extreme, he lived out the same principles which he preached. His preaching was done only with his life as an example.

The results of Orthodoxy in the world at large can also be seen throughout his writings, although they were small. Sonia influenced Raskolnikov, Myshkin influenced Kolya. Ivolgin and Alyosha – the children. It is assumed

---

93. *F. M. Dostoevsky v vospominaniyakh sovremennikov*, 358.

94. F. M. Dostoevsky, *Polnoe Sobranie Sochineniy, Stat'i i Kritika* [The Complete Works of Dostoevsky, Articles and Critical Works] [CD-ROM] (Izdatel'stvo Adept, 2002).

95. *Dnevnik Pisatelya*, 1876.

96. Grigory Florovsky, *O Dostoevskom* [About Dostoevsky], (Moscow: 1990), 15 May 2011, http://halkidon2006.orthodoxy.ru/bogoslovie/691_florovskii.htm.

97. F. M. Dostoevsky, *Polnoe Sobranie Sochineniy, Stat'i i Kritika* [The Complete Works of Dostoevsky, Articles and Critical Works] [CD-ROM] (Izdatel'stvo Adept, 2002).

98. *Brat'ya Karamazovy*, 272–275.

that this chain of influence would continue. Thus, Europe must be saved by Russia. Its impact on Europe should be positive. With all this, Dostoevsky still did not put the people of Russia above others.[99]

5.3 Conclusion

As the result of the overview of Dostoevsky's theology as one whole, some similarities and differences were identified. Differences are seen mostly between the periods of the life and work of Dostoevsky. The similarity of theology can be seen in the life and works of Dostoevsky belonging to the same period of life. The similarities relate to his understanding of Scripture, Christ, man, church and redemption. This is clearly evidenced in the way Dostoevsky proclaims his beliefs throughout his novels. The differences are seen in the emphasis. In his novels, Dostoevsky places a strong emphasis on each topic under consideration.

Thus, we can conclude that Dostoevsky wrote his works being driven by the same beliefs that he had at the time of writing of a given novel. His first task was to learn the secret of the happiness of man, later formulated in his beliefs and proclaimed through his works. During the post-Siberian period Dostoevsky's theology became more mature than in his pre-Siberian and Siberian periods. The dominant image was that of "Christ's Way."

---

99. *Pis'ma*, Vol. 28, 10 October, 1870.

CHAPTER 6

Influence of Dostoevsky's Theology on Society

6.1 Introduction

The purpose of first part of this chapter is to critically analyse the influence of Dostoevsky's theology on his contemporaries K. N. Leontiev, M. A. Antonovich, N. K. Mikhailovskiy and V. S. Soloviev. The choice of the above-mentioned thinkers and writers was made for three reasons. First, critical essays on Dostoevsky, investigated in this chapter, written by these thinkers, were written during the first three years after the death of Dostoevsky, from 1881 to 1883. During this short period of time, Russia had relatively the same political and socio-religious situation. Second, there is complete unanimity among scholars of Dostoevsky's work that Leontiev, Antonovich, Mikhailovsky and Soloviev were the first critics of Dostoevsky's faith immediately after his death.[1] Third, these thinkers represent different socio-political and religious movements. This allows one to see the influence of Dostoevsky, if not on all of society, then at least on much of it.

The purpose of the second part of this chapter is to see the relevance of Dostoevsky's "Christ Way" for a baptistic[2] contemporary community. To

---

1. See G. Pattison and D. O. Thompson, "Introduction: Reading Dostoevsky Religiously," in *Dostoevsky and the Christian Tradition*, ed. G. Pattison and D. O. Thompson, (Cambridge: 2001).

2. James McClendon used the term "baptist" for the Churches of the Radical Reformation (James McClendon, Jr. *Ethics: Systematic Theology, Vol. 1*, 19). For an extended

achieve this goal, Dostoevsky's "Christ Way" will be comparing with "The Gospel in Dostoevsky" from the Bruderhof Community[3] point of view.

6.2 Influence of Dostoevsky's Theology on the Society of His Time

6.2.1 Influence on Slavophilism: K. Leontiev

In K. N. Leontiev's[4] article "On Universal Love,"[5] "Dostoevsky's Speech on Pushkin Celebration," which was published in the Moscow News[6] was critically examined. Leontiev acknowledged that Dostoevsky's speech touched him so deeply that for a long time he could not find rest.[7] There was, however, a reason for Leontiev's worry. He was annoyed that Dostoevsky's speech

---

definition of the term "baptistic" see Lina Andronovienė and Parush Parushev, "Church, State, and Culture: On the Complexities of Post-Soviet Evangelical Social Involvement," *Theological Reflections*, EAAA Journal of Theology 3 (2004): 194; Rollin G. Grams and Parush R. Parushev, "Editors' Preface," in *Towards an Understanding of European Baptist Identity: Listening to the Churches in Armenia, Bulgaria, Central Asia, Moldova, North Caucasus, Omsk and Poland* eds. Rollin G. Grams and Parush R. Parushev (Prague, CZ: IBTS Publisher, 2006), 10; Parushev, "Theologie op een baptistenmanier," 8; and Parush R. Parushev, "Baptistic Convictional Hermeneutics," in *The Plainly Revealed Word of God? Baptist Hermeneutics in Theory and Practice*, ed. Helen Dare and Simon Woodman (Macon, GA: Mercer University Press, 2011), 173.

3. "The pacifist communitarian sect, known formally as the "Society of Brothers," and more colloquially as the "Bruderhof," today consists of three communities in the eastern United States, which together have a total population of between eight and nine hundred persons. In the half century of its existence, the sect has at various times established now defunct communities in Germany, Liechtenstein, England, Paraguay and Uruguay. The original community was founded in Germany in 1920 by Eberhard Arnold, who led the group until his death in 1935, and whose religious teaching and heirs continue to dominate the "Society of Brothers." John McKelvie, *Whitworth, God's Blueprints: A Sociological Study of Three Utopian Sects* (London; Boston: Routledge & Kegan Paul, 1975), 167. Bruderhof Community exhibits organically the marks of a baptistic community as defined earlier.

4. K. N. Leontiev (1831–1891) Russian diplomat, thinker of the religious conservative stream: philosopher, novelist, literary critic, essayist, late Slavophile (Entsiklopedicheskiy Slovar 'FA Brokgauza I IA Efrona ("Vehi" Library), 15 January 2011, http://www.vehi.net/brokgauz/).

5. Leontiev's article "On Universal Love" was first published in the book *Our New Christians: Dostoevsky and Count Leo Tolstoy* (in regard to Dostoevsky's speech at the celebration of Pushkin and Leo Tolstoy's story "What Do Men Live By?"), Moscow: 1882, (K. L. Leontiev, *O Vsemirnoy Liubvi* (Biblioteka "Vehi," 2001), 15 January 2011, http://www.vehi.net/leontev/dost.html).

6. Dostoevsky's speech on Pushkin was delivered by F. M. Dostoevsky on 8 June 1880 at a meeting of the Society of Lovers of Russian Literature, published 1 August in the *Diary of a Writer* (*Dnevnik Pisatelya*, 1 August 1880).

7. K. L. Leontiev, *O Vsemirnoy Liubvi* (Biblioteka "Vehi," 2001), 15 January 2011, http://www.vehi.net/leontev/dost.html.

at the Pushkin celebration, with which he disagreed, was received with such enthusiasm by the listeners. Leontiev recognized the ability of Dostoevsky to influence others: "A clear, sharp mind, faith, boldness of speech . . . Against all of this is hard for one's hearing to resist."[8]

In his speech Dostoevsky called for humility, patience, love and a world-wide unification of all people in Christ.[9] From the entire speech, only that part which calls for universal brotherhood seemed original to Leontiev,[10] so he left without comment Dostoevsky's appeal to humility and concentrated on the "original parts." Leontiev argued that Dostoyevsky's words about the universal reconciliation of all peoples were semi-Christian.[11] Therefore, he placed Dostoevsky with that part of Russian society "which neither wants to abandon their love for Europe, nor can accept the latest conclusions of its civilization."[12] Leontiev came to this conclusion on the grounds that he approached Dostoevsky's speech in his analysis from the perspective of a Slavophile.[13] Slavophilism was mainly represented by the religious-national movement. Therefore, as a convinced Slavophile, he defended his position by using religious and nationalist arguments common for the members of this movement.

Slavophiles believed the saying that the "West is decaying" and therefore everything that comes from that direction is harmful for the Russian people.[14]

Leontiev understood that for the implementation of universal reconciliation for which Dostoevsky called there must exist a love towards people of

---

8. Leontiev, *O Vsemirnoy Liubvi.*

9. *Dnevnik Pisatelya* (1 August 1880).

10. Leontiev, *O Vsemirnoy Liubvi.*

11. Leontiev.

12. Leontiev.

13. *Entsiklopedicheskiy Slovar' F. A. Brokgauza I I. A. Efrona* (Biblioteka "Vehi"), 15 January 2011, http://www.vehi.net/brokgauz/.

14. In the 1840s two lines had emerged in Russian philosophical thought: Slavophilism and Westernization. Public opinion tends to have reliable knowledge on the fate of the fatherland, the driving forces in its history, the mission that befell Russia. Opinions were divided. Some people thought that Russia was simply lagging behind the advanced countries of Europe and that it was doomed to continue the path traversed by the West, and will inevitably have to repeat it. Others, however, believed that as a result of Peter's reforms, Russia has lost its own way, lost its national roots, and that it was destined to revive the Old Russian Orthodox beginning of life and culture in order to tell the world its own, new message. Supporters of the first opinion formed a camp of adherents – Westerners; supporters of the second opinion, a camp of Slavophiles (A. S. Dolinin, *Dostoevskiy i drugie* [Leningrad: Hudozhestvennaiya Literatura, 1989], 132).

all nations. He correctly understood the appeal of Dostoevsky to universal reconciliation through love for all peoples.[15] But, being a nationalist, he did not understand how one can love people who are known for their arrogant attitudes towards the Russian people. For Leontiev love is a manifestation of pity and admiration, and he could find no reason why the Russian people could ever display pity or admiration especially to Europeans.[16] He came to this conclusion because he believed that a person should be loved for something rather than for no reason. Dostoevsky had another opinion. He was convinced that the human needs to be loved even if he is a great sinner.[17]

Leontiev as a Slavophile was in opposition to the Westerners and to the West in general.[18] He was so negatively opposed towards Western nations, especially against the French, that he was ready to learn to love a Turk, or an Asian, but never and especially a Frenchman.[19] For this he had a reason: historically Westerners were inspired by recent events in the West, especially by the French Revolution.[20] Leontiev shared the view of Dostoevsky that for the Russian people manifestation of mercy was easier than for other people: "I understand that that part of Christ's teachings which talks about forgiveness, that is, the highest manifestation of this moral love, is easier to comprehend for Russian people than for any other nation."[21] But he himself was against the manifestation of charity, behaving like the Good Samaritan to the French. Leontiev himself was not only against helping Western people,

---

15. *Dnevnik Pisatelya* (1 August 1880).

16. Leontiev, *O Vsemirnoy Liubvi*.

17. *Brat'ya Karamazovy*, 26.

18. Westerners were accused of their excessive predilection of all that was foreign, for their dislike of the fatherland and blind imitation of all European things, while Slavophiles were accused of failing to understand the natural course of history, defense of ignorance and barbarism, in clinging to the land and unneeded patriotism. Thus, some people appear in the halo of the progressive, advanced people, while others, in the best scenario, in the form of cultural reactionaries. In reality both Westerners and Slavophiles loved Russia. They loved it in their own way, taking into account philosophical, moral and religious characteristics inherent to their movements. Westerners liked to see Russia without the inherent flaws and imperfections, but sometimes this desire took the form of malicious criticism and hostility, going into naked hatred (Dolinin, *Dostoevskiy i drugie*, 131–132).

19. Leontiev preached "Byzantinism" (Church, monarchism, class hierarchy) and the union of Russia with Eastern countries as a protective agent of revolutionary change (*Entsiklopedicheskiy Slovar' F. A. Brokgauza I I. A. Efrona* (Biblioteka "Vehi"), 15 January 2011, http://www.vehi.net/brokgauz/).

20. Russkoe obshchestvo *40-50-h godov 19-go vekov*, 12–13.

21. Leontiev, *O Vsemirnoy Liubvi*.

but even viewed with true disdain those who did good to Europeans. He looked with the same disregard upon Dostoevsky.[22] But Dostoevsky was neither a Westerner nor a Slavophile. He wrote that "all our Slavophilism and Westernization is nothing but one great misunderstanding." He believed that on the part of Slavophiles there was, perhaps, something even more than an misunderstanding: rather a sin and a great one, because in the very foundation of their conception lay an unpardonable blindness in understanding the coming destiny of humanity. In their quest for national self-assertion they did not sufficiently appreciate that in the main feature of the Russian people, its universalism, they distorted the face of history according to their narrow-minded thinking.[23]

Leontiev derived his second block of arguments against universal reconciliation from his religious beliefs.[24] First, he resorted to the teachings of Jesus and the apostles. Unlike Dostoevsky, Leontiev did not find in the words of Jesus and the apostles a call for worldwide reconciliation, but a warning of the impending deterioration of relations between people:

> It is not a complete and universal triumph of love and universal truth in the land that was promised to us by Christ and His apostles, but on the contrary, something like the apparent failure of evangelical preaching in the world, because the proximity of the end should coincide with recent efforts to make all good Christians . . .[25]

Leontiev was convinced that people must prepare not for universal brotherhood, but for the impending catastrophe. To confirm his words, he quoted the Apostle Paul, "While people are saying, 'Peace and safety,' destruction will come on them suddenly, as labor pains on a pregnant woman, and they will not escape" (1 Thess 5:3). Then he quoted Jesus's words, warning about the appearance of false Christs:

> Jesus answered: "Watch out that no one deceives you. For many will come in my name, claiming, 'I am the Messiah,' and will

---

22. Leontiev.

23. Dolinin, *Dostoevskiy i drugie*, 112.

24. Dolinin. Leontiev believed the main danger for Orthodox Russia consisted in Western liberalism.

25. Dolinin.

deceive many. You will hear of wars and rumors of wars, but see to it that you are not alarmed. Such things must happen, but the end is still to come. Nation will rise against nation, and kingdom against kingdom. There will be famines and earthquakes in various places. All these are the beginning of birth pains." (Matt 24:4–8)

Citing this link Leontiev suggested that Dostoevsky's teaching of universal reconciliation in Christ contradicted the words of Jesus himself. He drew a parallel between the false Christs, of whom both Jesus and Dostoevsky warned, whose aim was to divert people from the truth. Leontiev blamed Dostoyevsky for his effort to appeal to the image of Christ apart from the church. All of this Leontiev perceived as a concession to European democracy.[26]

Leontiev explained how, according to his understanding of Orthodoxy, loving Europeans with all one's heart was only possible if Europeans were truly to repent.[27] "To put on Christ," in his opinion, meant to approach a priest and confess. Leontiev had even compiled a sample of repentance for the Europeans.[28] One must come to an Orthodox priest, and in humility say,

> My father, I realize that the republic is nonsense, that freedom is a worn platitude, that our nation, which in the past was truly great, now is no longer worthy of any attention, and to myself I seem so stupid and so low that I die of shame and anguish, teach me . . . Convert me . . . I know that Christians must have the force of will and humility of mind before your teaching . . . I agree to accept all, even that which is disgusting to me and what is disgusting to my stupefied mind, brought up with faith in progress, things to which it can not agree. Essentially, I decide to consider any sympathy for this funny, liberal mind to assume as an error, mistake, temptation.[29]

---

26. L. M. Rozenblium, *Tvorcheskie dnevniki Dostoevskogo* [Dostoevsky's Creative Diaries], (Moscow: Nauka, 1981), 141.

27. Westerners were little interested in religion; almost all of them were united by the idea of secularism in different spheres of public life. Most of all them valued political freedom and were advocates of socialism (Dolinin, *Dostoevskiy i drugie*, 132).

28. Leontiev, *O Vsemirnoy Liubvi*.

29. Leontiev.

As a religious conservative philosopher, he was an opponent of Western liberalism and a supporter of keeping the tradition and faith of the Russian community.[30] According to Leontiev, one can love a person, only if he were to repent and become Orthodox. A confession, in his view, should come from the fear of God. Therefore, if the Europeans would suffer some misfortune, then it would be possible for one to rejoice in it, referring to statements of Father Filaret of the need for corporal punishment which may lead a person to know the truth.[31] He saw some parallels between his understanding of the punishment of sinners and the understanding of Dostoevsky on the subject, since for the author without crime and punishment there would not be a Resurrection.[32] Therefore, the mission of the Orthodox Church was to help Europeans come to repentance. The path was not in the provision of love and mercy but in possible punishment.[33] Leontiev was enraged by Dostoevsky's call to love people, especially when this call applied to Europeans.[34]

From criticism of Dostoevsky's speech, Leontiev went into a general criticism of "Dostoevsky preaching." Of Dostoevsky's "sermons" on mutual love, forgiveness, only part of the orthodox doctrine, he said:

> He seems to speak to people constantly between the lines. He repeats by the mouths of his characters, portrays with his drama, and inspires them, "Do not be angry and dried-up, do not rush to rebuild in your ways your own civic life, occupy yourself first of all with life in your own heart, do not provoke, and you are good the way you are, try to be even kinder, love, forgive, regret, believe in God and Christ, pray and love. If the people themselves will be good, kind, noble and compassionate, then civil life will become much bearable, and most of injustice and

---

30. In conservatism the principal value is preserving the traditions of society, its institutions, beliefs, and even "prejudices." Its ideology emerged as a reaction to "the horrors of the French Revolution." It opposes liberalism, which requires economic freedom and socialism, which consequently calls for social equality (Russkoe obshchestvo *40-50-h godov 19-go vekov*, 12–13).

31. Leontiev, *O Vsemirnoy Liubvi.*

32. Leontiev.

33. Actually Dostoevsky was a radical Orthodox believer.

34. Dostoevsky and his works called for love of people even if they did not become part of the Orthodox faith (*Brat'ya Karamazovy*, 26).

hardships of civilian life will be eased under the healing influence of personal warmth.[35]

Leontiev concluded that Dostoevsky could be called a moralist but not a preacher of Orthodoxy.[36] The reason was that he was not talking about the impending disaster. According to Leontiev this was not Christianity, because Christianity is not so optimistic about the world. In his view, Orthodox teaching talks about the future development of evil. He could not understand why one needed to care about future generations, when everything will be destroyed. He concluded that it is necessary to care only about immediate things and loved ones and not for humanity as a whole.[37]

As proof of his accusations of the half-Christianity of Dostoevsky, Leontiev referred to the writer's novel *Crime and Punishment*. He argued that there was very little "Christian" in Sonya Marmeladova, one of the main characters who was called to serve as an example for the readers. The problem of Sonya, according to him, was that she read only the gospel. According to Leontiev this was not Orthodoxy. To be Orthodox means "to read the gospel through the perspective of patristic teaching, otherwise one could get from the Scriptures the ideas of eunuchism, Lutheranism, Molokanism and other false teachings that were so numerous and all of which themselves derive directly from the gospel or even from the Bible."[38] He further argued his position:

> We also note one detail: this young girl Marmeladova, somehow does not attend the public prayers, does not seek the advice of clergy and monks, does not kiss the miracle-working icons and relics, attends only a requiem for her father. Whereas in real life such a woman certainly would have done all of this, if only she woke up to a living religious feeling . . .[39]

He concluded "that Dostoevsky at the time when he wrote *Crime and Punishment*, thought very little about the present, that is, about Christianity."[40]

---

35. Leontiev, *O Vsemirnoy Liubvi*.

36. Leontiev.

37. Leontiev.

38. Leontiev.

39. Leontiev.

40. Leontiev.

Also, comparing the other works of Dostoevsky and his understanding of Orthodoxy, Leontiev came to the same conclusion, that through them, the writer did not preach the full teaching of Orthodoxy. Thus, in the novel *The Devils*, Leontiev saw general evangelical Christianity but not Orthodox Christianity. In *The Brothers Karamazov*, though he saw some approximation to the true Orthodoxy, as there was more written about monks, he was still not pleased with the image of monasticism in the novel.[41]

The general conclusion Leontiev arrived regarding Dostoevsky was as follows:

> It's too idealistic, introduced into Christianity by this speech of Dostoevsky, there is a novelty in relation to the Church, awaiting nothing particularly fruitful from mankind in the future, but this shade does not have in it anything personal, especially Russian, nor is particularly new in relation to the dominant European thought of the eighteenth and nineteenth centuries.[42]

He considered Dostoevsky as almost pernicious and almost a heretic. He was convinced that the only entity to which the love of the Russian people should be directed was the Orthodox Church.[43] In his arguments, he quoted K. P. Pobedonostsev, "Love above all else our holy Church, so the person who loves her, once having learned the supreme beauty will not want to trade her for anything else . . ."[44] Since Christ is only known through the Church, in Dostoevsky's speech Leontiev saw the proclamation of the way to Christ apart from the Orthodox Church. Paraphrasing Dostoevsky's words and giving them a negative tone, he turned to Europe:

> "Oh, how much we hate you, modern Europe, for destroying in yourself all that is great, elegant and holy, and continues to destroy it where we are, poor ones, by your precious pernicious

---

41. Leontiev.

42. Leontiev.

43. The main goal of Slavophiles was returning Russia to the beginnings of the Orthodox life. Slavophiles were the true bearers of the Orthodox culture (Dolinin, *Dostoevskiy i drugie*, 132).

44. Leontiev, *O Vsemirnoy Liubvi*.

breath!" He further says that if this kind of hatred is sin, then he agrees to live all his days in such a sin.[45]

Thus, according to the testimony of Leontiev himself, Dostoevsky had an impact on others and upon himself.

6.2.2 Influence on Westernism: M. Antonovich

M. A. Antonovich,[46] in his article "Mystic-Ascetic Novel"[47] critically analyzed Dostoevsky's novel *The Brothers Karamazov*. By his convictions, he was the direct opposite of Leontiev. Antonovich was a staunch materialist, the ideological successor of N. G. Chernyshevsky.[48] He was convinced that Dostoevsky wrote his novel *The Brothers Karamazov* based on his beliefs. Therefore, Antonovich explored the novel *The Brothers Karamazov* in the light of his opinion of the writer. According to him, Dostoevsky after prison became a convinced Slavophile.

Antonovich came to this conclusion from his understanding of Dostoevsky and his brother Michael as the publicists and editors of the journals "Time" and "Epoch."[49] According to him, after the end of his journalistic activities, Dostoevsky got involved in mysticism and asceticism.[50] But one cannot agree with Antonovich, as Dostoevsky simultaneously with the closure of magazines "Time" and Epoch" did not stop his journalistic activities. He published *Diary of a Writer* in which he included his articles from 1873 till his death.[51]

---

45. Leontiev.

46. Maxim Alexeevich Antonovich (1835–1918), Russian literary critic, essayist, philosopher. In the history of Russian philosophy, he took the place of a popularizer of materialist views. He was one of the first Darwinists in Russia, promoted Darwinism articles in the 1860s and published a book *Darwin and His Theory* (Sankt-Petersburg 1895), (*Entsiklopedicheskiy Slovar' F. A. Brokgauza I I. A. Efrona* (Biblioteka "Vehi"), 15 January 2011, http://www.vehi. net/brokgauz/).

47. M. A. Antonovich, *Mistiko-asketicheskiy roman* (Literatura, 2007), 10 January 2011, http://www.herzenlib.org/page21.php.

48. *Entsiklopedicheskiy Slovar' F. A. Brokgauza I I. A. Efrona* (Biblioteka "Vehi"), 15 January 2011, http://www.vehi.net/brokgauz/.

49. Antonovich led continuous arguments with such magazines as "Time" and "Epoch" and with their leaders N. N. Strahov and F. M. Dostoevsky (1861–1864). F. M. Dostoevsky, *Polnoe Sobranie Sochineniy, 'Stat'i i Kritika 1867 god'* [The Complete Works of Dostoevsky] [CD-ROM] (Izdatel'stvo Adept, 2002).

50. Antonovich, *Mistiko-asketicheskiy roman*, 10 January 2011, http://www.herzenlib. org/page21.php.

51. See *Dnevnik Pisatelya*, 1873.

Throughout the novel *The Brothers Karamazov* Antonovich saw a call to a mystical-ascetic life. Antonovich stated in the following way the essence of the mystical teachings of Dostoevsky:

> Russia with its simple and uneducated people, is the most religious nation in the world, it stands on the highest degree of perfection of the religious and spiritual education, so that it does not need any secular education. Russian people are "people-God-bearers," as expressed by the elder Zosima, pseudonym of Dostoevsky. Education is the spiritual light that illuminates the soul, illuminating the heart, and Dostoevsky speaks from his perspective that "our people were enlightened long ago, taking in them the essence of Christ and of His teachings, that while our land is poor, but Christ walked all over it blessing it."[52]

Consequently, according to Antonovich, Dostoevsky called for an ascetic monastic life. Antonovich arrived at this conclusion coming from the description of a Russian man in the novel *The Brothers Karamazov*: "Russian common people are different in their special love and respect to mysticism and asceticism, in the strong effort of fasting, obedience, chastity, and all other kinds of mortification of sinful flesh."[53] These features of the Russian people, according to Antonovich are inherent in monks. Therefore, as Dostoevsky called for a monastic-like life, then the European enlightenment and education was opposite to the "spirit of the simple Russian people," as it led to disbelief. This means that if a simple Russian man wanted to have mental development and get a scientific European education, "then together with education he would also receive the poison of disbelief, mental pride and alienation from the church."[54]

This approach was dictated by Antonovich's atheistic view. As a former editor of the "Contemporary," he rejected the path of faith for the Russian people. The only way he saw for the Russian people was in the social transformation

---

52. Antonovich, *Mistiko-asketicheskiy roman*, 10 January 2011, http://www.herzenlib.org/page21.php.

53. Antonovich, *Mistiko-asketicheskiy roman*, 10 January 2011, http://www.herzenlib.org/page21.php.

54. Antonovich.

of society and this issue he closely tied to the Europeanization of Russia.[55] To Antonovich, to be educated meant to be an atheist,[56] so it was difficult for him to understand the way of faith offered by Dostoevsky. Antonovich believed that Dostoevsky called all educated people to renounce Western education and humbly enter monasteries. In the monastery, they should choose as their leader some old man, to surrender to his full disposal, to be with him in obedience, to renounce their will and surrender to his will in everything, as did one of the characters of the novel, Alyosha Karamazov.[57] But Dostoevsky had not called for the abandonment of education; he called for a renunciation of godless doctrines that came from the West. Dostoevsky did not call Alyosha to go to a monastery but to the world, loving and helping people.[58]

Antonovich saw similarities between this appeal and the life of Dostoevsky himself. He cited the *Diary of a Writer*, in which the writer told us that he "once again accepted Christ in his soul, whom He knew in my parents' house as a child and who was lost when he was transformed into a European liberal."[59] Antonovich correctly notes that the basis of Dostoevsky's belief is faith in Christ, which is reflected in his works. But under "European liberalism" Dostoevsky did not mean education, but atheistic beliefs.[60] Antonovich, as a follower of Belinsky,[61] could not understand how the path of social transformation could be associated with faith in God, with inner freedom.[62]

---

55. "Antonovich was a follower of Belinsky, who in 1844 accepted the latest militant declaration of atheism. He was fascinated by the famous aphorism of Karl Marx, "religion is the opiate of the masses." The abolition of religion as the illusory happiness of the people is the demand for their real happiness. L. Grossman, *Dostoevskiy* (Moscow: Molodaya Gvardiya, 1965), 78.

56. Grossman, 78.

57. Antonovich, *Mistiko-asketicheskiy roman*, 10 January 2011, http://www.herzenlib.org/page21.php.

58. *Brat'ya Karamazovy*, 67.

59. See *Dnevnik Pisatelya* (August 1880).

60. *Brat'ya Karamazovy*, 466.

61. From the end of 1877 for three months Antonovich directed the Department of Criticism in the magazine "Word." In a number of articles, he criticized modern journalism and literature for the perversion of the ideals of V. G. Belinsky (*Entsiklopedicheskiy Slovar 'FA Brokgauza I IA Efrona* (Biblioteka "Vehi"), 15 January 2011, http://www.vehi.net/brokgauz/).

62. In the centre of the universe, Westerners placed personality, a living human ego. History for them has been synonymous with progress, whose ultimate aim was to create a society capable of ensuring the conditions of complete freedom, prosperity and harmonious development to the personality. The driving force of history is not the masses, but rationally-minded individuals. Social progress will advance simultaneously with the humanization of

He was not happy with the fact that in *The Brothers Karamazov* mystical-ascetics elements protruded instead of the humane element. In his view, the novel contains not all-forgiving love for all and everything, but a strict, unforgiving austerity.[63] Antonovich sees correctly in Dostoevsky's "sermon" that people without faith in God are doomed to misery and perdition but he could not accept this truth on the basis of his belief. Therefore, he perceived the division by Dostoevsky of people into saints and sinners as an insult by the writer. He argued,

> Real people with flesh and spirit, with a mixture of good and evil are not present here, but there is only the holy, righteous, standing above all human weaknesses on one side of, as if they were angels in the flesh, owing all their grandeur, and their righteousness, their strength to a strong and clear unwavering faith, but on the other hand unrepentant and sleeping sinners, doubters and unbelievers, and lost together with faith all spiritual love, shame and conscience, all of morality, all human likeness – in a word, incarnated devils, with pleasure giving themselves to evil and sowing it everywhere.[64]

He did not understand why people like Alyosha and Starets Zosima were happy, and Fyodor Pavlovich and Smerdyakov unhappy. It was annoying that Alyosha was loved by all, that wherever he was he brought peace, love, grace, good intentions and justice. All of this was because he believed in immortality and in God; he said, "I want to live for immortality, and do not accept a compromise."[65] Also he was annoyed by Starets Zosima:

> All his followers considered him a saint during his lifetime. All of his God-pleasing activity was ascetic teachings and moral charity. He was a refuge, spiritual support and consolation to all suffering, encumbered, grieving and angry and demanding assistance. All believers of all ages, ranks and states, and both

---

the individual consciousness and the whole system of social relations. (*Istoria Rossii v 19-go veke*, 489)

63. Antonovich, *Mistiko-asketicheskiy roman*, 10 January 2011, http://www.herzenlib.org/page21.php.

64. Antonovich.

65. *Brat'ya Karamazovy*, 24.

sexes, trustful, sincerely and frankly disclosed to him their hearts and minds, their doubts and perplexities, their spiritual needs and sorrows, their sins and sinful thoughts. And this holy man satisfied and reassured them all, and no one left him without relief and mental peace.[66]

Also, the negative statements of Zosima about Lutherans and Catholics, according to Antonovich, showed Dostoevsky's generally negative attitude towards the West.[67] In Dimitry Karamazov and in his repentance Antonovich saw the declaration of Dostoevsky's mysticism, as Dimitry turned from a rowdy and a fornicator into a saint, just because he admitted that he was "to blame for all and everything."[68]

Negative characters in the book, according to Antonovich, did not love anyone. For example, Rakitin: "He does not believe in anything, doesn't like anyone, and doesn't have higher interests. He despises Alyosha the angel, mocks Starets Zosima himself and all the monastic brethren."[69] Antonovich concluded that Dostoevsky "feels hatred and anger towards this his creation as his personal enemy and offender, who is a criminal, for whom there is no pity or compassion, and who does not deserve forgiveness."[70]

Antonovich did not understand the attitude of Dostoevsky to suffering. He argued,

> In terms of asceticism, why should we strive to minimize or mitigate the suffering of the earth? Are these sufferings a sin or are they wrong? Not at all, these sufferings are useful for people; they strengthen and purify the soul, like gold is purified by fire in the furnace, and generally they contribute to the moral standards of people. Therefore, not only must one endure the sufferings with pleasure, not only avoid and eliminate them, but one must still look for them. That is what the true ascetics do.

---

66. Antonovich, *Mistiko-asketicheskiy roman*, 10 January, 2011, http://www.herzenlib.org/page21.php.

67. Antonovich.

68. *Brat'ya Karamazovy*, 430.

69. Antonovich, *Mistiko-asketicheskiy roman*, 10 January, 2011, http://www.herzenlib.org/page21.php.

70. Antonovich.

Zosima gave Alyosha a covenant, if you remember, "In sorrow seek happiness."[71]

Thus, Antonovich concluded that Dostoevsky thought people do not need any new laws, reforms and measures to eliminate suffering; "it is only necessary to destroy that illusion, when people mistake something bad or unpleasant for something which they consider to be suffering and assure them that the sufferings are blessings and happiness as such."[72]

So, Antonovich concluded that Dostoevsky believed that religion should lay in the foundation of civil society and be a major guiding principle for both personal and public life and activity. By religion he means the church or even a monastery.[73]

Therefore, knowing that Dostoevsky continued to influence people through his works, even after his death, Antonovich considered it his rightful duty to oppose Dostoevsky's sermons. He acknowledged that "the voice of Dostoevsky is now silent for ever, but his works are still alive, speak loudly and preach, and, perhaps, their preaching became more real."[74]

Thus, Antonovich represented the extreme wing of the Westerners. Looking at *The Brothers Karamazov* from his atheist, materialist perspective, all the things that relate to faith in God he rejected. For him, the transformation of Russia lay in a social rather than a religious transformation of society. But despite his negative attitude, he well understood Dostoyevsky's main ideas. He could see that Dostoevsky proclaimed in *The Brothers Karamazov* transformation of man and society as a whole only through faith in God.

---

71. Antonovich.

72. In general, Slavophiles and Westerners shared a sense of discontent with Russia, and the established political and social conditions. They were united in the desire to find ways that they thought could alter the existing situation.

73. Antonovich, *Mistiko-asketicheskiy roman*, 10 January, 2011, http://www.herzenlib.org/page21.php.

74. Antonovich.

6.2.3 Influence on the Narodnik Movement: N. Mikhailovskiy

N. K. Mikhailovskiy[75] in his article "Cruel Talent"[76] explored Dostoevsky's work from the populist (Russian *narodnik*) position.[77] He spoke of Dostoevsky as of a great and original writer who was worthy of careful study and represented a great interest for the people of his time.[78]

In the beginning of his article, Mikhailovskiy stated his opinion of Dostoevsky and his works. He described Dostoevsky as a "cruel talent," who exalted suffering in his works. In his opinion, there were three reasons that allowed him to come to that conclusion. These were "respect for the existing general order, the thirst for personal preaching and the cruel talent" of Dostoyevsky.[79] A subjective view of the historic populism led him to such a generalized estimate of Dostoevsky's work.[80]

In his article, Mikhailovskiy's discussion was limited to only the last reason. For his research, he took only a few small works of Dostoevsky (in terms of volume), such as *Notes from Underground*, *The Gambler* and *The Village of Stepanchikovo*, in which, in his opinion, suffering is made very visible.[81] He argued that "violence and martyrdom have always occupied Dostoevsky, and that is part of their appeal, this peculiar craving for cruelty." In his opinion, Dostoevsky resorted specifically to scenes of cruelty, out of love for them.[82]

---

75. Nikolai Konstantinovich Mikhailovsky (1842–1904), Russian journalist, sociologist, literary critic and theorist of populism. From 1868 on participated in the journal "Notes of the Fatherland." After the death of N. A. Nekrasov (1877) he became one of the editors of the journal, together with Saltykov-Shchedrin and G. Z. Eliseev (*Mir na Rubezhe XIX – XX vekov: Tendentsiya, razvitiya, protivorechiya, revolyutsii* [Moscow: Izdatel'stvo MAI, 1991], 22).

76. N. K. Mihaylovskiy, *Zhestokiy talent*, 10 January 2011, http://az.lib.ru/m/mihajlowskij_n_k/text_0042.shtml.

77. Populists believed that Russia has its own way of development, which is non-capitalist. Initially, they opposed the violent methods of struggle. Populists have expressed the interests of the peasants, demanded the destruction of the remnants of serfdom, the elimination of landlordism and keeping capitalism away from Russia. They called for reforms. The main activities of populism were cultural and educational ("*Narodnichestvo*," [Onlain Entsiklopediya "Krugosvet," 2001–2009], 5 February 2011, http://www.krugosvet.ru/enc/istoriya/NARODNICHESTVO.html?page=0,3).

78. Mihaylovskiy, *Zhestokiy talent*.

79. Mihaylovskiy.

80. G. N. Pospelov, *Tvorchestvo F. M. Dostoevskiy* [F. M. Dostoevsky's Creative Work], (Moscow: Izdatel'stvo Znanie, 1971), 52.

81. Mihaylovskiy, *Zhestokiy talent*.

82. Mihaylovskiy.

To explain the martyrdom theme in Dostoevsky's works, Mikhailovskiy resorted to the image of a wolf devouring a sheep. According to him, at the beginning of his career, Dostoevsky thoroughly investigated the feelings of a sheep being devoured by a wolf, as in *The House of the Dead* and *The Oppressed and Insulted*, whereas towards the end of his literary career he used "wolf" much more for his illustration.[83] He believed that Dostoevsky was "rummaging in the deepest depths of the wolf's soul searching there for things that are subtle, complex, not just simple satisfaction of appetite, but mainly lust for anger and cruelty."[84] Mikhailovskiy came to the conclusion that Dostoevsky loved to "hunt a sheep by a wolf, and he was foremost particularly interested in the sheep and secondly in the wolf."[85]

He explained the love of Dostoevsky for cruelty in the following fashion:

> This thoroughly kept zoo, a nursery of various species of wolves, whose owner almost even doesn't take pride in his rich collection, and even more does not think about deriving from it direct benefits, knows his business so well and loves it, that a study of wolf-nature for him is something self-sufficient, and he deliberately teases his animals, shows a sheep to them, a piece of bloody meat, whips and beats them with a hot iron, to see this or other details of their malice and cruelty, to look upon them himself and, of course, to show it to the public.[86]

To confirm his findings Mikhailovskiy had recourse to examples from some of the works of Dostoevsky. The first example he took from *Notes from Underground*. In his view, the underground man in the beginning of the novel in his philosophical reflections "shows his soul in smallest details before the reader the soul, trying to get to the bottom and show this bottom to all, in all its dirt and filth."[87] Later in this same novel Dostoevsky showed in detail "wanton malice of the underground man against Lisa." The underground man tormented Lisa just because she happened to be close by.[88] There were

---

83. Mihaylovskiy.
84. Mihaylovskiy.
85. Mihaylovskiy.
86. Mihaylovskiy.
87. Mihaylovskiy.
88. Mihaylovskiy.

no other reasons for anger; he did not expect any results from the torment. He just loved to torment others, said Mikhailovskiy. The underground man tormented Lisa, not to direct her to the truth or to punish her for some offense; he simply hurt her to get pleasure from it.[89] He did not agree with Dostoevsky when he elevated the idea of patience. In his understanding, the reaction to evil against anyone should be a protest against inflicting suffering. Mikhailovskiy was outraged by the fact that the "sheep" of Dostoevsky, instead of protesting and resisting, simply allowed the "wolves" to devour them.[90] Therefore, he attributed to Dostoevsky the love of cruelty.

Mikhailovskiy was amazed by the strange understanding of love in the underground man. The underground man recognized that for him to love meant, "to tyrannize and be morally superior." He even throughout his life could not imagine love, so he thought that "love consists in the beloved object freely bestowing the right to tyrannize him."[91] But Mikhailovskiy did not notice the words of the underground man, who claimed that the "human soul, especially of the educated man of the nineteenth century, was so that the love and tyranny in it inevitably bloom next to each other."[92] Mikhailovskiy recognized that Dostoevsky found such subtlety in the human soul, which ordinary people could not see.

Another example to which Mikhailovskiy resorted is taken from "The Gambler." In this novel there is Paullina, a charming woman, though overbearing to cruelty.[93] A strange relationship develops between Paullina and the main character of the novel. She loves him and at the same time "treats him as a footman, and even worse than a footman."[94] Knowing that the gambler loves her, she "particularly for this reason mocks him in every way, ordering him to do different silly things, intentionally torments him with the cynicism and vulgarity of her conversations."[95]

In the story *The Village of Stepanchikovo* there is old man Yezhevikin, playing the role of the jester, appearing very good-natured, whom everyone

---

89. Mihaylovskiy.

90. Pospelov, *Tvorchestvo F. M. Dostoevskiy*, 122.

91. Pospelov, 122.

92. Pospelov, 122.

93. Mihaylovskiy, *Zhestokiy talent*.

94. Mihaylovskiy.

95. Mihaylovskiy.

wants to please, but in reality is very poisonous – a prototype of a number of old fools in the subsequent works of Dostoevsky.[96]

Mikhailovskiy believed that Dostoevsky, "choosing for himself the major theme of his works to be suffering, would cause his characters to suffer and so his readers."[97] The author of the article admitted that modern writers could incorporate in their novels the theme of suffering, because life is full of cruelty and suffering. He did not understand the approach of Dostoevsky, as in his works suffering and cruelty occur without cause, on reality without any purpose whatsoever.[98] Mikhailovskiy's conclusion showed that he looked from a different perspective and the cruelty of man and the world than Dostoevsky.

Mikhailovskiy saw only one explanation for the inclusion of such cruelty by Dostoevsky in his novels: a love for the imposition of cruelty upon other people. To argue his point, Michaelovskiy cited the example seen in Spain. He said,

> But in any case, relatively, even very recently, all travelers to Spain described the excitement and enthusiasm with which the audience, with the inclusion of the weaker and gentler sex, applauded the bull, the horns put on a picador, and matador plunging his sword into the bull. There was a time though, in poetic Spain, when the bullfight was an unnecessary thing, even when it wasn't considered one of the original Spanish customs. This need did not suddenly appear, as it is now being suddenly abolished.[99]

Mikhailovskiy did not agree with Dostoevsky, that man is a despot by nature and loves to be a torturer and that there are people who delight in tormenting not only those whom they hate but also their loved ones.

In conclusion, Mikhailovskiy wrote, "All the politics and journalism of Dostoevsky are a continuous vacillation and confusion, which have however,

---

96. F. M. Dostoevsky, *Polnoe Sobranie Sochineniy, Selo Stepanchikovo i ego obitateley* [The Complete Works of Dostoevsky] [CD-ROM] (Izdatel'stvo Adept, 2002).

97. Mihaylovskiy, *Zhestokiy talent.*

98. Mihaylovskiy. He called Dostoevsky a "cruel talent."

99. Mihaylovskiy.

one individual and original feature: unnecessary, unfounded, inconclusive brutality."[100]

Mikhailovskiy, just like Ivan Karamazov, operated with the same concept. Both built their arguments on injustice and suffering in the stories and novels.[101] However, it is acknowledged that he knew nothing about the very life of the writer but made his conclusions from some of the above works. He came to this conclusion because of his ideology as that of a populist. He was a supporter of the transformation of Russia without the use of violent methods of struggle. Mikhailovskiy had faith that one can change a person through cultural and educational activities.[102] Populists were convinced atheists, but in their minds socialism and Christian values freely coexisted, the release of public consciousness from the dictates of the church, and "Christianity without Christ," but with preservation of culture in general and of Christian tradition.[103] Mikhailovskiy wanted to see every human being living harmoniously and being a free subject of history. Introducing in Russian philosophy the term of "struggle for individuality," he made like-minded people feel the natural desire for freedom, privacy, and equality in rights, mutual aid and solidarity.[104] Dostoevsky had another opinion. He wrote, "Atheism is a disease . . . aristocratic, a disease of higher education and development, and therefore, must be repugnant to the people."[105]

Mikhailovskiy was right in saying that some of the characters of Dostoevsky behave badly without a cause. The author of *The House of the Dead*, while still in prison, was convinced that a person can fall to the state of a beast, so that he will do evil for fun.[106] Mikhailovskiy, being a populist, was convinced that evil is contained in the social order, rather than inside man. The key objectives of the populists were social justice and relative social equality.[107] In his understanding of man, if evil is done, then there is a reason for it, it cannot

---

100. Mihaylovskiy.

101. Rozenblyum, *Tvorcheskie dnevniki Dostoevskogo,* 128.

102. Rozenblyum.

103. Rozenblyum.

104. Rozenblyum.

105. F. M. Dostoevsky, *Polnoe Sobranie Sochineniy,* "*Zapisi, 1873–1878,*" [The Complete Works of Dostoevsky] [CD-ROM] (Izdatel'stvo Adept, 2002).

106. See *Zapiski iz Mjortvogo Doma.*

107. Dostoevsky saw a direct connection between socialism and atheism (Rozenblium, *Tvorcheskie dnevniki Dostoevskogo,* 123).

happen without any reason.[108] Dostoevsky was of a different opinion, as he saw it; the problem of evil is not in the social sphere, but in the spiritual.[109] Dostoevsky did not like violence, as Mikhailovskiy accused him of; he only represented the actual sinful state of some people. Dostoevsky wrote to N. Strakhov, "I have a special view of reality, and that which the majority calls fantastic and exceptional for me sometimes is the very essence of reality."[110] The reason why he portrayed this evil in man is precisely that he did not like violence and wanted people to see the way out of their situation through faith in Christ.

6.2.4 Influence on Radical Christian Thinkers: V. Soloviev

V. Soloviev[111] in his article "Three Speeches in Memory of Dostoevsky"[112] gave an estimate of Dostoevsky's work. He could hardly be considered either a Slavophile or a Westerner. Rather, he was a centrist, or was coming from the terms of its philosophical beliefs – a universalist.

Soloviev in all three of his speeches limited himself to the subject under discussion. He argued that the purpose of his speech was to express his understanding of who Dostoevsky was and what inspired all his activities.[113] He confirmed that in recent years Dostoevsky had a particular impact on people. Soloviev believed that the secret of conflicting assessments of Dostoevsky's work depends on whether the researchers took into account the opinion of the writer or not. He shared the same opinion as Antonovich that Dostoevsky wrote his works out of his beliefs.[114] But since not all scholars of Dostoevsky's works took into account his convictions, some perceived his works to be true

---

108. Mihaylovskiy, *Zhestokiy talent.*

109. Pospelov, *Tvorchestvo F. M. Dostoevskiy,* 52.

110. Pis'ma, Vol. 29, 26 February 1869, 15.

111. Vladimir Sergeyevich Soloviev (1853–1900), the Russian philosopher, theologian, poet, essayist, literary critic and honourary academician (*Entsiklopedicheskiy Slovar' F. A. Brokgauza I I. A. Efrona* (Biblioteka "Vehi"), 15 January 2011, http://www.vehi.net/brokgauz/).

112. Brochure of V. Soloviev's "Three Speeches in Memory of Dostoevsky" (1881–1883) contains the first published in this edition's speech, never read; a second speech, first printed in the newspaper "Novoe Vremya" (1882, # 2133) and given 1 February 1882. The third first saw light in the journal "Russia" (1883, #6) under the heading "The True Facts (In Memory of Dostoevsky)," given February 19, 1883 (V. Soloviev, "Tri rechi v pam'yat' Dostoevskogo."

113. Soloviev.

114. Soloviev.

and beneficial, while others viewed them as false and harmful.[115] Dostoevsky as a writer, according to Soloviev, differed from his predecessors and from his contemporaries. He said the following:

> The old art distracting people from the darkness and evil, which dominate the world, it has taken them away to its halcyon heights and entertained them with its bright images; the present art, by contrast, attracts people to the darkness and fury of everyday life with sometimes obscure desire to enlighten the darkness, pacify this anger.[116]

Soloviev saw the difference between the art of Dostoevsky and that art which preceded him and that which was in his time. According to him, preceding art raised man above the earth, leading him away from his reality; the art which was in his time returns to earth with love and compassion but not having the aim of plunging into darkness and the evil of life on earth. But Dostoevsky's art plunged into the darkness in order "to heal and refresh this life."[117] This was an important goal, said Soloviev, and it could not be achieved by a simple reproduction of reality; "to portray does not mean to transform, and the rebuke is not yet a correction."[118] He was confident that the transformation of man required help from outside, from God. Therefore, the real art was connected with faith in God. The true artist was he who "comes to religious truth, binds the task of his works to it, derives his social ideal from it, and sanctifies with it his public ministry."[119] Soloviev hoped that in the future there would be representatives of such art in Russia. But even in his time, he recognized only Dostoevsky as representative of this kind of art.

Soloviev's view ranged from Gnostic to Christocentric. Christ was his guide, who led him throughout life.[120] According to Soloviev, the subject of Dostoevsky's work was a social movement. He believed that only faith helped

---

115. Soloviev.

116. Soloviev.

117. Soloviev.

118. Soloviev.

119. Soloviev.

120. Tadeush Kondrusevich, "Slovo privetstviya," *Rossiya i Vselenskaya Tserkov': V. S. Soloviev i problema religioznogo I kul'turnogo edineniya chelovechestva* (Moscow: BBI Sv. Apostola Andreya, 2004), 10.

Dostoevsky to see the aim of the movement properly and its deviation from that goal. Therefore, he rightly judged, and rightly condemned them:

> Its just condemnation refers only to bad ways and bad methods of the social movement, but not to the movement itself, required and desired, it refers to the condemnation of the low-lying public's understanding of the truth, to the public's false ideals, but not to the search for social justice, not to a desire to implement social ideal. This last thing was ahead for Dostoevsky as well: he believed not only in the past, but in the coming kingdom of God, and understood the need for labour and heroic feat for its implementation.[121]

Soloviev saw the common sense of Dostoevsky's whole activities in this two-sided issue – "the resolution of the highest ideal of society and the path to its achievement."[122] The public ideal for Dostoevsky was the Church not the people, believes Soloviev.[123]

The same view was shared by Soloviev himself.[124] Soloviev concluded that "the ultimate ideal and goal is not in the nation, which in itself is only a useful instrument, but in the Church, which is the supreme object of service, requiring a moral life, not only from the individual, but from the whole nation."[125]

In the second speech, Soloviev addressed the theme of the Christian idea of "free universal brotherhood in Christ."[126] In his opinion, this is how Dostoevsky perceived the Orthodox Church and its mission.[127] The philosopher himself shared the idea of unity of believers.[128]

Soloviev was open to the fact that the study of Dostoevsky did not limit itself to the constraints of the Orthodox Church. For Dostoevsky, Christ is not a dead image worshipped in churches on Sundays, with no place in life, but the embodiment of truth; not only a picture in the temple, but "a

---

121. Soloviev, "Tri rechi v pam'yat' Dostoevskogo."

122. Soloviev.

123. Soloviev.

124. N. E. Smelova, "Vladimir Soloviev i Istinnoe Khristianstvo," *Rossiya i Vselenskaya Tserkov': V. S. Soloviev i problema religioznogo I kul'turnogo edineniya chelovechestva*, 48.

125. Soloviev, "Tri rechi v pam'yat' Dostoevskogo."

126. Soloviev.

127. Soloviev.

128. Smelova, "Vladimir Soloviev i Istinnoe Khristianstvo," 49.

living foundation and cornerstone of the universal church."[129] He argued that Dostoevsky preached precisely such universal Christianity, in which all human and universal relations must ultimately be controlled by Christ. With all that, Soloviev recognized that there is not presently "a universal earthly Church," but that is the goal. Whereas all universal things – politics, science, art, public sector, being outside of Christ, instead of bringing people together, separate them.[130]

But despite this reality, Soloviev believed that Dostoevsky continued to believe and preach "Christianity as being alive and active, the universal Church, the world's Orthodox cause."[131] With this he showed that he cared not only for the present but also for the future. To carry out this difficult task of unification of all of mankind in the name of Christ, a feat of love, mercy and sacrifice is required.

Soloviev believed that, according to Dostoevsky, the true Church is the universal one, especially in the sense that in it, division should disappear. Division between the tribes and nations related to hatred. He argued that:

> All of them, without losing their national character, but only getting rid from its national self-interest can and should unite in one common cause of worldwide revival. Indeed, he believed Russia to be the chosen people of God, but elected not to compete with other nations and not to dominate and be superior to them, but elected for the free service to all peoples and for the implementation, in a brotherly alliance with them, of the true universal Church.[132]

Soloviev shared Dostoevsky's view on the worldwide mission of Russia, because he agreed with him that the Russian people have certain qualities to carry out this mission. The first quality is "the ability to absorb the spirit and ideas of other nations."[133] The second quality is the realization of one's sinfulness, from which results the longing for a better life, and a thirst for purification and good deeds. Without this, there is no true activity, either for

---

129. Kondrusevich, "Slovo privetstviya," 11.
130. Soloviev, "Tri rechi v pam'yat' Dostoevskogo."
131. Soloviev.
132. Soloviev.
133. Soloviev.

an individual or for the entire nation. Soloviev talked about the importance of recognizing our sins:

> If a person or people do not put up with their bad reality and condemns it as sin that means that they already have an idea or a concept, or even just an anticipation of the other, better life than what should come. That is why Dostoevsky claimed that the Russian people, despite its apparent image of the beast in the depths of his soul contains another image – the image of Christ – and when the time comes, show Him alive to all nations and bring them to Him, and jointly with them will perform the all-human task.[134]

Dostoevsky's belief in a worldwide unity was based on a belief in finding the image of God in man. Dostoevsky believed, according to Soloviev, that people will come to faith themselves, because they have this infinity of their souls.[135] Soloviev agreed with Dostoevsky, as he himself saw the mission of the Russian people not to achieve a privileged position and to dominate, but to serve other people and all humanity.[136]

In his third speech, Soloviev began with a reminder of the difficult situation that prevailed in Russia in the 1860s. Representatives of revolutionary social movements, as a way out of the situation, proposed to "kill all the enemies, all defenders of this system."[137] But in contrast to them, there were only a few people who not being satisfied by any external goals and ideals "feel the need to proclaim the profound moral revolution, and indicate the conditions of a new spiritual rebirth of Russia and mankind."[138] Among these people the first one named by Soloviev was Dostoevsky. He believed that Dostoevsky saw more deeply than others the need not to have an external ideal, but the inner conversion of man and his birth from above. He knew all too well the depths of man's fall; he knew that anger and madness are at the core of our

---

134. Soloviev.

135. Soloviev.

136. L. A. Bessonova, "Printsip Vseedinstva v istoriosofii Vladimira Soloviev," *Rossiya i Vselenskaya Tserkov': V. S. Soloviev i problema religioznogo I kul'turnogo edineniya chelovechestva*, 191.

137. Solov'ov, "Tri rechi v pam'yat' Dostoevskogo."

138. Bessonova, "Printsip Vseedinstva v istoriosofii Vladimira Soloviev," 191.

perverted nature, and that if you accept perversion as the norm, it will not produce anything but violence and chaos.[139] Soloviev compared society to a crowd of people, blind, deaf, crippled and possessed. These people, above all, must be healed. Dostoevsky preached about it; he believed it.[140]

If a person did not see the need for healing, then such person is adopting the world to his own ways, and "by his very nature is a murderer, he will inevitably rape and kill others and himself would inevitably fall killed by violence."[141] So Soloviev saw several steps in Dostoevsky leading to salvation. The first step was that a person must "feel his helplessness and his bondage." Then he will not become a murderer but may become suicidal. The second step was faith in God. Those who resort to suicide are aware of the evil in mankind but do not believe in a supernatural Good. The next step was universal reconciliation. He argued that with faith in God, faith in man returns. For Dostoevsky, Soloviev said, it meant to recognize in man something more than what is seen, to recognize in him the power and the freedom that connects him to the Divine.[142] Soloviev explained that:

> The separation from God is evil. And acting on the basis of this evil man can do only bad things. The lowest thing the godless man does is murder or suicide. Only by abandoning his false position, with its manic focus on oneself, from one's evil loneliness, only connecting oneself to God in Christ and the world in the Church, we can now do God's work – what Dostoevsky called orthodox thing.[143]

From this follows a conclusion, "If Christianity is the religion of salvation, and if the Christian idea is healing, an inner joining of those principles, separation of which means death, the essence of true Christian deeds will be what is called in the language of logic – synthesis, and in the language of morality – reconciliation."[144] Soloviev believed that was what Dostoevsky called for in his Pushkin speech. Thus, the dispute between Slavophilism and

---

139. Bessonova.
140. Bessonova.
141. Bessonova.
142. Bessonova.
143. Bessonova.
144. Bessonova.

Westernism would be abolished and then vanish away and so would discord between East and West.

Thus, the activity of Dostoevsky, most certainly, influenced the great philosopher, V. Soloviev. He could see that Dostoevsky's appeal to inner change was possible only through the realization of one's lowliness and one's need for God. Faith in God enabled one to see the need for other people and would lead to a general reconciliation. The Russian Orthodox Church has this mission. Thus, Soloviev's assessment was influenced by his beliefs about the church and its relation to the Slavophiles and Westerners, which coincided with the beliefs of Dostoevsky.

6.3 Influence of Dostoevsky's Theology on a Baptistic Community

The book *The Gospel in Dostoevsky* is a collection of excerpts from several works of Dostoevsky to show that the gospel is in the writer's works. Each chapter of the book has an introduction which helps comprehend the Bruderhof Community's understanding of the quotations from Dostoevsky's novels. All the quotes are selected from Dostoevsky's works which were written in the post-Siberian period.[145] Thus the Bruderhof Community believes that Dostoevsky proclaimed the gospel through his literary works in the last period of his life.

6.3.1 Faith in God

According to Dostoevsky, a person who lives the life of Christ is a believer in God and he shares the importance of faith in God for the people. The follower of Christ is not indifferent to people's suffering because of their sin.[146] That's why he warns people that unbelief leads them to permissiveness and to tragedy.[147] The follower of Christ warns people that until they come to faith in

---

145. Quotes were taken from the following works: *Crime and Punishment* (1866), *The Idiot* (1868–69), *The Raw Youth* (1874) and *The Brothers Karamazov* (1880). The gospel, which the Bruderhof Community found in the aforementioned works of Dostoevsky, consists of four parts: "Faith in God", "Rebellion against God", "On the Way to God" and "Life in God."

146. *Brat'ya Karamazovy*, 134.

147. *Brat'ya Karamazovy*, 402.

God and immortality, they suffer.[148] But he proclaims the truth with kindness and humility,[149] understanding his own guilt in spreading evil in the world when he lived as they do.[150] A follower of Christ reads and explains the Bible to people[151] and calls other followers of Christ to do the same.[152] But the way to come to faith in God goes through inner struggle.

The Bruderhof Community believes that man's struggle of faith is better expressed in "The Legend of the Grand Inquisitor" from *The Brothers Karamazov*. That is why the quoted parable is named "Faith in God" in *The Gospel in Dostoevsky*. Ernest Gordon in the introduction of "The Gospel in Dostoevsky" said that the "The Legend of the Grand Inquisitor" is the climax of Dostoevsky's religious confession.[153] In his opinion in this parable, Dostoevsky gave readers a practical illustration of the universal truth that only in the light of the gospel can "the great, or cursed, questions" so characteristic of Dostoevsky's passion for the living gospel be solved.[154]

There are two reasons why the Bruderhof Community considered this parable the best expression of man's faith struggle. First, in the parable Jesus, without words, rejected the way for the temporary happiness of people proposed by the Grand Inquisitor. This way was based on violence, cheating and materialism. The Bruderhof Community shares Jesus's point of view of having a free society of followers based on love,[155] unity[156] and nonviolence.[157]

Second, the Bruderhof Community believes that the world is the principality of evil, the domain of anti-God whom most men worship in preference to God. Anti-God, or Mammon, stands "in contradiction to the future and to eternity." Eberhard Arnold, the founder of the Bruderhof Community,

---

148. *Brat'ya Karamazovy*, 61.

149. *Brat'ya Karamazovy*, 287–304.

150. *Brat'ya Karamazovy*, 140.

151. *Brat'ya Karamazovy*, 141.

152. *Brat'ya Karamazovy*, 375.

153. *The Gospel in Dostoevsky* (Farmington: Plough Publishing, Bruderhof Foundation, 2003), 5.

154. *The Gospel in Dostoevsky*, 5.

155. Benjamin Zablocki, *The Joyful Community: An Account of the Bruderhof – a Communal Movement Now in Its Third Generation* (Farmington: Plough Publishing House, 1971), 58.

156. Zablocki, *The Joyful Community*, 169.

157. John McKelvie, *Whitworth, God's Blueprints: A Sociological Study of Three Utopian Sects* (London; Boston: Routledge & Kegan Paul, 1975), 176.

believed that the world was "'quite literally peopled . . . by death-bringing spiritual beings." He stated that the spirit of anti-God and his demonic minions was manifested in all forms of violence.[158]

6.3.2 Rebellion against God

Dostoevsky explained to people how to come to faith by overcoming temptation: not to put themselves in the place of God[159] and not to give priority to material things over spiritual.[160]

Dostoevsky showed that the process of regeneration of convictions is a lengthy process, as a man would constantly have a struggle of belief and unbelief. Especially, in his opinion, the crimes committed in the world will sow doubts about the fairness of God.[161] Dostoevsky calls believers to solve these difficult issues in Christ, in His sufferings and resurrection. Only God can forgive the crimes of people and only He can condemn them.[162] To win this struggle between belief and unbelief, a person must believe in immortality. That is how man's rebellion against God is solved. Faith in Christ and immortality gives a sense of love towards people.[163]

The Bruderhof Community believes that "The Gospel in Dostoevsky" warns people about men's rebellion against God. To show this rebellion in the chapter "Rebellion Against God" from *The Gospel in Dostoevsky* there are quotes from "Rebellion" and "The Devil" from *The Brothers Karamazov* and "The Failure of Christendom" from *The Idiot*. These three passages contain a rebellion against God, but it is different in each of them. In "Rebellion" the rebellion of man against God is depicted by the fact that He allows the suffering of innocent children. It is strange that Ivan presents the claims of God. He himself confessed that he could not love his own neighbour. His rebellion is the position of an atheist who blames God for the lack of love. Dostoevsky taught that man is unhappy, not because God made the world bad but because man does not believe in God and therefore he is not capable

---

158. McKelvie, *Whitworth, God's Blueprints*, 174.

159. *Brat'ya Karamazovy*, 39.

160. *Brat'ya Karamazovy*, 39.

161. Dostoevskaya, *Vospominaniya*, 57.

162. Gus, *Idei i Obrazy F. M. Dostoevskogo*, 455.

163. *Dnevnik Pisatelya*, 1876.

of loving people.[164] In "The Devil" Dostoevsky showed to what extremes people can go in their atheism. His statements bordered on insanity at the time, when he saw the consequences of his evil actions, not only of direct, but also of indirect actions.[165] In "The Failure of Christendom," Dostoevsky, in the words of Prince Myshkin accused the Catholic Church of rebellion against God. In the actions of the pope, which Myshkin described as fraud, deception, bigotry, superstition and wickedness, he saw similarities with the teachings of the antichrist. It is interesting to note that Dostoevsky derived his teaching from actions, not words. According to Dostoevsky, actions speak louder about what a man believes in than his words.

The Bruderhof Community believes that the worst enemies of Jesus are often religious people, not unbelievers. The same as in Jesus's own lifetime, those who hated him most were not the soldiers who crucified him, but the very religious Pharisees and scribes.[166] In their teaching the Bruderhof Community, as did Myshkin, accused and condemned the Catholic Church which destroyed the capacity for men to enter into selfless relationships and so estranged mankind from God.[167]

6.3.3 On the Way to God

According to Dostoevsky, the follower of Christ looks with pain at people entangled in atheistic nets.[168] That's why he explained the meaning of repentance which leads people to a new life.[169] Also he shared his own repentance story.[170] Dostoevsky was convinced that everybody is a sinner and needs to repent[171] and that only sincere repentance gives forgiveness of sin.[172] He urged people not to follow the majority but to follow Christ and do it without coercion.

---

164. *Brat'ya Karamazovy*, 203–211.

165. See F. M. Dostoevsky, *Polnoe Sobranie Sochineniy, Bessy* [The Complete Works of Dostoevsky, The Devils], [CD-ROM] (Izdatel'stvo Adept, 2002).

166. J. Heinrich Arnold, *Discipleship: Living for Christ in the Daily Grind* (Farmington: Plough Publishing, Bruderhof Foundation, 1994), 11.

167. McKelvie, *Whitworth, God's Blueprints*, 174.

168. *Brat'ya Karamazovy*, 467.

169. *Brat'ya Karamazovy*, 474–475.

170. *Brat'ya Karamazovy*, 251–256.

171. *Brat'ya Karamazovy*, 269.

172. *Brat'ya Karamazovy*, 45–46.

So Dostoevsky called for a long, painful process of repentance. In his opinion, people should study their lives piece by piece, touching on all their beliefs, so that it would be possible to change them. If beliefs are based on the gospel, then one's life will be like that of Christ.[173]

Wishing happiness to everyone, Dostoevsky called upon all people by his example and the example of the characters of his novels, to experience regeneration of their convictions in line with the gospel and for their lives to become Christ-centred.[174]

In the chapter "On the Way to God" from *The Gospel in Dostoevsky*, the Bruderhof Community included quotations from three works of Dostoevsky.[175] The major part of this book is devoted to different ways in which people come to God. We find a way to God used by Dimitry, Grushenika, Starets Zosima, Raskolnikov and Alyosha. Also, in the book there are passages in which Dostoevsky showed the love of Myshkin and his sacrifice. Myshkin put himself in the place of Varya, when Ganya wanted to hit her. He took the blow, protecting the young girl.

The Bruderhof Community believes that the gospel begins with a call to repentance. Repentance in their understanding means that everything must be changed. It was the first call of Christ.[176] They consider that the radicalism of Christ's Way must challenge people, because He does not want to win numbers but dedicated hearts.[177]

6.3.4 Life in God

In the centre of Dostoevsky's "Christ's Way" there is love for God and for people. For Dostoevsky, to love God means first to communicate with God in prayer and then to share with God the sadness and joy of life.[178] Second, it means to read the Bible, trust it, to admire the gospel stories of Christ and

---

173. *Brat'ya Karamazovy*, 270–271.

174. *Brat'ya Karamazovy*, 260–266.

175. From *The Idiot* is quoted "The Story of Marie," "A Fool for Christ," "Reprieve," "Execution" and 'Crucifixion." From *Crime and Punishment* is quoted "The Awakening of Lazarus" and "The Last Judgment." From *The Brothers Karamazov* is quoted "Hymn of the Man from Underground" and "The Onion."

176. Arnold, *Discipleship: Living for Christ in the Daily Grind*, 11.

177. Arnold, 18.

178. *Brat'ya Karamazovy*, 138.

other Bible characters.[179] The life of Christ and that of other Bible characters have to be models to follow.[180] That's why love has to be unselfish and directed to each person including close relatives such as parents,[181] children,[182] brothers and sisters, and also strangers[183] and even enemies.[184]

The love of the follower of Christ has to be seen in helping people who are in need. It can be just listening to people who want to share their problems and needs[185] and when it is needed to give them advice according to the gospel,[186] or to comfort them with gospel words.[187]

A follower of Christ should live like Christ.[188] Like Christ, he should love people. In all his novels and in his life, Dostoevsky proclaimed the truth: love your neighbour. The life of Dostoevsky and his characters, such as Sonya Marmeladova, Makar Dolgoruky, Knyazh Myshkin, Starets Zosima and Alyosha Karamazov, are examples of love, humility and forgiveness of people. When Alyosha repented, it was said of him, "He wanted to forgive all and everyone, to ask for forgiveness, oh! not for himself, but for everyone and for all."[189] From their lives one can draw out some of the principles proclaimed by Dostoevsky as to what the life of a Christ-centred believer should be.

The follower of Christ should be concerned for the people, for society as a whole in which he lives.[190] Being concerned for other people, according to Dostoevsky, brings happiness; that is, it releases one from all cares about one's own life. In his life, pity and compassion for the people will be made manifest to all in need, regardless of who they are. Therefore, Dostoevsky condemns indifference. The follower of Christ should be willing to delve

---

179. *Brat'ya Karamazovy*, 250.

180. *Brat'ya Karamazovy*, 82–84.

181. *Brat'yu Karamazovy*, 189.

182. *Brat'ya Karamazovy*, 17.

183. *Brat'ya Karamazovy*, 19.

184. *Brat'ya Karamazovy*, 141.

185. *Brat'ya Karamazovy*, 48–49.

186. *Brat'ya Karamazovy*, 436–444.

187. *Brat'ya Karamazovy*, 41–44.

188. *Dnevnik Pisatelya*, 1873.

189. *Brat'ya Karamazovy*, 78.

190. F. M. Dostoevsky, *Polnoe Sobranie Sochineniy, Iz zapisnoy tetradi, 1880-1881gg.* [The Complete Works of Dostoevsky, From His Notebooks, 1880–1881] [CD-ROM] (Izdatel'stvo Adept, 2002).

into the problems of people to help them practically. A sacrificial spirit is the main characteristic of the follower of Christ. According to Dostoevsky, a Christ-centred believer, no matter what position in society he occupies, will treat others as equals.

The Bruderhof Community believes that part of the gospel consists of the life in God. That's why the chapter "Life in God" from *The Gospel in Dostoevsky* includes quotes from "Talks with an Old Friend of God" from the novel *The Raw Youth* and "Conversations and Exhortations" of Starets Zosima from *The Brothers Karamazov*. These stories are about two of Dostoevsky's positive characters – Makar Ivanovich Dolgoruky and Starets Zosima. The Bruderhof Community believes that the words of Starets Zosima were Dostoevsky's own words. They contain beliefs about Dostoevsky's life of faith in God. They stress the importance of love, prayers, not being judgmental, confidence in the afterlife and the proper attitude of followers of Christ to other people.[191] Makar Dolgoruky put the utmost importance on issues of faith, which were to be expressed in practical actions. He collected alms for the temple, prayed and took pilgrimages to holy places. He was interested in the problems of society and the entire country. Makar Dolgoruky was convinced that life without God is nothing but torment.

The Bruderhof Community quoted these stories because they are a community based upon obedience and brotherly love.[192] The moral basis of the Bruderhof consists in whatever enables the community to contain the Holy Spirit. Thus, the normative system is open and flexible.[193] Eberhard Arnold, the founder of the Bruderhof Community, did not attempt to develop a completely distinctive theology. He regarded himself as inspired by God to proclaim the continuing practical relevance of certain passages of Scripture, especially the Sermon on the Mount and a section from the Acts of the Apostles and to establish and promulgate a form of society based solely on Christ's ethical teaching.[194] Arnold became convinced that authentic Christian discipleship required an absolute break with the world and a total commitment to the fulfillment of the dictates of the Sermon on the Mount within an

---

191. *The Gospel in Dostoevsky*, 237.
192. Zablocki, *The Joyful Community*, 286.
193. Zablocki, 57.
194. McKelvie, *Whitworth, God's Blueprints*, 171.

alternative Christian community. His ideas crystallized during the Whitsun Conference in Marburg in October 1919. Erwin Wissman, correspondent for "The Furrow" wrote:

> The focus of all that was said and thought was Jesus's Sermon on the Mount. Eberhard Arnold burned it into our hearts with passionate spirituality, hammered it into our wills with prophetic power and the tremendous mobile force of his whole personality . . . Whoever wants to belong to this kingdom, must give himself wholly and go through with it to the last! To be a Christian means to live the life of Christ.[195]

6.3.5 The Mission of the Christian

The mission of the Christ-centred believer has two directions according to Dostoevsky. It is directed both towards one's neighbour, referring to one's people, and towards all mankind. Dostoevsky was convinced that "Christianity was the only refuge of the Russian Land from all its evils."[196]

Dostoevsky urged people to the worldwide mission, especially in his speech in memory of Pushkin.[197] The writer himself with his behaviour, his works, and his articles written in various magazines, was answering the problems of society by expressing the Christian way out of difficult situations.[198]

The follower of Christ is called not so much with his words, as with his life and acts to carry the message of God, of Christ, showing the reflection of his beliefs in daily life. One must feel a personal responsibility to everyone. One needs to feel himself obligated before everyone. This feeling should flow from the memory that we also wandered in the world, doing evil, not having the image of Christ before us. This is the secret of missions according to Dostoevsky. As soon as a Christian will start suffering for others, carrying responsibility before society, others will follow his example and so society will be transformed.[199]

---

195. Julius H. Rubin, *The Other Side of Joy: Religious Melancholy among the Bruderhof* (New York; Oxford: Oxford University Press, 2000), 24.

196. *Pis'ma*, 8 July 1866.

197. *Dnevnik Pisatelya*, 1 August 1880.

198. *Zapiski iz Mertvogo Doma*, 137.

199. *Brat'ya Karamazovy*, 269–273.

6.4 Conclusion

There is no classic writer in Russian literature other than Dostoevsky whose creativity would arouse such different, sometimes even opposing judgments.[200] The influence of Dostoevsky's theology on his contemporaries was strong, but varied, as is evidenced by all the authors of the articles examined in this chapter. His influence was different for several reasons.

First, in their research the authors of articles based their opinions on their own political and religious beliefs. Thus, Leontiev considered Dostoevsky's speech at the celebration of Pushkin from his position as a Slavophile with strong nationalist and Orthodox beliefs. Antonovich compared Dostoevsky with his materialistic beliefs. Mikhailovsky, a convinced populist, believed that by means of propaganda one could change a person. Soloviev also approached it from his more universal beliefs regarding the Church and Christianity in general.

Second, the acceptance or rejection of Dostoevsky's theology was also influenced by the method of "our" Dostoevsky or the "foreign" Dostoevsky, whom the authors of articles used in the assessment of the theology of the writer. At that time the basic interpretations of Dostoevsky's Russian philosophy evolved from an acute ideological struggle.[201] So Leontiev, Mikhailovsky and Antonovich all had a negative view of Dostoevsky's theology, as he was "foreign" to them, while Soloviev accepted him as "ours."

But, despite the acceptance or rejection of Dostoevsky's theology, the authors of articles were able to see some of the basic beliefs of the writer: Leontiev saw the appeal of Dostoevsky to universal brotherhood through Christ, Antonovich found in Dostoevsky the only way for Russia – the path of faith in God and humble Christ-like living; Mikhailovskiy saw in Dostoevsky's works, that a man so imbued with evil can resort to use of violence without any cause; Soloviev was convinced that Dostoevsky was a radical Orthodox Christian, who professed universal Christianity, in which man's deeds and relations should ultimately be directed by Christ.

Analyzing "The Gospel in Dostoevsky," we can come to three conclusions: first, the selected passages actually correspond to the name under which they

---

200. Pospelov, *Tvorchestvo F. M. Dostoevskiy*, 3.

201. *O Dostoevskom: Tvorchestva Dostoevskogo v russkoy mysli 1881–1931 godov* [About Dostoevsky: Dostoevsky's Work in Russian Thought 1880–1931], (Moscow: Kniga, 1990), 7.

are combined. Reading these passages together one can better see one or another theme that is dealt with in various works of Dostoevsky. Second, the Bruderhof Community did not include such important parts of Dostoevsky's gospel as the Christian mission to the neighbour and to society as a whole. Because "The Gospel in Dostoevsky" is limited to quotations from only part of Dostoevsky's works, the compilation does not have enough citations to create a complete picture of his gospel which would show the life of Dostoevsky from biographical sources.

Third, Dostoevsky's "Way of Christ" is relevant for a contemporary baptistic community as a living Christ-centred theology. True faith must necessarily have external manifestations in the life of a follower of Christ, in his actions and his relationships with people full of love in the example of Christ.

CHAPTER 7

Conclusion: The Challenge of Dostoevsky's "Christ's Way" for the MECBC

7.1 Introduction

This book has examined Dostoevsky's life and literature. The goal of the research has been to discover and analyse Dostoevsky's convictional theology expressed in his life and literature and its relevance for the life and mission of the MECBC – a network of baptistic communities in Moldova. The new contribution offered in this study is an attempt to discover Dostoevsky's lived out theology expressed in his life and works. The investigation which has been undertaken in this book reveals a great deal about Dostoevsky's implicit theology.

Dostoevsky's "Christ's Way" had a big influence on different people as seen in the previous chapter. His "Christ's Way" can also be an example for people from different cultures and religious denominations. As mentioned in the first chapter, my personal interest as a member of MECBC is to take some lessons from Dostoevsky's "Christ's Way," which can serve as an inspiration for improving the life and mission of MECBC in its Orthodox context. There are several reasons for doing this. First, Dostoevsky's theology, as well as the theology of MECBC, is a Christ-centred theology. It is seen in the way of life of Moldavian Baptists, which is yearning for "Christ's Way."[1] The way in which the Bruderhof have taken themes from Dostoevsky shows his relevance for a baptistic community.

Second, there is a similar Orthodox context in Dostoevsky's Russian society as in MECBC's Moldavian society. In Moldova 93 percent of the population consider themselves as belonging to the Orthodox Church.[2] MECBC is less than 1 percent of Moldova's population; and because they are radical Christians, people often do not understand them and criticize.[3] Dostoevsky associated himself with the Orthodox Church; but because he was a radical Orthodox Christian, many times he was not understood and was criticized by people of his time. In his day the Orthodox Church was corrupt, and Dostoevsky craved for improvements in Russian society.[4] Now the Moldavian society, which is predominantly Orthodox, is corrupt, and MECBC wants to regenerate it.[5]

Third, many of the Russian social issues of the nineteenth century, about which Dostoevsky was concerned, are also the issues of the contemporary Moldavian society: poverty, illness, corruption and lack of virtues.

7.2. Challenge for the Life of the MECBC

Dostoevsky's life and the life of his characters can become a role model for the life of the MECBC just as stories about the "heroes of faith," published in periodicals of the MECBC, serve as an example to follow. In each issue of the newspaper, "The Light of the Truth," an article is printed about "the heroes of faith."[6] The purpose of the stories is to inspire believers to follow

---

1. See 1.2 and Part I.

2. "Liga Islamică este nedumerită de faptul că Mitropolitul Vladimir condamnă înregistrarea acestui cult în Moldova" [Islamic League is puzzled that Metropolitan Vladimir condemns registration of this cult in Moldova], 25 April 2011, http://www.azi.md/ro/print -story/17954.

3. "Biserica baptista" [The Baptist Church], 13 June 2011, http://logos.md/2008/09/12/ biserica-baptista/.

4. Eroshkin, *Krepostnicheskoe samoderzhavie i ego politicheskie instituty*, 130.

5. See 1.2 and Alexandru Tanase, "Coruptie si coruptionisti" [Corruption and Corruption-ists], 28 July 2011, http://www.tanase.md/2011/07/02/coruptie-coruptioneri-si-crasa/.

6. These are Christians devoted to their ministry.

these examples. These articles are illustrations from the biographies of faithful Christians and their loyal service.[7]

These stories show that a living theology, in the centre of which is the Christ's "Living Way," is very important for the MECBC. All these and similar stories suggest that the MECBC is open to the possibility of learning from other people whose lives were an imitation of Christ's life no matter what Christian denomination they belonged to.[8]

The MECBC, as along with Dostoevsky, is convinced that a positive example could strongly influence the beliefs of man.[9] MECBC is confident

---

7. Thus, an example of love to a person's enemies was an article entitled "The Martyr of Love," which told the story of Pastor Yang Won Son (1902–1950) from South Korea who was able to forgive the murderers of his sons (Mihai Moscovici, "Martir al iubirii" [The Martyr of Love], *Slovo Istiny* 1 (April 2003), 6). An article from the biography of Abraham Lincoln (1809–1865) was an incentive to participate in the political life of the country (Mihai Moscovici, "Abraham Lincoln pilon al națiunii" [Abraham Lincoln Pilot of a Nation], *Slovo Istiny* 2 (May 2003), 4). Stories about Hudson Taylor (1832–1905), (Mihai Moscovici, "James Hudson Taylor missionarul Chinei" [James Hudson Taylor: Missionary to China], *Slovo Istiny* 3 (June 2003), 10); William Carey (1761–1834) (Mihai Moscovici, "Un model de transformare a oamenilor: William Carey" [A Model of People Transformation: William Carey], *Slovo Istiny* 8 (November 2003), 12); and Johann Gerhardt Onken (1800–1884) (Sergiu Matei, "Onken: Marele missionar German" [Onken: Great German Missionary], *Slovo Istiny* 1 (January 2007), 8) aimed to inspire young Christians to missionary service. An illustration of the importance of children's ministry was a story about George Muller (1805–1898) serving orphan children (Mihai Moscovici, "George Muller Incredere deplina in Dumnezeu" [George Muller: Full Trust in God], *Slovo Istiny* 4 (July 2003), 10). The story of James Clerk Maxwell (1831–1879) aimed to encourage Christians to be known for good deeds (Alexandr Sibilev, "James Clerk Maxwell," *Slovo Istiny* 5 (August 2003), 9). Parts of the biographies of Dwight L. Moody (1837–1899) (Mihai Moscovici, "Dwight L. Moody: Ce poate face un om consacrat lui Dumnezeu" [Dwight L. Moody: What Can a Person Dedicated to God Do?], *Slovo Istiny* 6 (September 2003), 12), and C. H. Spurgeon (1834–1892) (Mihai Moscovici, "Transformat pentru Dumnezeu: Charles Haddon Spurgeon" [Transformed for God: Charles Haddon Spurgeon], *Slovo Istiny* 7 (October 2003), 12) taught our readers to be persistent in preaching the word of God. The example of sacrificial love for people was told in the stories of Richard Wurmbrand (1909–2001) ("Glorie prin suferinte: Richard Wurmbrand" [Glory through Suffering: Richard Wurmbrand], *Slovo Istiny* 9 (December 2003), 12) and Martin Luther King Jr. (1929–1968) (Valentina Grinevici, "Martin Luther King: Odisseya k nenasiliyu" [Martin Luther King: Odyssey to Nonviolence], *Slovo Istiny* 3 (March 2005), 10).

8. These "heroes of faith" belonged to different Christian denominations. Thus Dwight L. Moody, C. H. Spurgeon, Martin Luther King, Jr., Johann Gerhardt Onken and William Carey were Baptists. Yang Won Son and James Clerk Maxwell were Presbyterians. James Hudson Taylor was Methodist. George A. Muller began to fellowship with members of the Brethren movement and was offered a position as pastor of a local church. Richard Wurmbrand belonged to the Lutheran church. Abraham Lincoln did not formally join the church.

9. Scanlan, *Dostoevsky the Thinker*, 91. Dostoevsky himself remembered throughout his life examples of the Bible characters and of numerous saints, heard in his childhood, which influenced his beliefs (Grossman, *Dostoevsky*, 15). In particular, he enthusiastically talked about the impact of Christ on his life. In the words of Prince Myshkin, the main character of *The Idiot*, one can see the importance of personal example in the life of Dostoevsky: "The good as such

that through personal example one can influence others. Dostoevsky also, as a writer, created characters so that their examples would be emulated.[10] Thus, the life of the writer and the lives of the characters of his novels, in the centre of which is Christ, can serve as role models for MECBC.

The MECBC believes, with Dostoevsky, that every person is sinful.[11] Some of Dostoevsky's stories can serve as illustrations for a deeper understanding that the greatest problem of humanity is inside of each person. Few people can so vividly illustrate the sinful condition of people as did Dostoevsky. All the characters in his works attested to the presence of a sinful nature. Sin permeated man so deeply that he sometimes did not realize that even the motivations of his good deeds were sinful. An example is how such a state could serve the life of Makar Devushkin, the main character of *The Poor Folk*. This story can be an example of how even unconscious sin leads man to misfortune, to tragedy.[12]

Some of Dostoevsky's stories, such as the life of Fyodor Pavlovich Karamazov, Ivan Karamazov, Smerdyakov and some convicts, such as Orlov and Petrov, can serve as an example for MECBC in understanding how life can be pathetic and disgusting, dominated by lies, vanity, selfishness, and cruelty. This kind of life brought suffering, even upon the characters themselves in these stories and caused pain and suffering to others. Dostoevsky offered his readers a chance to stop and look from the outside upon the sinfulness of people to understand the seriousness of sin.

The MECBC is convinced that there is an image of God in every person.[13] Several of Dostoevsky's stories can stimulate hope in people who have fallen down and seem to have lost any hope for transformation of their lives. Dostoevsky was not only convinced of the general sinfulness of people, but he also saw the image of God in every man. Chapters 6 and 7 of this study may

---

will always remain because it is the need of the personality, the living need to have influence upon another person," F. M. Dostoevsky, *Polnoe Sobranie Sochineniy, Idiot* [The Complete Works of Dostoevsky, The Idiot], [CD-ROM] (Izdatel'stvo Adept, 2002).

10. Dostoevsky was convinced that the Russian peasants, though not knowing the Orthodox teachings well, by knowing the lives of many saints and imitating them acted in a very Christian way (Scanlan, *Dostoevsky the Thinker*, 90).

11. MECBU's confession of faith. Taken from the report of the bishop of the MECBU, 20 February 2012, available from the author.

12. See chapter 5.

13. MECBU's confession of faith.

serve as an example of how even the most brutal man can fall in love with someone, like the Major from *The House of the Dead* and Fyodor Pavlovich Karamazov, who once expressed compassion for Smerdyakov who fell ill. It happened because God's image dwells inside of each person.[14]

According to the MECBC's confession of faith, repentance and faith in God is required for the transformation of a person's life.[15] Dostoevsky shared the same beliefs.[16] He wrote vivid stories about the conversion of such "big" notorious figures as Rodion Raskolnikov, Luchika, Dimitry Karamazov and the "saints" such as Alyosha Karamazov, Starets Zosima and Dostoevsky himself.[17] According to Dostoevsky, all are sinful; all are in need of repentance. Also, according to the writer, transformed lives should be visible in all respects and actions, following the example of Christ. A wonderful role model can be found in the story of "The Dream of the Ridiculous Man," in which the main character admitted that when he "saw the truth, his life got meaning." But the very meaning of his life was in acting morally, helping the girl whom he previously had refused to help.[18] Ethical maximalism reaches deeply and is given strong expression in Dostoevsky's works.[19]

Dostoevsky's own life in the post-Siberian period and the lives of some positive characters of his works such as Prince Myshkin, Starets Zosima, Makar Dolgoruky, Sonya Marmeladova and Alyosha Karamazov, can demonstrate how to live the life of Christ, overcoming various difficulties and temptations of life. Faith in God and the immortality of man's soul helped the characters to forgive the wrongs of people, to love, to sympathize and help.

All of these stories, including the life of Dostoevsky himself and the lives of his characters, should be printed in periodicals of the MECBC to serve as examples to follow in order to improve the quality of the lives of MECBC members.

---

14. Milikov, "Svetoch," in *Kriticheskie razbory "Zapisok iz Mernvogo Doma,"* 8.

15. MECBU's confession of faith.

16. *Brat'ya Karamazovy,* 45.

17. See chapters 2, 5, 6, and 7.

18. F. M. Dostoevsky, *Polnoe Sobranie Sochineniy, Son Smeshnogo Cheloveka* [The Complete Works of Dostoevsky, The Dream of a Ridiculous Man], [CD-ROM] (Izdatel'stvo Adept, 2002).

19. Zenkovsky, "Dostoevsky's Religious and Philosophical Views," in *Dostoevsky. A Collection of Critical Essays,* ed. Rene Wellek, 140.

7.3. Challenge for the Mission of the MECBC in Its Orthodox Context

To understand Dostoevsky's mission, one must "hear" his story, which is linked with the story of the people and with the greater story of Jesus.[20] Dostoevsky was a journalist as well as a novelist. N. Strakhov wrote that it was important for Dostoevsky to use his novels to influence Russian society. Even though Dostoevsky wrote almost all his novels in haste, he did not regret this, as it was far more important for him to deliver his "sermon." In this, he found his mission as a writer and journalist.[21]

That is why I am going to examine his perception of the situation of his time as a form of "mission as witness."[22] Also, I intend to explore two elements in the Orthodox Church mission – love and life[23] – as they are evident in the life of Dostoevsky, which can be an example for MECBC in its mission to secularized people in the Moldavian context where an Orthodox religious presence predominates.

The perception of the situation often begins by defining the "threat" and by "the questions of the desirability and speed of the presumably needed social change in the community."[24]

According to the MECBC's mission strategy, it is necessary to define the context and the situation for the mission's success.[25] The way Dostoevsky defined the threat and saw the way out for Russian society can serve as a model for MECBC. It is to see the danger in the way of rebellion and violence and to see the best way for society in humility and sacrificial living for the sake of helping people in need.

The situation in Russia at the beginning of the 1860s remained difficult. Reforms undertaken by Alexander II did yield the expected results.[26] In society, many people still suffered from poverty and were humiliated by the

---

20. McClendon, *Ethics. Systematic Theology, Volume 1*, 356.

21. Dolinin, *Dostoevskiy i drugie*, 101.

22. Parush R. Parushev and Rolling Grams, *Academic Reasoning, Research and Writing in Religious Studies: A Concise Handbook* (Librix.eu Tribun EU, 2008), 19.

23. David J. Bosch, *Transforming Mission: Paradigms Shifts in Theology of Mission* (Maryknoll: Orbis Books, 1991), 207–209.

24. Andronovienė and Parushev, *Church, State, and Culture*, 194–121.

25. MECBU's mission strategy. Taken from the report of the Bishop of the MECBU, 20 February 2012, available from the author.

26. Radzinskiy, *Alexandr II*, 254–255.

rich. At this time, there were ideological revolutionary-minded people who offered to rebel against their oppressors.[27] In their teachings, they justified such acts of violence, believing that some special people had the right to control the destinies of others for the well being of society.[28] As a response to this situation, Dostoevsky wrote his novel *Crime and Punishment*. The main characters of the novel are Rodion Raskolnikov and Sonia Marmeladova. They both are in difficult social situations. But each of them sees a different way out of the difficult situation. The rational theory of Raskolnikov led him to evil and murder, while the religious and moral beliefs of Sonia led her to humility and sacrifice for the sake of helping her neighbour. Through his novel, Dostoevsky showed the fallacy of the path chosen by Raskolnikov.[29] By showing the suffering and the internal punishment inside of Raskolnikov, the author cautioned the public to stay away from accepting Western ideas "preached" by revolutionary-minded Westerners.[30] The only way out that Dostoevsky saw was the acceptance of the gospel's good news, leading a person through repentance to a new life.[31]

Dostoevsky understood that to oppose the growing revolutionary ideas in society was possible only through the influence of some people upon others with their moral lives.[32] For him, there was only one ideal – Jesus Christ.[33] This was how the idea of writing the novel *The Idiot* came into being. In this novel, Prince Myshkin is the man who lived as Christ would have lived in a modern society. Myshkin was introduced in the novel as a moral antithesis to the proud, selfish, conniving, cunning of the Epanchins, the Totskys, and the Rogozhins. Mishkin had to morally oppose them, exercising moral influence on them.[34]

In late 1869 while abroad, Dostoevsky got interested in reports that the followers of the anarchists Mikhail Bakunin, Sergei Nechaev, and members

---

27. Radzinskiy, *Alexandr II*, 274.

28. Radzinskiy, 373–374.

29. "Dostoevsky condemned the notion that an action, which in itself is morally abhorrent, may be justified on the grounds that its good consequences would outweigh its inherent evil" (Scanlan, *Dostoevsky the Thinker*, 90).

30. Radzinskiy, *Alexandr II*, 241–242.

31. Pospelov, *Tvorchestvo F. M. Dostoevskiy*, 22–30.

32. Losskiy, *Bog i mirovoe zlo*, 93.

33. *Pis'ma*, Vol. 28, 20 February 1854, 175.

34. Pospelov, *Tvorchestvo F. M. Dostoevskiy*, 31–35.

of their clandestine circle killed one of their comrades in Moscow because of some disagreements with him. They were arrested and prosecuted.[35] The writer saw in this event a particularly vivid manifestation of the negative features of the secret political activities of the Russian revolutionaries of his time.[36] This situation prompted Dostoevsky to write the novel *The Devils*. In it, people like Nechaev and members of his underground group received negative, caricature-like images. In the spring of 1870, the writer had already told friends that he was working on a "tendentious thing, directed against the 'nihilists.'" Dostoevsky wrote:

> It's almost like a historical sketch, by which I wanted to explain the possibility of such monstrous events as the Nechaevsky movement. Our Belinsky and Granovsky would not have believed it if they had been told that they were the direct fathers of the Nechaevsky movement. This is the kinship and the continuity of thought, emerging from the fathers to the children that I wanted to express in my literary work.[37]

He used as a central character of the novel, the young Stavrogin, a man who had great religious and moral influence on others. His followers were Shatov and Kirillov. In the past, Stavrogin had been the organizer of an underground movement and having been abroad, had changed his beliefs. He himself believed in Christ and persuaded others in the correctness of the chosen path.[38]

In the mid-1870s in the atmosphere of a new public lift and "going to the people"[39] of the revolutionary-democratic minded youth, Dostoevsky wrote *A Raw Youth*. The content of this novel is Dostoevsky's response to the turmoil that had entirely gripped the old ways of social life in Russia, which had become quite noticeable in the middle of the 1870s. This situation was particularly painful to the writer for its negative moral consequences. "The deterioration is the main visible idea of the novel . . .," "general disorder, there

---

35. Radzinskiy, *Alexandr II*, 274.

36. Pospelov, *Tvorchestvo F. M. Dostoevskiy*, 36-37.

37. *Pis'ma*, Vol. 29, 10 February 1873, 260.

38. Pospelov, *Tvorchestvo F. M. Dostoevskiy*, 38.

39. Mihaylovskiy, *Zhestokiy talent*, 10 January 2011, http://az.lib.ru/m/mihajlowskij_n_k/text_0042.shtml.

and everywhere in society . . . in the governing ideas . . . in the beliefs, in the deterioration of the family foundation," "there are no moral ideas," wrote Dostoevsky in rough drafts of the novel. The entire novel is based on the antithesis between morally misguided people who are corrupt and depraved and people who embody kindness and spiritual purity. The first supports the expansion of general chaos, turmoil, and collapse. The second are carriers of moral values.[40] Of great significance for the teenager was to communicate with Makar Ivanovich who, like Myshkin in *The Idiot*, differed from all other people by "extraordinary candor and lack of the slightest self-esteem, as well as a penchant for 'tenderness.'"[41]

The content of his last novel, *The Brothers Karamazov*, continues in line with the previous great novels of the writer; but it raises the moral issues that the author dwelt on to a new, higher level. Moral decay and life in chaos received embodiment in the members of the same "Karamazov" family. This chaos had its antithesis here as well. Uprightness, total lack of self-love and a tendency to tenderness was disclosed in Starets Zosima and Alyosha. Here we find the denial of life based on wealth, pride, and vanity and the ideal of the Russian national fraternity, which can be achieved not by violence but only through moral regeneration of all members of society. To do this, people must realize their guilt before all and love everyone and all of God's creation. Sin is an evil that man can atone for by repentance and spiritual suffering. All the teachings of Zosima lead to the recognition of understanding one's own way through spiritual "harmony."[42] An opponent of such harmony in the novel is Ivan Karamazov, in his "rebellion." Thus, the ideological concept of the novel embodies the sharp antithesis of the church as based on coercion and temptation of believers as opposed to the church based on free faith, recognition of the spiritual world harmony and its rejection.[43]

Dostoevsky believed in the moral rebirth of men like Raskolnikov, Shatov, and Dimitry Karamazov by mentorship and the example of such moral people as Myshkin, Makar Dolgoruky, Alyosha Karamazov, Sonia Marmeladova, and

---

40. Mihaylovskiy, 41–42.

41. Mihaylovskiy, 43.

42. *Brat'ya Karamazovy*, 272–273.

43. *Brat'ya Karamazovy*, 45–46.

Starets Zosima.[44] His work is a manifestation of love and care towards Russian society and mankind in general. The value of Dostoevsky's novels increased greatly due to the fact that he realized the depth of the spiritual life of his characters in close connection with the resolution of critical issues of society.[45]

Dostoevsky's perception of the situation can serve as an example for MECBC in improving its mission. His examples can be shared at seminars for leaders of MECBC to help them first identify the threat of society and second to give a moral response in the centre, which will be the "Christ's Way" appropriate for the Moldavian situation.

According to David Bosch, God's love expressed in the sacrifice of Christ is the foundation for mission in an orthodox understanding. The followers of Christ are to display this same love beyond the limits of the flock.[46] The MECBU shares the same beliefs. It calls church leaders to encourage every believer to express his or her love, compassion and sacrificial attitude to people in need.[47]

Some of the issues faced by the Moldavian society are like those encountered by Dostoevsky's society. The poor, sick and oppressed Moldavian people are looking for love, compassion and help.

Dostoevsky lived in a difficult time, but during his life he acted as a person of compassion to the poor, sick and oppressed,[48] because his convictions were grounded in Jesus. Goryanchikov, the main character of *The House of the Dead*, in spite of a terrible life in penal servitude, remained a person of compassion to the sick and oppressed convicts.[49] For Dostoevsky and Goryanchikov, Christ's example and their faith in God helped them to love people in need. Their stories of love, compassion and help can be used as model – for example in sermon illustrations as a way of stimulating love and compassion of the members of MECBC churches for the poor, sick and oppressed.

According to Bosch, "For the Orthodox Church – love is the foundation of mission and life is its goal. Christ came not first of all to free men from

---

44. *Brat'ya Karamazovy*, 59.

45. *Brat'ya Karamazovy*, 61.

46. Bosch, *Transforming Mission*, 208–209.

47. MECBU's mission strategy.

48. Dostoevskaya, *Vospominaniya*, 293.

49. *Zapiski iz Mertvogo Doma*, 137.

their sins, but to restore them in their godly image and to give them life."[50] People are called not to simply get to know Christ; they are called to "share the glory of Christ."[51]

Dostoevsky's society was full of injustice, deceit, humiliation, selfishness and vanity. Unfortunately, in the Moldavian society, which is called a Christian society, nothing has changed for the better. Evil is increasing in people as a whole in society.

According to Dostoevsky, behind all of these vices is the unbelief of people, their rejecting of "Christ's Way." As a radical Christian, Dostoevsky tried to follow Christ in his life's attitude toward corruption, lying, selfishness and the excessive use of alcohol. His life during the Siberian and post-Siberian period and the life of Zosima, Alyosha, Prince Myshkin, Makar Dolgoruky and Sonya, which were honest, accurate, sober and self-sacrificing, can be an example for MECBC. MECBC can improve its mission in Moldavian society, which is full of corruption, lying, selfishness, excessive use of alcohol and indifference to the poor, sick and oppressed people.

Dostoevsky's above-mentioned stories will be included in the "Church and Society" course at CTE (College of Theology and Education) to stimulate "Christ's Way" as the only way of CTE students who are the future leaders of MECBC.

7.4 Conclusion

In the centre of Dostoevsky's life and mission is the image of Christ suffering and resurrected. He warned people of the danger of turning away from Christ and called upon them to follow Him through difficulties and hardships to "resurrection for new life." Through all these he would display a personal example of life in Christ in his relationships with Him and the people around him.

MECBC long for spiritual transformation of Moldavian society, which is predominantly nominal Orthodox. Dostoevsky's own life's story and sthe tories of his novel's characters can be a model for MECBC in improving love, compassion and justice to people in need.

---

50. Bosch, *Transforming Mission*, 208–209.
51. Bosch, 208–209.

This book argued that an analysis of the life and literature of Dostoevsky using McClendon's "biography as theology method" made it possible to discover the writer's implicit living theology and its influence on society. There is more work that can be done in this area. I did not explore all of Dostoevsky's novels in detail in chapters 2–4. In chapter 6, Dostoevsky's theology and its influence on his contemporaries during the first three years after the death of Dostoevsky, from 1881 to 1883, was explored. There is room for investigating the influence of Dostoevsky's theology on Russian society up until the Russian Revolution in 1917. This book contains new perspectives in the study of Dostoevsky's theology.

Bibliography

Primary Sources

Dostoevsky's Literature:

Dostoevskiy, F. M. *Brat'ya Karamazovy* [The Brothers Karamazov]. Kishinev: Cartea Moldoveneasca, 1984.

———. *The Brothers Karamazov*. Translated by Constance Garnett. Urbana, IL: Project Gutenberg, 2009. ePub edition. www.gutenberg.org/ebooks/28045.

———. *The House of the Dead or Prison Life in Siberia: With an Introduction by Julius Bramont*. Edited by Ernest Rhys. Urbana, IL: Project Gutenberg, 2011. ePub edition. www.gutenberg.org/eboooks/37536.

———. *Polnoe Sobranie Sochineniy v 30-i tomakh, T. 13, Podrostok* [The Complete Works of Dostoevsky in 30 Volumes, Vol. 13: *Raw Youth*]. Leningrad: Nauka, 1975.

———. *Polnoe Sobranie Sochineniy v 30-i tomakh, T. 4 Zapiski iz Mertvogo Doma* [The Complete Works of Dostoevsky in 30 Volumes, Vol. 4: *The House of the Dead*]. Leningrad: Nauka, 1972.

———. *Polnoe Sobranie Sochineniy v 30-i tomakh, T. 5, Zimnie zametki o letnikh vpechatleniyakh* [The Complete Works of Dostoevsky in 30 Volumes, Vol. 5: *Winter Notes on Summer Impression*]. Leningrad: Nauka, 1973.

———. *Polnoe Sobranie Sochineniy v 30-i tomakh, T. 1 Bednye Lyudi* [The Complete Works of Dostoevsky in 30 Volumes, Vol. 1: *The Poor Folk*]. Leningrad: Nauka, 1972.

———. *Polnoe Sobranie Sochineniy, Gospodin Procharchin* [The Complete Works of Dostoevsky: *Mister Procharchin*], [CD-ROM]. Izdatel'stvo Adept, 2002.

———. *Polnoe Sobranie Sochineniy, Netochka Nezvanova* [The Complete Works of Dostoevsky: *Netochka Nezvanova*], [CD-ROM]. Izdatel'stvo Adept, 2002.

———. *Polnoe Sobranie Sochineniy v 30-i tomakh, T. 5, Zapiski iz Podpolie* [The Complete Works of Dostoevsky in 30 Volumes, Vol. 5: *Notes from Underground*]. Leningrad: Nauka, 1973.

————. *Polnoe Sobranie Sochineniy v 30-i tomakh, T. 5, Idiot* [The Complete Works of Dostoevsky in 30 Volumes, Vol. 5: *The Idiot*]. Leningrad: Nauka, 1973.

————. *Polnoe Sobranie Sochineniy v 30-i tomakh, T. 5, Zimnie zametki o letnikh vpechatleniyakh* [The Complete Works of Dostoevsky in 30 Volumes, Vol. 5: *Winter Notes on Summer Impression*]. Leningrad: Nauka, 1973.

————. *Polnoe Sobranie Sochineniy, Belye Nochi* [The Complete Works of Dostoevsky: *White Nights*], [CD-ROM] (Izdatel'stvo Adept, 2002)

————. *Polnoe Sobranie Sochineniy, Bessy* [The Complete Works of Dostoevsky: *The Devils*], [CD-ROM]. Izdatel'stvo Adept, 2002.

————. *Polnoe Sobranie Sochineniy, Dvoynik* [The Complete Works of Dostoevsky: *The Double*], [CD-ROM]. Izdatel'stvo Adept, 2002.

————. *Polnoe Sobranie Sochineniy, Gospodin Procharchin* [The Complete Works of Dostoevsky: *Mister Procharchin*], [CD-ROM]. Izdatel'stvo Adept, 2002.

————. *Polnoe Sobranie Sochineniy, Idiot* [The Complete Works of Dostoevsky: *The Idiot*], [CD-ROM]. Izdatel'stvo Adept, 2002.

————. *Polnoe Sobranie Sochineniy, Netochka Nezvanova* [The Complete Works of Dostoevsky: *Netochka Nezvanova*], [CD-ROM]. Izdatel'stvo Adept, 2002.

————. *Polnoe Sobranie Sochineniy, Podrostok* [The Complete Works of Dostoevsky: *The Raw Youth*], [CD-ROM]. Izdatel'stvo Adept, 2002.

————. *Polnoe Sobranie Sochineniy, Prestuplenie i Nakazanie* [The Complete Works of Dostoevsky: *Crime and Punishment*], [CD-ROM]. Izdatel'stvo Adept, 2002.

————. *Polnoe Sobranie Sochineniy, Selo Stepanchikovo i ego obitateley* [The Complete Works of Dostoevsky: *The Village of Stepanchikovo*], [CD-ROM]. Izdatel'stvo Adept, 2002.

————. *Polnoe Sobranie Sochineniy, Son Smeshnogo Cheloveka* [The Complete Works of Dostoevsky: *The Dream of a Ridiculous Man*], [CD-ROM]. Izdatel'stvo Adept, 2002.

————. *Polnoe Sobranie Sochineniy, Belye Nochi* [The Complete Works of Dostoevsky: *White Nights*], [CD-ROM]. Izdatel'stvo Adept, 2002.

Dostoevsky's *Letters*:

Dostoevsky, F. M. *Polnoe Sobranie Sochineniy v 30-i tomakh, T. 28, Pis'ma* [The Complete Works of Dostoevsky in 30 Volumes, Vol. 28: *Letters*]. Leningrad: Nauka, 1985.

————. *Polnoe Sobranie Sochineniy v 30-i tomakh, T. 29, Pis'ma* [The Complete Works of Dostoevsky in 30 Volumes, Vol. 29: *Letters*]. Leningrad: Nauka, 1986.

———. *Polnoe Sobranie Sochineniy v 30-i tomakh, T. 30, Pis'ma* [The Complete Works of Dostoevsky in 30 Volumes: Vol. 30, *Letters*]. Leningrad: Nauka, 1990.

———. *Poor Folk*. Translated by C. J. Hogarth. Urbana, IL: Project Gutenberg, 2000. ePub edition. www.gutenberg.org/ebooks/2302.

Dostoevsky's *Diary of a Writer*:

Dostoevsky, F. M. *Polnoe Sobranie Sochineniy v 30-i tomakh, T. 21, Dnevnik Pisatelya za 1873g.* [The Complete Works of Dostoevsky in 30 Volumes, Vol. 21: *Diary of a Writer*, 1873]. Leningrad: Nauka, 1972.

———. *Polnoe Sobranie Sochineniy v 30-i tomakh, T. 22, Dnevnik Pisatelya za 1876g.* [The Complete Works of Dostoevsky in 30 Volumes, Vol. 22: *Diary of a Writer*, 1876]. Leningrad: Nauka, 1972.

———. *Polnoe Sobranie Sochineniy v 30-i tomakh, T. 25, Dnevnik Pisatelya za 1877g.* [The Complete Works of Dostoevsky in 30 Volumes, Vol. 25: *Diary of a Writer*, 1877]. Leningrad: Nauka, 1972.

———. *Polnoe Sobranie Sochineniy v 30-i tomakh, T. 26, Dnevnik Pisatelya za 1880g.* [The Complete Works of Dostoevsky in 30 Volumes, Vol. 26: *Diary of a Writer*, 1880]. Leningrad: Nauka, 1972.

———. *Polnoe Sobranie Sochineniy v 30-i tomakh, T. 27, Dnevnik Pisatelya za 1881g.* [The Complete Works of Dostoevsky in 30 Volumes, Vol. 27: *Diary of a Writer*, 1881]. Leningrad: Nauka, 1972.

———. *A Writer's Diary, Volume 1, 1873–1867*. Translated by Kenneth Lantz. Evanston, IL: Northwestern University Press, 1994.

Dostoevsky's *Notebooks*:

Dostoevsky, F. M. *Polnoe Sobranie Cochineniy v 30-i tomakh, T. 18, Stat'i i Zametri 1845–1861* [The Complete Works of Dostoevsky in 30 Volumes, Vol. 18: *Articles and Notes 1845–1861*]. Leningrad: Nauka, 1972.

———. *Polnoe Sobranie Sochineniy, Iz zapisnoy tetradi, 1860–1865gg.* [The Complete Works of Dostoevsky: *From His Notebooks, 1860–1865*] [CD-ROM]. Izdatel'stvo Adept, 2002.

———. *Polnoe Sobranie Sochineniy v 30-i tomakh, T. 19, Stat'i i Zametri 1861* [The Complete Works of Dostoevsky in 30 Volumes, Vol. 19: *Articles and Notes 1861*]. Leningrad: Nauka, 1972.

———. *Polnoe Sobranie Sochineniy, 'Zapiski, 1873–1878gg.* [The Complete Works of Dostoevsky] [CD-ROM]. Izdatel'stvo Adept, 2002.

———. *Polnoe Sobranie Sochineniy, Iz zapisnoy tetradi, 1880–1881gg.* [The Complete Works of Dostoevsky: *From His Notebooks, 1880–1881*] [CD-ROM]. Izdatel'stvo Adept, 2002.

———. *Polnoe Sobranie Sochineniy, Stat'i i Kritika* [The Complete Works of Dostoevsky: *Articles and Critical Works*] [CD-ROM]. Izdatel'stvo Adept, 2002.

———. *Neizdannyy Dostoevsky Zapisnye knizhki i tetradi 1860–1881гг* [Unpublished Dostoevsky: *Notebooks*]. Leningrad: Nauka, 1971.

Articles from Periodicals of MECBC:

Svet Zhizni [The Light of Life]:

Legcun, V. "Deschiderea Centrului Crestin pentru tineret" [Inauguration of a New Youth Centre]. *Svet Zhizni* 1 (January 1996): 15.

Mocan, O. "O sluzhenii zhenschin" [About Women's Ministry]. *Svet Zhizni* 3 (September 1995): 12.

Serghienco, G. "Isskustvo Propovedi" [The Art of Preaching]. *Svet Zhizni* 2 (July 1997): 9.

Plucci, N. "Spasay vzyatykh na smerti" [Deliver Those Who Are Being Taken Away to Death]. *Svet Zhizni* 3 (September 1995): 4.

Slovo Istiny [The Word of Truth]:

"Glorie prin suferinte: Richard Wurmbrand" [Glory through Suffering: Richard Wurmbrand], *Slovo Istiny* 9 (December 2003): 12.

"Rezolyutsia missionerskoy konferentsii Evro-aziatskoy federatsii soyuzov EHB" [Resolution of the Missions Conference of the Euro-Asiatic Federation of Unions of the ECB]. *Slovo Istiny* 3 (June 2003): 5.

"Samoe mnogochislennoe pokolinie vypusknikov TPK" [The Most Numerous Generation of the CTE Graduates]. *Slovo Istiny* 3 (June 2003): 12.

Alexeeva, Alla. "Svet Bozhiy liubvi v temnitse" [Light of God's Love in Prison]. *Slovo Istiny* 1 (January 2004): 9.

Burlacu, Ion. "Oportunitati pentru proclamarea evangheliei" [Possibilities for Proclamation of the Gospel]. *Slovo Istiny* 5 (May 2008): 10.

Filat, Vasile. "Tabara de limba engleza" [The Camp in English]. *Slovo Istiny* 8 (August 2008): 11.

Ghiletchi, V. "Obrashchenie glavnogo redaktora" [Chief Editor Speech]. *Slovo Istiny* 7 (October 2003): 1.

Grinevici, Valentina. "Martin Luther King: odisseya k nenasiliyu" [Martin Luther King: Odyssey to Nonviolence]. *Slovo Istiny* 3 (March 2005): 10.

Ivtodi, Rodica. "Membre in familia credintei" [Members in the Faith Family]. *Slovo Istiny* 5 (August 2003): 12.

Matei, Sergiu. "Onken – Marele missionar German" [Onken – Great German Missionary]. *Slovo Istiny* 1 (January 2007): 8.

Moscovici, Mihai. "Abraham Lincoln pilon al naţiunii" [Abraham Lincoln: Pilot of a Nation]. *Slovo Istiny* 2 (May 2003): 4.

———. "Dwight L. Moody: Ce poate face un om consacrat lui Dumnezeu" [Dwight L. Moody: What Can a Person Dedicated to God Do?]. *Slovo Istiny* 6 (September 2003): 12.

———. "George Muller Incredere deplina in Dumnezeu" [George Muller: Full Trust in God]. *Slovo Istiny* 4 (July 2003): 10.

———. "James Hudson Taylor missionarul Chinei" [James Hudson Taylor: Missionary to China]. *Slovo Istiny* 3 (June 2003): 10.

———. Martir al iubirii' [The Martyr of Love]. *Slovo Istiny* 1 (April 2003): 6.

———. "Transformat pentru Dumnezeu: Charles Haddon Spurgeon" [Transformed for God: Charles Haddon Spurgeon]. *Slovo Istiny* 7 (October 2003): 12.

———. "Un model de transformare a oamenilor: William Carey" [A Model of People Transformation: William Carey]. *Slovo Istiny* 8 (November 2003): 12.

Moosneaga, Igor. "Misiune prin sport" [Missions through Sports]. *Slovo Istiny* 3 (June 2003): 12.

Nezhel'skaya, Svetlana. "Deti kotorym my mozhem pomoch" [Children Who We Can Help]. *Slovo Istiny* 2 (February 2007): 4.

Stepaniuc, Valentina. "Facultatea de studio biblic inductive in limba engleza" [The Department of Bible Study in English]. *Slovo Istiny* 8 (August 2008): 3.

Ton, Iosif. "Cine suntem noi, baptistii?" [Who Are We, the Baptists?]. *Slovo Istiny* 9 (September 2003): 9.

Secondary Sources

Theses:

Grigorieff, Dimitry Felex. "Dostoevsky and The Russian Orthodox Church." PhD diss. Graduate School of the University of Pennsylvania, 1958.

Adam, Dejan. "'Character in the Community': Life and Convictions of Hans Meier (1902–1992)." MTh thesis. IBTS, Prague, 2006.

Books:

Abandonul copiilor in Republica Moldova [Abandonment of Children in Moldova]. Chisinau, Guvernul Republicii Moldova: UNICEF, 2005.

Akhshrumov, D. D. *Iz moikh vospominaniy1849 – 1851 гг.* [From My Memories 1849–1851]. Sankt-Petersburg, 1905.

Arnold, J. Heinrich. *Discipleship: Living for Christ in the Daily Grind.* Farmington: Plough Publishing House, Bruderhof Foundation, 1994.

Bakhtin, M. M. *Problemy poetiki Dostoevskogo* [Problems of Dostoevsky's Poetics]. Moscow: Sovetskiy Pisatel', 1979.

Bel'chikov, N. F. *Dostoevsky v processe petrashevcev* [Dostoevsky in Judicial Process of Petrashevists]. Moscow: Nauka, 1971.

Belinskiy, V. G. *Sobranie Sochineniy v 3 tomakh* [The Complete Works in 3 Volumes]. Moscow: OGIZ, 1948, 10 November 2010. http://az.lib.ru/b/belinskij_w_g/text_0090.shtml.

———. *Pis'mo Belinskogo Gogolyu* [Belinsky's Letter to Gogol]. 25 December 2010. http://ru.wikisource.org/wiki/.

Belopol'skiy, V. N. *Dostoevskiy i folosofskaya mysl' ego epokhi: Kontseptsiya cheloveka* [Dostoevsky and the Philosophical Thought of His Epoch: Concept of Man]. Rostov: Izd-vo Universiteta, 1987.

Berdyaev, N. A. *Mirosozertsanie Dostoevskogo* [Worldview of Dostoevsky]. Moscow: Vysshaya shkola, 1993.

Bogatov, V. V. *Osnovnye cherty mirovozzreniya vydayushhikhsya predstoviteley dvizheniya petrashevcev* [The Main Features of World-Famous Representatives of the Movement Petrashevists]. Moscow: Izd-vo Moskovskogo un-ta, 1958.

Bosch, David J. *Transforming Mission: Paradigms Shifts in Theology of Mission.* Maryknoll: Orbis Books, 1991.

Bulgakov, S. N. *Zhiznennyy podvig Dostoevskogo* [Life Deed of Dostoevsky]. Moscow: 1908.

Curle, Richard. *Characters of Dostoevsky.* New York: Russell & Russell, 1966.

De Kyuctin, Markiz Astol'f. *Nikolaevskaya Rossiya* [Nicholas Russia]. Moscow: Izdatel'stvo politicheskoy literatury, 1990.

De Vogue, E. M. *Le roman russe* [The Russian Novel]. 4th edition. Paris, 1897.

Dneprov, V. *Idei, Strasti, Postupki* [Ideas, Passions, Actions]. Leningrad: Sovetskiy Pisatel', 1978.

Dostoevskaya, A. G. *Vospominaniya* [Reminiscence]. Moscow: Prague, 1987.

Dostoevskiy [Dostoevsky]. Moscow: Molodaya Gvardiya, 1962.

Dostoevsky v Omske [Dostoevsky in Omsk]. Omsk: 1972.

Druzhinin, N. M. *Gosudarstvennye krect'yane i reforma P. D. Kiseleva, t.1.* [State Peasants and Kiselyov's Reform, Vol. 1. Moscow; Leningrad, 1946.

Engel'gardt, V. M. *Ideologicheskiy roman Dostoevskogo* [Ideological Novel of F. M. Dostoevsky]. Sankt-Petersburg: 1924.

Entsiklopedicheskiy Slovar' F. A. Brokgauza i I. A. Efrona (Biblioteka "Vehi"). 15 January 2011, http://www.vehi.net/brokgauz/.

Erickson, Millard J. *Christianskoe bogoslovie* [Christian Theology]. Sankt-Petersburg: Biblia dlya vseh, 1999.

Eroshkin, N. P. *Krepoctnicheskoe samoderzhavie i ego politicheskie instituty* [The Feudal Autocracy and Its Political Institutions]. Moscow: "Mysl," 1981.

F. M. Dostoevskiy: Materialy i isledovaniya [F. M. Dostoevsky: Materials and Studies]. Edited by A. S. Dolinina. Leningrad: Akademiya Nauk SSSR, 1935.

F. M. Dostoevsky v vospominaniyakh sovremennikov [F. M. Dostoevsky in the Memoirs of Contemporaries]. Moscow: Hudozhestvennaya literatura, 1990.

Florovsky, Grigory. *O Dostoevskom* [About Dostoevsky]. Moscow: 1990. 15 May 2011, http://halkidon2006.orthodoxy.ru/bogoslovie/691_florovskii.htm.

Frank, Joseph. *Dostoevsky. The Seeds of Revolt, 1821–1849.* Princeton, NJ: Princeton University Press, 1976.

Frank, L. *Dostoevskiy i krizis gumanizma* [Dostoevsky and the Crisis of Humanism]. Moscow, 1990.

Frank, S. L. *O Dostoevskom* [About Dostoevsky]. Moscow: n. p., 1990.

Gercen, A. I. *Sobranie Sochineniy v tridcati tomakh, t. VII* [Collected Works in 30 Volumes]. Moscow: Izd-vo AN SSSR.

Gessen, S. *Tragediya dobra v Brat'yakh Karamazovykh* [Tragedy of Good in Brothers Karamazov]. Moscow: Kniga, 1990.

Gibson, A. Boyce. *The Religion of Dostoevsky.* London: SCM Press, 1973.

Gogol, N. V. *Vybrannye mesta iz perepiski s druz'yami. Chetyre pis'ma k raznym licam i po povodu "Mertvykh dush."* [Selected Passages from Correspondence with Friends. Four Letters to Various People about the "Dead Souls."] Moscow: Nauka, 1889.

Grayson, James H. *Myths and Legends from Korea: An Annotated Compendium of Ancient and Modern Materials.* New York; Abingdon: Routledge Curzon, 2000.

Grossman, L. *Dostoevskiy* [Dostoevsky]. Moscow: Molodaya Gvardiya, 1965.

———. *Tvorchestvo Dostoevskogo* [Creative Work of Dostoevsky]. Moscow: Molodaya Gvardiya, 1959.

Gus, M. *Idei i obrazy F. M. Dostoevskogo* [Ideas and Images of F. M. Dostoevsky]. Moscow: Hudozhestvennaya Literatura, 1962.

Ivanets, S. K. *Alkogol'naya zavisimost.* [Alcohol Dependence]. Novosibirsk, 2006.

Istoricheskiy Vestnik, T. 2. [Historical Journal]. Sankt-Petersburg, 1904.

Istoriya Rossii v XIX veke [The History of Russia in the Nineteenth Century]. Sankt-Peterburg: Russkaya Skoropechatnya, T. 1–2, n.d.

Iz pisem i pokazaniy dekabristov [From the Letters and Testimony of the Decembrists]. Edited by A. K. Borozdina. Sankt–Peterburg, 1906.

Karyakin, Y. F. *Dostoevsky. Vse–ditya* [Dostoevsky: All Are Children]. Moscow: Nauka, 1971.

Kaye, Peter. *Dostoevsky and English Modernism 1900–1930.* Cambridge, UK: Cambridge University Press, 1999.

Kirpotin, V. *Dostoevsky i Belinskiy* [Dostoevsky and Belinsky]. Moscow: Khudozhestvennaya literatura, 1976.

Kleyman, R. Y. *Skvoznye motivy tvorchestva Dostoevsky* [Cross-Cutting Theme of Dostoevsky]. Kishinev: "Shtiinca," 1985.

Kniga dlya chteniya po istorii novogo vremeni. T. IV [A Book for Reading a History of Modern Time]. Moscow: Tipografiya T-va I. D. Sytina, 1914.

Komarovich, V. L. *Mirovaya garmoniya Dostoevskogo* [World Harmony of Dostoevsky]. Sankt-Petersburg: Molodaya Gvardiya, 1997.

Kotovich, A. *Dukhovnaya cenzura v Rossii 1799–1855* [Spiritual Censorship in Russia 1799–1855]. Sankt-Petersburg, 1909.

Kudryavtsev, Y. G. *Tri kruga Dostoevskogo* [Three Circles of Dostoevsky]. Moscow: Nauka, 1979.

Lauth, Reinhard. *Filosofiya Dostoevskogo v sistematicheskom izlozhenii* [Dostoevsky's Philosophy in Systematic Presentation]. Moscow: Respublika, 1996.

Leykina-Svirskaya, V. R. *Petrashevcy* [Petrashevists]. Leningrad, 1956.

Leont'ev, K. N. *Nashi novye khristiane* [Our New Christians]. Moscow, 1882.

Literaturnoe nasledstvo, T. III [Literary Heritage]. Moscow: Izd-vo AN SSSR, 1956.

Losskiy, N. O. *Bog i Mirovoe zlo* [God and World Evil]. Moscow: Respublika, 1994.

———. *Dostoevskiy i ego khristianskoe moroponimanie* [Dostoevsky and His Christian World Outlook]. New York, 1953.

Lunocharskiy, A. V. *Russkiy Faust* [Russian Faust]. Moscow, 1924.

McClendon, James Wm., Jr. *Biography as Theology.* Nashville, TN: Abingdon, 1974.

———. *Ethics: Systematic Theology, Volume 1.* Nashville: Abingdon, 1986.

McClendon, James Wm., Jr., and James M. Smith. *Understanding Convictions: Defusing Religious Relativism.* Revised edition. Valley Forge, PA: Trinity Press International, 1994.

McKelvie, John. *Whitworth, God's Blueprints: A Sociological Study of Three Utopian Sects.* London; Boston: Routledge & Kegan Paul, 1975.

Merezhkovskiy, D. S. *L. Tolstoy i Dostoevskiy* [L. Tolstoy and Dostoevsky]. Sankt-Petersburg, 1901–1903.

Mir na Rubezhe XIX – XX vekov: Tendentsiya, razvitiya, protivorechiya, revolyutsii [World at the Turn of the Nineteenth–Twentieth Centuries: The Trend, the Development, the Contradictions and the Revolution]. Moscow: Izdatel'stvo MAI, 1991.

Mironenko, S. V. *Samoderzhavie i Reformy: Politicheskaya bor'ba v Rossii v nachale XIX v.* [Autocracy and Reform: The Political Struggle in Russia in the Early Nineteenth Century]. Moscow: Nauka, 1989.

Molodoy Dostoevsky [The Young Dostoevsky]. Moscow: OGIZ, 1947.

Nikitin, V. A. *Dostoevskiy, pravoslavie i "Russkaya ideya"* [Dostoevsky, Orthodoxy and the "Russian Idea"]. Moscow: Nauka, 1989.

Noble, Ivana. *Theological Interpretation of Culture in Post-Communist Context.* Farnham, UK: Ashgate, 2010.

O Dostoevskom: Tvorchestva Dostoevskogo v russkoy mysli 1881–1931 godov [About Dostoevsky: Dostoevsky's Work in Russian Thought 1881–1931]. Moscow: Kniga, 1990.

Parushev, Parush R., and Rollin G. Grams. *Academic Reasoning, Research and Writing in Religious Studies: A Concise Handbook*. Librix.eu Tribun EU, 2008.

Pletnev, P. V. *Dostoevskiy i Bibliya* [Dostoevsky and the Bible]. Moscow, 1938.

Pokrovskiy, G. A. *Muchenik bogoiskatel'stva* [Martyr in a Search for God]. Moscow, 1929.

Petrashevcy [Petrashevists]. Moscow: Izd-vo AN SSSR.

Racu, A. *Interventia recuperative-terapeutica pentru copii cu dizabilitati multiple* [Recuperative-Therapeutic Intervention for Children with Multiple Disabilities]. Pontos, Chisinau, 2006.

Radzinskiy, E. *Aleksandr II Zhizn' i Smert'* [Alexander II: The Life and Death]. Moscow: Izdatel'stvo AST, 2006.

Reverent Iustin, *Dostoevsky o Evrope I slav'anstve* [Dostoevsky on Europe and the Slavs]. Moscow: Sretensky monastyr', 2001. 10 January 2011, http://www.pravoslavie.ru/sretmon/izdatel/justinpopovic-dostoevskij.htm.

Rossiya: Entsiklopedicheskiy spravochnik [Russia: Encyclopedic Reference]. Moscow: Izdatel, srijj dom "Drofa," 1998.

Rozanov, V. V. *O Dostoevskom* [On Dostoevsky]. Sankt-Petersburg, 1894.

Rozenblium, L. M. *Tvorcheskie dnevniki Dostoevskogo*. Moscow: Nauka, 1981.

Rubin, Julius H. *The Other Side of Joy: Religious Melancholy among the Bruderhof*. Oxford: Oxford University Press, 2000.

Rumyantseva, E. M. *Feodor Mikhaylovich Dostoevsky*. Leningrad: Prosveshhenie, 1971.

Russroe obshhectvo 40–50-kh godov XIX v. [Russian Society in the Forties and Fifties of the Nineteenth Century]. Moscow: Izd-vo Moskovskogo un-ta, 1989.

Sakkulin, P. *Russkaya literatura i socealizm* [Russian Literature and Socialism]. Moscow, 1924.

Scanlan, James P. *Dostoevsky the Thinker*. London: Cornell University Press, 2002.

Semenova, G. *Vysshaya ideya sushchestvovaniya u Dostoevskogo* [Higher Idea of Existence in Dostoevsky's Work]. Moscow: Nauka, 1989.

Shestov, L. *Kirkegard I Dostoevskiy* [Kierkegaard and Dostoevsky]. Paris, 1935.

———. *Dostoevsky i Nicshhe: Filocofiya tragedii* [Dostoevsky and Nietzsche: Philosophy of the Tragedy]. Berlin, 1922.

Shteynberg, A. Z. *Sistema svobody F. M. Dostoevskogo* [System of Freedom of F. M. Dostoevsky]. Paris, 1980.

Slonimskiy, A. L. *F. M. Dostoevskiy: Tvorchestvo i Religiya* [F. M. Dostoevsky: Creativity and Religion]. Sankt-Petersburg, 1915.

Ivanov, V. I. *Dostoevskiy i Roman tragediya* [Dostoevsky and the Novel-Tragedy]. Moscow: Kniga, 1990.

Statistika [Statistics]. 15 December 2010, http://www.statistica.md/index.php?l=en.

The Gospel in Dostoevsky. Farmington: Plough Publishing House, Bruderhof Foundation, 2003.

Timofeeva, V. V. *God raboty s znamenitym pisatelem* [A Year of Work with a Famous Writer]. Moscow: Istoricheskiy Vestnik, 1904.

Transnistria. 1 December 2010, http://www.ambasadamoldova.cz/ru/respublika-moldova/o-respublike-moldova/geografia.

Travers, Michael E. *Literary Motifs*. 12 December 2010, http://bible.org/seriespage/literary-motifs.

Troynitskiy, A. *Krepostnoe naselenie Rossii po 10-y narodnojj perepisi* [Serf Population in Russia According to the Tenth People's Census]. Sankt-Petersburg, 1861.

V. G. Belinskiy v spominaniyakh sovremenikov [V. G. Belinsky in the Memoirs of Contemporaries]. Moscow: Goslitizdat, 1962.

Vetlovskaya, V. E. *Tvorchestvo Dostoevskogo v svete literaturnykh I fol'klornykh parallekey. Stroitel'naya zhertva* [The Creative Work of Dostoevsky in Light of Literary and Folk Parallels]. Leningrad, 1978.

————. *Roman F. M. Dostoevskogo "Bednye Lyudi"* [Dostoyevsky's Novel *Poor Folk*]. Leningrad: Hudozhestvennaya literatura, 1988.

Vlaskin, A. P. *Ideologicheskiy kontekst v romane F. M. Dostoevskogo* [Ideological Context in Dostoevsky's Novel]. Chelyabinsk: "Chelyabinskiy rabochiy," 1987.

Volskiy. *Feodor Mihaylovich Dostoevskiy* [Fedor Mihailovich Dostoevsky]. Moscow: Knizhnyy magazin D. P. Efimova, 1906.

Volynskiy, A. L. *Dostoevskiy* [Dostoevsky]. Sankt-Petersburg: 1906.

Volzhskiy, A. S. *Fyodoer Michailovich Dostoevsky: Zhizni i Propoved'* [F. M. Dostoevsky: Life and Sermon]. Moscow: D. P. Efimov's Bookstoor, 1906.

Vvozniy, A. F. *Politicheskiy sysk i kruzhok Petrashevcev* [Political Spying and Petrashevists Circle]. Kiev: KVSh MVD SSSR, 1976.

Vysheslavtsev, B. P. *Russkaya stikhiyu u Dostoevskogo* [Russian Elements in Dostoevsky's Works]. Berlin, 1923.

Zablocki, Benjamin. *The Joyful Community: An Account of the Bruderhof – A Communal Movement Now in Its Third Generation*. Farmington: Plough Publishing, Bruderhof Foundation, 1971.

Articles:

"33 milioane de lei pentru "reamenajarea" complexului Condriţa" [33 Million Lei for "Redevelopment" of Condriţa Complex]. Timpul, 18 August 2009. 22 May 2011, http://www.azi.md/ro/print-story/5133.

Andronovienė, Lina and Parushev. Parush R. "Church, State, and Culture: On the Complexities of Post-Soviet Evangelical Social Involvement." *Theological Reflections: EAAA Journal of Theology* 3 (2004): 194–212.

Annikov, V. "Zamechatel'noe Desjatiletie 1888–1848" [Remarkable Decade 1888–1848]. *F. M. Dostoevskiy v vospominaniyakh sovremennikov*. Moscow: Hudozhestvennaya Literatura 1964. 5 November 2010, http://az.lib.ru/d/dostoewskij_f_m/text_0580.shtml.

Antonovich, M. A. "Mistiko-asketicheskiy roman" [Mystical-Ascetic Novel]. *Literatura* (2007). 10 January, 2011, http://www.herzenlib.org/page21.php.

"Barometrul de Opinie Publică" [Public Opinion Barometer]. 12 June 2011, http://www.azi.md/ro/print-story/18685.

Belinsky, V. "Pis'mo Belinskogo Gogolyu" [Belinsky's Letter to Gogol]. 25 December 2010, http://ru.wikisource.org/wiki/.

Bessonova, L. A. "Printsip Vseedinstva v istoriosofii Vladimir Soloviev." *Rossiya i Vselenskaya Tserkov': V. S. Soloviev i problema religioznogo I kul'turnogo edineniya chelovechestva*, 191.

"Biserica baptista" [The Baptist Church], 13 June 2011, http://logos.md/2008/09/12/biserica-baptista/.

"Noul parlament are 11 milionari" [The New Parliament Has Eleven Millionaires]. INFOTAG, 27 December 2010. 23 June 2011, http://www.azi.md/ro/print-story/15583.

"Comportamentul infantil al clasei politice din Republica Moldova" [Infantile Behaviour of Politicians in Moldova]. 14 May 2011, http://www.azi.md/ro/print-story/12916.

"Comunistii ataca din nou: AIE respecta democratia numai cand rezultatul le place" [Communists Attack AEI Again: They Respect Democracy Only When the Result Is Convenient for Them], 12 June 2011, http://www.inprofunzime.md/stiri/politic/html.

"Creşte numărul de persoane traficate în Moldova" [The Number of Trafficked Persons in Moldova Is Increasing]. INFOTAG, 16 June 2011. 12 June 2011, http://www.azi.md/ro/print-story/19072.

"Declaraţia PCRM" [PCRM Declaration]. 1 July 2011, http://www.pcrm.md/main/index_md.php.

"Deportarea romanilor din Basarabia, Bucovina, Herta" [Deportation of Romanians in Bessarabia, Bukovina, Herta]. 24 June 2011, http://civicnet.info/Procesulcomunismului.asp?ID=204.

"Deputatii primului Parlament sint ingrijorati de situatia social-economica si climatul politic din R. Moldova" [First Parliament Deputies are Concerned About the Socio-Economic and Political Climate of R. Moldavia]. INFOTAG, 6 March 2009. 18 September 2010, http://www.azi.md/ro/print-story/1644.

Eftode Alexandru, "Freedom House: R. Moldova – libertatea şi drepturile politice în declin." [Freedom House: R. Moldova – Freedom and Political Rights in Decline]. Radio Europa Libera, 17 July 2009. 14 April 2011, http://www.azi.md/ro/print-story/4516.

"Experţii europeni au prezentat strategia de reformare şi coordonare a sectorului justiţiei" [European Experts Presented Their Strategy and Coordination of Justice Reform]. INFOTAG, 7 July 2011. 28 July 2011, http://www.azi.md/ro/print-story/19562.

Filat, Vasile. "De ce creştinii adevăraţi frecventează serviciile divine ale bisericii?" [Why Do True Christians Attend Church Services?]. 20 May 2011, http://www.moldovacrestina.net/biserici/de-ce-crestinii-adevarati-frecventeaza-serviciile-divine-ale-bisericii/.

"F. M. Dostoevskiy: Materialy I isledovaniya" [F. M. Dostoevsky: Materials and Studies]. Edited by A. S. Dolinina. Leningrad, 1935.

Frolova, O. G. "Aborty v Moldove" [Abortion in Moldova]. 27 October 2010, http://tawhid.narod.ru.

Ghiletchi, Valeriu. 15 May 2011, ttps://valeriughiletchi.md/about/biography/.

Grams, Rollin G., and Parush R. Parushev. "Editors' Preface." In *Towards an Understanding of European Baptist Identity: Listening to the Churches in Armenia, Bulgaria, Central Asia, Moldova, North Caucasus, Omsk and Poland*, edited by Rollin G. Grams and Parush R. Parushev, 9–14. Prague, CZ: IBTS Publisher, 2006.

"Guvernantii moldoveni intensifica presiunea asupra businessului, Financial Times" [Moldavian Authorities Step Up Pressure on Business, Financial Times]. Info-Prim Neo, 29 May 2009. 14 March 2011, http://www.azi.md/ro/print-story/3350.

"Instanţele judecătoreşti economice dispar, dar nu consolidează alianţa de guvernământ" [Economic Courts Disappear, But Do Not Strengthen the Ruling Alliance]. Info-Prim Neo, 6 July 2011. 23 July 2011, http://www.azi.md/ro/print-story/19514.

"Interviu cu Vlad Filat, presedintcle PLDM" [Intervew with Vlad Filat, Chairman of PLDM]. 15 May 2011, http://www.azi.md/ro/interview/4/1.

"Interviu cu Mihai Ghimpu, presedintele PL" [Intervew with Mihai Ghimpu, Chairman of PL]. 16 May 2011, http://www.azi.md/ro/interview/8/1.

"Interviu cu Serafim Urechean, presedintele AMN" [Intervew with Serafim Urechean, Chairman of AMN]. 12 May 2011, http://www.azi.md/ro/interview/6/1.

Kirillovoy, Evgeniy. "Domashnee nasilie v Moldove" [Domestic Violence in Moldova], 21 July 2011, http://www.mtc-co.md/~wog/violence/moldova1.html.

Leontiev, K. L. "O Vsemirnoy Liubvi" [About Universal Love]. Biblioteka "Vehi" (2001). 15 January 2011, http://www.vehi.net/leontev/dost.html.

"Liga Islamică este nedumerită de faptul că Mitropolitul Vladimir condamnă înregistrarea acestui cult în Moldova." [Islamic League Is Puzzled that Mitropolitan Vladimir Condemns the Registration of This Cult in Moldova]. 25 April 2011, http://www.azi.md/ro/print-story/17954.

"Lista persoanelor vinovate de pedepsirea R. Moldova la CEDO" [The List of the People Who Are Guilty in Condemning of R. Moldova by the ECHR]. INFOTAG, 19 February 2009. 25 November 2010, http://www.azi.md/ro/print-story/1422.

Kondrusevich, Tadeush "Slovo privetstviya." *Rossiya i Vselenskaya Tserkov': V. S. Soloviev i problema religioznogo I kul'turnogo edineniya chelovechestva* [Word of Greeting. Russia and Universal Church]. Moscow: BBI Sv. Apostola Andreya, 2004.

Markov, E. "Russkaya Rechi" [Russian Speech]. In *Kriticheskie razbory "Zapisok iz Mernvogo Doma"* [Criticism of *The House of the Dead*], edited by V. Zelinskiy. Moscow: Tipografia Vil'de, 1907.

Maykov, A. "Iz pis'ma k P. A. Viscovatomu" [From the Letter to P. A. Viscovatom]. *F. M. Dostoevsky: Polnoe Sobranie Sochineniy* [The Complete Works of Dostoevsky] [CD-ROM]. Izdatel'stvo Adept, 2002.

Mihaylovskiy, N. K. "Zhestokiy talent" [Cruel Talent] (June 2007). 10 January 2011, http://az.lib.ru/m/mihajlowskij_n_k/text_0042.shtml.

Milikov, A. "Svetoch" [The Torch]. In *Kriticheskie razbory "Zapisok iz Mernvogo Doma,"* edited by V. Zelinskiy, 7.

"Mii de oameni au venit azi noaptea la catedrala metropolitan" [Thousands of People Came Last Night to the Metropolitan Cathedral]. 26 May 2011, http://www.prime.md/ro/news/mii-de-oameni-au-venit-azi-noapte-la-catedrala-metropolitana-1004694/.

Miller, O. "Russkie Pisateli posle Gogolya." In *Kriticheskie razbory "Zapisok iz Mernvogo Doma,"* edited by V. Zelinskiy, 86.

"Minimul de existenţă în Moldova a revenit la nivelul anului 2008" [Subsistence Minimum in Moldova Came Back to the Level of 2008]. INFOTAG, 7 April 2011. 22 May 2011, http://www.azi.md/ro/print-story/17619.

"Moldova fara saracie" [Moldova without Poverty]. 20 January 2011, http://pldm.md/index.php?option=com_content&view=category&layout=blog&id=73&Itemid=79.

"O Dostoevskom: Sbornik statey" [On Dostoevsky: Collection of Articles]. Edited by A. L. Blem. Prague, 1937.

Oprunenco, Alex. "Zona de Liber Schimb Aprofundat şi Cuprinzător dintre UE şi R. Moldova: o trambulină spre modernizare sau o cale spre ruinare?" [Free Trade Zone with Deep and Comprehensive between EU and Moldova:

A Springboard for Modernization or a Path to Ruin?]. Centrul Analitic Independent "EXPERT-GRUP", 11 mai 2011. 25 May 2011, http://www.azi.md/ro/print-story/18256.

Parushev, Parush R. "Baptistic Convictional Hermeneutics." In *The Plainly Revealed Word of God? Baptist Hermeneutics in Theory and Practice*, edited by Helen Dare and Simon Woodman, 172–190. Macon, GA: Mercer University Press, 2011.

———. "Convictional Perspectivism: A Constructive Proposal for a Theological Response to Postmodern Conditions." In *Mission in Context: Explorations Inspired by Andrew Kirk*, edited by John Corrie and Cathy Ross, 111–124. Farnham, UK: Ashgate, 2012.

———. "Convictions and the Shape of Moral Reasoning." In *Ethical Thinking at the Crossroads of European Reasoning*, Occasional Publications Series, Volume 7, edited by Parush R. Parushev, Ovidiu Creangă, and Brian Brock, 27–45. Prague, CZ: IBTS Publisher, 2007.

———. "Theologie op een baptistenmanicr" [Doing Theology in a Baptist Way]. In *Zo zijn onze manieren! In Gesprek over gemeentetheologie*, Baptistica Reeks (Series), Vol. 1, edited by Teun van der Leer, 7–22 and 66–75. Barneveld, Nederland: Unie van Baptisten Gemeenten in Nederland, September 2009, in Dutch.

Pattison, G., and D. O. Thompson. "Introduction: Reading Dostoevsky Religiously." In *Dostoevsky and the Christian Tradition*, edited by G. Pattison and D. O. Thompson, 13. Cambridge: Cambridge University Press, 2001.

"Pensia medie lunară nu acoperă minimul de existenţă" [Average Monthly Pension Does Not Cover Living Subsistence]. Info-Prim Neo, 21 December 2009. 23 February 2011, http://www.azi.md/ro/print-story/7923.

Pilli, Toivo. "Baptist History in Moldova." In *Dictionary of European Baptist Life and Thoughts*, edited by John Briggs. Milton Keynes, Colorado Springs, Hyderabad: Paternoster, 2009.

Pisarev, D.I. "Pogibshie i Pogibayuschshie." In *Kriticheskie razbory "Zapisok iz Mernvogo Doma,"* edited by V. Zelinskiy, 71.

Preasca, Ion. "De ce Moldova a devenit jucătorul nr. 1 pe piaţa contrabandei de ţigări în România" [Why Moldova Became the No. 1 Player in Smuggling Cigarettes to Romania], (15 March 2010). 12 April 2011, http://www.azi.md/ro/print-story/9963.

———. "PLDM, PL, PD şi AMN au semnat documentul de creare a coaliţiei" [PLDM, PL, PD, and AMN Have Signed the Document Creating the Coalition]. 20 September 2009, http://m.protv.md/stiri/politic/pldm-pl-pd-i-amn-au-semnat-documentul-de-creare-a-coali-iei.html.

Roberson, Ronald. "Pravoslavnaya tserkovi" [The Orthodox Church]. 4 July 2011, http://www.agnuz.info/tl_files/library/books/Ronald/page02.htm.

Rozanov, V. "Legenda o Velikom Inkvizitore" [The Legend of the Great Inquisitor]. In *F. M. Dostoevsky. Polnoe Sobranie Sochineniy* [The Complete Works of Dostoevsky] [CD-ROM]. Izdatel'stvo Adept, 2002.

"Samaya p'uschaya natsiya v mire: ne russkie" [The Nation That Drinks the Most in the World Is Not Russia]. 17 February 2011, https://www.kp.md/daily/25640/804812/.

Sibilev, Alexandr. "James Clerk Maxwell." *Slovo Istiny* 5 (August 2003), 9.

"Sindicalistele din Moldova anunţă proteste pentru 8 martie" [Trade Unions in Moldova Announced Protests on 8 March]. Info-Prim Neo, 25 February 2011. 24 April 2011, http://www.azi.md/ro/print-story/16790.

Smelova, N. E. "Vladimir Soloviev i Istinnoe Khristianstvo." Rossiya i Vselenskaya Tserkov': V. S. Soloviev i problema religioznogo I kul'turnogo edineniya chelovechestva, 48.

Soloviev, V. "Tri rechi v pam'yat' Dostoevskogo" [Three Speeches on Dostoevsky]. 15 January 2011, http://www.vehi.net/soloviev/trirechi.html.

"Spre sfârşitul campaniei electorale, presa devine tot mai partizană" [Towards the End of the Campaign, the Press Is Becoming More Partisan]. Centrul pentru Jurnalism Independent (CJI), Moldova Azi, 2 June 2011. 4 June 2011, http://www.azi.md/ro/print-story/18743.

"Statul va plăti despăgubiri cazurilor în instanţe, pentru a reduce numărul dosarelor depuse la CEDO" [The State Will Pay Compensation for Court Cases to Reduce the Number of Cases Submitted to the ECHR]. Info-Prim Neo, 13 April 2011. 2 February 2011, http://www.azi.md/ro/print-story/17740.

"Studiu IDIS: 2008 a fost dominat de tensiuni politice, regrupari pre-electorale si saracie" [IDIS Study: 2008 Was Dominated by Political Tensions, Pre-Election Regrouping and Poverty]. Info-Prim Neo, 29 January 2009. 2 May 2011, http://www.azi.md/ro/print-story/1121.

Sytkin, V. "Kogda govoryat" [When They Say]. 22 January 2010, http://www.analytique.md/index.

Tanase, Alexandru. "Coruptie si coruptionisti" [Corruption and Corruptionists]. 28 July 2011, http://www.tanase.md/2011/07/02/coruptie-coruptioneri-si-crasa/.

Vaculovsci, Ghenadie. 23 April 2010, http://vaculovschi.ppcd.md/?p=52.

"V Moldove ne hvataet vrachey fitiziatrov" [A Lack of Tuberculo-Therapists in Moldova]. 13 December 2010, http://vesti.md/?mod=news&id=3012.

"Voronin a depus flori la monumental lui Lenin" [Voronin Laid Flowers at the Monument of Lenin]. 25 April 2011, http://forum.md/Themes/basarabia/322195.

Zarin, E. "Biblioteka dlya chteniya," [Library for Reading]. In *Kriticheskie razbory "Zapisok iz Mernvogo Doma,"* edited by V. Zelinskiy, 10.

Zenkovsky, V. V. "Dostoevsky's Religious and Philosophical Views." In *Dostoevsky. A Collection of Critical Essays*, edited by Rene Wellek, 134. Englewood Cliffs: Prentice-Hall, 1962.

"Zlye dziny immonodifitsita" [The Evil Jinn of Immunodeficiency]. 20 March 2011, http://noutati.md.

Langham Literature, with its publishing work, is a ministry of Langham Partnership.

Langham Partnership is a global fellowship working in pursuit of the vision God entrusted to its founder John Stott –

> **to facilitate the growth of the church in maturity and Christ-likeness through raising the standards of biblical preaching and teaching.**

Our vision is to see churches in the Majority World equipped for mission and growing to maturity in Christ through the ministry of pastors and leaders who believe, teach and live by the word of God.

Our mission is to strengthen the ministry of the word of God through:
* nurturing national movements for biblical preaching
* fostering the creation and distribution of evangelical literature
* enhancing evangelical theological education

especially in countries where churches are under-resourced.

Our ministry

Langham Preaching partners with national leaders to nurture indigenous biblical preaching movements for pastors and lay preachers all around the world. With the support of a team of trainers from many countries, a multi-level programme of seminars provides practical training, and is followed by a programme for training local facilitators. Local preachers' groups and national and regional networks ensure continuity and ongoing development, seeking to build vigorous movements committed to Bible exposition.

Langham Literature provides Majority World preachers, scholars and seminary libraries with evangelical books and electronic resources through publishing and distribution, grants and discounts. The programme also fosters the creation of indigenous evangelical books in many languages, through writer's grants, strengthening local evangelical publishing houses, and investment in major regional literature projects, such as one volume Bible commentaries like the *Africa Bible Commentary* and the *South Asia Bible Commentary*.

Langham Scholars provides financial support for evangelical doctoral students from the Majority World so that, when they return home, they may train pastors and other Christian leaders with sound, biblical and theological teaching. This programme equips those who equip others. Langham Scholars also works in partnership with Majority World seminaries in strengthening evangelical theological education. A growing number of Langham Scholars study in high quality doctoral programmes in the Majority World itself. As well as teaching the next generation of pastors, graduated Langham Scholars exercise significant influence through their writing and leadership.

To learn more about Langham Partnership and the work we do visit **langham.org**